A Guide to the Mammals of the Southeastern United States

A Guide to the Mammals of the Southeastern United States

Larry N. Brown

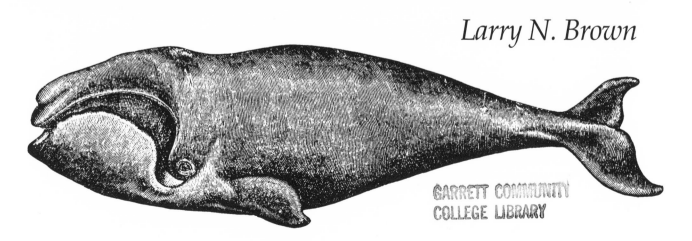

The University of Tennessee Press / Knoxville

Library of Congress Cataloging-in-Publication Data

Brown, Larry N.
A guide to the mammals of the southeastern United States /
Larry N. Brown.—1st ed.
       p. cm.
Includes bibliographical references (p.   ) and index.
ISBN 0-87049-965-3 (cloth : alk. paper).
ISBN 0-87049-966-1 (pbk. : alk. paper).
1. Mammals—Southern States—Identification.   I. Title.
QL719.S84B76 1997
599.0975—dc20   96-25272
                                                 CIP

To my father, Kermit Theodore Brown, of Springfield, Greene County, Missouri, who was an avid hunter, trapper, and sportsman in the Ozark Mountains of Missouri

and

To my son, Curtis Kermit Brown, of DeLand, Volusia County, Florida, who is a devoted wildlife officer, conservationist, and outdoorsman in the southeastern United States.

Contents

Preface

To date, there has been no general guide designed specifically for all the mammals of the southeastern United States and its adjacent waters. The general public has a great deal of difficulty identifying or obtaining comprehensive life-history information on southeastern mammals. This book is designed to provide descriptive information on the mammal species of the southeastern United States and serve as a general source of information about their life habits and natural history. Chapters on Studying Mammals, Mammal Characteristics and Adaptations, Mammal Conservation, and Mammal Affinities in the Southeast are also included.

I have been involved in the professional study of mammals for over thirty-five years and have visited forty-nine of the fifty states in that pursuit. Twenty-five of those years have been concentrated specifically on mammals of the southeastern United States. In this process, a wealth of information was accumulated on the natural history and ecology of both the native and introduced species found living there.

This book is designed to serve both the layperson interested in mammals, as well as the professional wildlife biologist, mammalogist, or natural resource manager who is making fauna evaluations and assessing the impacts of human activities in the southeastern United States.

Descriptive terms used in this text are as nontechnical as possible, but when technical language is necessary, every attempt is made to keep the terminology clear. I hope that this book, with its illustrations and clear language, will stimulate an even greater interest in the mammalian fauna of the southeastern United States among nature lovers and that it will stimulate them to appreciate this valuable natural resource along with the often more visible animals, such as birds and butterflies, etc.

Acknowledgments

Numerous friends and associates assisted with the preparation of this book during my many years of studying southeastern mammals and accumulating the life history information and ecological notes so vital to writing on each species. These people include the following: Clinton Conaway, Richard McGuire, Caleb J. Brown, Graham Hickman, Albert Maida, Gorgene Carson, Eugene Bakko, Stephen Adams, Kriss Brown, Marvin Maxell, C. Wright, Maron Davis, Curtis Brown, Al Baker, Tom Stombaugh, and Wesley Brown.

I am also very grateful to the people who helped secure or provide photographs, drawings, or other illustrations for this work. Their names are credited on each page where the photo or illustration appears.

The illustrations of skulls were primarily modified after Hall (1981). All were modified and altered in final form.

My thanks go to Paula M. Arico for computer help and final typing and editing. I would like to extend special thanks to my children, Wesley, Caleb, Curtis, Laurel, and Kriss, for providing help in the various phases of preparing, typing, and editing this large manuscript.

Introduction

There are a large number of mammal species found in the southeastern United States, but many people are aware of only a few of the larger or more easily visible kinds, such as deer, raccoons, opossums, squirrels, etc. There are dozens of others that are either secretive, nocturnal, or hidden from view of the casual observer. This book introduces the reader to these lesser-known mammals as well as to the more visible ones. It also covers the life history and identification of each species so that the observer may become versed in its biology and natural history.

Human beings should have more than a passing interest in mammals because this is the group of animals to which we belong and with which we share characteristics. Mammals, for example, are warm-blooded vertebrates, and the only animals on earth that possess mammary glands which secrete milk to nourish the young following birth. In fact, the term "mammal" comes from the Latin word which means breast or mammary gland. Also, mammals are the only animals on earth to have evolved hair that covers the body. Of course, some mammals, including whales, dolphins, manatees, and armadillos, have a greatly reduced amount of hair, which is limited to just a few bristles in the snout or belly area.

Another characteristic of mammals is the presence of four types of rooted teeth (incisors, canines, premolars, and molars). These teeth have different specialized functions which are reflected in their distinctive shapes, or morphologies. Mammals also exhibit two sets of teeth during their lifetimes. Young or juvenile mammals have a temporary set of small "milk or deciduous" teeth. These allow for rapid body growth and are later replaced by a permanent set of adult teeth that are larger. Mammals also have a four-chambered heart, and a single bone (the dentary) forms each half of the lower jaw.

The Southeast is home to a rich and varied mammal fauna totaling 132 species. Of this group, 97 are terrestrial and 35 are marine mammals recorded in the ocean and coastal waters adjacent to the southeastern United States. Within the terrestrial group, there are 12 species which were introduced from elsewhere and are now established in the Southeast (the house mouse, Norway rat, black rat, nutria, coyote, armadillo, black-tailed jackrabbit, red-bellied squirrel, sika deer, fallow deer, sambar deer, and wild pig). There are also 4 species which once occurred in the Southeast, but are now extirpated (the red wolf, elk, buffalo, and West Indian monk seal).

Many people have done research on the mammals found in the southeastern United States. I have relied extensively on this body of knowledge, as well as on my many years of mammal experience, in the preparation of this book.

I have listed those sources which are of most use to the general reader in the Selected References section at the end of the book. Geographical range maps are included for all the terrestrial mammal species which live in the Southeast. No distribution maps were included for the wide-ranging marine mammals which live along or off the Atlantic and/or Gulf coasts.

I am certain that this book will increase the reader's appreciation of our varied and diversified mammal fauna and stimulate additional interest in the life history and ecology of the southeastern species.

SOUTHEASTERN MAMMALOGY

Studying Mammals

Mammals are studied to gain new insight into their biology and natural history. Mammals are studied in a wide variety of methods. The simplest approach, which is not always feasible, is by direct observation of the animals. Unfortunately, most mammals (in contrast to the ever-popular birds) tend to be rather secretive and difficult to find or keep in view (about two-thirds of them are nocturnal). Because of this, observers usually turn to certain indirect methods of obtaining data on mammals. One of the most useful tools is to read the signs of their presence that mammals leave in a given area. These signs includes nests, tracks, feeding remnants, fecal droppings, tooth marks, food caches, burrows or dens, scent posts, and trails or runways. A knowledgeable observer can often use such signs to determine the kind of mammal making the signs and can also gain considerable natural-history information about the individual species.

The tracks that mammals leave are usually most easily identified if the substrate is mud, moist sand, or fresh snow. In many species, tail markings are also present along with the tracks. Each species leaves its own unique signature in terms of the number of toes and their shapes, claw imprints, palm prints, distance between tracks, tail marks, and so forth. The tracks of many larger mammals are usually the most easy to identify and interpret. Those of smaller mammals tend to be the most difficult to identify because several species may leave an almost identical sign.

The "scat," or fecal droppings, of mammals are also very useful in identifying them to species, especially in combination with tracks and other signs. The size, color, shape, and contents of scat often have clear, species-specific characteristics. The droppings of larger mammals, such as artiodactyls and carnivores, are frequently the most distinctive, while those of small species, such as mice and shrews, are rather similar to one another. Careful dissection of scats can usually provide very accurate information about the feeding habits of species, both in terms of what was eaten as well as the relative quantities of each food item consumed. For the reader who may wish to pursue the subject of mammal tracks, scat, and sign identification more actively, a book by O. J. Murie entitled *A Field Guide to Animal Tracks* is very useful. It is listed under field guides in the Selected References at the end of the book.

The home sites of many common mammal species are also easily recognized. They spend much of their time rearing young, avoiding predators, and resting or sleeping in their home sites. Burrowing and tree-dwelling species usually construct nests of grasses, leaves, sticks, fur, or other suitable materials. Aquatic mammals either build nests in and over the water or live in deep bank burrows, whose entrances are frequently concealed below the waterline. Well-worn trails often extend from terrestrial mammal nest and burrow entrances to feeding sites. Bats, wood rats, and several other nocturnal species often roost or nest in caves, rock crevices, hollow trees, and old buildings.

Some mammals produce excavations that are evidence of their presence. Pocket gophers and moles bring dirt to the surface to form earth mounds. Rabbits and hares make shallow depressions (called *forms*) on the ground's surface for resting and birthing sites. Tunnel entrances of burrowing species may be either vertical or dug at an acute angle and may either be plugged or left open, depending on the species of mammal involved.

In addition to fecal droppings, other signs indicate the feeding activities of mammals. Deer tend to browse on the twigs and leaves of trees and shrubs, sometimes pruning them rather severely. Rodents often leave shells of nuts and seeds that they have eaten, or sometimes grass cuttings, in runways. A number of species also cache uneaten food items as a hedge against leaner times in the future. The items stored include tubers, roots, bulbs, grasses, fruits, seeds, nuts, fungi, and arthropods.

In general, the types of indirect evidence of mammal presence are almost boundless and await discovery by the trained eye and clever mind of the observer.

To study many mammals, it is often necessary that they be trapped or collected. For some species, trapping and collecting are the only ways they can be seen at all. They must be brought into the laboratory for certain types of investigations, or they may be marked for individual identification and released for field study. Mammals are captured in a wide variety of sizes and kinds of traps, snares, and nets, etc. It is not unusual for a special kind of trap to be designed with only one type of mammal in mind, as in the case with mole traps or pocket gopher traps.

Many state and federal laws or regulations control the capture, possession, transport, and deposition of various mammal species. At the state level the state Game and Fish departments are primarily responsible for enforcing these regulations. At the federal level this responsibility falls mainly upon the U.S. Fish and Wildlife Service.

The marking of mammals that are to be released back into the field for various ecological or population studies is accomplished through several different methods. The procedure may be as simple as ear or toe marking to give each animal a number or a unique character which can always be recognized and identified. Other marking methods include applying colored fur dyes, attaching numbered or colored tags and bands, branding, fur clipping, tattooing, affixing radio transmitters, or having the animal ingest radioisotopes, food dyes, or related methods. The proper marking method must be carefully tailored to the scientific objective of the mammal study to be undertaken.

Some of the newer methods of studying mammal movements involve 1) the use of fluorescent powders to show the marked animal's tracks; 2) the use of radio transmitters to signal its position at all times; 3) the use of cameras, set along prescribed runways or trails, which record the passage of each mammal at a given point in the environment. It is clear that the various methods of studying mammals in the field are becoming increasingly more sophisticated with each passing year. Advances in technology and equipment are making new techniques available to the researcher almost on a daily basis.

Finally, the keeping of detailed and accurate field notes and data sheets is a vital ingredient of any mammal study. To have any scientific importance, all specimens collected must be accompanied by recorded data on the precise location, date of capture, physical characteristics and measurements, age and sex, reproductive status, method of collection, and name of collector. In these ways, very important and interesting information on the ecology and life histories of southeastern mammal species can be obtained.

Mammal Characteristics and Adaptations

Fossil evidence indicates that the first mammals on earth evolved about 260 million years ago during the late Paleozoic era from a group of advanced reptiles called Thecodonts. The first mammals were small and rather inconspicuous contemporaries of the huge dinosaurs which dominated the world at that time. When the giant reptiles finally became extinct near the end of the Mesozoic era, about 65 million years ago, the mammals evolved rapidly into many diverse forms which dominated the earth. This occurred during the Cenozoic period, which is called the "Age of Mammals." Many of the mammal groups which appeared later became extinct during the Pleistocene period (from a million to 10,000 years ago).

Mammals are placed in the class Mammalia as the group of vertebrate animals in which the young develop inside the mother's uterus (rather than developing in eggs surrounded by a shell to be incubated outside the body). There are, however, two kinds of primitive egg-laying mammals (the platypus and spiny anteater) living in Australia and New Guinea. In all other mammals, the embryos attach to the uterine wall via a placenta which provides nourishment and oxygen from the mother's bloodstream. After birth, baby mammals are nourished with milk produced by the mammary glands. No other animals on earth nourish their babies with milk.

Another unique mammalian characteristic is the presence of hair. It is a derivative of the outer layer (epidermis) of the skin and is usually responsible for the external coloration and general appearance of a mammal. Hair is lubricated by oil (sebaceous) glands in the skin, and a fur coat provides insulation against the loss of body heat. Since mammals are warm-blooded (that is, *homiotherms*), they must carefully regulate heat loss through the skin to remain healthy and functional. The pelage (another name for the fur or hair of the animal) also often provides cryptic coloration to hide a mammal from enemies or predators, and it usually distinguishes males from females (a very important factor in courtship and mating behavior).

The fur of many mammals is shed either once or twice a year (a process called molting) and replaced by a new growth. The winter fur is much thicker and heavier than the summer coat. The pelage often contains two types of hair: 1) long guard hairs that are somewhat stiff; and 2) shorter, soft underfur, which may be dense and woolly or sparse and straight. Hair is always present in mammals, but it is rather restricted in whales, manatees, and armadillos (sometimes represented by only a few bristles).

Mammals which are active nocturnally often have enlarged eyes and other light-gathering adaptations in the eyeballs. This is exhibited by the large eyes of flying squirrels compared with those of diurnal squirrels. Mammals which are adapted for living underground tend to have smaller or poorly developed eyes and external ears compared to mammals adapted for living above ground. This is readily evident in examining these two features in moles and pocket gophers. Moles possess vestigial eyes and no external ears (just ear openings, no external structure, or "pinna"), and gophers have small eyes and very tiny external ears that fold tightly shut to keep dirt out of the ear canal. These adaptations and the many others described in this book fit mammals to their great variety of ecological lifestyles.

Mammal Conservation

The mammal species living today have been here for centuries, so one can assume that they are well adapted to specific environmental situations of their habitats, and their survival is insured by the package of naturally selected genes found in their bodies, but there are some overriding trends in the world's ecology that may affect the long-term survivability of many mammal species. The most prominent forces of change are related to human exploitation and pollution of the world's ecosystems. The vast expanses of mature climax communities—i.e., "the wilderness"—in which many mammals have evolved over the millennia have been or are being rapidly destroyed or significantly altered. These expanses include the tropical rain forests, temperate hardwood forests, temperate tall-grass prairies, and so on. Thus, all those mammals which require large tracts of virgin wilderness are becoming rare or extinct around the globe. Species such as cougars, bears, wolves, bison, elk, and many others are in great danger. In sharp contrast, those species that are adapted to live in ecotones, where different communities meet, or in ecologically disturbed situations have gone from relatively low numbers to higher total populations and greatly expanded their geographical ranges within the last 200 years. Some examples include the black rat, Norway rat, house mouse, woodchuck, armadillo, cotton rat, opossum, coyote, etc.

Another more subtle effect is the ever-increasing release of chemicals and waste products by humans into the environment. This includes insecticides, fungicides, herbicides, rodenticides, etc., as well as air pollutants, sewage, industrial wastes, water pollutants, solid wastes, combustible engine discharges, and an impressive array of other chemical pollutants. Many of these enter the mammal food chains or are picked up directly from other environmental contacts. Chemical pollutants are almost always concentrated by animals in increasing amounts as one climbs the food chain. Therefore, the "top carnivores" (such as whales, cougars, wolves, and seals) generally accumulate the highest concentration of pollutants, which in turn can block reproduction or be life-threatening via some metabolic pathway (tumors, cancer, direct toxicity, etc.). Insect-eating mammals are especially at risk when the prey carries a sublethal dose of pesticides. In such cases, even a primary or secondary carnivore runs a high risk of concentrating biological lethal doses of persistent pesticides. The decline in some populations of bats, shrews, and moles is no doubt caused by pesticide accumulations.

Competition between mammal species for space and food resources is often influenced by human alteration of habitats. For example, the cutting of nearly all the virgin hardwoods in the eastern United States allowed the coyote to invade, out-compete, and replace the red wolf. Also, the introduction of nonnative species has sometimes had disastrous effects. The importation of nutria from South America, for example, has led to the decline and near-disappearance of the native muskrat in the Louisiana marshlands and other aquatic habitats. Exotic species such as the nutria and armadillo readily adapt to a wide range of habitats and food supplies. In the future, better care must be taken to protect our native species from the introduction of exotics.

One measure of the hardships many species of mammals face for future survival in the coming century is the long lists of endangered and threatened forms that we see nationally and state-by-state today. The U.S. Fish and Wildlife Service currently lists many different forms of mammals that are endangered or threatened with extinction. It is easy to see that, as human population numbers continue to climb and as critical natural habitats continue to decline or disappear, existing species will compete for less and less suitable space, leading to the extinction of the more vulnerable forms. The only way that increased competition and extinction can be avoided is to reduce or reverse the rate of human population growth (which probably will not happen) and to set aside in permanent preservation larger quantities of undisturbed natural habitats, free of pollution and encroachment by human beings.

In the United States there are already numerous national and state wildlife refuges, state and national parks, federal wilderness areas, and other managed habitats that attempt to protect wildlife species. Unfortunately, many of the critical habitats which need to be in permanent preservation are not presently represented in the system in significant amounts. This is especially true in the eastern United States because most of the natural environments were already in private ownership and/or highly modified by human use well before the park and refuge system came into existence in the late 1800s and early 1900s. If more of these shrinking critical habitats can be added to the preservation and conservation system in the coming decades, the survival outlook for many species of endangered and threatened mammals will improve as we enter the twenty-first century. The human overpopulation and environmental pollution problems are the "major catastrophes" which *must be solved* on a global level if the present mammal diversity is to survive.

The Southeastern Region and Mammal Affinities

The southeastern region of the United States covered in this book extends from Maryland in the East, all the way to the Mississippi River in the West, to the Ohio River in the Northwest, and includes all the South Atlantic and Gulf Coast states. The 12 states included are Georgia, Florida, South Carolina, North Carolina, Virginia, Maryland, West Virginia, Kentucky, Tennessee, Alabama, Mississippi, and the portion of Louisiana located east of the Mississippi River.

The southeastern states exhibit great variation in physiography and climate, ranging from the cool, moist spine of the Appalachian Mountains to the hot, humid coastal lowlands and tropical islands at sea level in the Florida Keys.

The Coastal Plains

Much of the Southeast is occupied by a great coastal plain of varying width, once covered by ocean and greatly shaped by wave action. It varies from perfectly flat (the lower coastal plain) to moderately rolling (the upper coastal plain). The coastal plain region possesses many diverse habitats with wide divides between drainage systems, broad slow-moving streams, and extensive floodplains. River swamps (with vegetation consisting mostly of hardwoods) and marshes

(with their aquatic grasses and forbs) form an important habitat in the coastal plain, as do sand hills derived from old beach dunes. Sand hill habitats have infertile, low-organic soils and are dominated by various types of pines and scrubby hardwoods.

The Atlantic Coastal Plain extends from Maryland through Virginia, North and South Carolina, Georgia, and Florida. The Gulf Coastal Plain then stretches from Florida through Alabama, Mississippi, and Louisiana. Both coastal plains often reach inland as much as 200 miles. As one approaches the coast, forested wetlands often give way to marshes and shallow bay systems. Prime examples are the Chesapeake marshes in Maryland and Virginia, the Everglades ("River of Grass") in Florida, and the vast marshes of Louisiana near the mouth of the Mississippi River.

Typically, a strand of barrier islands are found seaward of the coastal plain all along the Atlantic and Gulf coasts in the Southeast. These barrier islands contain many unique and isolated environments for mammals and are critical to protecting the mainland from erosion by oceanic storms. Some of the most famous barrier islands are the Outer Banks of North Carolina, the Sea Islands of Georgia, the Cape Canaveral region of Florida, and the Gulf Coast Islands of Florida,

Mississippi, and Alabama. Hurricanes are notorious for periodically changing the shape and configuration of the barrier islands in the southeastern states.

The Appalachian Mountains

Probably the most striking and beautiful region of the Southeast is the Appalachian Mountains. These mountains include the Allegheny, Blue Ridge, and Great Smoky Mountain ranges and several smaller chains. While the Appalachians are very ancient and worn down by erosion, they still form a group of moderately high peaks (several over 6,000 feet tall) which run northeast to southwest, bisecting the southeastern United States almost in half. The mammal habitats located in the mountains are characteristic of more northern portions of the United States and Canada. The tallest peaks are topped with spruce-fir-hemlock evergreen forests, which reach their southernmost sites of occurrence in the eastern United States. Mid- and lower-mountain slopes are dominated by a "mixed mesophytic" forest composed of maples, beech, tulip poplar, basswood, sweet gum, and various other hardwoods. Another dominant component of this beautiful forest, the chestnut tree, has been killed by the chestnut blight imported accidentally by humans from Europe in the 1800s. The foothills and dryer slopes of the Appalachians are typically dominated by oak-hickory forests. Mountain habitats often feature strong understory components of mountain laurel, rhododendrons, and azaleas, plus other shrubs and vines. Unique grasslands, called "mountain balds," also occur on the tops of some of the highest Appalachian peaks. Representative examples are Gregory Bald and Clingmans Dome located along the Tennessee–North Carolina border.

The climate of the mountain regions of the Southeast is much more characteristic of northern latitudes than the rest of the South. Summers tend to be moist, cool, and pleasant, while the winters are wet and cold, with a good deal of the precipitation falling as sleet, snow, or freezing rain.

The Plateau Areas

Surrounding the mountains are uplifted plateaus which form a rolling series of hills that are highly eroded. These foothills of the Appalachian Mountains are dissected by numerous streams into sharp hills, steep ridges, and valleys that are narrow compared with the upper coastal plains. East of the Appalachian Mountains, the plateau is called the Piedmont, but west of the mountains it is called the Cumberland or Appalachian Plateau. The latter region is dissected by rivers flowing to the Ohio and Mississippi Valleys. Isolated mountains and very large hills also occur extensively as occasional features in the Appalachian Plateau country. In the Piedmont a distinct "fall line," or steep escarpment having waterfalls, normally marks the boundary between the plateau and the upper coastal plain. No such fall line occurs clearly in the Cumberland Plateau region, although individual waterfalls and rapids do occur there.

Since agriculture is heavily practiced in the plateau regions, natural woodlands tend to occur today in remnants and isolated blocks compared with earlier days. These are primarily oak-hickory forests with flowering dogwood or various species of pine also present. Fallow fields in various stages of "oldfield succession" back to forest are abundant features in both the plateau and coastal plains regions. Annual and perennial weeds and grasses tend to predominate in the early stages of oldfield succession, followed by vines, brush, and various invading trees at later stages.

Mississippi and Ohio River Valleys

As one travels westward, the Appalachian Plateau gives way to the low, rolling hills of Kentucky and central Tennessee, which are drained by several major rivers that flow to the Ohio River and thus into the Mississippi. These include the Kentucky River, Green River, Cumberland River, and Tennessee River, among others. In western Kentucky and Tennessee are found the alluvial valleys of the major rivers in the region. Nearly all of the giant hardwood forests of the rich river valleys were long ago cut and replaced by agricultural fields. The deep floodplain soils deposited in the Ohio and Mississippi Valleys are among the most productive croplands in the country. In a few places, remnants of the hardwood forest (usually second-growth stands) still serve as mammal habitats.

Mammal Affinities

With regard to habitat restrictions placed on mammals, most medium-sized and larger species tend to range over several different plant communities or, occasionally, even over more than one physiographic region, but small mammals, on the other hand, are usually quite restricted in their mobility. They are usually confined to a specific habitat in a specific physiographic region. For example, deer, foxes, raccoons, and bobcats range over several habitats, but a pigmy shrew or bog lemming may be found in only one or two narrow habitat types.

It is also clear that many of the mammal species living in the Appalachian Mountains are quite distinctive from the mammal species found living in the coastal plains or plateau regions, both of which have rather similar faunas. Most of the mountain mammals found in the Southeast have direct affinities to Arctic and northern species rather than temperate or southern species of mammals. That is to say, colonization of the region by land mammals probably took place repeatedly from the north as climates fluctuated back and forth, north to south. The great ice sheets of the Pleistocene geological era pushed a number of northern mammal species southward into what is now the Southern Appalachians. These species include the red squirrel, five species of shrews, the hairy-tailed mole, the rock vole, the bog lemming, the red-backed vole, the Appalachian cottontail, the least weasel, the ermine, and the northern flying squirrel.

In contrast to terrestrial mammals, the marine mammals living along the Atlantic and Gulf Coasts tend to show affinities to southern and tropical species. This is reasonable, because there is little or no physical barrier to prevent warm-water whales or dolphins from swimming northward in the ocean to the Gulf and Atlantic Coasts. Clearly, major ocean barriers to terrestrial mammals do exist to colonization northward from the Caribbean Islands or the mainland of South America. Only three flying species, Wagner's mastiff bat, the little mastiff bat, and the Jamaican fruit bat, seem to have colonized the southeastern United States directly from the south. All other terrestrial mammals in the Southeast appear to have affinities to the west along the Gulf lowlands or from the north via the Appalachian Mountain chain or Atlantic lowlands.

Preservation of Mammal Specimens

Occasionally, private mammal collections are made and maintained by individuals interested in mammals, but most studies today are by specialists at institutions. Thus, mammal specimen collections usually are maintained by public and private institutions because of the continued expense and special long-term curatorial problems. There are, however, many valuable contributions regarding the behavioral patterns, life history, and geographical distribution of mammals that can be made by nonprofessionals and by the interested members of the public. Such contributions are achieved by careful observations of mammals coupled with accurate note taking and recording of the information.

Mammals are normally preserved in museums as study skins along with the skulls or skeletons. Because the preparation of a series of mammal study skins is a highly involved and laborious process which requires special skills, training, and experience, the layperson would be well advised to collect mammals with a camera. For the reader who is specifically interested in learning the techniques for preparing museum specimens, I would recommend E. R. Hall, *The Mammals of North America* (1981). It is listed in the Selected References at the end of this book.

To prevent decomposition of a mammal until it can be prepared as a museum skin or autopsied for other purposes, it should be properly tagged and labeled, then placed in a plastic bag, and kept frozen (or refrigerated) until prepared. For the person who obtains a specimen that needs identification by a specialist but lacks freezer space, smaller specimens may be preserved in 70-90 percent alcohol or in 5-10 percent formaldehyde. An incision made in the abdominal wall of the mammal will speed penetration of the chemicals and result in better preservation. For larger species, they should be frozen or refrigerated, if at all possible, until they can be examined by a mammalogist or wildlife biologist.

It should be emphasized that collecting permits are often required by state game and fish agencies before an individual conducts any trapping activities and/or scientific studies of mammals. Always check with the proper state agency in advance of any proposed field work.

Checklist of Southeastern Mammals

Key to Symbols
A = Abundant   C = Common   U = Uncommon   R = Rare
* = Some or all populations or subspecies are listed as endangered or threatened by U.S. Fish and Wildlife Service
+ = Nonnative species that has been introduced and now established in the southeastern United States

Mammal	Southeast Range	Typical Habitat	Relative Abundance
Class Mammalia			
Order Didelphimorpha—Pouched Mammals			
Family Didelphidae—Opossums			
Virginia Opossum	Regionwide	Most habitats	A
Didelphis virginiana			
Order Insectivora—Insectivores			
Family Soricidae—Shrews			
Pigmy Shrew	NE corner	Rocky slopes	R
Microsorex hoyi			
Water Shrew	Mountains	Stream banks	R
Sorex palustris			
Smoky Shrew	N mountains	Moist	C
Sorex fumeus			
Long-tailed Shrew	Mountains	Rocky slopes	R
Sorex dispar			
Southeastern Shrew	Regionwide, N 1/2 Florida	Most habitats	U
Sorex longirostris			
Masked Shrew	Mountains	Moist forests	C
Sorex cinereus			

Continued on next page

Mammal	Southeast Range	Typical Habitat	Relative Abundance
Northern Short-tailed Shrew *Blarina brevicauda*	N 1/3	Woodlands	C
Southern Short-tailed Shrew *Blarina carolinensis*	S 2/3	Woodlands	C
Least Shrew *Cryptotis parva*	Regionwide	Fields	C
Family Talpidae—Moles			
Eastern Mole *Scalopus aquaticus*	Regionwide	Fields	A
Star-nosed Mole *Condylura cristata*	Mountains & SE coast	Wet soils	R
Hairy-tailed Mole *Parascalops breweri*	Mountains	Moist soils	R
Order Chiroptera—Bats			
Family Vespertilionidae—Twilight Bats			
Little Brown Bat *Myotis lucifugus*	N 3/4	Caves, buildings	C
Southeastern Bat *Myotis austroriparius*	S 1/3, W 1/5	Caves, buildings	C
Gray Bat *Myotis grisescens*	C 1/3	Caves	R*
Keen's Bat *Myotis keenii*	N 1/3, SC 1/4	Caves	R
Indiana Bat *Myotis sodalis*	N 1/3, SC 1/4	Caves	R*
Small-footed Bat *Myotis leibii*	Mountains	Caves, rocks	R
Silver-haired Bat *Lasionycteris noctivagans*	NE 3/5	Trees	C
Eastern Pipistrelle *Pipistrellus subflavus*	Regionwide	Caves, trees	C
Big Brown Bat *Eptesicus fuscus*	Regionwide & buildings	Caves, trees	R
Red Bat *Lasiurus borealis*	Regionwide	Trees	C
Seminole Bat *Lasiurus seminolus*	Coastal plain	Trees	C
Hoary Bat *Lasiurus cinereus*	Regionwide	Trees	C
Yellow Bat *Lasiurus intermedius*	Lower coastal plain	Trees	C
Evening Bat *Nycticeius humeralis*	Regionwide	Trees, buildings	A
Rafinesque's Big-eared Bat *Plecotus rafinesqii*	S 3/4	Trees, buildings	R

Continued on next page

Mammal	Southeast Range	Typical Habitat	Relative Abundance
Townsend's Big-eared Bat	Mountains,	Caves	U*
Plecotus townsendii	E Kentucky		
Family Molossidae—Free-tailed Bats			
Brazilian Free-tailed Bat	S 1/2	Trees, buildings	C
Tadarida brasiliensis			
Wagner's Mastiff Bat	S Florida	Trees, buildings	R
Eumops glaucinus	S Florida	Trees, buildings	R
Little Mastiff Bat			
Molossus molossus			
Family Phyllostomidae—Leaf-nosed Bats			
Jamaican Fruit Bat			
Artibeus jamaicaensis			
Order Xenarthra—Armadillos, Anteaters, and Sloths			
Family Dasypodidae—Armadillos			
Nine-banded Armadillo	S 1/3	Most Habitats	C+
Dasypus novemcinctus			
Order Lagomorpha—Rabbits and Hares			
Family Leporidae—Rabbits			
Eastern Cottontail	Regionwide	Fields	A
Sylvilagus floridanus			
Appalachian Cottontail	Mountains	Dense shrubs	R
Sylvilagus obscurus			
Swamp Rabbit	W 3/5	River bottoms	C
Sylvilagus aquaticus			
Marsh Rabbit	Lower coastal plain	Wet areas	A
Sylvilagus palustris			
Snowshoe Hare	Mountains	Conifers	R
Lepus americanus			
Black-tailed Jackrabbit	Virginia, Maryland,	Fields	U
Lepus californicus	& Florida		
Order Rodentia—Gnawing Mammals			
Family Sciuridae—Squirrels			
Woodchuck	N 1/2	Field borders	A
Marmota monax			
Eastern Chipmunk	W 2/3	Mesic forests	C
Tamias striatus			
Gray Squirrel	Regionwide	Woodlands	A
Sciurus carolinensis			
Fox Squirrel	Regionwide	Oak, pine	C*
Sciurus niger			
Red-bellied Squirrel	Florida Keys	Tropical forest	U+
Sciurus aureogaster			
Red Squirrel	NE edge &	Conifers	C
Tamiasciurus hudsonicus	Mountains		
Southern Flying Squirrel	Regionwide	Mature forests	A
Glaucomys volans			

Continued on next page

Southeastern Mammalogy 15

Mammal	Southeast Range	Typical Habitat	Relative Abundance
Northern Flying Squirrel *Glaucomys sabrinus*	Mountains	Conifers	R*
Family Geomyidae—Pocket Gophers			
Southeastern Pocket Gopher *Geomys pinetis*	S 1/4	Sandy soils	C
Family Castoridae—Beavers			
Beaver *Castor canadensis*	Regionwide, N 1/3 Florida	Streams, lakes	C
Family Muridae—Mice, Rats, and Voles			
Eastern Woodrat *Neotoma floridana*	W 4/5	Forests	C*
Cotton Rat *Sigmodon hispidus*	Regionwide	Fields	A
Rice Rat *Oryzomys palustris*	Regionwide	Fields	C*
Eastern Harvest Mouse *Reithrodontomys humulis*	Regionwide	Fields	R
Fulvous Harvest Mouse *Reithrodontomys fulvescens*	Mississippi, Louisiana	Fields	C
Common Deer Mouse *Peromyscus maniculatus*	Mountains	Forests	C
Old-field Mouse *Peromyscus polionotus*	S 1/3	Fields	C*
White-footed Mouse *Peromyscus leucopus*	N 2/3	Hardwoods	C
Cotton Mouse *Peromyscus gossypinus*	S 1/2	Forests	A*
Florida Mouse *Peromyscus floridanus*	Florida	Scrub	C
Golden Mouse *Ochrotomys nuttalli*	Regionwide	Forests	C
Rock Vole *Microtus chrotorrhinus*	Mountains	Rocky slopes	C
Meadow Vole *Microtus pennsylvanicus*	NE 1/3, & W Florida	Moist meadows	C*
Prairie Vole *Microtus ochrogaster*	NW 1/5	Fields	C
Woodland or Pine Vole *Microtus pinetorum*	Regionwide, N 1/2 Florida	Woodlands	C
Southern Bog Lemming *Synaptomys cooperi*	Mountains & N 1/4	Forest edges	R
Southern Red-backed Vole *Clethrionomys gapperi*	Mountains	Conifers	R
Round-tailed Muskrat *Neofiber alleni*	Florida, S Georgia	Marshes, lakeshores, & farmlands	C

Continued on next page

Mammal	Southeast Range	Typical Habitat	Relative Abundance
Muskrat *Ondatra zibethicus*	NW 2/3	Marshes, lakeshores	C
Norway Rat *Rattus norvegicus*	Regionwide	Buildings, farms	A+
Roof Rat *Rattus rattus*	Regionwide	Buildings, farms	A+
House Mouse *Mus musculus*	Regionwide	Buildings, farms	A+
Family Dipodidae—Jumping Mice			
Meadow Jumping Mouse *Zapus hudsonius*	N 1/2	Wet meadows	U
Woodland Jumping Mouse *Napaeozapus insignis*	Mountains	Wooded brooks	U
Family Myocastoridae—Nutrias			
Nutria *Myocaster coypu*	Scattered colonies	Marshes, lakes	C+
Family Erethizontidae—Porcupines			
Porcupine *Erethizon dorsatum*	Mountains	Forests	R
Order Carnivora—Flesh-eating Mammals			
Family Ursidae—Bears			
Black Bear *Ursus americanus*	Mountains, coastal plains	Most habitats	R*
Family Procyonidae—Raccoons			
Raccoon *Procyon lotor*	Regionwide	Most habitats	A
Family Mustelidae—Weasels and Skunks			
Mink *Mustela vison*	Regionwide, parts of Florida	Near water	C
Fisher *Martes pennanti*	Mountains	Conifers	R
Pine Marten *Martes americana*	N Mountains.	Conifers	R
Long-tailed Weasel *Mustela frenata*	Regionwide	Most habitats	R
Short-tailed Weasel *Mustela erminea*	NE Corner	Conifers	R
Least Weasel *Mustela nivalis*	Mountains	Conifers	R
Striped Skunk *Mephitis mephitis*	Regionwide	Most habitats	C
Eastern Spotted Skunk *Spilogale putorious*	Regionwide	Open areas	R
River Otter *Lutra canadensis*	Regionwide	Streams, lakes	C

Continued on next page

Mammal	Southeast Range	Typical Habitat	Relative Abundance
Family Canidae—Foxes and Coyotes			
Coyote	Regionwide	Open country	C+
Canis latrans			
Red Fox	Regionwide	Field borders	C
Vulpes vulpes			
Gray Fox	Regionwide	Most habitats	A
Urocyon cinereoargenteus			
Family Felidae—Cats			
Cougar	S Florida	Most habitats	R*
Felis concolor			
Bobcat	Regionwide	Most habitats	A
Lynx rufus			
Family Phocidae-Hair Seals			
Harbor seal	Atlantic	Coastal marine	R
Phoca vitulina			
Hooded Seal	Atlantic	Coastal marine	R
Cystophora cristata			
Order Sirenia—Manatees			
Family Trichechidae—Manatees			
Manatee or Sea Cow	Atlantic, Gulf	Rivers, coastal	R*
Trichechus manatus			
Order Artiodactyla—Even-Toed Hoofed Mammals			
Family Suidae—Pigs			
Wild Boar	Regionwide	Most habitats	C+
Sus scrofa			
Family Cervidae—Deer			
White-tailed Deer	Regionwide	Most habitats	C
Odocoileus virginianus			
Sambar Deer	St. Vincent, Island, Florida	Wetland borders	C+
Cervus unicolor			
Sika Deer	Virginia, Maryland	Forests	C+
Cervus nippon			
Fallow Deer	Virginia, Maryland	Forest	U+
Dama dama			
Order Cetacea—Whales			
Family Delphinidae—Dolphins and Porpoises			
Rough-toothed Dolphin	Atlantic, Gulf	Marine	R
Steno bredanensis			
Long-snouted Spinner Dolphin	Atlantic, Gulf	Marine	R
Stenella longirostris			
Short-snouted Spinner Dolphin	Atlantic, Gulf	Marine	R
Stenella clymene			
Striped Dolphin	Atlantic, Gulf	Marine	C
Stenella coeruleoalba			
Spotted Dolphin	Atlantic, Gulf	Marine	C
Stenella frontalis			

Continued on next page

Mammal	Southeast Range	Typical Habitat	Relative Abundance
Bridled Dolphin *Stenella attenuata*	Atlantic, Gulf	Marine	R
Saddle-backed Dolphin *Delphinus delphis*	Atlantic. Gulf	Marine	C
Bottle-nosed Dolphin *Tursiops truncatus*	Atlantic, Gulf	Marine	A
Fraser's Dolphin *Lagenodelphis hosei*	Atlantic, Gulf	Marine	R
False Killer Whale *Pseudorca crassidens*	Atlantic, Gulf	Marine	R
Killer Whale *Orcinus orca*	Atlantic, Gulf	Marine	R
Pigmy Killer Whale *Feresa attenuata*	Atlantic, Gulf	Marine	R
Risso's Dolphin *Grampus griseus*	Atlantic, Gulf	Marine	R
Short-finned Pilot Whale *Globicephala macrorhynchus*	Atlantic, Gulf	Marine	A
Long-finned Pilot Whale *Globicephala melaena*	Atlantic	Marine	R
Melon-headed Whale *Peponcephala electra*	Atlantic, Gulf	Marine	R
Family Phocoenidae—Porpoises			
Harbor Porpoise *Phocoena phocoena*	Atlantic	Marine	R
Family Physeteridae—Sperm Whales			
Pigmy Sperm Whale *Kogia breviceps*	Atlantic, Gulf	Marine	U
Dwarf Sperm Whale *Kogia simus*	Atlantic, Gulf	Marine	R
Giant Sperm Whale *Physeter macrocephalus*	Atlantic, Gulf	Marine	R
Family Ziphiidae—Beaked Whales			
Goose-beaked Whale *Ziphius cavirostris*	Atlantic, Gulf	Marine	R
Dense-beaked Whale *Mesoplodon densirostris*	Atlantic, Gulf	Marine	R
Antillean Beaked Whale *Mesoplodon europaeus*	Atlantic, Gulf	Marine	R
True's Beaked Whale *Mesoplodon mirus*	Atlantic, Gulf	Marine	R
North Sea Beaked Whale *Mesoplodon bidens*	Atlantic, Gulf	Marine	R
Family Balaenopteridae—Fin Whales			
Fin Whale *Balaenoptera physalus*	Atlantic, Gulf	Marine	R*

Continued on next page

Mammal	Southeast Range	Typical Habitat	Relative Abundance
Minke Whale	Atlantic, Gulf	Marine	R
Balaenoptera acutorostrata			
Sei Whale	Atlantic, Gulf	Marine	R*
Balaenoptera borealis			
Bryde's Whale	Atlantic, Gulf	Marine	R
Balaenoptera edeni			
Blue Whale	Atlantic, Gulf	Marine	R*
Balaenoptera musculus			
Humpbacked Whale	Atlantic, Gulf	Marine	R*
Megaptera novaeangliae			
Right Whale	Atlantic, Gulf	Marine	R*
Balaena glacialis			
Extirpated Native Species			
Red Wolf	Regionwide	Mature forests	
Canis rufus			
Elk or Wapeti	Regionwide	Meadows, forests	
Cervus canadensis			
Bison or Buffalo	Regionwide	Meadows, forests	
Bison bison			
West Indian Monk Seal	Atlantic, Gulf	Coastal marine	
Monachus tropicalis			

Key to Orders of Terrestrial Mammals in the Southeast

Key	Order	Page
1. Forelimbs form wings Forelimbs form legs	Chiroptera (bats)	53
2. Feet with 2 or more large, hard hoofs Feet with 4 or 5 clawed toes		
3. Each foot with 2 or 4 hoofs	Artiodactyla (deer, pigs, etc.)	179
4. Innermost toe of each hind foot thumb like, opposable, and without claw; tail long, nearly naked, and capable of grasping; female with pouch for young	Didelphimorpha (opossum)	33
Innermost toe of each hind foot not thumb like and with claw; tail either short or long, haired or naked, not grasping; female without pouch for young		
5. Upper part of body and tail completely covered with a hard, bone-like plate	Xenarthra (armadillo)	80
Body and tail not covered with a bonelike plate		
6. Tail a cotton-like tuft; ear longer than tail	Lagomorpha (rabbits)	84
Tail not a cotton-like tuft; ear longer than tail		
7. Snout long and pointed, highly flexible; eyes very small	Insectivora (shrews & moles)	36
Snout normal, not flexible; eyes normal		
8. A conspicuous gap (diastema) between front teeth (incisors) and cheek teeth (molars); no canines present	Rodentia	94
9. No conspicuous gap between incisor and molar teeth in upper and lower jaw; prominent canines behind incisor teeth	Carnivora	147

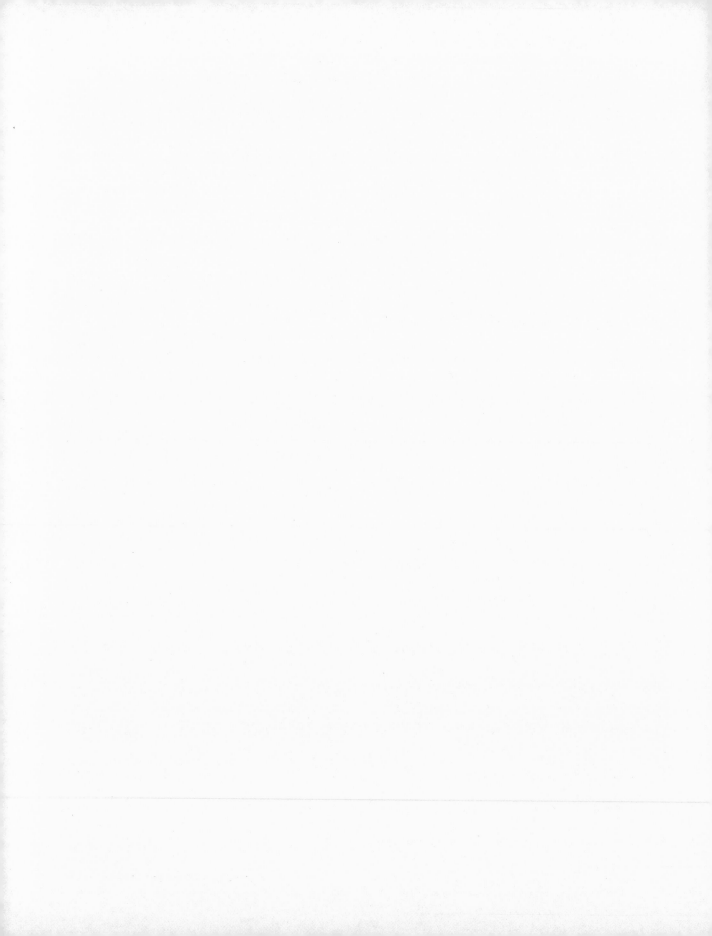

Southern short-tailed shrew, *Blarina carolinensis*. Larry Brown

Star-nosed mole, *Condylura cristata*. American Society of Mammalogists

Red bat, *Lasiurus borealis*. Merlin Tuttle

Hoary bat, *Lasiurus cinereus*. American Society of Mammalogists

Nine-banded armadillo, *Dasypus novemcinctus*. Larry Brown

Fox squirrel, *Sciurus niger.* Barry Mansell

Eastern woodrat, *Neotoma floridana.* Larry Brown

Old-field mouse, *Peromyscus polionotus.* Larry Brown

Black bear, *Ursus americanus*. Florida Game & Fresh-Water Fish Commission

River otter, *Lutra canadensis*. Larry Brown

26 Color Illustrations

Coyote, *Canis latrans.* U.S. Fish & Wildlife Service

Cougar, *Felis concolor.* Florida Game & Freshwater Fish
Commission

Harbor seal, *Phoca vitulina.* Tom French

Manatee, *Trichechus manatus.* Florida Game & Freshwater Fish Commission

Wild Boar, *Sus scrofa*. Larry Brown

White-tailed deer, *Odocoileus virginianus*. Florida Game & Freshwater Fish Commission

American bison, *Bison bison*. Barry Mansell

SPECIES ACCOUNTS

Order Didelphimorpha
Pouched Mammals

Members of this group differ from other mammals by the presence of a pouch on the abdomen of the female, where the young are sheltered as they suckle. Order Didelphimorpha is a very primitive one, with the skeleton showing certain affinities to reptiles.

Most species of pouched mammals (or marsupials) inhabit South America, Australia, and nearby islands. These include kangaroos, opossums, wallabies, wombats, koalas, marsupial moles, bandicoots, Tasmanian devils, and marsupial wolves. Only one species, the Virginia opossum, is found north of Mexico. The gestation period of marsupials tends to be very short, and young are poorly developed and very small at birth. They complete their development over a period of several weeks after attaching to a nipple in the pouch. There is often considerable mortality of the poorly developed offspring at the time of birth and before they reach the pouch and attach to a mammary gland. Young marsupials are also rather vulnerable to predation after they complete development and leave the safety of the pouch to be on their own.

Marsupials are generally at a competitive disadvantage compared with the more advanced placental mammals. They are sluggish, slow, and possess a low order of intelligence. Also, reproductive processes are inefficient (only a primitive type of placenta develops), and they are subject to more mortality than the advanced mammals. Still, it is hard to argue with the wide distribution and overwhelming success of some of the more generalized types of marsupials such as the Virginia opossum. They have overcome the evolutionary drawbacks of being primitive forms by being adaptable to almost every type of ecological situation and climate, and they can survive on almost any kind of food available, whether it be animal or vegetable in nature. Also, their primitive reproductive system makes up for breeding losses by out-producing any potential competitor that occupies their habitat. In this way, the opossum and several other generalized marsupials have survived and thrived many millions of years, despite the subsequent evolution of thousands of more advanced mammalian species.

Virginia Opossum
Didelphis virginiana

Virginia opossum, *Didelphis virginianus.* Unknown

Identification: The "possum" in the Southeast is about the size of a house cat, has a long, naked grasping (prehensile) tail and small, leaflike ears. The feet are shaped somewhat like human hands with the inner toe being thumblike. The fur color is quite variable and ranges from the common gray form to an almost all-white or all-black coloration. Females have a fur-lined pouch on the abdomen, but males lack pouches. Also, males are heavier and larger than females.

The skull is identified by a prominent median ridge on the top, small brain size, and 50 teeth present in the jaws. No other terrestrial mammal in the southeast has more than 44 teeth.

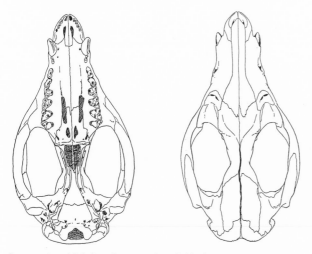

Lower view (right) and upper view (left) of an opossum (*Didelphis virginiana*) skull.

Geographical Range: The opossum occurs throughout the southeastern states and in virtually all habitats. It also occurs throughout most of the United States except for a few western and northern states. It has been expanding its range northward and westward in historic times, aided greatly by people's activities, such as ranching, farming, timbering, and outright releases of opossums into new areas.

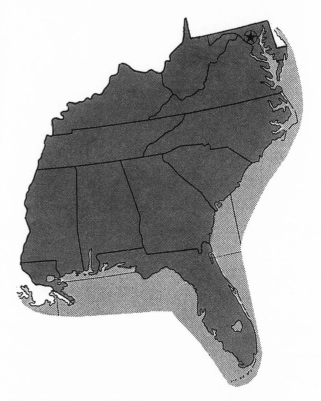

Geographical range of the Virginia opossum in the Southeast.

Habitat: Opossums show no clear-cut habitat preference and can be found virtually anywhere there are trees. They are excellent climbers and often seek safety in the treetops. In residential and suburban areas, opossums are surprisingly abundant, nesting in yard trees, attics, and outbuildings.

Natural History: Opossums forage extensively on the ground as well as in trees. They are mainly nocturnal, and have a slow ambling gait. In the Southeast, they are probably the most common "road-kill" found on the highways.

When cornered, opossums appear to be slow-witted and nonaggressive. They often open their mouths and hiss or growl at the offender, but rarely attack. If tormented extensively, they sometimes feign death in a behavioral pattern commonly called "playing possum." When handled in this condition, opossums are limp and appear dead. However, they quickly regain consciousness and escape after the tormentor has lost interest.

The breeding season is long, extending from January to mid-summer. Each female usually produces two litters per year and the gestation period is an incredibly short 13 days long. As many as 18–25 young may be born at one time, but since there are only 13 milk-producing nipples in the pouch, this an upper limit for the number of young that can complete development. The actual number of young opossums leaving the pouch averages around six or seven. When young opossums finally leave the pouch, they are about the size of a small rat and 70–80 days old. For a time they hang on to the mother's back or tail and are carried about as she forages. They are on their own for the first time when about three months old, and some are known to breed at six months of age.

The opossum is omnivorous and will eat almost any animal or vegetable food available. In residential areas they often can be found foraging in garbage cans if they can gain access to them. On farms opossums frequently kill poultry which they corner in pens or on the roost at night when the birds are helpless.

The maximum longevity of opossums in the wild is not known, but in captivity, they have lived as long as eight to ten years. Population turnover in the southern states appears to occur every four to six years for natural populations. They are preyed upon by many carnivores, including dogs, cats, foxes, bobcats, owls, and humans.

Remarks: Opossums are sometimes hunted by humans for food in the Southeast, but are not considered an important game animal. The pelt is sometimes sold, but is of very low fur value in southern states. Opossums cause some crop damage in certain truck-gardening operations, but are seldom a serious economic problem except in poultry farming.

The forked penis of male opossums is sometimes a subject of interest, leading to the myth that opossums copulate via the female's nose. Instead, the bifurcate penis enters the paired lateral vaginae of the female reproductive tract to deposit sperm. In other mammals, the two female reproductive tubes fuse in the midline to form a single canal, the vagina, but in the primitive marsupials they remain separate.

Selected References:

Fitch, H. S., and L. L. Sandridge. 1953. Ecology of the opossum on a natural area in northeastern Kansas. University of Kansas, Publication of the Museum Natural History, No. 7: 305–38.

Gardner, A. L. 1973. The systematics of the genus *Didelphis* (Marsupialia: Didelphidae) in North and Middle America. Texas Tech University, Special Publication of the Museum, No. 4: 81 pp.

Hartman, C. G. 1952. *Possums*. University of Texas Press, Austin. 174 pp.

———. 1953. Breeding habits, development and birth of the opossum. Smithsonian Report for 1952, Pp. 347–63.

Llewellyn, L. M., and F. H. Dale. 1964. Notes on the ecology of the opossum in Maryland. J. Mamm. 45: 113–22.

McManus, J. J. 1974. Virginia Opossum *(Didelphis virginiana)*. Mammalian Species, No. 40: pp. 1–6.

Petrides, G. A. 1949. Sex and age determination in the opossum. J. Mamm. 30: 364–78.

Reynolds, H. C. 1945. Some aspects of the life history and ecology of the opossum in central Missouri. J. Mamm. 26: 361–79.

Shirer, H. W., and H. S. Fitch. 1970. Comparison from radio tracking of movements and denning habits of the raccoon, striped skunk, and opossum in northeastern Kansas. J. Mamm. 51: 491–503.

Order Insectivora
Insectivores

The insectivores are a group of mammals whose name reflects their dietary habits; that is, insects usually form the bulk of their food (however, they also consume a wide variety of other invertebrates and small animals). They all possess long, pointed, flexible snouts that are sensitive organs of touch and smell. Their eyes are tiny and beadlike, and in some the eyelids are permanently closed. Their ears are leaflike or absent, buried in the fur, and not clearly visible.

This order contains one of the smallest kinds of mammals alive on earth, the shrew. One species native to the Southeast, the pigmy shrew, has a body weight of one-tenth of an ounce or slightly less. Insectivores also have a high metabolic rate and may consume nearly twice their body weight in food each day. Since most members of the order do not hibernate, they must have a constant and dependable supply of invertebrates available to feed upon. Insectivores have a reputation for being aggressive foragers, and sometimes they kill and consume prey somewhat larger than themselves. In one group, the moles, the eyes are poorly developed or vestigial, and they can tell only light from dark.

Most insectivores have a short life span and a rather high reproductive rate. Mortality is also high, and populations turn over rapidly (sometimes even annually).

Insectivores are relatively primitive and considered to be the evolutionary stem group that gave rise to all the advanced mammals. The order has a worldwide distribution, except for Australia, the polar regions, and part of South America. They include hedgehogs, solenodons, tenrecs, shrews, and moles. Insectivores are very well represented in the Southeast with twelve species known to live within the boundaries of the region. This diversity of species is at least partially due to the large variety of ecological communities within the southeastern United States, most of which are rich in the various types of invertebrates that serve as an annual food supply.

Pigmy Shrew
Microsorex hoyi

Pigmy shrew, *Microsorex hoyi*. Unknown

Geographical range of the pigmy shrew in the Southeast.

Identification: The pigmy shrew is the smallest mammal in the Southeast and the United States. Its body weigh is about the same as that of a dime. The pelage is grayish brown to reddish brown on the back and grayish tan on the belly. This is a long-tailed shrew like all those of the *Sorex* group, and the tail is about one-half the length of the rest of the body.

The skull of the pigmy shrew is extremely small and forms an elongated, narrow triangle when viewed from above. It is identified by its small size and the fact that only three unicusps are readily visible when the skull is viewed from the side (unicusps are small, cone-shaped teeth located near the front of the upper jaw). For positive identification of all shrew skulls, an expert should be consulted.

Geographical Range: This species is one of the most rarely trapped mammals in North America. It is almost never taken by conventional traps, but the use of pitfall traps (sunken cans) normally reveals its presence. In the southeastern states, the pigmy shrew is known only from the Appalachian Mountains, and it has been recorded as far south as northern Georgia. In the United States, the pigmy shrew is considered a boreal species which ranges southward primarily in the western and eastern mountain ranges.

Habitat: The pigmy shrew has been taken on steep, rocky slopes in moist mountain woodlands (birch-basswood-hemlock stands) having heavy leaf litter and a rhododendron understory. It is probably more common than trapping suggests because this shrew will not enter the traps traditionally used by mammalogists to study most small species. Pitfall traps are the best way to collect pigmy shrews.

Natural History: Very little is known about the life history of the pigmy shrew, primarily because few have ever been captured. In Wisconsin one was observed eating the larvae from a dung beetle burrow. The stomach contents of pigmy shrews have been found to contain beetle grubs, flies, and unidentifiable arthropod fragments. Pigmy shrews apparently produce large litters, because the few pregnant females that have been taken contained five to eight embryos. They apparently produce only one or two litters per year, these during the summer months.

Remarks: The pigmy shrew has no economic importance. It is mainly remarkable for its small body size, which approaches the theoretical lower limit at which a mammal can maintain its body heat. According to mathematical calculations involving the surface area of a mammal in relationship to its overall volume (biomass), the pigmy shrew would lose body heat faster than it could be produced if it were any smaller.

Selected References:

Diersing, V. E. 1980. Systematics and evolution of the pigmy shrews (subgenus *Microsorex*) of North America. J. Mamm. 61: 76–101.

Feldhamer, G. A., R. S. Klann, A. S. Gerard, and A. C. Driskell. 1993. Habitat partitioning, body size, and timing of parturition in pigmy shrews and associated soricids. J. Mamm. 74: 412–21.

Long, C. A. 1974. Pigmy Shrews *(Microsorex hoyi* and *M. thompsoni)*. Mammalian Species, No. 33: pp. 1–4.

Water Shrew
Sorex palustris

Water shrew, *Sorex palustris.* Roger W. Barbour

Geographical range of the water shrew in the Southeast.

Identification: The water shrew is the largest long-tailed shrew found in the Southeast, with a total length approaching six inches. The fur is soft, woolly, and blackish on the upper side. The underparts are silver white, and the tail is long, hairy, and distinctly bicolor. The feet are large and covered with stiff, silvery bristles which aid greatly its locomotion through the water.

The skull is identified by its robust size for a shrew and chestnut brown pigment on the teeth. It possesses one more unicusp (a simple peglike tooth near the front of the upper jaw) than the short-tailed shrew in the same size range.

Geographical Range: The water shrew occurs only in a few relict populations at high altitude along the Appalachian Mountain chain from western Virginia and eastern West Virginia southward to western North Carolina and eastern Tennessee. In North America, it also ranges across New England, Canada, the Great Lakes region, and the northern Rocky Mountains of the United States.

Habitat: The water shrew lives along the banks of mountain brooks and streams located at higher elevations. The forests surrounding these streams are generally conifers (spruce-fir-hemlock) or a mixture of broadleaf trees and conifers. These shrews never venture far from running or standing water.

Natural History: Water shrews are powerful swimmers and forage for insects, arthropods, and other invertebrates by diving into streams or by searching along stream banks. When moving rapidly, water shrews can sprint along the top of the water on their enlarged, bristled feet, supported by surface tension; therefore, they are often called "water walkers." Water shrews also trap air in their thick fur, which adds to their buoyancy while swimming. They tend to float like a cork when resting in the water. Both the forefeet and hind feet are used in paddling.

The diet varies with the seasonal availability of prey, but includes stone flies, caddis flies, mayflies, planarians, fish eggs, minnows, leeches, and many other small aquatic organisms.

The breeding season starts in late winter and extends through the spring and summer months. Ovulation in adult females is induced by copulation, and the gestation period is about 21 days. The litter size ranges from three to eight and averages five. Females produce two to three litters during the breeding season. Postpartum pregnancies are known to occur in this species. Young water shrews born early in the spring often breed in their first summer.

Remarks: Water shrews are seldom captured, but they are fairly abundant along high mountain streams. Traps must be set along stream banks and at the water's edge to be successful.

Selected References:
Beneski, J. T. 1988. American Water Shrew *(Sorex palustris)*. Mammalian Species, No. 296: pp. 1–6.

Conaway, C. H. 1952. Life history of the water shrew, *Sorex palustris navigator*. Amer. Midl. Nat. 48: 219–48.

Sorenson, M. W. 1963. Some aspects of water shrew behavior. Amer. Midl. Nat. 68: 445–62.

Smoky Shrew
Sorex fumeus

Smoky shrew, *Sorex fumeus.* Roger W. Barbour

Identification: The smoky shrew is one of the larger long-tailed shrews occurring in the Southeast. Its tail is also quite long (one and two-thirds inches to two inches), so the total length of the species is four and one-quarter inches to four and three-quarters inches. The pelage is grayish brown to dusky brown on the back, and the belly is gray.

The skull is robust for a shrew and identified by the third unicusp, which is larger than the fourth unicusp. For positive identification, all shrew skulls should be examined by a mammalogist.

Geographical Range: In the Southeast, this shrew occurs only in the Appalachian Mountain chain. It is a boreal species whose geographical range extends southward in the United States only in the higher mountains. In North America the smoky shrew ranges through New England to southeastern Canada, but not westward.

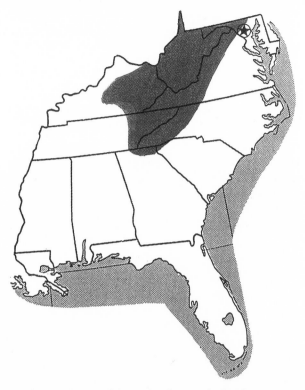

Geographical range of the smoky shrew in the Southeast.

Habitat: The smoky shrew lives in cool, moist deciduous and coniferous forests having a thick leaf litter and strewn with mossy rocks, logs, and stumps. It seems to prefer mixed stands of hemlock and deciduous hardwoods.

Natural History: This species is active both day and night under the leaf-litter of the forest floor. It often utilizes the tunnels of moles, rodents, and other species of shrews.

Smoky shrews are aged by using a combination of tooth wear and body weight. Breeding commences in April and after a gestation period of three weeks, litters of two to eight young are born (the average is five and one-half per litter). There is a postpartum estrous period (females come into heat right after giving birth), and another litter is soon on its way. Two or three litters are normally produced each breeding season. By late August the reproductive season ends, and most of the adult shrews die off before the next breeding season. Studies have shown that almost the entire population is composed of immature shrews, born the previous spring and summer. Sexual maturity does not occur until after the first winter in young smoky shrews. Adults rarely ever reach two years of age before dying.

In a New York study, the smoky shrew's diet included (in order of preference) insects, earthworms, centipedes, millipedes, snails, salamanders, and other small animals. When kept alive in captivity, smoky shrews have eaten about one-half their body weight each day.

Remarks: Known predators of this shrew include hawks, owls, weasels, foxes, bobcats, and raccoons.

Smoky shrews are ecologically and economically beneficial because of the large number of insects and other arthropods consumed.

Selected References:

Hamilton, W. J., Jr. 1940. The biology of the smoky shrew (*Sorex fumeus* Miller). Zoologica 25: 473–92.

Owen, J. G. 1984. Smoky Shrew (*Sorex fumeus*). Mammalian Species, No. 215: pp. 1–8.

Long-tailed Shrew
Sorex dispar

Long-tailed shrew, *Sorex dispar*. Roger W. Barbour

Identification: This species, also called the rock shrew, is a medium-sized, slim-bodied shrew with a much longer tail than the other members of the *Sorex* group. The masked shrew, southeastern shrew, and pigmy shrew are much smaller, and the water shrew and smoky shrew are much more robust then the long-tailed shrew. The fur of this species is a dark slate gray both above and below. The long tail is somewhat darker, stout, and not noticeably bicolored.

The skull is relatively small, slim, and difficult to distinguish from the other shrews in its size range. A shrew expert should be consulted for positive identification.

Geographical Range: This shrew ranges only along the higher mountains of the Appalachian chain, from Maine to western North Carolina and eastern Tennessee. It has not yet been captured in northern Georgia or Alabama, but could possibly be in both states at higher elevations.

Geographical range of the long-tailed shrew in the Southeast.

Habitat: The long-tailed shrew prefers moist, rocky slopes, rock slides, cliffs, and talus slopes in cool, coniferous forests at higher altitudes. I found them to be abundant in moss-covered rockpiles located several miles east of Gatlinburg, Tennessee, in Great Smoky Mountain National Park.

Natural History: Little is known of this shrew's life history, but it feeds heavily on spiders, centipedes, beetles, flies, roaches, and other invertebrates common to boulder fields.

The breeding season begins in the late spring and continues through the summer with two to six young produced per litter. Females average two to three litters each year. The length of gestation or duration of maternal care is not known.

Remarks: The long-tailed shrew is beneficial because of the large numbers of arthropods and other invertebrates it consumes.

This shrew appears to have very narrow habitat requirements and is restricted to very specific mountain environments. However, within those ecological limits it often is locally rather abundant and easily taken in traps set in rock slides and boulder fields.

Selected References:

Kirkland, G. L., Jr. 1981. Rock Shrew and Gaspe Shrew *(Sorex dispar* and *Sorex gaspensis)*. Mammalian Species, No. 155: pp. 1–4.

Richmond, N. D., and W. C. Grimm. 1950. Ecology and distribution of the shrew, *Sorex dispar*, in Pennsylvania. Ecology 31: 279–82.

Southeastern Shrew
Sorex longirostris

Southeastern shrew, *Sorex longirostris*. Tom French

Identification: The southeastern shrew is one of the smallest long-tailed shrews in the Southeast; only the pigmy shrew is smaller. The long-tailed shrew and smoky shrew both are significantly larger than the southeastern shrew. The fur is reddish brown above, paler on the belly, and the tail extends at least a half inch beyond the length of the back leg.

The skull is identified by small size and the fact that the third unicusp is smaller than the fourth.

Geographical Range: This shrew has a regionwide distribution, except the southern half of Florida, and is widely scattered through the various ecological communities present in the Southeast. In the United States, the range of the southeastern shrew fits approximately the southeastern quadrant of the country.

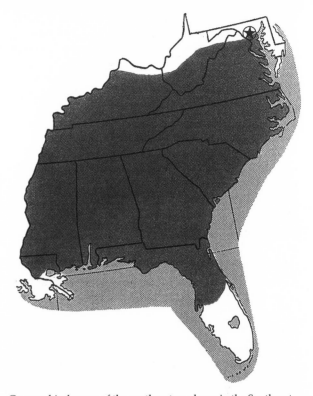

Geographical range of the southeastern shrew in the Southeast.

Habitat: Many records of this shrew are from swamp borders and floodplain forests; however, it has also been frequently taken in drier upland locations, including fields and pastures, so it probably occurs in most habitats.

Natural History: The life history of the southeastern shrew is poorly known because it is seldom captured. This apparent rareness generally reflects nothing more than the reluctance of this shrew to enter standard mammal traps. It can readily be taken in pitfall traps (sunken cans) placed in the ground, but this labor-intensive sampling method is unfortunately seldom utilized by investigators. My first southeastern shrew was collected in a snap trap over 30 years ago (the shrew had never been recorded in that state before), but in many thousands of trap nights since then, I have never taken another one in a snap trap. Pitfall traps have shown that the southeastern shrew is really rather common in many different kinds of habitats, including fields, swamps, forests, thickets, etc.

Southeastern shrews spend most of their time under the leaf litter of the forest floor and in subterranean tunnels. Their nests are fairly bulky and made of leaf litter lined with fine grasses and plant fibers. Nests are usually located under logs, stumps, and tree roots.

Analysis of stomach contents reveals they feed primarily on spiders, lepidoptera larvae, snails, centipedes, and slugs.

Southeastern shrews are known to breed during the spring and summer months when arthropods are most abundant, and produce two to six young per litter (the average is four). The length of gestation or duration of maternal care is unknown. The young shrews probably mature, breed, and die on an annual turnover basis.

Remarks: This species is sometimes taken by owls, opossums, cats, and snakes. All shrews have strong musk glands, and the shrews may be killed by predators but may not be eaten.

The southeastern shrew has little or no economic importance, except as a voracious eater of arthropods and other invertebrates.

Selected References:

Brown, L. N. 1961. *Sorex longirostris* in southwestern Missouri. J. Mamm. 42: 527.

French, T. W. 1980. Southeastern Shrew (*Sorex longirostris*). Mammalian Species, No. 143: pp. 1–3.

Whitaker, J. D., Jr., and R. E. Mumford. 1972. Food and ectoparasites of Indiana shrews. J. Mamm. 53: 329–35.

Masked Shrew
Sorex cinereus

Masked shrew, *Sorex cinereus*. Roger W. Barbour

Identification: The masked shrew, or cinereus shrew, is a long-tailed species somewhat smaller than the smoky shrew and slightly larger than the southeastern shrew. The pelage is gray-brown above and pale smoke-gray below. Tail length is one and one-quarter inches to one and one-half inches and body length ranges from three and one-half inches to four and one-eighth inches. Contrary to the common name, this species does not have an obvious facial mask.

The skull is rather similar to that of the smoky shrew but smaller and more delicate. The third unicusp is distinctly larger than the fourth. As with the other shrews living in the southeastern states, positive identification of skulls requires an expert.

Geographical Range: In the Southeast, this shrew lives only in the Appalachian Mountains. In North America, the masked shrew occurs widely over the northern half of the United States, most of Canada, and southward into the Rocky Mountains.

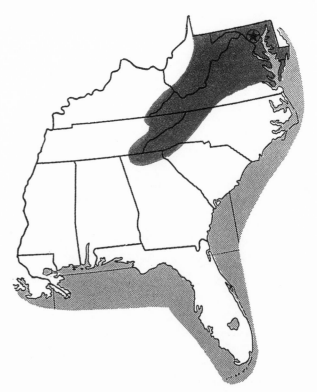

Geographical range of the masked shrew in the Southeast.

Habitat: The masked shrew occurs in moist deciduous forests or in mixed conifers and hardwoods having heavy leaf litter and mossy rocks, stumps, and logs.

Natural History: Like many other species, this shrew is active both day and night. It feeds voraciously, consuming at least half its body weight each day. Stomach contents have been found to contain caterpillars, beetle larvae, centipedes, millipedes, spiders, earthworms, crickets, adult beetles, snails, insect eggs, pupae, and other invertebrates.

The breeding season lasts from early March until mid-September, and several litters are produced each year. Litter size ranges from two to ten (the average is six), and the gestation period is 22 days. All baby shrews are blind, naked, and helpless. The eyes open when they are about 12 days old. Young masked shrews exhibit an interesting behavior of follow-the-leader, or "caravaning," once they are able to crawl about well. They form a single file behind the mother, each maintaining contact with the rump of the one in front by burying its nose in the fur at the base of the tail. The mother weans her offspring at about three weeks of age. Masked shrews can become sexually mature when three weeks old. The maximum life span is about 15 months in this species.

The population densities of the masked shrew can sometimes exceed 40 per acre, as shown in a Wisconsin study, but are usually much lower. The home-range size of a shrew is small, not exceeding one-fourth acre (1,200 square feet).

Masked shrews, like other species, have strong musk or scent glands in the flank area. Their musky smell apparently protects them from predators, but I have seen many of them killed by cats and dogs and left uneaten. The principal predators of masked shrews appear to be owls, foxes, weasels, and bobcats.

Remarks: This shrew is usually common in a variety of habitats, so it has an impact on a variety of invertebrates.

Selected References:

Brown, L. N. 1967. Ecological distribution of six species of shrews and comparison of sampling methods in the Central Rocky Mountains. J. Mamm. 48: 617–23.

Zyll de Jong, C. C., and G. L. Kirkland, Jr. 1989. A morphometric analysis of the *Sorex cinereus* group in central and eastern North America. J. Mamm. 70: 110–22.

Northern Short-tailed Shrew
Blarina brevicauda

Northern short-tailed shrew, *Blarina brevicauda*. Roger W. Barbour

Identification: The northern short-tailed shrew is slightly larger than the southern short-tailed shrew, but they are very difficult to separate in some areas. The fur is slate gray, velvety to the touch, and often slightly darker in tint than the southern short-tailed shrew. The tail is short and barely extends beyond the hind foot when stretched out. This separates it from any of the long-tailed shrews (*Sorex* and *Microsorex*).

The skull is quite robust for a shrew and not as elongate in the snout area as the other species in the Southeast. The teeth are large and heavily pigmented (a deep chestnut color) at the tips. The third and fourth unicusps are of equal size.

Geographical Range: This species occurs only in the northern third of the southeastern region. Since the geographical ranges of the northern and southern short-tailed shrews show only slight overlap in the Southeast, specimens can be placed in the correct species by location of capture. The North American range extends from northern Georgia northward to eastern Canada and westward through the Great Lakes region.

Habitat: This shrew lives in almost every forested habitat having a thick layer of leaf litter or other suitable ground cover, including grass and weeds. They are sometimes also found living in brushy areas, old fields, thickets, and marsh edges.

Natural History: The northern short-tailed shrew is normally very abundant throughout its range. Population estimates have ranged from as few as 4 to as

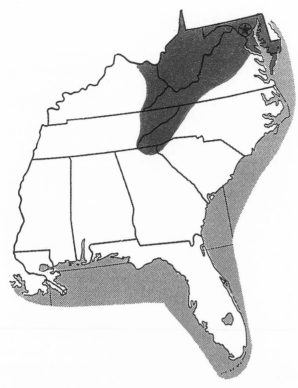

Geographical range of the northern short-tailed shrew in the Southeast.

many as 100 short-tailed shrews per acre in some northern states. A figure of around 25 shrews per acre is considered average for the species in favorable habitat.

This species has a reputation for being very aggressive in its foraging behavior. It will attack and kill animals larger than itself without hesitation. This predatory behavior is greatly assisted by the presence of a poison in this shrew's saliva, which is produced by the submaxillary glands. The poison present in the saliva readily enters the wounds of any animal bitten by the shrew. This poison acts to slow heart rate and breathing in the prey, thereby paralyzing it.

The home range of the northern short-tailed shrew varies from one-eighth to one-half acre, depending on the food supply, cover, and time of year. This species makes characteristic runways and tunnels through the leaf-litter or grass which have a diameter of only one-half to three-quarters of an inch. They also often use the runways of voles, cotton rats, and moles for foraging.

The diet of northern short-tailed shrews includes earthworms, insects, centipedes, millipedes, spiders, slugs, snails, mice, frogs, salamanders, and other shrews. They sometimes make food caches or hordes.

Breeding has been recorded from March to late November. Two or three litters are produced each season, with number of young ranging from three to nine, averaging six. The gestation period is about three weeks. The newborn shrews are blind, naked, and helpless. By the end of a week they start growing hair, but still lack teeth. When they are two weeks old, the eyes open and the incisor teeth erupt through the gums. They are weaned at about three weeks of age and mature sexually when almost three months old.

Short-tailed shrews live a maximum of about two years in captivity, but in nature few reach that age. This species has very strong scent glands which emit a pungent musk when the shrew is aroused. Many predators are known to kill this shrew occasionally, but seldom do they eat it because of the offensive smell. The musk glands are probably also used to mark the territory or home range of each individual.

Remarks: The northern short-tailed shrew is large enough and abundant enough to have considerable impact on insect and other invertebrate populations. It is doubtful whether they have nearly as much influence on mice and amphibian populations.

Selected References:

George, S. B., J. R. Choate, and H. H. Genoways. 1986. Northern Short-Tailed Shrew (*Blarina brevicauda*). Mammalian Species, No. 261: pp. 1–9.

Getz, L. L. 1989. A 14-year study of *Blarina brevicauda* populations in east-central Illinois. J. Mamm. 70:58–66.

Hamilton, W. J., Jr. 1929. Breeding habits of the short-tailed shrew, *Blarina brevicauda*. J. Mamm. 10: 125–34.

Southern Short-tailed Shrew
Blarina carolinensis

Southern short-tailed shrew, *Blarina carolinensis*. Larry Brown

Identification: The southern short-tailed shrew is slightly smaller than the northern short-tailed shrew and has a velvety slate gray fur. The tail is short and barely extends beyond the hind foot when stretched out. The gray coloration of the fur is only slightly darker on the back than on the belly. The summer pelage is a bit lighter and more brown than the winter pelage, suggesting there are two molts a year.

The skull morphology is virtually identical to that of the northern short-tailed shrew described above, but slightly smaller.

Geographical Range: This species ranges throughout the southern two-thirds of the southeastern region. In the United States, the geographical range is confined to the southeastern quadrant of the country.

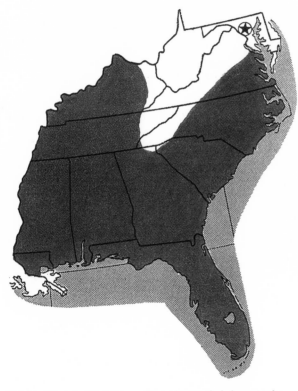

Geographical range of the southern short-tailed shrew in the Southeast.

Habitat: The southern short-tailed shrew is most common in wooded localities, but sometimes it occurs in old fields, weedy or bushy areas, and openings in the forest. It is often found associated with the runways and tunnels of mice and moles.

Natural History: All shrews, including this species, have high metabolic rates and spend most of their time actively foraging for food. They have a heart rate that averages 160 beats per minute and respiration is around 150 per minute.

The diet of this species is presumably very similar to that of the northern short-tailed shrew. It likewise will attack and kill prey much larger than itself, utilizing the poison present in the saliva to help subdue the prey.

Southern short-tailed shrews breed primarily from early spring to late fall, but sporadic reproduction is also reported in the winter months. Two or three litters are born annually containing two to eight young each (the average is five and one-half). The gestation period is about 21 days. The young are weaned at an age of just over one month, and they can breed when three months old.

Remarks: The southern short-tailed shrew was, until recently, considered to be a subspecies of the northern short-tailed shrew. The two shrews are sibling species that are very closely related and probably hybridize where the ranges meet.

People who are bitten by southern short-tailed shrews (which almost never happens) sometimes experience considerable pain, irritation, and swelling in reaction to the salivary poison. Individual humans vary greatly in their sensitivity to shrew bites, but there is no health hazard.

Southern short-tailed shrews kept in captivity are fairly gregarious and get along well together so long as they are kept well fed. Fighting and cannibalism will occur, however, if food is in short supply.

Domestic cats often kill this shrew but seldom eat them. My cat just drops them at the back door for me to dispose of.

Selected References:

Brown, J. K., and M. I. Kennedy. 1983. Systematics of the genus *Blarina* in Tennessee and adjacent areas. J. Mamm. 64: 414–25.

George, S. B., H. H. Genoways, J. R. Choate, and R. J. Baker. 1982. Karotypic relationships within the short-tailed shrews, genus *Blarina*. J. Mamm. 63: 639–45.

Least Shrew
Cryptotis parva

Least shrew, *Cryptotis parva*. James Parnell

Geographical range of the least shrew in the Southeast.

Identification: The least shrew is a pint-sized version of the short-tailed shrews. Its pelage is grayish brown on the upper parts and distinctly paler on the underside. The feet are white or light gray and the tail is short, being only slightly longer than the hind leg when extended. The skull is delicate, and there are a total of 30 teeth.

Geographical Range: The least shrew occurs throughout the entire Southeast. Its United States range includes all the eastern two-thirds of the country, south of the Great Lakes.

Habitat: This species usually lives in dry grassy areas, fallow fields, and brushy, weedy sites. Occasionally, they are taken in woodlands and marshy habitats as well. Least shrews often use the runways and tunnels of mice and moles.

Natural History: The diet of this shrew is very similar to that of the larger short-tailed species, except that smaller prey items are taken. The major food items recovered from stomachs are insects, centipedes, millipedes, spiders, slugs, snails, and earthworms. Preferred insects include beetles, crickets, grasshoppers, and lepidoptera. They actively forage both day and night in order to supply their high metabolic needs. Least shrews have been reported to consume their body weight in food each day under captive conditions. The species is quite gregarious and social; several can be housed together as long as plenty of food is available. If food should run short, cannibalization occurs.

Least shrews make a globular nest about four to five inches in diameter, consisting of dried grasses and leaves and lined with finely shredded grass. Males and females nest together and cooperate in caring for the young.

This shrew can breed every month of the year and produce several litters each year. The litter size varies from two to eight, with five being the average number. The gestation period in more northern populations has been reported to be 21–23 days. The young are naked and helpless at birth, but in two weeks they are fully furred with eyes open. The babies are weaned at three weeks of age and reach adult size when one month old. In captivity, I have observed breeding of individuals at five weeks of age. Females normally come into estrus and breed again on the day they give birth (which is known as postpartum estrus).

Remarks: Least shrews consume large numbers of insects and other invertebrates. Occasionally, they also enter commercial beehives to feed on larvae and pupae, which results in some loss in honey production. They can be readily controlled by using small mammal traps.

The major predators of the least shrew are hawks, owls, snakes, cats, weasels, and skunks. They have the musky, pungent odor characteristic of all shrews; therefore, least shrews are sometimes killed and not eaten by predators.

Selected References:

Conaway, C. H. 1958. Maintenance, reproduction and growth of the least shrew in captivity. J. Mamm. 39: 507–12.

Hamilton, W. J., Jr. 1944. The biology of the little short-tailed shrew, *Cryptotis parva*. J. Mamm. 25: 1–7.

Kivett, V. K., and O. B. Mock. 1980. Reproductive behavior in the least shrew (*Cryptotis parva*) with special reference to the aural glandular region of the female. Amer. Midl. Nat. 103: 339–45.

Whitaker, J. O., Jr. 1974. Least Shrew (*Cryptotis parva*). Mammalian Species, No. 43: pp. 1–8.

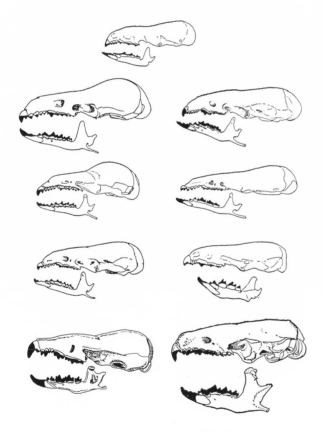

Skulls of the nine species of shrews found in the Southeast. Top-middle: pigmy shrew (*Microsorex hoyi*). Left column (top to bottom): water shrew (*Sorex palustris*); masked shrew (*Sorex cinereus*); southeastern shrew (*Sorex longirostris*); southern short-tailed shrew (*Blarina carolinensis*). Right Column (top to bottom): smoky shrew (*Sorex fumeus*); long-tailed shrew (*Sorex dispar*); least shrew (*Cryptotis parva*); northern short-tailed shrew (*Blarina brevicauda*).

Eastern Mole
Scalopus aquaticus

Eastern mole, *Scalopus aquaticus*. Unknown

Identification: Eastern moles are highly specialized anatomically for living under the ground all their lives. These characteristics are called fossorial adaptations and include broad, shovel-like front paws with large digging claws and a long, flexible snout for probing the soil. The powerful forelimbs are wider than they are long, and the body is stout and muscular. The eastern mole is covered with a silvery gray-brown fur that is soft and velvety to touch. Their tiny degenerate eyes have sealed eyelids, and they can only distinguish light from dark. Skin glands on the belly sometimes stain the fur a bright orange color in that area. Moles molt twice a year, in the spring and fall. The tail is short, virtually naked, and functions as an important organ of touch at the posterior end of the body.

The skull has a flat, triangular shape, narrow, delicate cheekbones, and white teeth (they are not stained chestnut brown as in shrews). There are 36 teeth in the skull of the eastern mole, compared with 44 teeth in the skulls of both the star-nosed mole and hairy-tailed mole.

Geographical Range: The eastern mole occurs throughout the entire southeastern region. In the United States, this species is widespread, being found throughout the eastern two-thirds of the country from the Great Lakes south to Texas and Florida.

Habitat: The eastern mole is present in virtually all types of soil and in all terrestrial habitats from forest to grassland. It is often absent from saturated muck or peat soils.

Geographical range of the eastern mole in the Southeast.

Natural History: This species spends its entire life under the ground, living in a labyrinthine tunnel system, closed off from the surface. The underground tunnels are of two different types. One tunnel is a pushed-up elevated ridge that marks the mole's passage just beneath the surface of the ground. These are temporary foraging tunnels (one and one-quarter inches to one and three-quarters inches in diameter), and they are only used for a few days each. The other type of tunnel is located several inches to three feet beneath the surface and is more permanent in nature. When constructing the deep tunnels, the mole sometimes opens up a vertical shaft to the surface, through which it pushes up excess dirt to form surface mounds. In sandy soils, the eastern mole makes these surface mounds much less often than it does in heavier soils. Often, the mole redistributes the excavated soil beneath the surface into older portions of its tunnel system rather than making surface mounds. The small, linear elevated foraging tunnels are always present and serve as the main evidence for the presence of eastern moles at any locality.

Eastern moles can dig rapidly and have been observed to excavate surface tunnels in sandy loam at a rate of over one and one-half feet per minute. Deeper tunnels are extended at a slower rate because of the need to redistribute excavated dirt. The eastern mole's nest chamber is always constructed in one of the deeper tunnels of the system and is four to eight inches in diameter with multiple entrances. The bottom of this round cavity is normally lined with a thick bed of fine grasses and leaves.

Eastern moles produce only one litter per year, born during the spring months. The litter size ranges from two to five and averages three. Breeding in eastern moles usually takes place from March to May. The length of gestation is not clearly known, but falls between four and six weeks. Eastern moles are naked and blind at birth, but grow rapidly and are able to fend for themselves when about four weeks old.

Eastern moles are active both day and night and in all seasons of the year. Activity peaks tend to occur in the early morning and late evening hours. They live a solitary lifestyle and are quite antisocial except at the time of breeding. I have placed two healthy adult moles together in a large terrarium filled with dirt, and they will fight almost continuously until one is dead.

A mole's diet is variable depending upon habitat and season of year, but is composed of earthworms, insects, and every other kind of soil-dwelling invertebrate. The eastern mole has a high metabolic rate and consumes a sizable percentage of its body weight in food each day.

Eastern moles appear to be fairly long-lived, especially for an insectivore. Their low annual breeding output would suggest that they live several years, but there is little or no data on their actual longevity.

Remarks: The tunnel systems of eastern moles often cause damage to lawns, flower beds, farm crops, and golf courses. There are also instances where moles have caused extensive losses to earthworm farms. However, the damage to plant bulbs, roots, and tubers, is caused by foraging rodents, which tend to invade and utilize the extensive tunnel systems of moles.

Moles are best controlled by trapping rather than poisoning. The poisons used are seldom if ever consumed by moles, and many poisons utilized in past years persist in the soil or damage the environment. In order to successfully trap eastern moles, a specially designed trap is required. Ordinary rat or mammal box traps are useless. Three types of mole traps are available: 1) the choker-loop trap, 2) the harpoon or pitchfork trap, and 3) the scissor-jaw trap. The scissor-jaw trap is generally the most effective, but unfortunately is seldom available at retail outlets. The mole traps all operate on the principle that a mole will return to repair damage to its surface feeding tunnel, which has been artificially closed by the trapper. The mole traps must, therefore, be placed astride freshly dug surface tunnels in order to increase the probability that a mole will return to forage and be caught.

Eastern moles, because of their fossorial lifestyle, tend to have very few predators. They also have strong musk glands, which make them less palatable to many carnivores. Some species of snakes occasionally take moles, as do skunks, foxes, owls, and cats.

Moles have a positive value in tilling and turning the soil and in distributing organic matter and nutrients to plants. They also feed on certain types of destructive insects, such as lepidoptera larvae and pupae.

There was once a lucrative business in mole pelts in both Europe and America: during the eighteenth and nineteenth centuries, they were utilized for making soft plush linings in hats, purses, pockets, and other garments. But styles changed, and pelts are not sold today.

Selected References:

Arlton, A. V. 1936. An ecological study of the common mole. J. Mamm. 17: 344–71.

Brown, L. N. 1972. Unique features of eastern mole tunnel systems in Florida. J. Mamm. 53: 394–95.

Christain, J. J. 1950. Behavior of the mole (Scalopus) and the shrew (Blarina). J. Mamm. 31: 281–87.

Conaway, C. H. 1959. The reproductive cycle of the eastern mole. J. Mamm. 40: 180–94.

Davis, F. W., and J. R. Choate. 1993. Morphologic variation and age structure in a population of the eastern mole, Scalopus aquaticus. J. Mamm. 74: 1014–25.

Harvey, M. J. 1976. Home range movements and diel activity of the eastern mole, Scalopus aquaticus. Amer. Midl. Nat. 95: 436–45.

Yates, T. L., and D. J. Schmidly. 1978. Eastern Mole (Scalopus aquaticus). Mammalian Species, No. 105: pp. 1–4.

Star-nosed Mole
Condylura cristata

Star-nosed mole, *Condylura cristata*. American Society of Mammalogists

Identification: The star-nosed mole is probably the most easily distinguished small mammal in the Southeast. This is because there are 22 fleshy pink appendages on the nose. These appendages are delicate touch (tactile) receptors that form a unique rosette, or "star," around the nasal openings. The mammal's thick fur is black to blackish brown on the back and slightly paler on the belly. The front paws are longer than they are wide and equipped with long, heavy digging claws on each toe. This mole has functional eyes, but they are very small, beadlike organs that suggest it has very weak eyesight. The tail is long, scaly, moderately haired, and serves as a fat-storage organ (thus the tail's diameter is large). The tail also functions as a sensitive tactile organ at the rear end of the body and as a rudder when the star-nosed mole is swimming.

The skull is more narrow, delicate, and elongated than that of the eastern mole. A weak, slender zygomatic arch (cheekbone) is present, as it is in the eastern mole skull. However, the star-nosed mole has 44 teeth in the skull (which is equaled by the hairy-tailed mole but not the eastern mole, which has far fewer teeth).

Geographical Range: This species occurs in the Appalachian Mountains as far south as northeastern Georgia. Surprisingly, it also occurs in scattered locations in a very different type of environment along the Atlantic Coastal Plain as far south as northern Florida.

The coastal lowland collection records almost certainly represent a disjunct population that occurs well east and south of the main range down the Appalachian chain. The United States range of the star-nosed

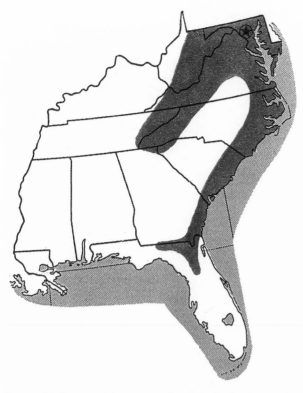

Geographical range of the star-nosed mole in the Southeast.

mole encompasses the Great Lakes area, the northeastern states, and the southward extensions mentioned for the southeastern states.

Habitat: Moist, saturated soils are the preferred habit of this semiaquatic mole. Its tunnels usually border streams, swamps, marshes, and some of the burrows lead directly into the water.

Natural History: Star-nosed moles are excellent swimmers and frequently forage for food in the aquatic environment. They also travel above ground and forage in the leaf litter like a shrew. They are active both night and day. The diet consists of aquatic and terrestrial insects, aquatic worms, crayfish, minnows, frogs, salamanders, snails, and various other invertebrates.

Only one litter is produced each spring or early summer, consisting of three to seven young (the average is five). The gestation period is about 45 days. Newborn moles are naked, helpless, blind, and pink in color. Hair first appears at about ten days of age and the eyes open at two weeks. They first leave the nest to forage for themselves when about four weeks old.

Reproductive maturity does not occur until the following spring when the moles are about ten months old.

Star-nosed moles are often difficult to trap with standard mole traps. I once spent five days trying to catch a single animal using both scissors and pitchfork type mole traps. Every day the mole very delicately probed the traps with its sensitive fleshy nose and usually dug its way around them without setting off the trap mechanisms. Twice a day I kept resetting the traps, using "hair-trigger" positions for the trap mechanisms. Finally, on the evening of the fifth day, I caught a specimen of this wily star-nosed mole in a scissors trap at the edge of the small brook.

The list of carnivores who occasionally prey on this mole includes owls, hawks, foxes, cats, dogs, raccoons, mink, skunks. They have even been found in the stomachs of large game fish such as bass, pike, and trout.

Remarks: The star-nosed mole has not been taken in the swamps of the southeastern coastal plain by scientists for a number of decades. An intensive survey needs to be made to see if the relict populations still survive there. Since the area was first settled, humans have drained swamps, channelized streams, logged forests, and altered the basic ecology in those areas where the lowland star-nosed moles were once captured.

Since this mole consumes large numbers of aquatic and terrestrial invertebrates, it may help control certain species. They also are beneficial in turning, mixing, and aerating wet soils.

Selected References:

Gould, E., W. McShea, and T. Grand. 1993. function of the star in the star-nosed mole. *Condylura cristata*. J. Mamm. 74: 108–16.

Peterson, K. E., and T. L. Yates. 1980. Star nosed mole (*Condylura cristata*). Mammalian Species, No. 129: 1–4.

Hairy-tailed Mole
Parascalops breweri

Hairy-tailed mole, *Parascalops breweri*. Roger W. Barbour

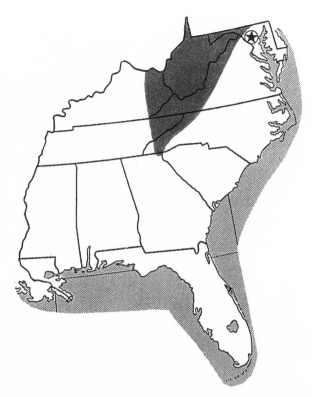

Geographical range of the hairy-tailed mole in the Southeast.

Identification: The hairy-tailed mole has a short, well-haired tail, a characteristic which separates it from the eastern mole and star-nosed mole. The tail hair is black, and some individuals have a white tuft at the end of the tail. The fur is black to dark slate gray above and slightly paler below with occasional irregular white spots. The forefoot is highly modified for digging, is as broad as it is long, and is equipped with strong claws. The eyes are small, allowing this species only to tell light from dark.

The skull contains 44 teeth, as does the skull of the star-nosed mole. The snout is shorter and broader than in *Condylura* and longer and narrower than in *Scalopus*.

Geographical Range: In the Southeast, this mole occurs in the Appalachian Mountain chain as far south as northeastern Georgia. In the United States, this mole has a geographical range extending from the New England states southwestward to eastern Kentucky, eastern Tennessee, and northeastern Georgia.

Habitat: This species lives in the mountains in a variety of soil types with various plant dominants, including conifers, hardwoods, rhododendrons, meadows, fields, and pastures. It prefers a much higher altitude than the eastern mole, and, in most instances, the hairy-tailed mole is found living in somewhat drier habitats than the star-nosed mole.

Natural History: The hairy-tailed mole digs a large, irregular complex of shallow subsurface tunnels, plus a few deeper tunnels that reach from 10 inches to 20 inches in depth. The deep tunnels are used more extensively during the winter months, and the shallow tunnels are traveled more extensively during the warmer months. The mole constructs a spherical nest of leaves and grass in a deep tunnel, usually located under a boulder or tree stump. The nest chamber always has several exit runnels. Hairy-tailed moles forage extensively above ground on the forest floor, especially at night. Because of this habit, they are often caught by owls, cats, opossums, foxes, weasels, snakes, and other nocturnal predators. This mole feeds chiefly on beetles, moths, ants, insect larvae, earthworms, and other invertebrates of the forest floor. Hairy-tailed moles in captivity have consumed their body weight in food every day, indicating a high metabolic rate. They do not hibernate and are active throughout the winter months.

Breeding occurs in March and April and only one litter of four to eight young is produced by each adult female. The moles lead a solitary life during the bulk of each year, but during the spring mating period both sexes have been found within the same tunnel system.

Remarks: This mole sometimes damages lawns, gardens, golf courses, and parks with their extensive tunnel systems. In other areas they are beneficial in tilling and aerating soil.

Selected References:

Hallett, J. G. 1978. Hairy-Tailed Mole *(Parascalops breweri)*. Mammalian Species, No. 98: pp. 1–4.

Jensen, I. M. 1983. Metabolic rates of the hairy-tailed mole, *Parascalops breweri.* (Bachman, 1842). J. Mamm. 64: 453–62.

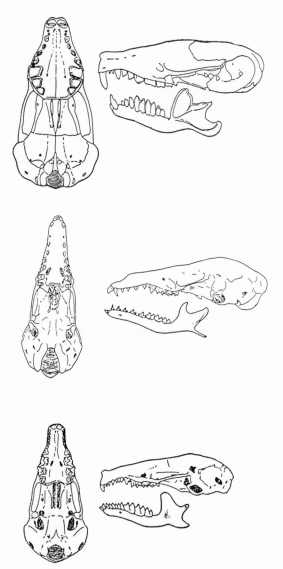

Skulls of the three species of moles found in the Southeast (top to bottom): eastern mole *(Scalopus aquaticus)*; star-nosed mole *(Condylura cristata)*; hairy-tailed mole *(Parascalops breweri)*.

Order Chiroptera
Bats

Bats are the only mammals with the ability to fly. All bats have the forearms and hands modified into large wings covered with a soft, membranous skin. The word *Chiroptera* means "hand-winged" in Latin. A broad tail membrane is also present and serves as a very effective rudder for changing directions in the air. Also, some species use the tail (or interfemoral) membrane as a basket to snare insects in flight. Nearly every feature of a bat's anatomy is specialized to aid in the process of flight. For example, all bones are thin-walled, hollow, and tubular in structure, which makes the skeleton lighter. The chest (or pectoral) muscles are massive and well vascularized to provide the strong wing beats necessary to fly.

Bats have the ability to reduce their metabolisms and hibernate on a day-to-day or seasonal basis, depending on ambient temperatures and relative availability of food. Nearly all bats have a finely tuned echolocation system, or "biological radar," for use in catching insects and avoiding objects in their flight path. Bats emit supersonic squeaks and clicks from their mouths which bounce off objects. Their extremely sensitive ears then pick up the sound pulses that bounce back. They can easily discriminate between food items and other objects located in their flight path.

This large order has a worldwide distribution, but by far the greatest number of species occur in the tropics rather than in the temperate zones. The southeastern states have a total of 20 species of bats, all but one of which feed exclusively on insects. Bats are extremely beneficial in consuming the hordes of nocturnally flying insects found everywhere in the region. Bat specimens and bat skulls are very difficult to identify for the layperson and should always be examined by an expert in mammalogy for the final determination of the species. Identification is particularly important when medical or health questions are involved. If, for example, a dead or injured bat tests positive in the laboratory for rabies or histoplasmosis, then it is vital to know which species of bat is involved so that other species of bats will not be listed as disease risks to humans. Most species of bats do not carry rabies or any other disease transmittable to humans, so the few that do have to be carefully identified and the others protected from harm.

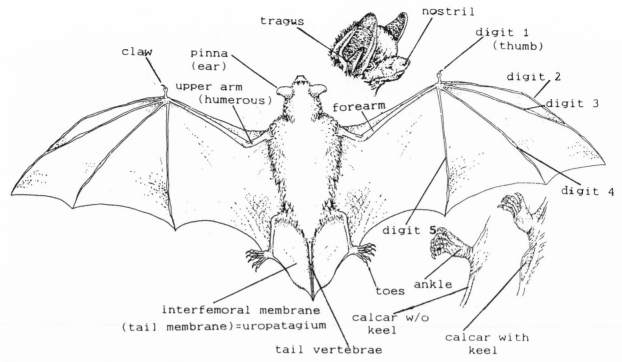

Important anatomical features found in bats.

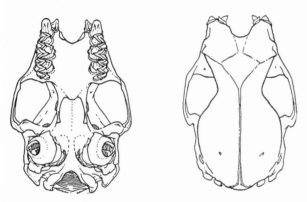

Lower view (left) and upper view (right) of a representative bat skull, the yellow bat (*Lasiurus intermedius*).

Little brown bat, *Myotis lucifugus*. American Society of Mammalogists

Little Brown Bat
Myotis lucifugus

Identification: This species has a glossy olive-brown fur with a slight metallic or burnish tint to the hair on its back. The ears are fairly narrow and naked, with bluntly rounded tips. When the ears are laid forward, they just barely extend beyond the nostrils. The tragus (a leaflike spike projecting upward in the ear) is pointed and only about one-half the ear length. The tail membrane is not furred and the calcar (the ankle bone which supports the tail membrane) is not keeled.

Geographical Range: The little brown bat ranges over the northern three-fourths of the southeastern states, but does not appear to be common in most areas. This bat has a broad distribution in North America, ranging throughout the southern three-fourths of the United States and much of Canada.

Habitat: In many parts of its range, the little brown bat shows a preference for forested areas, living in caves during the winter and in attics or tree hollows during the summer months. They often forage for insects along streams, lakes, ponds, or rivers.

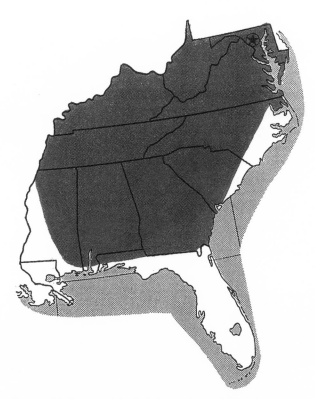

Geographical range of the little brown bat in the Southeast.

Natural History: During the late spring and summer months, female little brown bats form nursery colonies with their offspring, living apart from the males. The adult males are either solitary or live in small bachelor groups during the warmer months of the year. In the fall and winter months, sexes rejoin and live in large hibernating colonies in some protected location, such as caves or buildings. When hibernating, the bats hang upside down by their back feet from the ceiling in extremely closely packed groups of several dozen to several hundred individuals.

Mating takes place in the fall just before hibernation begins, and it often occurs again in the spring when the bats become active again. The female ovulates one egg in the spring shortly after arousal from hibernation. The sperm present in the female's reproductive tract from the preceding fall remains viable all winter and is capable of fertilizing the egg released the following spring (a process called delayed fertilization). Bats have the longest period of sperm storage in a female's reproductive tract known for any mammal species.

The gestation period in the little brown bat varies from 50 to 60 days, and each female produces one offspring per year. Most of the young are born in May or June. Young bats are relatively large when born, averaging one-fifth to one-fourth the weight of their mothers. They are naked and blind at birth, but the eyes open when they are only two days old. When mother bats depart the nursery colony to feed each evening, they leave the young behind. Later, when the mothers return, they search diligently through the baby bats until they unerringly locate their own offspring for nursing. Each little bat is apparently identified by its different scent.

The young bats can fly when three weeks old, but are not weaned until three months of age. They reach their adult size when about two months old. Some young females breed their first fall, but most males do not mature sexually until they are one year old. In the late summer and fall, little brown bats put on a thick layer of fat in order to hibernate successfully through the winter months.

Analysis of the stomach contents of foraging little brown bats reveals they show a dietary preference for moths, beetles, flies, and wasps.

Remarks: This bat eats large quantities of flying insects, which is a very beneficial function. Studies have shown that a little brown bat can catch up to 500 insects per hour using its biological radar system. A large colony of these bats can account for the removal of tons of potentially harmful insects each year.

The life span of the little brown bat has been studied extensively by using tiny numbered aluminum bands placed on the wings. They exhibit remarkable longevity for so small a mammal. I once banded an adult little brown bat that was found still wearing the numbered aluminum band 25 years later, and it was still living in the same small town where it was originally released. Since this individual bat was an adult when first banded, it had to be at least a year old or possibly older at the time of the original capture. It is probable that the maximum longevity of little brown bats thus approaches 30 years.

Humans appear to be the most serious enemy of bats, because so many colonies are exterminated each year. This is truly unfortunate since bats are so beneficial in consuming hordes of insects. Bats are usually feared and misunderstood by humans for no good, compelling reason. A few bats are also killed and eaten by such predators as owls, raccoons, cats, and snakes. Bats only rarely carry diseases such as histoplasmosis or rabies.

Selected References:

Brown, L. N. 1989. A longevity record for the little brown bat, *Myotis lucifugus*, in the western states. Southwestern Nat. 34: 287.

Burnett, C. D., and T. H. Kunz. 1982. Growth rates and age estimation in *Eptesicus fuscus* and comparison with *Myotis lucifugus*. J. Mamm. 63: 33–41.

Fenton, M. B., and R. M. R. Barclay. 1980. Little Brown Bat (*Myotis lucifugus*). Mammalian Species, No. 142: pp. 1–8.

Humphrey, S. R., and J. B. Cope. 1976. Population ecology of the little brown bat, *Myotis lucifugus*, in Indiana and north-central Kentucky. American Society of Mammalogists Special Publ. No. 4, 81 pp.

Kunz, T. H., and E. L. P. Anthony. 1982. Age estimation and post-natal growth in the bat, *Myotis lucifugus*. J. Mamm. 63: 23–32.

Southeastern Bat
Myotis austroriparius

Southeastern bat, *Myotis austroriparius*. Merlin Tuttle

Identification: In the southeastern bat, the fur on the upper side is dull grayish brown or, very rarely, a dull reddish brown. The hair, when parted, is slightly darker at the base than toward the tips. The underparts vary from grayish white to tan. The southeastern bat is very similar to the little brown bat and difficult to identify, but it exhibits a much duller coloration and shorter hair on the back. The ears are short and, when folded forward, extend only as far as the tip of the nose. The tragus of the ear is fairly short, slender, and pointed; the calcar of the ankle is not keeled.

Geographical Range: The southeastern bat is found in the southern one-third of the southeastern states as well as along the western border of the region. Its range in the United States is confined to the lower Mississippi Valley, Ohio Valley, and adjacent areas, as well as to the Deep South.

Habitat: The southeastern bat prefers limestone caves, hollow trees, attics of buildings, crevices of bridges, concrete storm sewers, and other dark, hollow cavities. The species is quite adaptable to a variety of locations

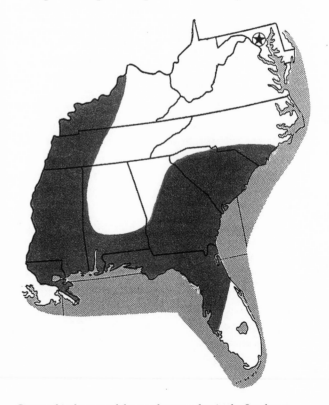

Geographical range of the southeastern bat in the Southeast.

and physical conditions. They are sometimes found roosting in mixed species groups with evening bats, free-tailed bats, gray bats, or Indiana bats.

Natural History: In the northern portion of its range, the southeastern bat hibernates in colonies from October to late February or early March. However, in the southern portion of the range, colonies are active during much of the winter and only hibernate for short periods during cold spells when the nighttime temperatures fall to 45 degrees Fahrenheit or below.

Females become pregnant in the spring and normally give birth to twins 50–60 days later. This is the only *Myotis* that commonly produces more than one young per pregnancy. The mother bats and their offspring form large maternity colonies, sometimes numbering in the thousands (often a few adult males are present also). Births occur from late April or early May to the end of May or early June. The young bats can fly when about five weeks old.

It is not unusual for predators to take southeastern bats from the roost where they are sleeping or hibernating in large groups. Predators of this species include owls, rat snakes, corn snakes, opossums, skunks, and foxes.

Remarks: Since southeastern bats form large colonies, they help control excessive insect populations within the foraging range of the colony.

Since this species is so adaptable to human-made structures, it appears to be holding its own in much of the range. The fungal disease histoplasmosis is sometimes associated with colonies of the southeastern bat.

Selected References:
Jones, C., and R. W. Manning. 1989. Southeastern Myotis (*Myotis austroriparius*). Mammalian Species, No. 332: pp. 1–3.
LaVal, R. K. 1970. Infraspecific relationships of bats of the species *Myotis austroriparius*. J. Mamm. 51: 542–52.
Rice, D. W. 1957. Life history and ecology of *Myotis austroriparius* in Florida. J. Mamm. 38: 15–32.
Zinn, T. L., and S. R. Humphrey. 1981. Seasonal food resources and prey selection of the southeastern brown bat (*Myotis austroriparius*). Florida. Fla. Sci. 44: 81–90.

WITHDRAWN

Gray Bat
Myotis grisescens

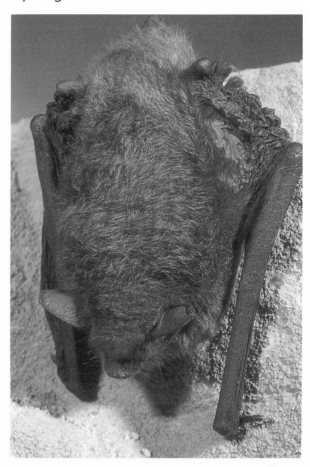

Gray bat, *Myotis grisescens.* American Society of Mammalogists

Identification: In the gray bat, the upper pelage is a uniform grayish brown, and the hairs on the back, when parted, are the same color all the way to the base (in other similar bats, the hair is darker at the base than at the tips). The body size is slightly larger than other *Myotis* species, and it is the only one in which the wing membrane is attached at the ankle rather than at the base of the toes. The calcar of the ankle is not keeled and the tragus is narrow and pointed.

Geographical Range: This species occurs in the central portion of the southeastern region, from Kentucky through Tennessee and Alabama to northern Florida. Its geographical range in the United States occupies the mid-Mississippi and Tennessee valleys and areas of the Deep South, especially Alabama.

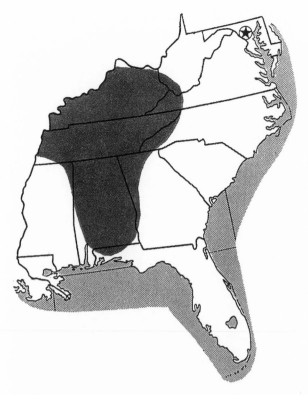

Geographical range of the gray bat in the Southeast.

Habitat: The gray bat is considered to be exclusively a cave-dwelling species. It shows a distinct preference for large, moist caves in limestone strata, where very sizable colonies frequently occur.

Natural History: The gray bat forms maternity colonies during the late spring and early summer. The females select large caves containing streams for the nursery colonies. Males form bachelor colonies in separate caves at this time of the year. In the winter months, both sexes reassemble in large hibernating colonies, often selecting inaccessible caves that have vertical shaftlike entrances and constant humidities.

Gray bats emerge from the cave at dusk and usually forage over bodies of water and in nearby forested areas. They show dietary preferences for flying aquatic insects such as mosquitoes, stone flies, caddis flies, mayflies, and beetles.

Mating takes place at the hibernation colony in the fall. Each female ovulates one egg (or ovum) the following March or April after she becomes active from hibernation and the sperm that overwintered in her reproductive tract fertilizes the egg. Gestation lasts 50–

60 days after fertilization, and each pregnant female gives birth to a single offspring in late May or early June. The young bats grow rapidly, and some can fly when 25 days old. All gray bats become sexually mature when they are two years old, in contrast to the little brown bat.

Remarks: Because gray bats roost in only a few select caves in a given area, they are extremely vulnerable to decimation by humans. For this reason, the state and federal agencies have officially classified the gray bat as "endangered." The reproductive potential of gray bats is very low, so the recovery rate of a partially decimated colony is painfully slow even under ideal conditions. It is probably advisable to close caves containing nursery colonies to the public in order to help save this unique endangered species from extinction.

Selected References:

Stevenson, D. E., and M. D. Tuttle. 1981. Survivorship of the endangered gray bat. J. Mamm. 60: 244–57.

Tuttle, M. D. 1974. Population ecology of the gray bat (*Myotis grisescens*): Factors influencing early growth and development. Museum of Nat. History, Univ. of Kansas. Occasional Papers No. 36: 1–24.

———. 1976. Population ecology of the gray bat (*Myotis grisescens*): Philopatry, timing and patterns of movements, weight loss during migration, and seasonal adaptive strategies. Mus. Nat. Hist., Univ. of Kansas, Occasional Papers No. 54: 1–38.

———. 1979. Status, causes of decline, and management of endangered gray bats. J. Wildl. Mgmt. 43: 1–17.

Keen's Bat
Myotis keenii

Keen's bat, *Myotis keenii*. Merlin Tuttle

Identification: Keen's bat, sometimes referred to as the long-eared myotis, is very similar to other species of *Myotis*. Its fur is light reddish brown or olive-brown above and buff-gray below. The fur on the back, when parted, is dark at the base, in contrast to the fur of the gray bat. Also, the hair is shorter and less glossy than that of the little brown bat, and the ankle calcar is slightly keeled. The tragus of the ear is long, narrow, and pointed. The ears are large and, when laid forward, extend well beyond the nose (three-sixteenths of an inch to one-quarter inch beyond). The scientific name, *Myotis septentrionalis*, is sometimes applied to this species, but *Myotis keenii* is more widely used.

Geographical Range: In the Southeast, this species occurs in the northern third of the region and in a band down the center states of Alabama and western Georgia to north Florida. In the United States, the geographic range spans most of the northern three-quarters of the country east of the Rocky Mountains, as well as a distinct population in the Pacific Northwest.

Habitat: Keen's bat is primarily a cave dweller in winter, but in summer it may be found in hollow trees, under loose bark, in attics and barns, and under the eaves of houses, as well as in caves. These bats show a preference for cooler hibernation sites, and they are less gregarious than most other species of *Myotis*.

Natural History: Females form small maternity colonies during the late spring and summer, but during the rest of the year individuals tend to live a solitary existence. Very little is known about their reproductive cycle, but it is apparently very similar to other members of the genus. Females annually give birth to a single young in June or July.

In late summer, Keen's bat, like other hibernators, accumulates substantial amounts of body fat. Copulation has been observed in caves, just before the onset of hibernation in the northern part of its range (September and October).

During hibernation, Keen's bat roosts singly or in groups of two or three, often seeking out deep crevices in the ceiling to spend the winter months. A hibernation cave may contain several hundred Keen's bats dispersed in this manner, but most hibernating colonies are much smaller.

Remarks: This bat tends to forage in forests beneath the crowns of trees and is beneficial because of the large numbers of insects consumed. Their semisolitary habits make them less vulnerable to decimation by humans than most gregarious cave-dwelling species. Like the other hibernating species of bats, Keen's bat is long-lived. One banded specimen lived 18 1/2 years in a midwestern field study.

Selected References:

Caire, W., R. K. LaVal, M. L. LaVal, and R. Clawson. 1979. Notes on the ecology of *Myotis keenii* (Chiroptera, Vespertillionidae) in eastern Missouri. Amer. Midl. Nat. 102: 404–7.

Easterla, D. A. 1968. Parturition of Keen's myotis in southwestern Missouri. J. Mamm. 49: 770.

Fitch, J. H. and K. A. Shump Jr. 1979. Keen's Myotis (*Myotis keenii*). Mammalian Species, No. 121: pp. 1–3.

van Zyll de Jong, C. G. 1979. Distribution and systematic relationships of long-eared *Myotis* in western Canada. Canad. J. Zool. 57: 987–94.

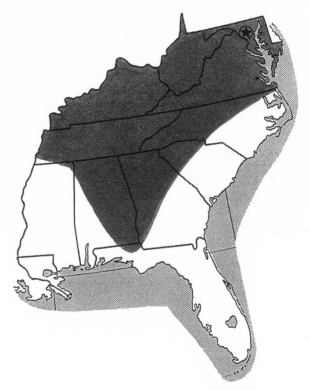

Geographical range of the Keen's bat and the Indiana bat in the Southeast.

Indiana Bat
Myotis sodalis

Indiana bat, *Myotis sodalis.* Merlin Tuttle

Identification: The fur on the back of the Indiana bat is dull grayish brown or pinkish brown, and when the hairs are parted it is distinctly darker at the base. The underside fur is pinkish white or gray. The ears, when laid forward, barely project beyond the nose. The wing membrane joins the foot at the base of the toes, and the calcar of the ankle has a well-developed keel visible. The tragus of the ear is short, narrow, and pointed.

Geographical Range: In the Southeast, this species occurs in the northern third of the region and in a band through the center states of eastern Alabama and western Georgia to Florida. The rest of the geographical range in the United States includes the midwestern and northeastern states south of the Great Lakes. A number of colonies have declined in populations in recent decades.

Habitat: The Indiana bat spends the winter months in just a few large, cool, and moist limestone caves (water pools and streams are always present) scattered throughout its range. In the spring and summer, they disperse widely throughout the forests, forming small colonies under the loose bark of dead trees, in small caves, and in other types of dark cavities.

Natural History: The Indiana bat forms extremely large wintering colonies which, like the gray bat, make them especially vulnerable to repeated disturbance and decimation by humans. Human disruption has occurred extensively over the past few decades, and their overall populations have declined sharply.

This species enters hibernation in the late fall, and copulation occurs just prior to their winter torpor. They often gather in large, tightly packed clumps hanging from the ceiling near the entrance of the caves, where the air is coldest during the winter months. It is not unusual to find a few little brown bats and gray bats among the clumps of Indiana bats. They awake from hibernation and leave the caves in March or in April at more northern locations. Ovulation and fertilization occur shortly after the females emerge from hibernation. A single young is born, usually in late June, under the loose bark of dead trees located along wooded streams. Indiana bats prefer moths to other food items, but they also consume beetles, flies, and miscellaneous aquatic insects from various riparian and floodplain forest habitats. Bat banding studies in the Midwest show that the maximum longevity of the Indiana bat exceeds twenty years.

Remarks: This is another highly beneficial species of bat that consumes large quantities of insects within the flying range of the colony. Because of its vulnerability and declining population numbers, the Indiana bat is officially listed as an endangered species by the federal government. Steps need to be taken to locate and protect all the large colonies from human depredations or the Indiana bat could eventually become extinct.

Selected References:
Brock, V., Jr., and R. K. LaVal. 1985. Food habits of the Indiana bat in Missouri. J. Mamm. 66: 308–15.
Hall, J. S. 1962. A life history and taxonomic study of the Indiana bat, *Myotis sodalis.* Reading Publ. Mus. and Art Gallery, Science Publ. No. 12, 68 pp.
Humphrey, S. B. 1978. Status, winter habitat, and management of the endangered Indiana bat, *Myotis sodalis.* Florida Sci. 41: 65–76.
Thomson, C. E. 1982. Indiana Bat (*Myotis sodalis*). Mammalian Species, No. 163: pp. 1–5.

Small-footed Bat
Myotis leibii

Small-footed bat, *Myotis leibii*. Roger W. Barbour

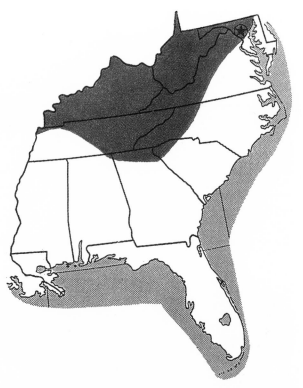

Geographical range of the small-footed bat in the Southeast.

Identification: The small-footed bat is the smallest species in the *Myotis* group of bats. The fur is chestnut brown above and gray-brown below. The muzzle and face are black, which gives the species a "masked" appearance. The ears are also black, short, and the tragus of the ear is pointed. The calcar of the ankle is clearly keeled, which distinguishes the small-footed bat from the somewhat larger little brown bat. Also, as the common name indicates, this species has a very tiny foot compared to other similar bats.

Geographical Range: The small-footed bat in the Southeast ranges down the Appalachian Mountains as far south as northern Georgia. Its geographical range in the United States spans the north-central portion of the country.

Habitat: This bat prefers caves, crevices, and rocks in the mountain zone. They often spend the winter hibernating in inconspicuous locations, such as in cracks in cave floors or ceilings, under boulders and rocks, or in deep crevices of other kinds. During the summer months, they sometimes roost in buildings, hollow trees, and even rockpiles.

Natural History: The small-footed bat is generally the last cave-dwelling species to enter hibernation in the autumn and the first species to wake up and start flying in the spring. When hibernating, this bat hangs with its forearms partially outstretched rather than closely folded to the body like other bats.

Little is known about the reproductive cycle of the small-footed bat, but it is probably similar to other members of the *Myotis* group. Only one young is born per female in the early summer, usually in small nursery colonies composed of 10 to 20 females. Insemination of the females by the males probably takes place in the late fall or early winter just before hibernation begins.

Remarks: This bat is probably not as rare as the few specimens taken in the Southeast would indicate. Its peculiar life habits of roosting and hiding under rocks and in crevices have undoubtedly caused it to be overlooked even in those areas where it might be relatively common.

Selected References:

McDaniel, V. R., M. J. Harvey, R. Tumlison, and K. Paige. 1982. Status of the small-footed bat, *Myotis leibii*, in the southern Ozarks. Proc. Ark. Acad. Sci. 36: 92–94.

Tuttle, M. D., and L. R. Heaney. 1974. Maternity habits of *Myotis leibii* in South Dakota. Bulletin Southern Calif. Acad. Sci. 73: 80–83.

Silver-haired Bat
Lasionycteris noctivagans

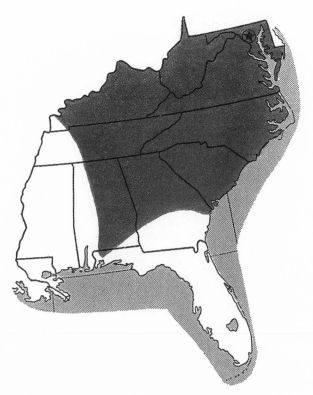

Silver-haired bat, *Lasionycteris noctivagans*. Merlin Tuttle

Geographical range of the silver-haired bat in the Southeast.

Identification: The silver-haired bat's fur on its back and belly is very striking in color: it is brownish black washed with silvery white at the tips of the hair. The frosted coloration is most conspicuous on the back. The wing and tail membranes are black, and the upper surface of the tail membrane is well furred near the body. The ears are short and rounded and contain a broad, blunt tragus. The wing membrane attaches to the foot at the base of the toes, and the calcar of the ankle is unkeeled.

Geographical Range: This bat has been recorded over the northern three-fifths of the Southeast. The southernmost record is in the Florida Panhandle. It appears to be a characteristic bat of the Appalachian plateaus, mountain foothills, and ridges and valleys, but is rare in the coastal plain. Its geographical range in the United States extends from coast to coast, with records in every state.

Habitat: The silver-haired bat is a forest dweller that roosts in dense foliage, under loose bark, in hollow trees, in rock crevices, and in cabins and sheds. These bats usually forage along wooded streams and lake borders.

Natural History: The silver-haired bat is a migratory species, moving north in the spring and south in the fall. Most of them winter in the southern states, but a few enter caves or buildings elsewhere and hibernate all winter. Others have been observed off the East Coast of the United States. Where these bats are migrating for the winter is something of a mystery. These East Coast individuals were probably blown off course by winds, storms, or other atmospheric problems. During migration, silver-haired bats occasionally fly during the daytime as well as during the normal nighttime period.

The males of this species are always solitary, but females are more gregarious, especially during the summer months, when they form small roosting and nursery colonies. Mating occurs in the fall, but females do not ovulate until spring. The gestation period is 50–60 days long after fertilization of the egg. Females normally give birth to twins (but the number of young varies from one to three) in late June or early July in northern locations. The babies grow rapidly and can fly when three to four weeks of age. They are weaned when a little over a month old, and they breed their first fall.

Remarks: Beetles form the main dietary item for silver-haired bats, but they also eat moths and other sizable nocturnal insects. Since many beetles and moths are considered forest pests, this species is especially beneficial in helping to control harmful insects.

A few silver-haired bats are nonmigratory and hibernate at northern locations from November to March in buildings, mines, and other protected sites. Little is known about the basic population biology of this bat because it is so secretive.

Selected References:

Brown, L. N. 1986. First record of the silver-haired bat, *Lasionycteris noctivagans* (Le Conte) in Florida. Fla. Scientist 49: 167–68.

Easterla, D. A., and L. C. Watkins. 1970. Breeding of *Lasionycteris noctivagans* and *Nycticeius humeralis* in southwestern Iowa. Amer. Midl. Nat. 84: 254–55.

King, T. H. 1982. Silver-haired bat (*Lasionycteris noctivagans*). Mammalian Species, No. 172: pp. 1–5.

Eastern Pipistrelle
Pipistrellus subflavus

Eastern pipistrelle, *Pipistrellus subflavus*. Barry Mansell

Identification: The eastern pipistrelle is one of the Southeast's smaller bats. The upper fur is pale yellowish brown or yellowish gray, and the belly fur is yellowish brown. The hairs, which can be separated by blowing into the fur, are dark at the base. This is the only southeastern bat having black wing membranes combined with burnt-orange skin covering the arm bones. The ears are fairly large for a small bat. When the ears are placed forward, they extend slightly beyond the nose. The tragus is fairly long, narrow, and pointed. The ankle calcar is not keeled, and the tail membrane is slightly haired only where it joins the body.

Geographical Range: This bat occurs throughout the entire southeastern region in many different habitats. Its range in the United States includes the eastern half of the country. The species also occurs in Mexico and Central America.

Habitat: In the northern part of their range, eastern pipistrelles hibernate singly in caves. In the Southeast, they hibernate that portion of the winter when night temperatures are cold, but they may forage on warm

Geographical range of the eastern pipistrelle in the Southeast.

nights. In the summer they roost in old cabins, hollow trees, culverts, attics, bridges, and other dark cavities in forested areas.

Natural History: Females form small nursery colonies away from the males during the spring and summer months. Mating among members of this species has been observed in the fall, winter, and spring. Sperm is viable after overwintering in the female reproductive tract. Females give birth to one litter each year of one to three offspring (normally twins) from mid-May to mid-July. The baby bats grow rapidly and can fly when they are about four weeks old. Pipistrelles do not reach sexual maturity until they are nearly one year old.

This species has a weak, erratic, and fluttering type of flight which is somewhat reminiscent of a moth. They are easy to distinguish on the wing from other bats because of this slow, characteristic flight pattern. Pipistrelles feed on tiny nocturnal insects such as moths, flies, beetles, mayflies, and caddis flies. They prefer to forage over bodies of water, and they catch many flying aquatic insects.

Remarks: Pipistrelles, like other bats, are beneficial insect consumers. However, because of their small body size and semisolitary lifestyle, they probably have less impact on insect numbers than most colonial species of bats.

This species is one of the deepest hibernators of all bats, and thus they are less easily aroused by disturbances than other species. They usually stay in one spot in the cave for weeks during the winter hibernation period. It is common to find a layer of water droplets condensed on the surface of the pipistrelle's fur (they shimmer like jewels in the beam of a flashlight as they hang from the cave ceiling). Banding has revealed a maximum longevity of about 15 years.

Selected References:

Cockrum, E. L. 1952. Longevity in the pipistrelle, *Pipistrellus subflavus subflavus*. J. Mamm. 33: 491–92.

Fujita, M. S., and T. H. Kung. 1984. Eastern pipistrelle (*Pipistrellus subflavus*). Mammalian Species, No. 228: pp. 1–6.

MacDonald, K., E. Matsui, R. Stevens, and M. B. Finton. 1994. Echolocation calls and field identification of the eastern pipistrelle (*Pipistrellus subflavus:* Chiroptera: Vespertillionidae), using ultrasonic bat detectors. J. Mamm. 75: 462–65.

Big Brown Bat
Eptesicus fuscus

Big brown bat, *Eptesicus fuscus*. Merlin Tuttle

Identification: The big brown bat is fairly large; it is bigger than any of the *Myotis* species. It has a rich, chestnut brown fur that is rather long and glossy. The underparts are cinnamon, and the wing membranes are black. The ears are not large, and the tragus is short and rounded at the tip. The calcar of the ankle is keeled, and the tail membrane is devoid of hair.

Geographical Range: The big brown bat ranges over the entire southeastern region. It also occurs throughout the entire country from coast to coast. The big brown bat also occupies most of the larger Caribbean Islands.

Habitat: This bat lives in a wide variety of habitats. It roosts in attics, hollow trees, caves, chimneys, storm sewers, bridges, outbuildings, and many other human-made structures.

Natural History: In the northern part of its range, the big brown bat hibernates during the winter, but in the southern states it is often on the wing on warm winter nights. In caves, these bats almost always select a roosting place near the entrance and may roost in partial daylight.

Geographical range of the big brown bat in the Southeast.

Hibernation in the big brown bat has been studied extensively. The body temperature falls to that of the environment, and they can survive temperatures as low as 30 degrees Fahrenheit. When their metabolism returns to normal, the body temperature rises to around 99 degrees Fahrenheit. In hibernation, big brown bats may go as long as four to eight minutes without taking a breath, but when active they may breathe at a rate of 200 times per minute.

Compared to many bats, this species is very sedentary. Banding studies show that most live their lives within 10 miles of where they were born. Like many other bats, females form nursery colonies in the spring, separate from the males. These colonies break up by mid-summer, and the males and females roost together again.

Mating takes place in the fall, winter, and again in the spring. The females may ovulate two to seven eggs in the spring, but normally only two complete development. The babies are usually born in May or early June after a gestation period of about 60 days. They are naked at birth, and their eyes open when they are two days old. Young big brown bats can fly when three weeks old, and most breed their first autumn.

Remarks: Big brown bats eat mainly beetles, including tree borers and other forest pests. These bats are relatively slow, straight fliers, and they do not veer about erratically like some species of bats.

Maximum longevity appears to be around 10–12 years, based on banding studies conducted in the New England states. Big brown bats occasionally carry rabies. One study reported that 10 percent of the bats in one population were infected with the virus.

Selected References:

Beer, J. R. 1955. Survival and movements of banded big brown bats. J. Mamm. 36: 242–48.

Burnett, C. D., and T. H. King. 1982. Growth rates and age estimation in *Eptesicus fuscus* and comparison with *Myotis lucifugus*. J. Mamm. 63: 33–41.

Christian, J. J. 1956. The natural history of a summer aggregation of the big brown bat, *Eptesicus fuscus fuscus*. Amer. Midl. Nat. 55: 66–95.

Davis, W. H., R. W. Barbour, and M. D. Hassell. 1968. Colonial behavior of *Eptesicus fuscus*. J. Mamm. 49: 44–50.

Kurta, A., and R. H. Baker. 1990. Big Brown Bat (*Eptesicus fuscus*). Mammalian Species, No. 356: pp. 1–10.

Whitaker, J. O., Jr., and S. L. Gummer. 1992. Hibernation of the big brown bat, *Eptesicus fuscus*, in buildings. J. Mamm. 73: 312–16.

Red Bat
Lasiurus borealis

Red bat, *Lasiurus borealis*. Merlin Tuttle

Identification: The red bat is the most brightly colored southern bat, and one of the few which is sexually dimorphic. In males the upper pelage is brick red, and in females it is dull red with pronounced white frosting on the tips of the fur. The ears are small, broad, and rounded, and the tragus is short and blunt at the tip. There is a yellowish white patch on each shoulder at the base of the wing. The underparts are paler than the back and usually white frosted. The tail membrane is heavily furred over the entire upper surface and the calcar of the ankle is keeled.

Geographical Range: This bat occurs over the entire southeastern region except possibly south Florida. In the United States, the red bat lives in nearly every region except portions of the Rocky Mountains and the Great Basin. It also ranges throughout Mexico, Central America, and South America.

Habitat: The red bat is strictly a tree dweller and almost never roosts in caves or buildings. It sleeps in dense foliage, under loose bark, in hollow trees, and in clumps of Spanish moss during the daylight hours. These bats often hang upside down by one foot from a tree limb, and they look for all the world like a dead leaf.

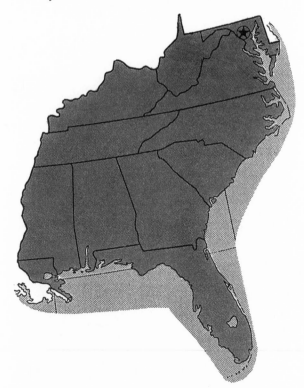

Geographical range of the red bat in the Southeast.

Natural History: Red bats, like the silver-haired bat and the hoary bat, are extremely migratory, spending their winters in the southern states, and returning north each spring to a specific summer range. They lead largely solitary lives, and the females rarely form nursery colonies. They are sometimes observed migrating in small unisex groups, however. A few red bats do not migrate but remain in the north year round, hibernating in well-sheltered locations, such as caves, large hollow trees, and deep crevices. Red bats mate in the late summer and fall (often while flying) before they start the migration southward. Females store the sperm in their reproductive tracts over the winter months and ovulate in the early spring. Copulation in the spring has also been recorded. The gestation period is 80–90 days after fertilization of the ova, with one to four baby bats (usually two) born in late May or early June, after the females arrive at the summer range. The young are naked and blind at birth, but their eyes open when three days old. They start flying when about four weeks of age, but remain with the mother until weaned at about six weeks. Mother red bats are frequently captured with several nearly full-grown young attached to them. The combined load sometimes becomes too heavy for the mother to support when she tries to carry them from one roost to another. There is considerable mortality in red bats at this time of the year. This species puts on a heavy layer of fat prior to the fall and spring migrations to sustain them on the long journey.

Red bats consume many types of flying insects, including moths, flies, bugs, crickets, beetles, cicadas, bees, and wasps. They tend to forage at low levels among the trees, over meadows, and along watercourses. The flight speed is fairly slow, but extremely erratic, as they veer this way and that to capture elusive insects. They sometimes even land on a branch or bush to capture a choice insect before resuming flight.

Remarks: Like all the insectivorous bats, the red bat is a useful consumer of many flying pests. On the negative side, they are occasionally found to carry rabies. No bat, regardless of species, should be handled if it is found fluttering about in the daytime or is apparently sick.

Red bats show the tendency to return to the same spot night after night to forage. The same individual often returns to catch insects at the same street light or security light in the back yard for weeks during the summer. For example, I have captured a single banded red bat on numerous occasions, using a long-handled insect net, as she circled her favorite security light with its thousands of attracted insects.

The red bat possesses a great tolerance to cold weather compared with most bats. They are occasionally observed foraging during the afternoon or evening on cool winter days in their southern wintering areas. Due to the red bat's habit of roosting in trees, its major predators are hawks, owls, crows, jays, rat snakes, raccoons, and opossums.

Selected References:

Davis, W. H., and W. Z. Lidicker Jr. 1956. Winter range of the red bat, *Lasiurus borealis*. J. Mamm. 37: 280–81.

LaVal, R. K., and M. L. LaVal. 1979. Notes on reproduction, behavior, and abundance of the red bat, *Lasiurus borealis*. J. Mamm. 60: 209–12.

Shump, K. A., Jr., and A. V. Shump. 1983. Red bat *(Lasiurus borealis)*. Mammalian Species, No. 183: pp. 1–6.

Seminole Bat
Lasiurus seminolus

Seminole bat, *Lasiurus seminolus*. Roger W. Barbour

Identification: The Seminole bat is a sibling species to the red bat, so its characteristics are very similar. Instead of being brick red on its upper parts, the Seminole bat is a rich mahogany or reddish brown color. It is sometimes referred to as the mahogany bat for this reason. Females tend to have the upper fur frosted white, while the males are much less likely to have this color characteristic. Like the red bat, Seminole bats have small, rounded ears, a short, blunt tragus, and a fully furred tail membrane. The belly fur is paler than the back fir, and they have white shoulder patches.

Geographical Range: The Seminole bat occurs throughout the coastal plains of the southeastern region. In the United States it is confined to the Gulf and Atlantic coast states as far north as New York and as far west as Texas.

Habitat: This species shows a preference for cypress stands and floodplain forests which border lakes and streams. It roosts in clumps of Spanish moss, in dense foliage, and occasionally under tree bark.

Natural History: Seminole bats leave the roost at early twilight and tend to forage at treetop levels. They also

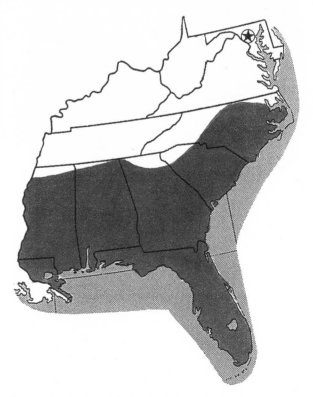

Geographical range of the Seminole bat in the Southeast.

sometimes feed at lower levels, especially when they are over water. They are fast fliers and not as erratic as red bats.

Seminole bats may move seasonally to other areas, but they do not imitate the long-distance, north–south migration characteristic of red bats. They tend to be active on a year-round basis in the southeastern lowlands whenever the air temperature is 60 degrees Fahrenheit or higher.

Very little is known about reproduction in Seminole bats, but it is apparently very similar to that of the red bat. The normal litter size is two (but it ranges from one to four), and the offspring are born in May or June. I have observed Seminole bats copulating in the air on one occasion in mid-August. They fell from the air locked *in copulo* at 2:00 A.M. under a bright light. It is possible that sperm remain viable in the female reproductive system until ovulation occurs the following early spring.

Remarks: The Seminole bat feeds on a variety of insects that occur in the tree canopy, including small moths, beetles, flies, bugs, and mosquitoes. Predators which consume Seminole bats in their tree roost locations are generally the same as those listed for the red bat.

Some mammalogists have speculated that the Seminole bat is nothing more than a southern color phase of the red bat, but I believe it is a distinct species. No intermediate forms or mixed-color litters have ever been found where both bats occur in the same region. Also, there are consistent minor differences in the skull and body morphologies that separate the two bats into distinct species.

Selected References:

Constantine, D. G. 1958. Ecological observations on lasiurine bats in Georgia. J. Mamm. 39: 64–70.

Sherman, H. B. 1935. Food habits of the seminole bat. J. Mamm. 16: 224.

Wilkins, K. T. 1987. Seminole Bat *(Lasiurus seminolus).* Mammalian Species, No. 280: pp. 1–5.

Hoary Bat
Lasiurus cinereus

Hoary bat, *Lasiurus cinereus.* American Society of Mammalogists

Identification: This species is one of the largest bats living in the Southeast (the wing span is 12–14 inches) and one of the most attractive bats in the world. The fur on the back is a beautiful mixture of deep browns and yellows tipped with a heavy white frosting. The underparts are mostly yellow and buff with slight white frosting. There is also a yellowish white shoulder patch at the base of each arm that usually extends across the chest. The wing and tail membranes are brownish black, and the tail membrane is heavily furred and frosted on the upper side. The ears are relatively small, broad, rounded, and contain a short, blunt tragus. The calcar has a well-developed keel.

Geographical Range: In the southeastern states, the hoary bat occurs regionwide, primarily as a winter resident and migrant. In the United States, this species has a nationwide distribution, with records from every state except Alaska. These bats also occur throughout most of Mexico, Central America, South America, and there is also a population in Hawaii.

Geographical range of the hoary bat in the Southeast.

Habitat: Hoary bats are found in pine woodlands, hardwood forests, and mixed pine-hardwood stands in the Southeast. It is a strong, high flier and is often seen foraging well above the tree canopy. In the northern states, hoary bats are associated with coniferous forests.

Natural History: These bats are solitary forest dwellers and almost never seek shelter in caves or buildings. They roost in dense foliage, under loose bark, and in clumps of Spanish moss where available. Hoary bats are highly migratory and spend winters in the southern states or in Mexico, and summers in the northern states or Canada.

Breeding occurs in the fall and winter months, and females are pregnant when they head northward in the spring. The litter size is usually twins (but ranges from one to four), and the offspring are born from late May to early June on the summer range. Babies are naked and blind at birth, but the eyes open about 10–12 days after birth. Young hoary bats are able to fly when about four weeks old.

This species feeds mainly on moths, but it also consumes dragonflies, beetles, bugs, wasps, large flies, mosquitoes, and other sizable insects.

Remarks: The hoary bat usually flies late, venturing forth right at dark, and is seldom noticed by the casual observer. However, during the colder winter months in the southern states, they may forage in the late afternoon or early evening when temperatures are warm enough for insects to be flying. They are usually overlooked by observers, who think they are swallows, nighthawks, or other insectivorous birds.

Because of their large size, hoary bats are valuable insect consumers, but a small percentage of them sometimes carry the rabies virus. They should not be handled if encountered.

Selected References:

Rolseth, S. L., C. E. Koehler, and R. M. R. Barclay. 1944. Differences in the diets of juvenile and adult hoary bats, *Lasiurus cinereus*. J. Mamm. 75: 394–98.

Shump, K. A., and A. V. Shump. 1982. Hoary Bat (*Lasiurus cinereus*). Mammalian Species, No. 185: pp. 1–5.

Zinn, T. L., and W. W. Baker. 1979. Seasonal migration of the hoary bat, *Lasiurus cinereus*, through Florida. J. Mamm. 60: 634–35.

Yellow Bat
Lasiurus intermedius

Yellow bat, *Lasiurus intermedius*. Roger W. Barbour

Identification: The yellow bat is only slightly smaller than the hoary bat, so it is one of the larger bats in the Southeast. The upper side is yellowish tan or grayish yellow, and the underside is slightly paler. The wings are dark brown, and the anterior half of the tail membrane is furred on its upper side. The ears are fairly small, broad, and rounded, and the tragus is short and blunt as it is among other members of this group.

Geographical Range: This species occurs throughout the lower coastal plains of the Southeast, from southeastern Virginia all the way to Louisiana and beyond. The geographical range in the United States is restricted to the Gulf Coastal Plain from Mexico northeastward and to the Atlantic Coast from Florida north to Virginia. The species also occurs southward through Mexico into northern Central America, and it also lives on the island of Cuba.

Habitat: Yellow bats are closely associated with woodlands which have the epiphyte Spanish moss growing on the trees. They are probably most abundant in live oak hummocks and open pine-oak forests. Yellow bats roost by day in the clumps of Spanish moss or among the hanging dead fronds of palm trees.

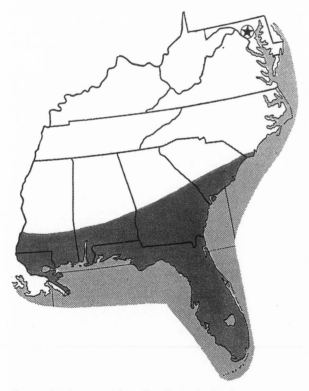

Geographical range of the yellow bat in the Southeast.

Natural History: Yellow bats start flying in the evening well before dark and are normally the earliest bat to appear each day. They are slow, straight fliers and tend to move back and forth over the same course repeatedly.

Yellow bats are active the year round, providing the temperature is warm enough at night for flying insects. They take a wide variety of large and medium-sized insects, including bugs, beetles, moths, wasps, and dragonflies.

The reproductive cycle of yellow bats is poorly known, but it is probably rather similar to that of other members of the genus. The number of offspring averages three (and ranges from two to four), which are usually born in May or June. Mating has been observed in the fall, and ovulation occurs the following spring. Foraging mothers leave the babies at the roost until the young bats can fly at three to four weeks of age. Most yellow bats appear to live a solitary existence, but small unisex groups are sometimes found roosting together in a favored palm or oak tree.

Remarks: Predators which are known to consume yellow bats on occasion include owls, hawks, raccoons, foxes, opossums, rat snakes, corn snakes, and cats. One unusual case of predation turned up in southern Georgia. A fisherman cut open an eight-pound largemouth bass he hooked one evening and was shocked to discover a recently swallowed yellow bat in its stomach. Presumably the bat had swooped low over the pond to drink, as the bats often do after leaving the roost, and the bass ate it.

Yellow bats have turned up fairly consistently as rabies carriers. One study in Florida reported that 20 percent of those yellow bats analyzed for rabies carried the virus. This figure is probably not representative of populations as a whole, since sick bats are more likely to be captured and examined than viable ones.

Selected References:

Hall, E. R., and J. K. Jones, Jr. 1961. North American yellow bats, *"Dasypterus,"* and a list of the named kinds of the genus *Lasiurus.* Gray. Univ. of Kansas Publ. Mus. Nat. Hist., No. 14: 73–98.

Jennings, W. L. 1958. The ecological distribution of bats in Florida. Ph.D. diss., Univ. of Fla., Gainesville, Fla., 125 pp.

Webster, W. D., J. K. Jones, and R. J. Baker. Northern Yellow Bat *(Lasiurus intermedius).* Mammalian Species, No. 132: pp. 1–3.

Evening Bat
Nycticeius humeralis

Evening bat, *Nycticeius humeralis*. Roger W. Barbour

Geographical range of the evening bat in the Southeast.

Identification: The evening bat is most likely to be confused with the *Myotis* group of species, because they are in its size range and rather similar in color. The upper parts are a rich, chocolate brown, and the underparts are paler and more buff. The fur on the back, when parted, is dark at the base. Evening bats have short narrow wings, and the wing membranes are black. The tail membrane is unfurred, and the wing membrane joins the foot at the base of the toes. The calcar of the ankle is not keeled.

The diagnostic features that identify the evening bat are small black ears containing a short, blunt-tipped tragus, which is less than half the length of the ear.

Geographical Range: This species occurs throughout the entire southeastern region. In the United States, the geographical range falls within the southeastern quadrant of the country, from Kansas eastward to the Atlantic Coast and from Michigan southward through Florida.

Habitat: Colonies of the evening bat live in hollow trees, culverts, old bridges, abandoned buildings, attics, barns, cabins, and other dark cavities. They prefer mature forests containing many old hollow trees.

Natural History: Evening bats leave the roost to forage at early twilight, so they are one of the bats commonly observed by people. For example, I have a small colony of evening bats which live in my back yard inside a hollow cavity in the top of an old utility pole. They fly forth in a short but steady stream just before dark to forage each night.

Mating occurs in the autumn, winter, and sometimes again in the spring. Females form nursery colonies separate from the males in the late spring and early summer. The average number of young is two (and ranges from one to four), and they are born in late May or early June. The babies are blind and naked at birth, but by the ninth day they are fully furred. The eyes open when they are two days old.

During the first 10 days of life, the baby bats squeak and chirp almost constantly, and it appears that, in this species, individualized vocalizations probably aid the mother in locating her young when she returns to the nursery colony from foraging. Young evening bats can fly when they are about three weeks old, but they continue to nurse until about eight weeks of age.

Remarks: Documented predators of the evening bat include raccoons, cats, dogs, owls, hawks, and various snakes. Banding studies suggest that the maximum longevity for this species is 10–12 years.

Selected References:

Jones, C. 1967. Growth, development, and wing loading in the evening bat, *Nycticeius humeralis* (Rafinesque). J. Mamm. 48: 1–19.

Watkins, L. C. 1970. Observations on the distribution and natural history of the evening bat *(Nycticeius humeralis)* in northwestern Missouri and adjacent Iowa. Trans. Kan. Acad. Sci. 72: 330–36.

———. 1971. A technique for monitoring the nocturnal activity of bats (with comments on activity patterns of the evening bat, *Nycticeius humeralis.* Trans. Kansas Acad. Sci. 74: 261–68.

———. 1972. *Nycticeius humeralis.* Mammalian Species, No. 23: pp. 1–4.

Rafinesque's Big-eared Bat
Plecotus rafinesqii

Rafinesque's big-eared bat, *Plecotus rafinesqii.* Merlin Tuttle

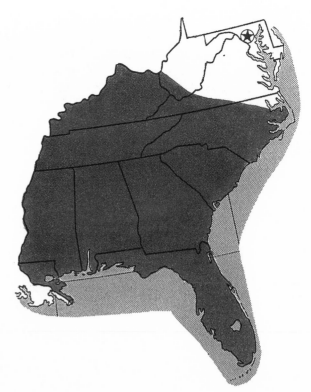

Geographical range of Rafinesque's big-eared bat in the Southeast.

Identification: Rafinesque's (or eastern) big-eared bat is easily identified by its huge ears, which are approximately one and one-quarter inches long, and by the presence of two prominent lumps on the nose. The ears are held slightly coiled backwards like a ram's horns and reach the middle of the back when pressed down. The fur is buff brown above and whitish buff below. The tragus of the ear is also very long (half the ear length) and pointed. In addition, there are prominent bristles or large hairs on the feet of Rafinesque's big-eared bat which are long enough to project beyond the ends of the toes.

Geographical Range: This species ranges over the southern three-quarters of the southeastern region. In the United States, the geographical range is roughly confined to the southeastern quadrant of the country.

Habitat: Rafinesque's big-eared bat roosts in hollow trees, under bark, in old cabins and barns, in wells and culverts, and in attics of houses located in forested areas. It shows a particular preference for abandoned, dilapidated shacks in remote, wooded locations. In northern areas, it also sometimes roosts in caves.

Natural History: This bat becomes active late in the evening, well after dark, so it is almost never visible on the wing. In the lower coastal plains, it most often forages in mature pine flatwoods or open pine-oak woodlands.

Copulation apparently takes place in the autumn and winter months, but the exact length of gestation is not known. Small groups of females form nursery colonies in the late spring and early summer months. Each female gives birth to one young per year, usually born in late May or early June. The babies grow rapidly and can fly in about three weeks, but are not weaned until around two months old. Young big-eared bats molt from their juvenile to adult pelage when they are about three months old.

In Florida and the warmer Gulf Coast areas, this bat appears to be active year round when the nights are warm enough for insects to be flying. Further north, they enter caves or deep crevices and hibernate for the winter. Banding studies of Rafinesque's big-eared bats reveal a maximum life span of over 10 years. Known predators include rattlesnakes, rat snakes, pine snakes, opossums, raccoons, cats, and owls.

Remarks: The main food item of Rafinesque's big-eared bats is moths. They undoubtedly reduce the numbers of several forest pest species as result of their nightly foraging activities. These bats are very swift fliers and are extremely agile in changing directions to pursue their quarry.

When at rest, Rafinesque's big-eared bat usually coils its large ears back spiral fashion along the sides of the back, like ram's horns, but the tragus remains forward like small ears.

Selected References:

Brown, L. N., and Curtis K. Brown. 1993. First record of the Eastern Big-eared Bat *(Plecotus rafinesqii)* in southern Florida. Fla. Scientist 56: 63–64.

Jones, C. 1977. Rafinesque's Big-eared Bat *(Plecotus rafinesqii).* Mammalian Species, No. 69: pp. 1–4.

Jones, C. and R. D. Suttkus. 1971. Wing loading in *Plecotus rafinesqii.* J. Mamm. 52: 458–60.

———. 1975. Notes on the natural history of *Plecotus rafinesqii.* Mus. Zool., Louisiana State Univ., Occasional Papers No. 47: 1–14.

Townsend's Big-eared Bat
Plecotus townsendii

Townsend's big-eared bat, *Plecotus townsendii.* American Society of Mammalogists

Identification: Both Townsend's and Rafinesque's big-eared bats are easily distinguished from all other southeastern bats by huge ears, which, when laid back, are half the length of the body. The ears are parchment-like, furred only along the inner edges, and joined across the forehead at their bases. They are sometimes called "lump-nosed" bats because of two winglike glands extending forward from the nostrils.

The fur is long, soft, and brownish above, grading to buff on the belly. The presence of buff-colored ventral fur separates Townsend's from Rafinesque's big-eared bat, whose underparts are washed with white. Also, the dorsal fur of Townsend's bat shows little contrast between the tips and bases of the hairs, but in Rafinesque's bat the hairs of the dorsum are black at their bases.

The skull of Townsend's big-eared bat has an accessory cusp on the first upper incisors, which is lacking in Rafinesque's big-eared bat.

Geographical Range: Townsend's big-eared bat is rather common in the western United States, but rare in the Southeast. It occurs in isolated colonies located

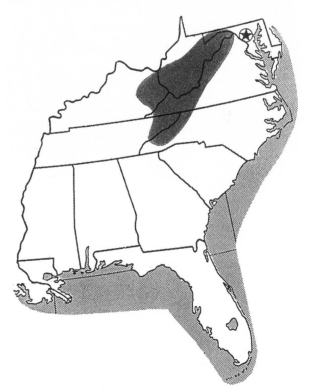

Geographical range of Townsend's big-eared bat in the Southeast.

in the mountains of northern and western Virginia, eastern and southern West Virginia, western North Carolina, eastern Tennessee, and in eastern Kentucky. These relict southeastern populations are distinct from the populations in the western United States.

Habitat: Townsend's big-eared bat appears to be restricted to limestone caves located in the mountains above 1,500 feet elevation. Rafinesque's big-eared bat, in contrast, occurs at much lower elevation in the Southeast. Individual Townsend's big-eared bats tend to congregate in small groups, hanging from the ceilings and walls, usually near the mouth of the cave in the "twilight zone" where the light is dim even at mid-day.

Natural History: This species uses one cave for its summer colonies and a separate cave—normally only a few miles away—for hibernation during the winter months. Hibernation lasts from October or November until late March or early April. These bats, when hanging upside down from the cave ceiling to sleep or hibernate, coil their ears spirally and flatten them against their neck and sides. When they awaken, the ears straighten out and are held erect. These are among the wariest of bats, taking flight at the least disturbance.

In the summer months, females establish small nursery colonies and usually return to the same cave year after year.

Mating takes place in the fall before hibernation, during the winter when the females are dormant, and again in the spring when the colony becomes active. Ovulation occurs in the spring, and a single offspring is born in May or June. Gestation lasts for 56–100 days in the spring; the shorter gestation occurs in females that maintain a higher body temperature as a result of clustering very close together.

Newborn bats are naked, pinkish gray, and the eyes are closed. Dark gray lumps on the nose are conspicuous, and the ears are long and pointed. The young are left hanging in the nursery colony each night while the mother forages. Upon returning, each female relocates her baby by smell, even in a large cluster of young bats. They are nursed during the daytime, and the eyes first open when they are about eight days old. Big-eared bats first fly when three weeks old, but they do not venture forth to forage until about six weeks of age. The young bats are weaned when approximately two months old. Males do not mate their first fall, but young females do breed at that time.

Remarks: This species flies later than most bats, and it does not leave the cave to forage until well after dark. The prey consists almost totally of moths, an eating pattern which is very beneficial to agricultural interests.

Since this bat has been very vulnerable to human disturbances in the few caves it occupies, and since it occurs in low population numbers in the Southeast, it is listed as an endangered species in Kentucky, North Carolina, West Virginia, Virginia, and Tennessee by the U.S. Fish and Wildlife Service.

Selected References:

Adam, M. D., M. J. Lacki, and T. G. Barnes. 1994. Foraging areas and habitat use of the Virginia big-eared bat in Kentucky. J. Wildl. Mgmt. 58: 462–69.

Humphrey, S. R., and T. H. Kung. 1976. Ecology of a Pleistocene relict, the western big-eared bat (*Plecotus townsendii*) in the southern Great Plains. J. Mamm. 57: 470–94.

Kunz, T. H., and R. A. Martin. 1982. Townsend's Big-eared Bat (*Plecotus townsendii*). Mammalian Species, No. 175: pp. 1–6.

Lacki, M. J., M. D. Adam, and L. G. Shoemaker. 1993. Characteristics of feeding roosts of Virginia big-eared bats in Daniel Boone National Forest. J. Wildl. Mgmt. 57: 539–42.

Pearson, O. P., M. R. Koford, and A. K. Pearson. 1952. Reproduction of the lump-nosed bat (*Corynorhinus townsendii*) in California. J. Mamm. 33: 273–320.

Sample, B. E., and R. C. Whitmore. 1993. Food habits of the endangered Virginia big-eared bat in West Virginia. J. Mamm. 74: 422–27.

Brazilian Free-tailed Bat
Tadarida brasiliensis

Brazilian free-tailed bat, *Tadarida brasiliensis*. American Society of Mammalogists

Identification: In this species the tail continues beyond the tail membrane one inch to one and one-half inches, or half its length, which gives it the "free-tail" in the common name. The upper and lower pelage varies from blackish brown to dark chocolate-brown, mixed with charcoal gray. The ears are very broad, short, and funnel-like. When laid forward, the ears do not touch the tip of the nose. Numerous hairs or bristles, which are as long as the foot itself, grow from the tips of the toes. Free-tailed bats have small, narrow, black wings and a short tail membrane.

Geographical Range: Brazilian free-tailed bats live in the southern half of the southeastern region and are most common on the coastal plains. In the United States, the geographical range encompasses the entire southern half of the country. The species also occurs in Mexico, Central America, and South America.

Habitat: Free-tailed bats live in colonies the year round in a wide variety of locations, including attics, tile roofs, hollow trees, caves, culverts, storm sewers, and outbuildings. They are common in the heart of cities, as well as in the suburbs and in rural areas.

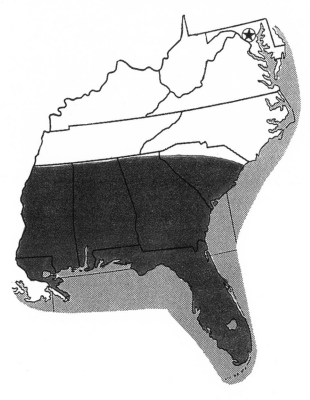

Geographical range of the Brazilian free-tailed bat in the Southeast.

Natural History: This is one of the most gregarious bats known to mammalogists. In some western caves, single colonies number in the double-digit millions, but in the Southeast the colonies only contain hundreds or thousands of bats each.

Free-tailed bats in the Southeast are rather sedentary and do not migrate. In the western states by contrast, free-tailed bats migrate several hundred miles from a summer range to a warmer winter range.

Studies have shown that breeding is quite synchronized and occurs during a short span of a few days in the spring. Females ovulate right after copulation, and one offspring is born after a gestation period of 75–85 days. The babies are born from early to mid-June, and they are naked and blind at birth. The young bats do not fly until they are about five weeks of age, which is somewhat longer than for most bats.

Free-tailed bats have a very penetrating, musky odor, which can be detected at some distance from the colony. The musky scent emanates from powerful skin glands.

These bats feed extensively on small moths, winged ants, small beetles, midges, mosquitoes, chalcid wasps, and many other small insects. Free-tailed bats are considered to be the most rapid fliers of American bats, and their flight pattern is very erratic and difficult to follow with the eye.

Remarks: A large free-tailed bat colony makes a great impact on local nocturnal insect populations, because each bat is estimated to consume three grams of insects per night. Some large western bat colonies also generate substantial amounts of guano (droppings) on cave floors. The guano is mined and sold as a rich nitrate fertilizer.

The maximum longevity for this species is about 15 years.

Selected References:

Davis, R. B., C. F. Herreid II, and H. L. Short. 1962. Mexican free-tailed bats in Texas. Ecological Monographs, No. 32: 311–64.

Edgerton, H. E., P. F. Spangle, and J. K. Baker. 1966. Mexican free-tailed bat photography. Science 153: 201–3.

Pagels, J. F. 1975. Temperature regulation, body weight, and changes in total body fat of the free-tailed bat, *Tadarida brasiliensis cyncocephala* (Le Conte). Comp. Bioch. Physio. 50: 237–46.

Spenrath, C. A., and R. K. LaVal. 1974. An ecological study of a resident population of *Tadarida brasiliensis* in eastern Texas. Museum, Texas Tech Univ., Occasional Papers No. 21: 1–14.

Wilkin, K. T. 1989. Brazilian Free-Tailed Bat *(Tadarida brasiliensis)*. Mammalian Species, No. 331: pp. 1–10.

Wagner's Mastiff Bat
Eumops glaucinus

Wagner's mastiff bat, *Eumops glaucinus*. Roger W. Barbour

Geographical range of Wagner's mastiff bat in the Southeast.

Identification: This species, sometimes called the Florida mastiff bat, is by far the largest bat living in the Southeast. It looks like the Brazilian free-tailed bat, but it is several times larger. The upper fur is grayish brown and the belly is gray. The ears are broad, short, funnel-shaped, and, when laid forward, do not reach the tip of the nose. The wing and tail membranes are small and narrow, dark brown in color, and naked. The tail extends beyond the tail membrane for half its length (one and one-quarter inches to one and one-half inches). The toes also have long, bristlelike hairs extending from them.

Geographical Range: In the United States, Wagner's mastiff bat is known only from the southern part of Florida. It has been captured as far north as Ft. Lauderdale in Broward County, and across the peninsula at Punta Gorda in Charlotte County. This tropical bat also lives in Cuba, Jamaica, southern Mexico, Central America, and parts of South America.

Habitat: This species prefers to roost among the fronds of tall palms, under the Spanish tiles of roofs, in the upper reaches of tall buildings, and in the hollows of trees, such as pines and royal palms.

Natural History: Wagner's mastiff bat is considered to be a rare species throughout its range, but since it forages late at night and at high levels, it may be just difficult to collect. It was first reported in the United States in 1936. At the time, the single specimen was thought to have been accidentally imported on a banana boat. However, since then over 50 other specimens have been taken, so there is certainly a well-established population living in southern Florida, regardless of the source. The species has also been found in fossil deposits from eastern Florida, so it is possible that a relict population could have survived in southern Florida. It is also conceivable that a hurricane could have blown a "founding population" of these strong, fast fliers to our shores from Cuba (a distance of about 90 miles). At the speed these bats fly, they could make the flight across the Florida Straits in well under two hours, even without a tailwind. Since there are no living records of this bat in Florida prior to the second third of the twentieth century, colonization by storm-blown refugees from Cuba seems most plausible.

Very little is known about the life history of Wagner's mastiff bat in the United States. In Panama they have been found roosting in small colonies of 10–12 individuals in the attics of houses. However, in September 1979, a small colony of eight Wagner's mastiff bats (seven females and one male) was found living in an old woodpecker nest cavity in a longleaf pine tree near Punta Gorda, Florida. Five of these females were post-lactational and one was pregnant with a single, two-inch-long fetus. In Cuba, the species is polyestrous and therefore breeds throughout the year, so in southern Florida its reproduction cycle is probably similar. The sex ratio of the Punta Gorda colony suggests that this group may represent a male and his harem. In Cuba, however, males and females in approximately equal numbers have been found roosting together throughout the year in tree hollows. Litter sizes of both one and two offspring have been recorded.

Remarks: Analysis of fecal pellets of this species reveals that, by volume, the diet is 55 percent beetles, 15 percent flies, and 10 percent true bugs. Mastiff bats are thus beneficial as insect consumers.

Mastiff bats make a characteristic high-pitched call as they fly overhead at night. This vocalization is being used by wildlife biologists to locate colonies of this rare creature. The Florida Game and Fresh Water Fish Commission has listed Wagner's mastiff bat as a threatened species.

Selected References:

Belwood, J. J. 1981. Wagner's mastiff bat, *Eumops glaucinus floridanus*, molossidae in southwestern Florida. J. Mamm. 62: 411–13.

Owre, O. T. 1978. The Florida mastiff bat, *Eumops glaucinus floridanus*. In Rare and endangered biota of Florida. Vol. I. Mammals. Univ. Presses of Fla., Gainesville, Fla., pp. 43–44.

Robson, M. S., F. J. Mazzotti, and T. Parrott. 1989. Recent evidence of the mastiff bat in southern Florida. Fla. Field Nat. 17: 81–82.

Little Mastiff Bat
Molossus molossus

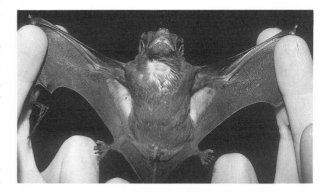

Little mastiff bat, *Molossus molossus*. American Society of Mammalogists

Identification: This species is rather similar to the Brazilian free-tailed bat, but slightly larger in body size. There are two color phases, one with short, velvety hair of uniform color throughout, and one with longer fur and bicolored banded hairs. The pelage is variable in color from chestnut brown to rusty dark brown to blackish. The base of each ear joins the other in the middle of the forehead.

The skull has one upper premolar on each side in the upper jaw, which distinguishes it from the Brazilian free-tailed bat, which has two upper incisors on each side.

Geographical Range: The little mastiff bat was recently recorded for the first time in the United States in the lower and middle Florida Keys (Boca Chica, Key West, Stock Island, and Marathon). This species ranges throughout Central America, South American, and many islands of the Caribbean, including Cuba.

Natural History: This bat is found in moist, tropical broadleaf forests and dry, tropical deciduous forests. Females congregate in nursery colonies at the start of the summer rainy season in hollow trees, building, caverns, or palm fronds. The colonies in the Florida Keys are often found in the roofs of buildings. They leave to forage for insects on the wing at dusk. These bats fly very rapidly and veer from side to side a great deal, much in the manner of swifts. They appear to feed on most types of flying insects, but especially moths and beetles.

In Puerto Rico, members of *Molossus molossus* mate in February or March and give birth to a single young in June, then mate again and produce a second off-spring in September or October. Females suckle the young for about six weeks and leave them at the roost in a cluster when foraging. Juveniles are on their own when about 65 days old.

Remarks: The little mastiff bat has probably been an overlooked resident of the Florida Keys for some years because the colonies discovered there appear to be well established, ranging in size from 50 to 300 indivduals. Since there are large hordes of flying insects throughout the Keys, this bat should be beneficial in reducing their numbers.

Selected References:
Eisenberg, J. *Mammals of the Neotropics, Vol. 1 Northern Neotropics.* Univ. of Chicago Press. 449 pp.
Frank, P., and J. Lazelle. 1995. *Molossus molossus* in the Florida Keys (Personal Comm.).
Jones, J., Jr., and C. Phillips. 1970. Comments on the systematics and zoogeography of bats in the lesser Antilles. Studies Fauna, Carib. Islands 32: 131–45.

Geographical range of the little mastiff bat and the Jamaican fruit bat in the Southeast.

Jamaican Fruit Bat
Artibeus jamaicensis

Jamaican fruit bat *(Artibeus jamaicensis)* with young. American Society of Mammalogists

Identification: The Jamaican fruit bat, or Antillean fruit bat, is a large brown bat with no tail and is the only bat in the eastern United States with a nose leaf. It is also the only fruit bat found in the eastern United States, and it lives only in the Florida Keys. The upper parts are various shades of brown, and the underparts are often grayish and somewhat paler than the back. White facial markings are usually present, and the body weight averages 40 grams or slightly more.

The skull is large and broad, with a slightly elevated brain case, and there are 30 teeth in the upper and lower jaws.

Geographical Range: In the United States, the Jamaican fruit bat has been reported only from the southern Keys (especially Key West, Ramrod Key, and Cudjoe Key), but probably lives on others. This species ranges throughout many islands of the Caribbean Sea, including Cuba, Jamaica, Puerto Rico, Hispaniola, and the islands of the Lesser Antilles. It also occurs in Mexico, Central America, and parts of South America. In the tropics, this species lives in a wide range of forest habitats. It roosts in caves, hollow trees, tents of folded leaves made by biting the midribs, and in buildings.

Natural History: This species is mainly frugivorous and feeds primarily on figs and other fruits. However, it also feeds on pollen, nectar, flower parts, and occasional insects. Preferred fruits besides figs are mangos, avocados, and bananas. Food can pass through the digestive tract in as little as 15 minutes, and fecal material usually has the odor of the food being eaten.

The reproductive period of this species is tied closely to maximum abundance of figs. In Panama, births peak in March and April. There is a postpartum estrus followed by a second birthing period in July and August. This is followed by estrous, fertilization, and implantation, but the implanted embryos remain dormant from September to November.

Development then proceeds normally until birth occurs in March or April. The species is polygynous, and the males accumulate harems of up to 25 females. A single young is born to each female, although occasional cases of twinning are known. Females have a daytime roost and leave their young during each nightly feeding foray.

Remarks: Jamaican fruit bats often forage in small groups, and they are much less active on bright moonlight nights. Besides harems, this species also forms groups of bachelor males or nonbreeding females. Individual fruit bats have been known to live eight to ten years. Owls, snakes, and bat falcons are known predators.

Selected References:

Humphrey, S., and L. Brown. 1986. Report of a new bat in the United States is erroneous. Florida Scientist 49: 262–63.

Kunz, T., P. August, and C. Burnett. 1983. Harem social organization in cave roosting Jamaican fruit bats. Biotropica 15: 133–38.

Morrison, D. 1978. Foraging ecology and energetics of the frugivorous bat, *Artibeus jamaicensis*. Ecology 59: 16–123.

———. 1979. Apparent male defense of tree hollows in the fruit bat, *Artibeus jamaicensis*. J. Mamm. 60: 11–15.

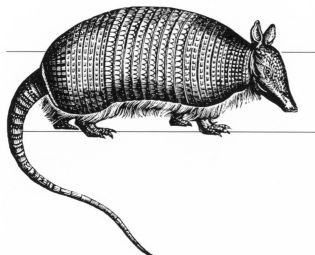

Order Xenarthra
Armadillos, Anteaters, and Sloths

Order Xenarthra is made up of a bizarre-looking group of mammals which includes the armadillos, anteaters, and sloths. All are characterized by having reduced degenerate teeth or no teeth at all. Armadillos and anteaters feed mainly on insects, using their long mucus-covered tongue to capture ants, termites, and other arthropods. The prey is swallowed whole, and only simple, peglike teeth are required. Sloths are sluggish tree dwellers that feed on leaves. They have degenerate but functional teeth that chew up the food.

The three families (armadillos, anteaters, and sloths) are placed in a common order because of some similarities in the skeletons, but outwardly they look very dissimilar. Many experts think they are not too closely related and that the skeletons are somewhat similar because of convergence in their evolution from unrelated ancestors.

Some xenarthrans are quite large, such as the giant anteaters of South America, which is over 6 feet long and weighs up to 120 pounds. Most xenarthrans, however, are small to medium-sized mammals less than two feet long and weighing only a few pounds. The largest xenarthrans that ever lived are now fossils. They were the giant ground sloths, some of which stood as high as an elephant. Their fossilized bones often turn up in numerous locations throughout the southern states.

Only one xenarthran, the nine-banded armadillo, occurs in the United States, but a number of other species live in Mexico, Central America, and South America.

Nine-banded Armadillo
Dasypus novemcinctus

Nine-banded armadillo, *Dasypus novemcinctus*. Larry Brown

Identification: This species is about the size of an opossum and is a strange-looking mammal because it is nearly hairless and covered with armor plates. Along the back, there are nine connected moveable plates which give the armadillo its name. There is also a broad shoulder shield plate and a smaller hip shield plate. The head and snout are small, tapered, and narrow. The tail is also long, tapered, and encased in 12 armor rings. All the feet are armed with long white claws which are specialized for digging. The color of the armored body plates is brownish black, and there are white hairs sparsely scattered over the thinner skin of the belly. The head, sides, and tail have ivory-yellow spots on the armor plates. The bare ears are shaped like two leathery funnels that nearly join each other at the midline.

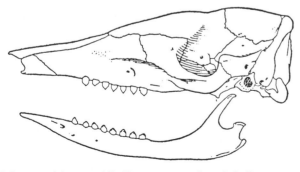

Side view of the armadillo *(Dasypus novemcinctus)* skull showing the simple peglike teeth in both upper and lower jaws.

Geographical Range: Armadillos were not native to the Southeast in early historic times, but were introduced by humans into Florida several times during the early 1900s. They became well established in Florida and eventually expanded their range northward into the coastal plains of Georgia, Alabama, and Mississippi by the 1950s and 1960s. The native armadillos in Texas and Louisiana also expanded eastward to hook up with the introduced eastern populations. Presently, the geographical range of the armadillo extends over the southern half of the southeastern region. In the United States, the armadillo ranges across the southern third of the country and as far west as New Mexico. It also occurs in much of Mexico, Central America, and South America.

Habitat: Armadillos prefer both forested and semi-open habitats having deep sandy soils. They are most common in areas with dense ground cover and a loose-textured soil that make digging easy. There tend to be few armadillos in areas having heavy clay or rocky soils, as well as in regions dominated by marshes and swamps.

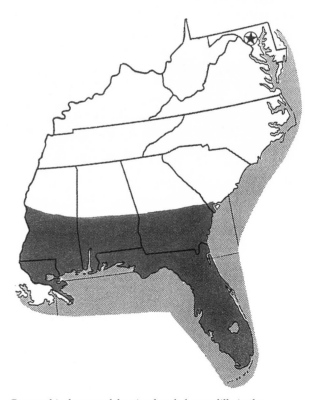

Geographical range of the nine-banded armadillo in the Southeast.

Natural History: The armadillo is a burrowing mammal that digs a series of dens scattered throughout its home range. They often locate a den's entrance at the base of stumps, trees, palmettos, bushes, brush piles, or other protected locations. At the end of a downward-sloping tunnel, armadillos make a slightly enlarged nest chamber containing a sizable mass of leaves and grasses. Armadillos also occasionally build massive above-ground nests consisting of leaves and grasses. Many other animals, including snakes, lizards, rabbits, toads, frogs, rats, mice, skunks, opossums, and arthropods, also use armadillo burrows for homes or refuge. Armadillo burrows usually have at least two or more entrances, which provide additional escape routes for the inhabitant.

When pursued, armadillos can dig a burrow and disappear underground in just a few seconds, and they are very difficult to pull out of a partially completed burrow when grasped by the tail. They cannot, however, roll themselves up into a protected ball as is often alleged (although there is a small South American armadillo that does form a tight ball).

Breeding in the nine-banded armadillo occurs in July or August. Ovulation follows insemination, and fertilization of an egg takes place in short order. However, implantation of embryos in the uterus is delayed until late November or December (this process is called "delayed implantation"). Prior to further embryonic development, the single fertilized egg (called a zygote) divides into four different cells that separate and ultimately develop into four different identical embryos. The gestation period averages about 120 days. Normally, the nine-banded armadillo produces a litter of identical quadruplets (all four are genetically alike and of the same sex). I have occasionally collected pregnant females with embryo counts of three and six. Presumably, a litter of three armadillos results when resorption of one embryo occurs early in gestation. An embryo count of six is a little more complicated, but might be explained by the simultaneous ovulation of two eggs, prior to the splitting of both into four individuals, then followed by the loss of two of the eight. Also, a single fertilized egg could possible give rise to eight individuals under certain conditions of excessive splitting.

Birth of the young armadillos usually occurs in late March or April, but a few are born in May. The offspring are precocious; the eyes are open within a few hours, and the babies can walk and follow their mother on their first day.

Armadillos do not hibernate during cold weather, and this fact probably restricts their northward geographical range expansion. Even if individuals on the edge of northerly expansion do not freeze during a long cold spell, they probably do starve from lack of food. They forage for all kinds of insects and other invertebrates, as well as for some plant material. One study of stomach contents found that beetles and beetle larvae composed 45 percent of the armadillo's diet.

Armadillos are primarily nocturnal, but on cloudy days they are frequently seen probing the ground along roadsides or heard scratching about in the bushes. They have very poor eyesight but a keen sense of hearing, so they can often be approached and captured with a hand net, as long as no sound gives the collector away.

Armadillos are fairly sedentary and often remain in the same general area for long periods of time. They forage within a home range which is only a few acres in size. Their maximum longevity in the field is not known, but in captivity they have lived as long as 10 years.

Remarks: Armadillos are generally beneficial since they consume certain destructive insects such as termites, ants, ground-dwelling beetles, and beetle larvae. On the negative side, armadillo diggings often damage lawns, golf courses, corn, peanut fields, cantaloupes, watermelons, and other truck garden crops. They occasionally eat the eggs of ground-nesting birds such as quail and sparrows, but eggs account for only a tiny fraction of their normal diet.

This species is used extensively in biomedical and genetic research because of its unique characteristic of bearing identical quadruplets. Armadillos are also used in research on leprosy because the bacteria that causes this disease will also grow on them.

Some states consider the armadillo a game animal and encourage hunters to kill and eat them. The meat has a very rich taste, and recipes for its preparation often appear in print. Most people remain unconvinced of its palatability, however. Armadillo hides are sometimes made into baskets and handbags in parts of the United States.

Armadillos are one of the most common animals killed on southern highways, trailing only the opossum. Their high morbidity is partially explained by their unwary nature and tendency to forage on road shoulders, but they also have a tendency to jump straight up when startled and strike the bottom of the automobile as it passes over them.

Selected References:

Clark, W. K. 1951. Ecological life history of the armadillo in the eastern Edwards Plateau region. Amer. Midl. Nat. 46: 337–58.

Enders, A. C. 1966. The reproductive cycle of the nine-banded armadillo *(Dasypus novemcinctus)*. In *Comparative Biology of Reproduction in Mammals*. Zool. Soc. Symp. 15: 295–310.

Fitch, H. S., P. Goodrum, and C. Newman. 1952. The armadillo in the southeastern United States. J. Mamm. 33: 21–37.

Humphrey, S. R. 1974. Zoogeography of the nine-banded armadillo *(Dasypus novemcinctus)* in the United States. Bioscience 24: 457–62.

Johansen, K. 1961. Temperature regulation in the nine-banded armadillo *(Dasypus novemcinctus mexicanus)*. Physiol. Zool. 34: 126–44.

Kalmbach, E. R. 1944. The armadillo: Its relation to agriculture and game. Texas Game, Fish and Oyster Commission, Austin, Texas, 60 pp.

McBee, K., and R. J. Baker. 1982. Nine-banded Armadillo *(Dasypus novemcinctus)*. Mammalian Species, No. 162, pp. 1–9.

McDonough, C. M. 1944. Determinants of aggression in nine-banded armadillos. J. Mamm. 75: 189–98.

Talmage, R. V., and G. D. Buchanan. 1954. The armadillo *(Dasypus novemcinctus)*, a review of its natural history, ecology, anatomy, and reproductive physiology. The Rice Institute Pamphlet 41, 135 pp.

Order Lagomorpha
Rabbits and Hares

Rabbits and hares resemble rodents rather closely and were once considered a subgroup of that order. Like rodents they have a pair of large, chisel-shaped upper incisors, but differ from them in that there is a second smaller pair right behind the first pair. Rabbits and hares also have very large hind feet compared to the front feet, and their ears are very large and elongated. The males lack a baculum, or penis bone, which is present in rodents. The tail is always short and covered with fluffy, cottonlike hairs. Rabbits and hares eat only vegetable matter. Lagomorphs and rodents are no longer considered to be close relatives, and their superficial resemblance is probably due to their similar herbivorous adaptations.

Lagomorphs are unusual in that they produce two types of fecal pellets from the digestive tract. One is a soft, green pellet that is only partially digested. These are re-eaten, passed through the digestive tract a second time, and virtually all remaining nutrients are extracted. The second type is a dry, brownish pellet which is the true feces. The whole process of food reingestion is called "pseudo-rumination," because it is functionally analogous to the method used by cattle to extract more nutrients from grass (which involves regurgitation, chewing of the cud, and swallowing the food a second time).

Six species of rabbits occur in the Southeast (five native species plus one introduced). Lagomorphs now have virtually a worldwide distribution because of introductions by humans. They were once absent from Australia, but they were introduced by the English colonists and are now a considerable pest. All rabbits exhibit a hopping or "saltatorial" type of locomotion because of their enlarged, powerful hind legs and relatively small, weak front legs.

Hares and rabbits have very different reproductive strategies. The rabbits all have fairly short gestation periods, large litter sizes, the young are altricial, and the babies remain in the nest for considerable time and mature slowly. Hares, on the other hand, have long gestation periods, small litter sizes, the young are precocial, and the babies spend almost no time in a nest and mature rapidly. Rabbits thus sustain much more infant mortality than do hares, which they offset by producing more litters of much larger size.

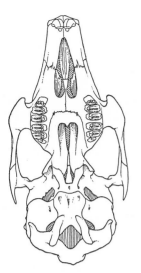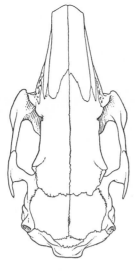

Lower view (left) and upper view (right) of a representative rabbit skull, the marsh rabbit (*Sylvilagus palustris*).

Eastern Cottontail
Sylvilagus floridanus

Eastern cottontail, *Sylvilagus floridanus*. Florida Game & Freshwater Fish Commission

Identification: This species is slightly smaller than a cat and its upper parts are grayish to reddish brown sprinkled with black. The nap of the neck is rusty red, as are the forelegs. There is a cream-colored ring around the eye and often a white star or blaze on the forehead. The underparts are white except for a brown throat patch. The tail hair forms a cottonlike tuft, which gives the species its common name.

The skull is identified by the presence of a posterior supraorbital process that is only partially fused to the cranium, leaving a slitlike opening when viewed from above. An anterior supraorbital process and supraorbital notch are both well developed in the eastern cottontail, but absent in the Appalachian cottontail.

Geographical range of the eastern cottontail in the Southeast.

Geographical Range: The eastern cottontail occurs throughout the entire southeastern region. In the United States, the geographical range occupies the eastern two-thirds of the country.

Habitat: This species is highly adaptable and lives in virtually every upland plant community except dense forest. It is most abundant in fallow weedy fields, in brush lands with grassy openings, and in open forest edges. The eastern cottontail is normally absent from the wetter habitats occupied by the marsh rabbit or swamp rabbit.

Natural History: The eastern cottontail is primarily nocturnal, but it is often seen actively foraging at dawn and dusk. These rabbits rest in a shallow depression, or "form," usually concealed in a dense clump of grass. It consists of nothing more than a well worn and slightly scratched depression. Eastern cottontails eat the leaves of a wide variety of plants, but prefer legumes, grasses, and various broadleaf weeds.

In Florida and the warmer Gulf Coast areas, there appears to be a nearly year-round breeding season, but in the rest of the Southeast this species exhibits seasonal breeding that coincides with the length of the growing season. Most litters are born between March and October. Eastern cottontails are noted for their high reproductive output. The litter size varies from one to eight and averages about three and one-half in southern states. The gestation period averages 28 days (ranging from 26 to 32), and females generally produce four to six litters per year.

Dominant-subordinate interactions take place during the reproductive season in the eastern cottontail. The establishment of male hierarchies tends to prevent fighting over females at the time of breeding. Normally, the dominant males inseminate more females than do subordinate males.

The nest is a shallow, saucerlike depression in the ground lined with fine grass and soft fur plucked from the female's breast with her teeth. When she leaves the nest to forage, she also covers the young with a top layer of hair and grass to hide them. The babies are born altricial, i.e., naked, blind, and helpless at birth.

A mother cottontail normally comes into estrus and is bred immediately after giving birth (called a postpartum estrus and pregnancy). Thus, an adult female is pregnant and nursing young most of the breeding season. Baby rabbits grow rapidly; their eyes are open and they are fully furred in a week. At the end of three to four weeks they leave the nest and are weaned, as the female is ready to deliver another litter. Young cottontails have been known to breed when as young as three to four months of age, thus they can produce several litters their first year of life.

Mortality is high in juvenile cottontails, with only 55 percent surviving to reach the age of one month. They are preyed upon by virtually every terrestrial carnivore big enough to catch them. These predators include foxes, coyotes, dogs, cats, owls, snakes, hawks, crows, weasels, and bobcats. The maximum life span of the eastern cottontail is about ten years. However, in natural populations few rabbits live more than two years. Home range size varies from one to ten acres, depending on the quality and density of the plant cover.

Remarks: Cottontail rabbits are one of the most important game animals in the United States. They are not hunted as extensively in southern states as they are in northern states, but they are still a valuable small-game mammal. Eastern cottontails are also a vital link in many ecological food chains for animals.

Eastern cottontails are occasionally infected with the disease tularemia, a bacterial disease which can be contracted through a break in the person's skin while handling or skinning an infected animal. If the disease is not diagnosed and treated with antibiotics, it will do serious damage to the human nervous system. Various species of ticks are the primary transmitter of tularemia between rabbits. Thorough cooking of a wild rabbit before eating eliminates any danger of acquiring tularemia from the meat.

Eastern cottontails frequently cause damage to garden vegetables and commercial agricultural crops. They are best controlled by trapping or shooting in such situations, or by eliminating nearby rabbit cover if direct removal is not feasible. For permanent protection of a garden, rabbit-proof fencing can be utilized.

Selected References:

Chapman, J. A., A. L. Harman, and D. E. Samuel. 1977. Reproductive and physiological cycles in the cottontail complex in western Maryland and nearby West Virginia. Wildl. Monogr. 56: 1–73.

Chapman, J. A., J. G. Hockman, and M. M. Ojeda 1980. Eastern Cottontail (*Sylvilagus floridanus*). Mammalian Species, No. 136: pp. 1–8.

Hill, E. P., III. 1972. The cottontail rabbit in Alabama. Auburn University, Agr. Exper. Station Bull. 440: 1–103.

Jacobson, H. A., R. L. Kirkpatrick, and B. S. McGinnes. 1978. Diseases and physiologic characteristics of two cottontail populations in Virginia. Wildl. Monogr. 60: 1–58.

Lord, R. D., Jr. 1963. The cottontail rabbit in Illinois. Illinois Dept. Cons., Tech. Bull. No. 3, 96 pp.

Schribner, K. T., and R. K. Chesser. 1993. Environmental and demographic correlates of spatial and seasonal genetic structure in the eastern cottontail (*Sylvilagus floridanus*). J. Mamm. 74: 1026–44.

Appalachian Cottontail
Sylvilagus obscurus

Appalachian cottontail, *Sylvilagus obscurus*. U.S. Fish & Wildlife Service

Identification: The Appalachian cottontail is very similar to the eastern cottontail in coloration, but is slightly smaller in body size and has a black patch (never white) between the ears, which are slightly shorter and more rounded than those of the eastern cottontail.

The skull is identified by its smaller size and by the absence of an anterior supraorbital process or anterior supraorbital notch (both are present in the skull of the eastern cottontail).

Geographical Range: This species occurs at scattered locations at high elevations along the Appalachian Mountain chain as far south as Georgia and Alabama. In the United States, the geographical range of the Appalachian cottontail extends along the Appalachian Mountains from Pennsylvania to northeastern Alabama in the mountains.

Habitat: The Appalachian cottontail inhabits dense forests and bushy thickets at high elevations in the mountains. It prefers thick cover, such as rhododendron, mountain laurel, and blueberries, to open meadows.

Natural History: The diet of this species is less varied than that of the eastern cottontail. Their summer foods

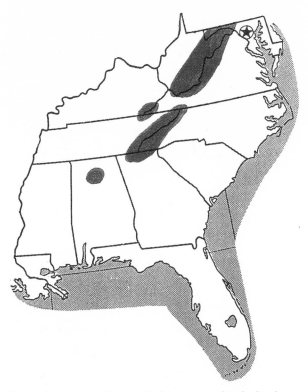

Geographical range of the Appalachian cottontail in the Southeast.

consist of grasses, legumes, and herbs of several kinds. In winter, they eat the twigs and buds of maple and oak trees and various shrubs which project above the snow blanket.

Breeding activities usually begin in January or February. The gestation period is 28 days, and the first litter is usually born in March or April. Three or four litters of three to eight young each (the average is five) are produced each spring and summer. The nest is a fur-lined cup in the ground covered with leaves and twigs and located in dense cover. The newborn cottontails are altricial.

Over much of its range the Appalachian cottontail is declining in numbers because of the extensive cutting of mature mountain forests for lumber and pulpwood.

Remarks: A great deal of the biology of the Appalachian cottontail is not known and needs to be studied. There are also reports that crossbreeding (or hybridization) of the eastern cottontail with the Appalachian cottontail occurs in some areas of their overlapping geographical ranges. Research is needed on the frequency of these interspecific matings and on the characteristics of the resulting hybrid cottontails.

Until recently, the New England cottontail (*Sylvilagus transitionalis*) was lumped with the Appalachian cottontail as a single species. They are indeed very similar and both occupy identical mountain habitats in the Appalachian Mountains. More studies are needed to ascertain whether splitting them into two species is truly justified.

Selected References:

Chapman, J. A. 1975. New England Cottontail (*Sylvilagus transitionalis*). Mammalian Species, No. 55: pp. 1–4.

Chapman, J. A., and R. P. Morgan II. 1973. Systematic status of the cottontail complex in western Maryland and nearby West Virginia. Wildl. Monogr. 36: 1–54.

Chapman, J. A., A. L. Harman, and D. E. Samuel. 1977. Reproduction and physiological cycles in the cottontail complex in western Maryland and nearby West Virginia. Wildl. Monogr. 56: 1–73.

Swamp Rabbit
Sylvilagus aquaticus

Swamp rabbit, *Sylvilagus aquaticus.* William Sanderson

Identification: The swamp rabbit is the largest species of the cottontail rabbit group, weighing as much as six pounds. The upper pelage is rusty brown to yellowish brown with a heavy sprinkling of black guard hairs, and the belly is white. The tail is rather small, dark, and inconspicuous. This rabbit closely resembles the marsh rabbit but is two to three times larger.

The skull is very similar to that of the marsh rabbit, with the posterior portion of the supraorbital process being fused to the cranium, but it is much larger.

Geographical Range: This species lives in the western three-fifths of the southeastern region. In the United States, the geographical range includes the Mississippi Valley north to eastern Missouri and then eastward to northwestern South Carolina.

Habitat: The swamp rabbit prefers river swamps, wet river floodplains, and thickets of cane (a native bamboo). This species is found in the wet bottomlands of most streams cutting through the Appalachian Plateau and ridge and valley areas. Studies need to be conducted to determine whether this large rabbit is increasing or decreasing in numbers in the Southeast.

Natural History: As the species name *aquaticus* suggests, the swamp rabbit is a water lover. It readily takes to the water, dives, and swims away from potential enemies, then comes up for air under a stump or overhanging roots where it is safe from intruders. Nests are simple depressions on high ground above the water level, lined with the rabbit's own fur and occasionally with dead leaves, grasses, and twigs.

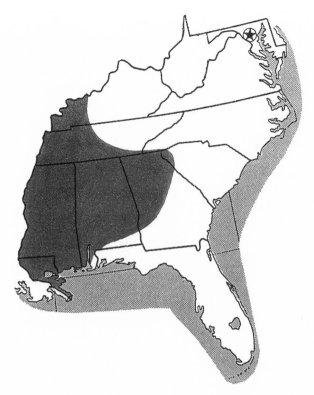

Geographical range of the swamp rabbit in the Southeast.

During the growing season, the diet includes grasses, sedges, herbs, succulent aquatic vegetation, and cane. The swamp rabbit's preference for eating cane has given it the common name "cane-cutter" by many locals. In the winter months, swamp rabbits feed on the buds, twigs, and bark of woody plants and shrubs which grow in wet areas.

The breeding season is long, beginning in late winter and extending to late autumn. The gestation period varies from 35 to 40 days and averages 38. Females usually experience a postpartum heat period and become pregnant immediately after giving birth, even though they are nursing a new litter. The longer gestation periods are recorded when the females are pregnant and lactating at the same time. Up to five litters are produced annually, consisting of two to six young each (the average is approximately four). There is normally a synchrony of the start of the breeding season in swamp rabbits. All females will come into estrus and breed within a one- or two-day period each year. This is apparently an adaptation to ensure the survival of more young. Theoretically, if all the young are produced at about the same time, there are too many for predators to eliminate.

At birth swamp rabbits are somewhat precocial, i.e., they are fully furred, the eyes open two days after birth, and they are able to leave the nest when about eight days old. Since the gestation period is a good deal longer than in the eastern and Appalachian cottontails, the offspring are correspondingly further along in development at birth. Young swamp rabbits are weaned at about four weeks of age. They do not become sexually mature until the late winter following the spring or summer of their birth.

Within their home range, swamp rabbits tend to defecate and urinate on elevated sites such as stumps, logs, and hummocks. These signposts serve as good clues to the presence of swamp rabbits for the hunter or for the wildlife biologist.

Remarks: Where cultivated fields adjoin wet floodplains or swamps, these rabbits often do extensive damage by foraging on various crops. Many hunters consider the meat of the swamp rabbit very palatable.

One danger facing this species is progressive loss of habitat. The continued drainage of wetlands and filling of swamps for other uses is gradually eliminating their populations in many parts of the Southeast.

Selected References:

Chapman, J. A., and G. A. Feldhammer. 1981. Swamp Rabbit *(Sylvilagus aquaticus)*. Mammalian Species, No. 151: pp. 1–4.

Hunt, T. P. 1959. Breeding habits of the swamp rabbit with notes on its life history. J. Mamm. 40: 82–91.

Lowe, C. E. 1958. Ecology of the swamp rabbit in Georgia. J. Mamm. 39: 116–27.

Terrel, T. L. 1972. The swamp rabbit *(Sylvilagus aquaticus)* in Indiana. Amer. Midl. Nat. 87: 283–95.

Marsh Rabbit
Sylvilagus palustris

Marsh rabbit, *Sylvilagus palustris*. U.S. Fish & Wildlife Service

Identification: The marsh rabbit is slightly smaller and somewhat darker than the eastern cottontail. The tail is small, gray-brown in color, and lacks any white "powder-puff" appearance. The back is dark reddish brown, sprinkled with black hairs. The nape of the neck is rufous brown and the underparts range from gray to buff. The ears are shorter than those of the eastern cottontail, but about the same size as those of the Appalachian cottontail.

The skull is identified by its small overall size and a posterior supraorbital process that is completely fused to the cranium, leaving no slitlike openings when viewed from above.

Geographical Range: This species occurs only in the Atlantic and Gulf Plains portion of the Southeast. In the United States, it occurs throughout the Atlantic and Gulf coastal plains from Virginia to Alabama. It is replaced by its sibling species, the swamp rabbit, on the northwestern fringes of its range. Marsh rabbits and swamp rabbits differ very little except that the marsh rabbit is a good deal smaller (and some experts believe these two groups should be considered a single species).

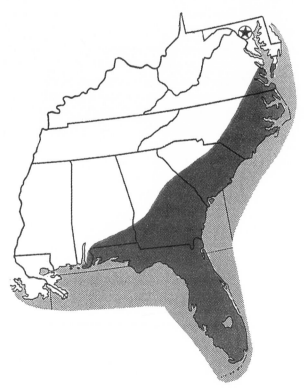

Geographical range of the marsh rabbit in the Southeast.

Habitat: As the common name implies, marsh rabbits occur in both freshwater and brackish marshy areas. They are seldom found far from standing water and occur in most floodplain habitats and in wet upland areas as well. They occur in coastal and freshwater marshes, swamp borders, canal banks, lowland meadows, and cypress edges. Marsh rabbits swim readily and for considerable distances. They are truly semiaquatic in their habits, and there are records of them swimming strongly as far as one-quarter mile from the nearest shoreline.

Natural History: The "nest," or form, is located in thickets, under stumps, in logs, and in various other slightly elevated, sheltered locations. These rabbits often make runways through dense vegetation and habitually travel a network of paths or trails running throughout their home ranges.

The breeding season extends year round; however, there is a peak in breeding from March through July, after which it continues at lower levels. In the northern part of the range there appears to be only a limited amount of breeding from November to February, probably due to cold weather. The mean litter size averages just under three young and ranges from one to six. The gestation period averages 37 days (and ranges from 35 to 39).

The nest, like that of the eastern cottontail and Appalachian cottontail, is a cup-shaped depression in the ground lined with grass and breast fur. Babies are born well furred, and their eyes open when they are two days old. They leave the nest when just over one week old, but remain with their mother until they are weaned at about four weeks of age. Adult females usually come into estrus at the time they give birth and are bred again. Juvenile marsh rabbits become sexually developed when they are five to six months old.

Marsh rabbits eat a wide variety of emergent aquatic vegetation and wetland plants, including grasses, sedges, maiden cane, broadleaf herbs, and various aquatic weeds. Most foraging occurs at night, but they are also quite active at dawn and dusk, as well as almost anytime on cloudy days. Home range size varies from one to six acres, depending on the density of the cover type and location.

Remarks: Marsh rabbits are not hunted as extensively as the eastern cottontails are, but they constitute a worthwhile small-game mammal. They sometimes cause considerable damage to field crops and home gardens situated adjacent to wetlands.

Predators of the marsh rabbit include the same extensive list of species that prey on the eastern cottontail. Another mortality factor is the flooding of their habitat by heavy rains. This is mainly destructive to young rabbits and nestlings when floods occur during the nesting season.

Selected References:

Chapman, J. A., and G. R. Willner. 1981. Marsh Rabbit *(Sylvilagus palustris)*. Mammalian Species, No. 153: pp. 1–3.

Holler, N. R., and C. H. Conaway. 1979. Reproduction of the marsh rabbit *(Sylvilagus palustris)* in south Florida. J. Mamm. 60: 769–77.

Howe, S. E. 1988. Lower Keys marsh rabbit status survey. Report to U.S. Fish and Wildl. Serv., Jacksonville, Fla., 8 pp.

Tomkins, I. R. 1935. The marsh rabbit: An incomplete life history. J. Mamm. 16: 201–5.

Snowshoe Hare
Lepus americanus

Snowshoe hare, *Lepus americanus*. U.S. Fish & Wildlife Service

Identification: This species is also called the varying hare and is the only hare native to the southeastern United States. It is larger than the eastern cottontail or Appalachian cottontail and has much enlarged hind legs and feet well adapted for running and jumping on snow (thus the name snowshoe hare). The soles of the feet are entirely furred to insulate them from the cold ground or snow. There are two distinctly different seasonal color patterns in the snowshoe hare. The summer pelage is generally dusky gray or brownish gray on the back, the head is brown to buff-cinnamon, and the undersides are white with some buff markings. The winter pelage is all white, except the ear tips, which are black to dusky. The ears are fairly short for a species of hare (three and one-half inches to four inches).

The skull is considerably larger than those of cottontails in its range and considerably smaller than the skull of the introduced black-tailed jackrabbit. The interparietal bone at the back of the cranium is fused and not visible as a separate bone in the snowshoe hare.

Geographical Range: The snowshoe hare is confined to the higher Appalachian Mountains in small, disjunct populations as far south as the Great Smoky Mountains of North Carolina and Tennessee. There are also a few scattered records from western Maryland, West Virginia, and western Virginia. In the rest of North America, it ranges northward through New England across Canada, the Great Lakes region, and down the Rocky Mountains in the West.

Habitat: The snowshoe hare lives in evergreen forests, such as spruce-fir-hemlock, especially in thickets of laurel and rhododendron, or similar bushy openings in the conifers. From the paucity of records, this hare has been apparently rather rare in the southern Appalachians over the past 30 years.

Natural History: Like many other northern species, the snowshoe hare exhibits a population cycle whereby it is superabundant in some years but very scarce in other years. Hare populations in Canada are known to peak only once every 6 to 13 years, with the average being about once every 10 years. Such peaks and valleys in the number of snowshoe hares are less pronounced in the United States.

The summer diet consists of succulent grasses and forbs, but in the winter months they live on the buds, twigs, bark, and evergreen leaves of woody plants.

Geographical range of the snowshoe hare in the Southeast.

The reproductive season begins in late winter and extends until late summer. Unlike the cottontails, snowshoe hares give birth to precocial young, which are born in an advanced state of development, having dense fur and open eyes. The gestation period is 36 days, and the litter size varies from one to six (the average is four). There are usually two or three litters produced between March and August. They are weaned when about three weeks of age.

Snowshoe hares are preyed upon by many carnivores, including foxes, bobcats, great-horned owls, goshawks, coyotes, and lynx (in northern latitudes). Like most prey species, this hare has a fairly short life span in the wild, estimated to be four to five years on the average.

Remarks: The apparent decline in the numbers of snowshoe hares in the southern Appalachians in recent decades may reflect habitat loss or modification in its restricted, high-altitude environment. Research is needed into possible reasons for the decline and to determine what management steps might be taken to increase snowshoe hare populations. This hare should probably be given endangered or threatened species status in most of its range in the Southeast.

Selected References:

Aldous, C. M. 1937. Notes on the life history of the snowshoe hare. J. Mamm. 18: 46–57.

Keith, L. B., and L. A. Windberg. 1978. A demographic analysis of the snowshoe hare cycle. Wildl. Monogr. 58: 1–70.

Keith, L. B., J. R. Cary, O. J. Rongstad, and M. C. Brittingham. 1984. Demographics and ecology of a declining snowshoe hare population. Wildl. Monogr. 90: 1–43.

Litvaitis, J. A. 1990. Differential habitat use by sexes of showshoe hares (*Lepus americanus*). J. Mamm. 71: 520–23.

MacLulich, D. A. 1937. Fluctuations in the numbers of the varying hare (*Lepus americanus*). Univ. of Toronto Studies, Biology Series No. 43, pp. 5–136.

Black-tailed Jackrabbit
Lepus californicus

Black-tailed jackrabbit, *Lepus californicus*. U.S. Fish & Wildlife Service

Identification: This species is a large, robust hare with extremely long ears and large hind limbs. The dorsal pelage of the black-tailed jackrabbit is grayish brown or grayish buff with wavy black markings. There is also a dense, whitish underfur. A black area extends from the rump onto the upper surface of a short, fluffy tail. The outer borders and under surface of tail are pure white. The tops of the long ears are tipped in black, the inside of each ear is buff, and the back of each ear is whitish. The underparts are mostly white with a buff band across the neck and chest. A small white star or blaze is usually present on the forehead.

The skull is about twice the size of the skulls of the eastern cottontail, Appalachian cottontail, and marsh rabbit, and about one-third larger than the skull of the snowshoe hare or swamp rabbit.

Geographical Range: The black-tailed jackrabbit has been introduced and become established at several lo-cations in the southeastern states. It has been repeatedly brought in to train greyhounds, and many have escaped into the surrounding countryside. Local black-tailed jackrabbit populations now live in the vicinity of the Miami International Airport, on Cobb Island in Northampton County, Virginia, and on the eastern shore of Maryland. The natural range of this species is the western half of the United States.

Habitat: This hare naturally occupies the open arid grasslands of the West. In southern Florida it lives in the mowed grass along runways and in open fields around Miami International Airport. In Virginia, they thrive in the sparse, sandy vegetation on coastal dunes and barrier islands. In Maryland the hares live in plant nurseries featuring ornamental plants and also in closely cropped agricultural lands. They only do well and avoid predators where the cover is limited.

Natural History: Jackrabbits spend most of the day resting in a shallow depression or a bare area scratched out in a clump of cover. They generally become active at dusk and forage nocturnally, but on cloudy days

Geographical range of the black-tailed jackrabbit in the Southeast.

they often venture forth. Jackrabbits consume a wide variety of grasses and forbs, in addition to a long list of cultivated crops and vegetables.

Breeding takes place year round in the western states, but is most intense from January to September. The gestation period ranges from 41 to 47 days (and averages 43 days). Litter size ranges from one to eight, but averages three. Baby hares are precocial at birth and can hop about on the first day. They usually stay in or near the nest for only the first three or four days. Juvenile jackrabbits are weaned and totally on their own at about three weeks of age. A few breed late in their first year of birth, but most do not become reproductively active until the next year. Most hares live no longer than three or four years in the wild.

Remarks: Foraging jackrabbits consume large amounts of vegetation and can damage gardens and row crops extensively.

Black-tailed jackrabbits are impressive jumpers, traveling 20–25 feet in a single leap, and attaining speeds of 35–40 miles per hour for short distances. They can also jump vertically 3–5 feet in order to obtain a better view of the surrounding area. They will also stand erect upon the hind feet for the same general purpose. Jackrabbits rely extensively on their keen eyesight, good hearing, and substantial speed to escape predators. Their reliance on these specialties to avoid enemies probably accounts for their inability to colonize southeastern areas having heavy cover. They are just too vulnerable to "ambush"-type predators that can hide in the good cover characteristic of a high rainfall region.

Like all lagomorphs, this species can transmit tularemia and leptospirosis. Precautions should always be taken to wear gloves when handling or skinning wild hares or rabbits of any kind. The offending germs are normally transmitted to humans via a cut, scratch, or lesion in the person's skin.

Selected References:

Goodwin, D. L., and P. O. Currie. 1965. Growth and development of black-tailed jack rabbits. J. Mamm. 46: 96–98.

Haskell, H. S., and H. G. Reynolds. 1947. Growth, developmental food requirements, and breeding activity of the California jack rabbit. J. Mamm. 28: 129–36.

Lechleitner, R. R. 1958. Certain aspects of the behavior of the black-tailed jackrabbit. Amer. Midl. Nat. 60: 145–55.

———. 1959. Sex ratio, age classes, and reproduction of the black-tailed jackrabbit. J. Mamm. 40: 63–81.

Tiemeier, O. W., and M. L. Plenert. 1964. A comparison of three methods for determining the age of black-tailed jack rabbits. J. Mamm. 45: 409–16.

Order Rodentia
Gnawing Mammals

Rodents are the largest group of mammals that live in the southeastern United States, both in number of species and in population numbers. They are quite a diverse group, ranging from a tiny harvest mouse, which weighs only a few ounces, to the sizable beaver, which may weigh over 80 pounds. All rodents are unified anatomically by the presence of one pair of large, chisel-like incisors located in the upper and lower jaws at the front of the mouth, adapted for gnawing plant material. In addition, the canine teeth are absent in rodents, leaving an extensive gap (called the "diastema") between the incisors and cheek teeth. The large incisors continue to grow throughout the rodent's life and must be worn down by being used or they will become too long to function properly. In some species the incisors grow as rapidly as one inch per month.

Most rodents exhibit a high reproductive potential. Most species are specialized to produce large litters of offspring and to breed several times a year. Rodents have a number of specializations that are rather advanced and unusual. These include induced ovulation and induced estrus, as well as postpartum pregnancies. In induced ovulation, the act of copulation with a male stimulates the release of eggs in the female rodent. The presence of a male also induces estrus in the females of some rodents. These reproductive specializations and other adaptive features make rodents one of the most successful mammal groups on earth.

Rodents have a worldwide distribution and occur in virtually every terrestrial habitat that supports plant growth. There are approximately 2,000 living species of rodents in the world, which is the largest group of mammal species. A total of 36 different kinds of rodents live in the southeastern states.

Woodchuck
Marmota monax

Woodchuck, *Marmota monax*. Roger W. Barbour

Identification: The woodchuck, or groundhog, is the largest member of the squirrel family living in the Southeast. The upper pelage is a coarse, grizzled gray or grayish brown, and the belly is lighter, usually reddish brown or buff-gray. The guard hairs are broadly tipped with buff-white, which produces the frosted or grizzled effect. The woodchuck's body is broad, flat, and squat, with short, powerful legs and a flattened, bushy tail of black or dark brown, fringed in buff-white. The ears are short, round, and close over the ear opening to keep out dirt.

The skull is of large size and broad, with a sizable depressed or concave area located on top, between the orbits. The large, chisel-shaped incisors are white rather than pigmented brown on the front side like other rodents.

Geographical Range: This large, semifossorial rodent occurs in the northern mountains, plateau lands, and foothills of the Southeast. In North America, the geographical range includes nearly all of the eastern United States except the lower Gulf Coast and Florida, as well as much of eastern Canada.

Habitat: The woodchuck is an animal of field borders, fencerows, and forest edges. It also prefers rocky outcrops and openings in heavily forested mountain areas. Woodchucks dig a large burrow in whatever soil or rocky substrate is available.

Natural History: The burrow dug by the woodchuck is usually conspicuous because of the presence of a mound of fresh dirt situated in front of the opening. Several nest chambers, lined with leaves and grasses, are usually scattered throughout each burrow system, and there are normally several different entrances to the burrow system, which allows for a quick exit if a predator enters. Single individuals or a family group (an adult female and her offspring) occupy the burrow system.

Woodchucks are primarily diurnally active, feeding on a wide variety of herbaceous plants. Their diet is

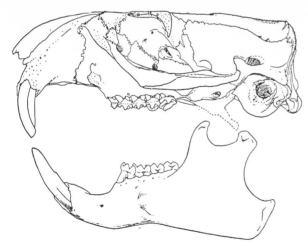

Side view of a representative rodent skull, the woodchuck (*Marmota monax*). Note large anterior incisors and diastema (or gap) behind them.

Geographical range of the woodchuck in the Southeast.

almost totally vegetarian, as they consume less than 1 percent animal material. They tend to be most active in the early morning and late afternoon and typically remain in the burrow during the middle of the day. By late summer and early fall, they accumulate a thick layer of fat under the skin and in body cavities. By late October or early November most woodchucks are curled up and hibernating in their nest chambers. The oldest and fattest tend to enter hibernation first, while the youngest and leanest wait a few days or weeks longer.

During the winter months, woodchucks have a sharply reduced metabolic rate, slow heartbeat (four beats per minute), slow breathing rate (one breath every three to four minutes), and the body temperature falls to a low level (about 40 degrees Fahrenheit). During this winter hibernation, the animals occasionally rouse from their deep sleep to urinate and defecate. During these brief periods of arousal (which usually occur at about two-week intervals) they may leave the burrow, but more commonly they remain below ground.

Woodchucks usually emerge from hibernation by March or April. Males also become active a few days earlier than females. Fat stores are largely depleted by spring, and there is a lot of loose skin on each woodchuck.

Mating occurs shortly after the females emerge from hibernation. The gestation period is 31–33 days. A single litter of two to nine altricial young (the average is four or five) are born in April or May. Young females breeding for the first time average smaller litters than older females. Newborn woodchucks are naked, blind, and helpless. Their eyes do not open until they are about four weeks of age, and they rarely leave the burrow until they are six to seven weeks old (when they are weaned). By midsummer they leave the family group and establish their solitary burrow. There are reports of a few one-year-old woodchucks breeding, but the majority are nearly two years old before becoming reproductively active.

Predators include foxes, dogs, coyotes, bobcats, large hawks, and bears, which feed mostly on young woodchucks. Humans are the greatest enemies of the woodchuck. They are considered good target practice in many places, and woodchucks are shot for sport (but some are eaten) every year.

Woodchucks have an interesting alert posture of standing on their hind legs and straining for a better view. They often do this at the entrance of the burrow, and, if alarmed or disturbed, the woodchuck will give a sharp whistle followed by soft, chuckling notes as it descends into the burrow to safety. Because of this characteristic vocalization, my grandfather, I. B. Brown, an old-time farmer in the Missouri Ozarks, used to call them "whistle-pigs" rather than groundhogs.

Remarks: The interesting holiday called Groundhog Day occurs on February 2 each year and is based on a European legend that the woodchuck will emerge from hibernation and predict the weather. If it sees its shadow, the woodchuck will supposedly re-enter hibernation because six more weeks of winter are to follow. If the groundhog fails to see its shadow, winter is supposed to be over for that year. The whole myth serves to underwrite a delightful tongue-in-cheek celebration. Apparently the only biological truth that helps support the annual occurrence of Groundhog Day is the fact that this famous hibernator wakes up periodically during the winter to go to the bathroom. As a biologist, I find this a very amusing factor upon which to build a minor holiday.

Woodchucks do considerable damage to farm crops and gardens when their dens are located within foraging distance. I have seen cornfields with the ears destroyed and the stalks ripped down for several hundred feet adjacent to a woodchuck den. Their dirt piles in front of the den entrance also break or dull mower blades, and horses and cattle sometimes injure or break legs by stepping into unseen den openings.

On the positive side, woodchuck burrows provide good refuge for many other animals, including rabbits, opossums, skunks, raccoons, foxes, snakes, lizards, box turtles, rodents, arthropods, amphibians, and many others.

It is not too unusual to encounter woodchucks which are melanistic (that is, individuals with black-colored fur) or erythristic (individuals with reddish cinnamon–colored fur), and true albinos (individuals with completely white fur and pink eyes) are not unknown. Such coat color variations are apparently due to spontaneous mutations in the genes which control pigment deposition in the fur.

Selected References:

Anthony, M. 1962. Activity and behavior of the woodchuck in southern Illinois. C.C. Adams Center, Occasional Papers 6: 1–24.

Davis, D. E. 1967. The role of environmental factors in hibernation of woodchucks. Ecology 48: 683–89.

Grizell, R. A., Jr. 1955. A study of the southern woodchuck, *Marmota monax monax*. Amer. Midl. Nat. 16: 187–200.

Hayes, S. R. 1976. Daily activity and body temperature of the southern woodchuck, *Marmota monax monax,* in northwestern Arkansas. J. Mamm., 57: 291–99.

———. 1977. Home range of *Marmota monax* (Sciuridae) in Arkansas. Southwestern Nat. 22: 547–50.

Swihart, R. K. 1992. Home-range attributes and spatial structure of woodchuck populations. J. Mamm. 73: 604–18.

Eastern Chipmunk
Tamias striatus

Eastern chipmunk, *Tamias striatus*. James Parnell

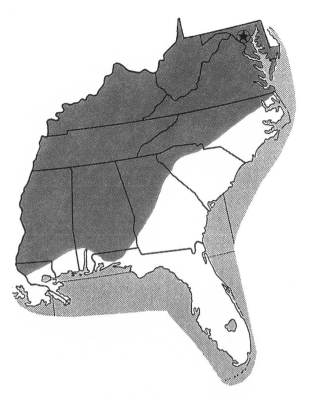

Geographical range of the eastern chipmunk in the Southeast.

Identification: The eastern chipmunk is a small, ground-dwelling squirrel having conspicuous, longitudinal stripes down the back and on the face. The back fur is reddish brown, with five dark stripes alternating with light buff stripes, ending at a prominent rusty red rump patch. The belly and sides are buff to white and the feet are tan. The tail is blackish above and rusty below, with a narrow fringe of white or yellow hairs. The ears are short, rounded, and held erect.

The skull looks like that of a small squirrel, but with a broader interorbital area. Only four cheek teeth are present on each side, and the two tooth rows converge slightly toward the rear of the palate. In contrast to the flying squirrel, no notch is present in the frontal bone at the upper rim of the eye socket.

Geographical Range: The eastern chipmunk ranges over approximately the western two-thirds of the southeastern region. It is absent from most of the upper and lower coastal plains, except at the western portion of its range. In the United States, its geographical range occupies the eastern half of the country, exclusive of nearly all of the southeastern coastal plains.

Habitat: The eastern chipmunk inhabits rich deciduous forests, forest edges, and moist, wooded ravines having rocky outcrops, as well as brushy woodlands having numerous fallen logs, woodpiles, and rocks. Chipmunks are primarily ground dwellers but will climb trees readily to forage.

Natural History: Chipmunks are solitary animals that are active diurnally (in the daytime), with peaks in the early morning and late afternoon. They dig a burrow system which is fairly extensive and complex, usually placed under a tree, rock, bank, or similar protected location. There are normally two or three burrow entrances, and the nest is an enlarged chamber about 10 inches in diameter, containing dried leaves. Other special chambers are dug to provide for storage of nuts and seeds (acorns, pecans, hickory nuts, etc.). They also eat considerable numbers of insects, including grasshoppers, large beetles, katydids, and cicadas. On some occasions, they will eat frogs, salamanders, young mice, small snakes, bird eggs, mushrooms, and berries.

Chipmunks have cheek pouches located inside the mouth (called internal cheek pouches). Food crammed into cheek pouches while foraging is then carried back to the burrow in large quantity. When the cheek pouches are full of seeds and nuts, the face bulges so much the chipmunk appears to have the mumps. Besides storing food in several underground chambers, chipmunks also cache food in shallow excavations on the forest floor in a manner identical to that of tree squirrels. During periods of food scarcity, they utilize these various caches.

When alarmed or agitated, eastern chipmunks emit a trilling "chip" sound, which serves to warn others. In the Southeast chipmunks hibernate during the winter months.

Two seasonal breeding peaks occur, one in the early spring and another in the summer. The first litter is usually born in April after a gestation period of 31 days. The second litter follows in July or August. Litter size is two to seven and averages four and one-half young. In some years, the females produce only one litter in the spring, but, if conditions are favorable, a second litter is born in the summer. The babies are naked and blind, and they remain in the underground nest chamber for five to six weeks. Eyes do not open until the young chipmunks are 30 days old; they are weaned when two months of age. A few females born in the spring will breed later in the summer, but most do not breed until the following spring. All young males mature and produce sperm their first summer.

Eastern chipmunks have lived as long as eight years in captivity, but maximum longevity in wild populations is rarely more than three years, due to predators and other mortality factors.

Remarks: The chipmunk's habit of burying seeds throughout its home range promotes the dispersal and germination of many forest trees. Tunneling by chipmunks provides aeration and mixing of the soil's organic and inorganic components.

Selected References:

Allen, E. G. 1938. The habits and life history of the eastern chipmunk, *Tamias striatus lysteri*. N.Y. State Mus. Bull. 314: 7–119.

Getty, T. 1981. Structure and dynamics of chipmunk home range. J. Mamm. 60: 726–37.

Schooley, J. P. 1934. A summer breeding season in the eastern chipmunk, *Tamias striatus*. J. Mamm. 15: 194–96.

Snyder, D. P. 1982. Eastern Chipmunk (*Tamias striatus*). Mammalian Species, No. 168: pp. 1–8.

White, M. M., and G. E. Svendsen. 1992. Spatial-genetic structure in the eastern chipmunk, *Tamias striatus*. J. Mamm. 73: 619–24.

Yerger, R. W. 1953. Home range, territoriality, and populations of the chipmunk in central New York. J. Mamm. 34: 448–58.

Gray Squirrel
Sciurus carolinensis

Gray squirrel, *Sciurus carolinensis*. Florida Game & Freshwater Fish Commission

Identification: This is a medium-sized tree squirrel with a long, flattened bushy tail. In the southern states, people often call this species the "cat squirrel," presumably because of its agile climbing abilities. The upperside is grayish brown, and the underside is usually white or grayish white. A fairly common variation has a yellowish or orangish belly instead of white. Albino gray squirrels are also fairly common, as are color variants known as "blondes," which have a diluted, whitish upper pelage with a gray stripe down the middle of the back only. The ears are small, rounded, erect, and brown in color, often with a prominent patch of white hair on their posterior side. The tips of the tail hairs are also white or pale gray. Melanistic squirrels are also common.

The skull is distinguished from the fox squirrel by its smaller size and the presence of five upper cheek teeth on each side instead of four (also, the first cheek tooth is very small).

Geographical Range: The gray squirrel has a region-wide distribution in the Southeast and is one of the area's most visible mammals. In the United States, the natural range of the gray squirrel occupies the eastern half of the country. It has also been introduced and established as the "town squirrel" in several western states.

Habitat: Gray squirrels occur in all types of wooded habitats. They probably reach maximum numbers in mature hardwood forest, which is considered the eco-

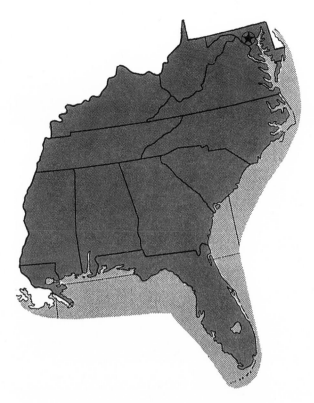

Geographical range of the gray squirrel in the Southeast.

logical climax forest for most of the southern states. They also are abundant in all suburban and residential areas of cities, where many of their natural predators are absent. Gray squirrels are amazingly adaptable and even occur in some urban areas that have only a few scattered trees and vast expanses of mowed lawns between widely separated buildings. They prefer to nest in hollow trees, but if these are not available, they build bulky leaf nests in the treetops and take refuge there.

Natural History: Gray squirrels forage both in trees and on the ground. They habitually bury individual acorns and other nuts in numerous shallow pits scattered throughout their home range. They also eat various fruits, mushrooms, buds, insects, bird eggs, and berries. It has recently been found that they will even leave their normal home range and travel some distance to feed on an attractive nut crop (such as pecans) which mature in the early fall. They apparently detect the nuts by scent carried on the wind.

Eastern gray squirrels are strictly diurnal and forage mainly in the early morning and late afternoon hours. They do not hibernate and are active the year round. Population size varies directly in response to the abundance of foods. In years of good acorn and nut crops (also known as "mast"), mortality of young is low and populations increase. A poor mast crop in the fall will be followed by a population decline resulting from starvation and emigration of individuals in search of food.

The breeding season tends to have two peaks. The first occurs in the late winter and early spring, and the second in the late spring and early summer. The gestation period is 44–45 days, and each adult female normally produces two litters per year of two to six young, each averaging three. The first litter is born from February to April and the second from June to August. Newborn young are hairless, with eyes and ears tightly closed. The eyes finally open when they are about 28 days old, and they are also well furred at this time. Young squirrels may continue to suckle until they are two to four months old, depending on the season. When a new litter is due, the mother will abandon the den to the juveniles and select a new site in which to bear the second litter. As the newly weaned young squirrels disperse and try to establish their own homes, a great deal of mortality occurs. Nearly all young squirrels fail to breed until the second year.

Gray squirrels are often vocal and will scold intruders with a barking chatter that can continue for some time. Such warning vocalizations are usually accompanied by vigorous pumping and wagging of the bushy tail. Males exhibit a great deal of antagonism toward one another, especially during the mating season. Mating chases are common, with several males ardently following and quarreling over a female in heat.

Remarks: The eastern gray squirrel is a very important small game species, harvested in large numbers by southern hunters. Squirrels also have a certain aesthetic value to humans in parks and back yards, where they often become so tame that they can be sometimes be hand-fed. On the negative side, they may also bite the hand that feeds them, and their ability to steal food intended for birds is legendary. They can overcome almost every "squirrel-proof" bird feeder designed by humans, and they are so habitual about eating food put out for birds that they can become a notable pest.

Gray squirrels sometimes nest in attics and outbuildings, doing damage by gnawing and depositing fecal material. Occasionally, they damage the insulation on electrical wiring, and they frequently short-out transformers in urban areas. Local power failures induced by electrocuted gray squirrels are fairly common in the southeastern states.

On the plus side, the caching of seeds and nuts by gray squirrels results in dispersal and germination of many oaks, hickories, pecans, walnuts, and other hardwoods. This not only ensures that future generations of squirrels will have food and shelter, but also eventually provides timber for future generations of people as well.

Heavy agricultural losses can occur when gray squirrels live near pecan groves, cornfields, or certain garden vegetables. I personally fight a battle every year with gray squirrels that harvest my crop of pecans, tomatoes, peaches, pears, and plums in the yard and garden. Squirrels invariably pick fruit or nuts when they are too green for human consumption, which makes it much harder to beat the squirrels to the punch.

Gray squirrels and the larger fox squirrels rarely occur together in numbers in habitats suitable for both species. Usually one species of squirrel or the other will dominate to the apparent exclusion of the other. This mutual exclusion could be caused by interspecific behavioral aggressiveness, but the actual reasons are not clear. Some southerners believe that gray squirrels and fox squirrels can hybridize, but this a myth. The two species never interbreed anywhere in their broadly overlapping geographical ranges.

It is fairly common for one of the coat-color variations (such as albino, black, or blond) of the gray squirrel to become dominant in "town squirrels." This is because there is no natural selection against showy coat colors in an urban squirrel population, while such a noncryptic squirrel would be quickly seen and eaten by predators in natural populations.

Selected References:

Brown, L. N. 1986. Sex ratio bias among gray squirrels foraging at a single attractive seasonal food source. J. Mamm. 67: 582–83.

Cordes, C. L., and F. S. Barkalow, Jr. 1973. Home ranges and dispersal in a North Carolina gray squirrel population. Proc. Annu. Conf. S.E. Assoc. Game and fish Comm. 26: 124–35.

Fischer, R. A., and N. R. Holler. 1991. Habitat use and relative abundance of gray squirrels in southern Alabama. J. Wildl. Mgmt. 55: 52–58.

Flyger, V. 1960. Movements and home range of the gray squirrel, Sciurus carolinensis, in two Maryland woodlots. Ecology 41: 365–69.

Hougart, B. 1975. Activity patterns of radio-tracked gray squirrels. Unpubl. M.S. thesis, Univ. of Maryland, College Park, Md. 37 pp.

Koprowski, J. L. 1994. Eastern Gray Squirrel (Sciurus carolinensis). Mammalian Species, No. 480: pp. 1–10.

Uhlig, H. C. 1956. The gray squirrel in West Virginia. Cons. Comm., West Virginia. Div. Game Mgmt., Bull. No. 3: 1–83.

Fox Squirrel
Sciurus niger

Fox squirrel, *Sciurus niger*. Barry Mansell

Identification: Fox squirrels are much larger than the eastern gray squirrel, and have a more robust, squarish profile. The fox squirrel occurs in several dorsal color phases, including grizzled brown, brownish orange, gray-brown, blackish brown, steel gray, or all black. The underside likewise varies from creamy yellow, to rusty orange, to black. Regardless of the coat-color combination, fox squirrels have a darker head, and some have a white patch on the muzzle and white on the back of the ears. The tail is quite long, bushy, and variable in color depending on the phase. Our largest and most variably colored fox squirrels live in the coastal plain.

The skull is distinguished from the gray squirrel by its much greater size and the presence of four upper cheek teeth on each side rather than five.

Geographical Range: The fox squirrel has a regionwide distribution in the Southeast The geographical range in the United States is the eastern half of the country. Fox squirrels have also been introduced and established in several western states where they are not native (usually as "town squirrels" living in parks and residential areas, but also invading rural riparian areas).

Habitat: Fox squirrels inhabit open hardwoods, open pine flatwoods, open pine-oak forests, and open oak-hickory woodlands. They forage extensively on the ground and do not do well where there is a heavy ground cover. In pine lands, periodic fires which kill hardwoods and promote grassy ground cover are considered necessary for fox squirrel populations to thrive.

Natural History: Eastern fox squirrels spend more of their time foraging on the ground than do gray squirrels. They bury large numbers of acorns, nuts, and/or pine seeds as a hedge against low food supplies. They also eat fungi, bulbs, tubers, buds, fruits, berries, insects, and bird eggs.

Fox squirrels are strictly diurnal, but they are later risers than gray squirrels. They usually forage in the mid-morning hours, again around noon, and then close the day with a late-afternoon foraging period. They are active year round and do not hibernate during cold weather.

Fox squirrel numbers have declined steadily over the last several decades in the South, due primarily to fire suppression and habitat destruction. For this reason, in parts of Florida the fox squirrel has been placed on threatened or endangered species lists to draw attention to its needs. In those areas where seasonal prescribed burning is practiced in the pine forests, fox squirrels are doing well and not declining.

The reproductive season of the fox squirrel is rather similar to that of the gray squirrel. There are two breeding peaks, one in late winter and early spring, and another in the summer. Older females usually produce two litters per year, but young females only produce one litter the year following. The litter size ranges from one to six and averages two and one-half offspring. The gestation period averages 45 days long, and the young are naked and blind at birth. The ears and eyes open at about 28 days of age, by which time they are fully furred. They do not leave the nest until they are about eight weeks old, they are weaned at 10-12 weeks, and they are on their own at three months of age. Fox squirrels have lived as long as 10 years in captivity.

This species prefers to nest in hollow pines or oaks, but also build large leaf nests in the treetops. The scolding chatter of a fox squirrel is very similar to that of gray squirrels, but deeper and stronger.

Remarks: The fox squirrel is a highly sought species by small-game hunters. Because of their impressive size, striking coloration, and large size, many fox squirrels end up as mounted trophies rather than on the dinner table.

Fox squirrels are beneficial in dispersal and germination of oaks, beech, pecans, walnuts, hickories, pines, and various other hardwoods found in their habitat. In certain local areas, they may reduce pecan harvests or damage cornfields where their home ranges include such agricultural endeavors. The Delmarva fox squirrel of the eastern shore of Maryland is listed as endangered by the U.S. fish and Wildlife Service.

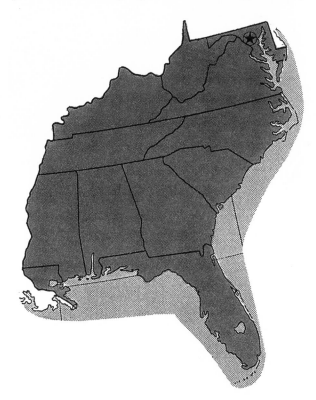

Geographical range of the fox squirrel in the Southeast.

Selected References:

Allen, D. L. 1942. Populations and habits of the fox squirrel in Alleyan County, Michigan. Amer. Midl. Nat. 27: 338–79.

———. 1943. Michigan fox squirrel management. Dept. of Conservation, E. Lansing, Michigan. 404 pp.

Jodice, P. G. R., and S. R. Humphrey. 1992. Activity and diet of an urban population of Big Cypress fox squirrels. J. Wildl. Mgmt. 56: 685–92.

Kantola, A. T., and S. H. Humphrey. 1990. Habitat use by Sherman's fox squirrel *(Sciurus niger shermani)* in Florida. J. Mamm. 71: 411–19.

Koprowski, J. L. 1994. Eastern Fox Squirrel *(Sciurus niger).* Mammalian Species, No. 479: pp. 1–10.

Moore, J. C. 1957. The natural history of the fox squirrel, *Sciurus niger shermani.* Bull. Amer. Mus. Nat. History 113: 1–71.

Williams, K. S., and S. R. Humphrey. 1979. Distribution and status of the endangered big cypress fox squirrel *(Sciurus niger avicennia)* in Florida. Fla. Sci. 42: 201–5.

Zelley, R. A. 1971. The sounds of the fox squirrel, *Sciurus niger rufivanter.* J. Mamm. 52: 597–604.

Red-bellied Squirrel
Sciurus aureogaster

Red-bellied squirrel, *Sciurus aureogaster.* Larry Brown

Identification: This introduced species is slightly larger than the eastern gray squirrel and smaller than the eastern fox squirrel. The upper parts are light to dark gray, frosted with white. The underparts are rich mahogany red, which also extend high up on the sides of the mid-flank region, almost to the back. The ears are small, rounded, and erect with reddish brown on their posterior sides. The tail is large, bushy, and salt-and-pepper gray with white frosting on the tips of the hair. This squirrel also has a totally black color phase that is quite common in many populations.

The skull is very similar to that of the gray squirrel and must be examined by an expert for positive identification.

Geographical Range: The red-bellied squirrel was introduced from Mexico to Elliott Key, Dade County, Florida, in 1938 by a wealthy resident of the island. Only two pairs were released, but the species thrived, gradually increasing in numbers, and presently covers the entire eight-mile-long island. It does not occur on the mainland of the southeastern United States or on the other Florida Keys. The native range of the red-bellied squirrel occupies the southern half of Mexico and a portion of Guatemala.

Habitat: In Florida, this squirrel is established in a dense, second-growth, tropical, hammock type of forest, containing such trees as mahogany, stopper, gumbo limbo, strangler fig, mastic, poisonwood, Jamaican dogwood, manchineel, pigeon plum, and coconut palm. In Mexico the red-bellied squirrel lives in various lowland and foothill tropical forests.

Geographical range of the red-bellied squirrel in the Southeast.

Natural History: Red-bellied squirrels spend almost all their time in the tree canopy (they live an arboreal lifestyle) and rarely come down to the ground to forage. These squirrels are shy and difficult to observe.

On Elliott Key, Florida, a live-trapping study in 1972 revealed a density of approximately one squirrel per acre. It was also found that 50 percent of the trapped squirrels were melanistic, and the other half had the normal frosted gray and red pelage. The original introduction included one black-phase squirrel, so this color phase was perpetuated. The black squirrels are much easier to see in the tropical forest, and the gray-red phase blends into the background so well that researchers virtually never saw them except in the live traps. There is a strong possibility that these color phases are sex-linked, because 68 percent of the gray-red squirrels were males and only 36 percent of the black squirrels were males.

The home range size of male red-bellied squirrels on Elliott Key, Florida, averages 5.9 acres, but for females the range is less than half that at 2.2 acres. In most mammals, it should be noted, the home range size of males is significantly larger.

Red-bellied squirrels are frugivorous, feeding primarily on tropical fruits, berries, and seeds. In Mexico, they eat mangos, figs, jubo plums, tamarind pods, zapote, and maize. On Elliott Key, Florida, they were found to consume the fruit and seeds of a wide variety of tropical trees, including sea grape, wild mastic, papaya, coconut palm, and gumbo-limbo. The huge nut of the coconut palm is heavily utilized, but requires hours of effort for the squirrel to cut through the thick outer hulk and hard shell. Once the squirrel finally penetrates the shell, it will return repeatedly to feed, up to a week or so, until all the nut meat has been consumed.

Red-bellied squirrels are diurnally active, with most foraging taking place between one-half hour after sunrise and about 11:00 a.m. They are rarely active in the afternoon and evening, except on cloudy days. This species makes extensive use of temporary leaf nests constructed in the canopy, as well as permanent nests constructed in tree hollows. Leaf nests are of a dome type, consisting of a base of interwoven twigs supporting an inner cup of tightly packed leaves. The inner surface of the nest cup is sometimes lined with a thin layer of soft fibers stripped from the trunk of palm trees, papaya plants, or other tropical trees.

The breeding season extends throughout the year in the red-bellied squirrel. Data are meager, but the litter size ranges from one to four and averages two. Adult females generally breed two or three times a year, but sometimes more often in years of high food abundance. Young squirrels do not become sexually active until they are about one year old.

Remarks: Red-bellied squirrels are so beautifully marked that they have considerable aesthetic value to humans. In Mexico, they are often kept as caged pets because of their beauty.

In Florida, red-bellied squirrels have no economic importance at present, and this should continue as long as they remain on an island, eight miles from the mainland. However, since they are tropical frugivores, if they should ever colonize the south Florida mainland, there would be considerable impact on commercially grown and back yard fruit trees (especially mangos, papaya, avocados, and citrus).

Selected References:

Brown, L. N., and R. J. McGuire. 1975. field ecology of the exotic Mexican red-bellied squirrel in Florida. J. Mamm. 56: 405–19.

McGuire, R. J., Jr., and L. N. Brown. 1973. Coconut feeding behavior of the Mexican red-bellied squirrel on Elliott Key, Dade County, Florida. Amer. Midl. Nat. 89: 498.

Musser, G. G. 1968. A systematic study of the Mexican and Guatemalan gray squirrel, *Sciurus aureogaster*, F. Cuvier (Rodentia: Sciuridae). Univ. Mich., Misc. Publ. Mus. Zool. 137: 1–112.

Red Squirrel
Tamiasciurus hudsonicus

Red squirrel, *Tamiasciurus hudsonicus.* Larry Brown

Identification: The red squirrel, or pine squirrel, is reddish brown or grayish brown above, has a white eye ring, is smaller than the gray squirrel, and larger than the southern flying squirrel. The underside is uniformly white or grayish white. The summer and winter pelages are somewhat different. In summer they have a distinctive lateral black stripe separating the brown dorsal fur from the white belly fur. The winter pelage is rusty red on the back and tail, the black lateral stripe disappears, and there are short tufts of hair on the ears.

The skull is intermediate in size between that of the gray squirrel and the southern flying squirrel, and its cranial features are similar to both.

Geographical Range: This squirrel is found only in the Appalachian Mountains (as far south as northern Georgia) and in the northeastern corner of the region. In the United States, the geographical range covers the northern half of the country, extending further southward into the Rocky Mountains and Appalachian Mountains.

Habitat: The red squirrel lives in both mixed hardwoods and coniferous forest (specifically hemlocks), as well as in mixed conifers and hardwoods throughout its range.

Geographical range of the red squirrel in the Southeast.

Natural History: The diet of the red squirrel consists of tree seeds and nuts (from both conifers and hardwoods), buds, twigs, berries, fungi, fruits, and occasionally insects. Red squirrels are noted for establishing large and well-defined "food caches" or "food middens," which are usually located in a hollow tree, log, or stump. Over a period of several years, each squirrel may accumulate several bushels of cones and seeds. Red squirrels have a territory which they defend against other squirrels and which includes the seed-cache sites. From a tree perch, they will scold loudly in a long staccato chatter and also flick their tails and stamp their feet. Many hunters have had their hiding places announced to the world by a scolding red squirrel. The seed caches serve as the main source of food for each red squirrel during the long winters characteristic of mountain regions.

This squirrel is strictly diurnal, with peaks in foraging activity occurring in the early morning and late afternoon. They spend a good deal of time on the ground hunting food as well as in the trees. I have even located nests constructed in the ground at the base of trees and in rockpiles during the winter months when cold temperatures are the norm. In the summer, red squirrels sometimes live in globular leaf nests constructed in the tree canopy instead of relying on tree hollows. Nests are composed of leaves or conifer needles, shredded bark, grasses, and mosses, and they are about the diameter of a basketball (gray squirrels have larger, coarse-looking nests).

Breeding begins in late winter or early spring when females allow neighboring males into their territories briefly for mating. There is almost always an extensive mating chase through the trees and over the ground prior to copulation. The gestation period ranges from 35 to 40 days (and averages about 38 days). Usually only one litter is produced each year in April or May, of two to eight young (the average is five or six). A few females also give birth to a second litter in August or September in years of high food availability. Baby red squirrels are quite altricial, as the eyes do not open until they are about four weeks old. Young red squirrels reach sexual maturity and breed when about 10 months old.

The maximum longevity of this species is six to eight years, but very few probably reach that age under natural conditions. Predators include hawks, owls, bobcats, foxes, raccoons, and snakes, among others.

Remarks: The seed-caching habits of the red squirrel have long been known to foresters, who often raid them for large quantities of high-quality tree seeds. After such seeds are cleaned and sorted, they are used for nursery plantings or for direct reseeding of clearcut areas of the forest.

Red squirrels are seldom hunted for food because of their small body size and questionable flavor. There are, however, documented cases of lost hunters or travelers surviving by eating these readily available and noisy little squirrels.

Selected References:

Hamilton, W. J., Jr. 1939. Observations on the life history of the red squirrel in New York. Amer. Midl. Nat. 22: 732–45.

Hatt, R. T. 1929. The red squirrel: Its life history and habits. Roosevelt Wild Life Annals, N.Y. State College, Forestry 2: 3–146.

Layne, J. N. 1954. The biology of the red squirrel, *Tamiasciurus hudsonicus loquax* (Bangs), in central New York. Ecol. Monogr. 24: 227–67.

MacClintock, D. 1970. *Squirrels of North America.* Van Nostrand Reinhold Co., New York, N.Y., 184 pp.

Southern Flying Squirrel
Glaucomys volans

Southern Flying Squirrel, *Glaucomys volans.* Larry Brown

Identification: This a very small tree squirrel having a loose fold of skin (the gliding, or alar, membrane) running along the side of the body from wrist to ankle. When both the front and hind limbs are spread laterally, the gliding membrane creates a winglike surface as the squirrel glides from tree to tree. On the back, the flying squirrel is buff-brown to gray, and the fur is ex-

ceptionally soft, dense, and silky in texture. The fur of the underside is completely white. The body is horizontally flattened, and the tail is also very broad, flat, heavily furred, and serves as a rudder and stabilizer during flight.

The skull is very small for a squirrel and has five cheek teeth on either side of the upper jaw. There is also a deep notch in the frontal bone located at the upper rim of the eye socket.

Geographical Range: The southern flying squirrel occurs throughout the entire southeastern region. Its geographical range in the United States is confined to the eastern half of the country. There are also several isolated populations scattered through the mountains of Mexico and Central America.

Habitat: Flying squirrels occur in most forested habitats, but tend to reach highest densities in mature pine-oak and oak-hickory woodlands. In all habitats, they need hollow, dead snags or hollow cavities in living trees for nest sites. They are largely dependent upon woodpeckers to provide such hollows.

Geographical range of the southern flying squirrel in the Southeast.

Natural History: The flying squirrel is seldom noticed because it sleeps all day, becomes active at dusk, and forages during the nighttime hours. They are sometimes glimpsed gliding from tree to tree on a bright, moonlit night or with the aid of a flashlight. Flying squirrels have very large eyes that glow red in the light and are well adapted for night vision. The tail, serving as a rudder, enables them to execute sharp turns and maneuvers during each glide. Their forward momentum is checked by an upward swoop, executed just before they land at the base of a tree, feet first and head up. Each glide is normally about 30–50 feet long, but extremely long ones of 100–200 feet have been reported (the higher the tree, the longer the glide).

Flying squirrels do very little foraging on the ground, concentrating instead on the treetops, trunks, and branches. Their favorite foods are hickory nuts, pecans, acorns, fungi, berries, fruits, insects, bird eggs or nestlings, seeds, and buds of many different trees. They eat more insects and other types of protein than any other native squirrel. Flying squirrels even occasionally feed on the carcasses of dead animals. They also horde and cache seeds and nuts in tree cavities to use when food supplies are low.

Flying squirrels are rather gregarious, especially in the colder months of the year (from November to March). At Tall Timbers Research Station near Tallahassee, Florida, I have found as many as 28 southern flying squirrels sleeping together in a single large tree cavity, but a more normal number is three to eight. The nest is usually made of shredded bark or moss mixed with pieces of nut shells and leaves. During the warmer times of the year, males and females are found in pairs in the nests. The male leaves before the young are born (probably driven out by the female in late pregnancy), and the mother takes care of the babies alone. The male and female again form a pair after weaning of the offspring. This is the only species of squirrel found in the Southeast known to have a strong pair bond.

Mating takes place twice a year, with litters produced in the spring and again in the fall. Mating for the first litter usually occurs in January or February, and young are born in March or April in the southern states. Reproduction is probably delayed by a month or more in the colder parts of the Southeast. The gestation period is 39–40 days, and the average number of young is around two and one-half (but ranges from one to six). The babies are tiny, blind, pink, and hairless at birth. They grow rapidly, and in 14 days they are fully furred, but the eyes do not open until the squirrels are about 28 days old. They are weaned and able to fend for themselves by six weeks of age, but often remain with the mother for some time after that. Mating for the second litter takes place in August or September, and the young are born in October or November. Juveniles do not breed until one year old.

At night, flying squirrels can often be detected by the faint, birdlike chirps and twitters that they make while foraging in the trees. They sometimes also utter a soft chattering noise similar to the sounds made by their larger relatives, the red, gray, and fox squirrels.

Remarks: Flying squirrels are often kept as pets. They are easily tamed, rather docile, and seldom bite unless handled roughly. However, they do tend to sleep all day and frolic at night when most people want to sleep.

Flying squirrels sometimes gain access to attics and become a nuisance because of the noise and accumulation of fecal droppings. The place of entry can be plugged at night while they are gone, or they can be live-trapped and moved.

In stands of young timber lacking many hollow trees, flying squirrels can actually be attracted and the population greatly increased by placing artificial nest boxes on tree trunks, eight to ten feet above the ground. The squirrels are not a all particular about the size of wooden box used. I once nailed up a large number of nest boxes designed to attract fox squirrels, but they soon filled with flying squirrels, much to my surprise.

Selected References:

Bendel, P. R., and J. E. Gates. 1987. Home range and microhabitat partitioning of the southern flying squirrel *(Glaucomys volans)*. J. Mamm. 68: 242–55.

Dolan, P. G., and D. C. Carter. 1977. Southern Flying Squirrel *(Glaucomys volans)*. Mammalian Species, No. 78: pp. 1–6.

Layne, J. N., and M. A. V. Raymond. 1994. Communal nesting of southern flying squirrels in Florida. J. Mamm. 75: 110–20.

Sollberger, D. E. 1940. Notes on the life history of the small eastern flying squirrel. J. Mamm. 21: 282–93.

Weigl, P. D. 1978. Resource overlap, interspecific interactions, and the distribution of the flying squirrels, *Glaucomys volans* and *G. sabrinus*. Amer. Midl. Nat. 100: 83–96.

Northern Flying Squirrel
Glaucomys sabrinus

Northern flying squirrel, *Glaucomys sabrinus*. American Society of Mammalogists

Geographical range of the northern flying squirrel in the Southeast.

Identification: The northern flying squirrel is much larger and more heavily built than the southern flying squirrel. The upper pelage is soft, fluffy, and cinnamon-brown in color. The underparts are gray to buff-gray, but never white as in the southern flying squirrel. The tail is broad, flat, gray above, and buff-gray underneath. Individuals from the southern Appalachians tend to be darker than flying squirrels from farther north.

The skull is twice as large as that of the southern flying squirrel and much more rugged looking.

Geographical Range: This species occurs at higher elevations down the Appalachian Mountain chain as far south as the Great Smoky Mountains of North Carolina and Tennessee. In North America, it also ranges through New England, across Canada, and southward in the Rocky Mountains in the western states.

Habitat: The northern flying squirrel prefers to live in dense coniferous forests and occasionally is found in mixed stands of hardwoods and conifers, such as yellow birch-hemlock.

Natural History: The northern flying squirrel is very social, as is its southern cousin, especially during the winter months when they den up in sizable groups. They are totally nocturnal and leave the communal tree cavity to forage most of the night. Northern flying squirrels eat nuts, fungi, buds, insects, conifer seeds, and many similar items. During the summer months they cache food in cavities for the long, snowy winter season. Flying squirrels glide from treetop to the base of a tree some distance away. They travel through the forest via a series of climbs, leaps, and long glides.

The breeding season begins in winter, and two litters are normally produced each year, one in April or May, and the second in mid-summer. The gestation period is about 40 days, with a range of one to five young per litter, and the average being three. Newborn flying squirrels are altricial, but the lateral gliding membrane, or "alar fold," is very well developed. Their eyes open when the young are three to four weeks old, and they are weaned when 45–50 days of age. Juvenile squirrels begin gliding from tree to tree at about the time of weaning.

Remarks: Northern flying squirrels have a fondness for meat and protein in general. They often set off traps baited for furbearers during the winter months, and they consume substantial numbers of large insects (beetles and moths mainly).

The northern flying squirrel appears to have become rarer in recent years, especially in the Appalachians. The reasons for the population decline are not known, but the U.S. fish and Wildlife Service lists it as an endangered species in Virginia and West Virginia. It is also considered rare in the Great Smoky Mountain National Park by most naturalists.

Selected References:

Booth, E. S. 1946. Notes on the life history of the flying squirrel. J. Mamm. 27: 28–30.

Weigl, P. D. 1978. Resource overlap, interspecific interactions and the distribution of the flying squirrels (Glaucomys volans and G. sabrinus). Amer. Midl. Nat. 100: 83–96.

Wells-Gosling, N., and L. R. Heaney. 1984. Northern Flying Squirrel (Glaucomys sabrinus). Mammalian Species, No. 229: 1–8.

Southeastern Pocket Gopher
Geomys pinetis

Southeastern pocket gopher, *Geomys pinetis*. Barry Mansell

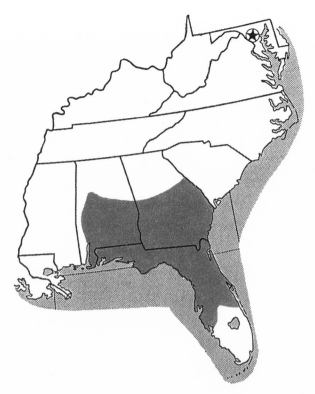

Geographical range of the southeastern pocket gopher in the Southeast.

Identification: The southeastern pocket gopher, or "salamander," as some natives call it, is a peculiar-looking, ratlike mammal having huge "buck-teeth" at the front of the mouth, enlarged front feet with claws, a stocky body, and a fairly short, naked tail. the upper pelage is short and chestnut brown or cinnamon-brown in color and tan or buff on the underside. The forearms are greatly enlarged for digging, and each of the five toes is armed with a large, slightly curved claw. The gopher's most distinctive characteristic is a pair of large, fur-lined cheek pouches, or "pockets," which open by vertical slits on each side of the face just outside the entrance to the mouth. They extend backward as far as the shoulders and are used for carrying food and nest material.

Gophers have oversized, orange-stained incisor teeth which are always exposed because the furry lips guarding the mouth close behind them. This characteristic allows pocket gophers to dig dirt and cut roots using their gigantic incisors without getting soil inside the mouth. Pocket gophers have fairly small, beady eyes and presumably weak vision. The ears are tiny, rounded, and fold shut to keep soil out of the auditory canal. Large facial whiskers, called vibrissae, located on the snout are very sensitive tactile organs.

The skull is identified by the presence of very large upper incisors, which have two lengthwise grooves on the anterior surface of each. The skull also has a large, square rostrum and is broad and flattened.

Geographical Range: This species is restricted to the Southeast, living only on the coastal plains. In the United States, the geographical range extends only from central Alabama and central Georgia southward into Florida.

Habitat: The southeastern pocket gopher prefers deep, sandy soils throughout its range. It is rare or absent from most hard clay or rocky soils, as well as from saturated hydric or mucky soils. Pocket gophers are most abundant in open pine-oak woodlands, open pine flatwoods, and in weedy or grassy fields.

Natural History: Like moles, the pocket gopher is well adapted to live under the ground (practicing a fossorial lifestyle) in an extensive series of tunnels having no openings to the surface. They build two types of tunnels: 1) a shallow feeding tunnel system located in the plant root zone within a foot or so of the surface; and 2) a deep tunnel system located 18–36 inches below the surface, which contain a single nest chamber and several food-storage areas. The southeastern pocket gopher normally builds a tightly spiraling ramp, or "spiral staircase," which connects the surface feeding tunnels to the deep tunnel system. It is probable that a spiraling tunnel confuses predators that enter the gopher's system (such as snakes and weasels), and, if plugged by the pocket gopher, the sharply curving trail is difficult to follow.

In the course of excavating a tunnel system, the pocket gopher generates a great deal of loose dirt that is pushed up a sloping tunnel to the surface to form large mounds. The large front paws and chest are used to thrust the dirt "bulldozer style" along the tunnels and out onto the surface of the ground. The dirt forms a flat, fan-shaped mound in front of the tunnel entrance. The opening is eventually plugged at the entrance when the mound nears completion. Thus, the plugged tunnel tends to be located at one edge of each surface mound, rather than being in the center of the mound, as moles construct them. A single pocket gopher usually produces a series of mounds in a line, marking the approximate course of its underground tunnel system. The surface mounds vary a great deal in size, but tend to be large (12–18 inches across and 4–8 inches high in freshly constructed ones). Rain and wind gradually erode them, but each mound scar usually persists on the surface for a year or more.

Pocket gophers are solitary, antisocial animals that will not tolerate one another except briefly at breeding time. Only one individual lives in each tunnel system, except when females are nursing offspring. Breeding in the southeastern pocket gopher can occur any month of the year, but there are two peaks (February–March and June–July), when most females are involved. The average litter size is slightly less than two, and the range is only one to three young. Gestation takes about four weeks. At birth, baby gophers are approximately two inches long, have hairless, pink, wrinkled skin, and the eyes are closed. They develop fairly slowly, and the eyes do not open until they are five weeks old, at which time the young disperse and dig their own tunnel systems near the female's tunnel system. Breeding begins at about six months.

How the highly territorial pocket gophers locate one another at the time of breeding is not clear. It appears that the males may leave their tunnel systems and travel above ground in search of receptive females. Females may also come to the surface and emit a sexual attractant (called a pheromone), which is detected downwind by males, who then follow the scent to the female, where they copulate.

The southeastern pocket gopher feeds on a wide variety of roots, tubers, bulbs, and other plant parts. They show a special liking for Bahia grass tubers in lawns and pastures. Food is cached in special storage chambers and utilized when supplies are short. The nest chamber usually contains a shallow pad of grasses, plant tubers, or dried roots. Pocket gophers extend their tunnels less actively during the cooler months of the year than during the warmer months, but they do not hibernate. They may be active any time of the day in the tunnel system, but foraging tends to peak in the late evening and nighttime hours. They are often taken by owls, which indicates that they spend a certain amount of time above ground at night. Green plant cuttings are also often abundant on the floor of tunnels, suggesting the same conclusion.

Adult females appear to produce an average of two litters per year. This is a low reproductive output (because of few litters and small litter size), yet pocket gophers are common in most habitats where they occur. This viability strongly suggests that there is a high survival rate for the young pocket gophers. In the closed, subterranean tunnels, they are largely free of predators; they are vulnerable mainly to snakes and weasels that sometimes penetrate the tunnel systems.

Remarks: Pocket gophers become a considerable nuisance when they live in lawns, gardens, parks, golf courses, and in the fields of various agricultural crops. They are best controlled by trapping, since most poisons are largely ineffective and hazardous to the environment. Poisonous gases, such as automobile exhaust fumes, which are funneled into their tunnel systems are also generally not effective, because the pocket gopher quickly plugs off the tunnel through which the gas is coming. The most effective trap is the small, metal MacAbee gopher trap, which fits inside a tunnel entrance. In order to catch a pocket gopher, the tunnel system must be opened up at some point with a shovel, which requires digging through the dirt plug associated with a surface mound until the open subterranean tunnel is reached. The tunnel traps are especially effective because pocket gophers will not tolerate a surface opening into their tunnel system and always respond by trying to plug it with dirt. The jaws of the trap are designed to catch them as they push a load of dirt forward to plug the open end of the tunnel. These traps are almost 100 percent effective if properly placed and set.

The southeastern pocket gopher is a great soil mixer and is especially beneficial in redistributing organic matter and surface nutrients in sterile, sandy soils.

The colloquial name "salamander" sometimes used for the southeastern pocket gopher is probably derived from a corruption of "sandy mounder," which describes their prominent surface mounds. Pocket gophers certainly bear no resemblance to true salamanders.

The maximum longevity of the southeastern pocket gopher in natural situations probably approaches five years. They do not do well in captivity and almost always die within a few days, apparently from stress.

Selected References:

Brown, L. N. 1971. Breeding biology of the pocket gopher (Geomys pinetis) in southern Florida. Amer. Midl. Nat. 85: 45–53.

Hickman, G. C., and L. N. Brown. 1973a. Mound-building behavior of the southeastern pocket gopher (Geomys pinetis). J. Mamm. 54: 786–90.

———. 1973b. Pattern and rate of mound extension of the southeastern pocket gopher (Geomys pinetis). J. Mamm. 54: 971–75.

Pembleton, E. F., and S. L. Williams. 1978. Southeastern Pocket Gopher (Geomys pinetis). Mammalian Species, No. 86: pp. 1–3.

Wing, E. S. 1960. Reproduction in the pocket gopher in North Central Florida. J. Mamm. 41: 35–43.

Beaver

Castor canadensis

Beaver, *Castor canadensis*. Larry Brown

Identification: The beaver is the largest rodent living in the Southeast, and one of the most recognizable. Adults usually weigh 30–50 pounds, but individuals up to 85 pounds have been recorded. The dorsal fur is a rich, glossy brown, with a fine dense underfur that is grayish. The underside is grayish tan, and the feet and tail are black or brownish black. The back feet are webbed for swimming, and the tail is broad, flat and scaly, and used as a rudder and propeller when swimming. The two inner toes on the back feet have specialized double claws that are used for combing and grooming the fur.

The massive skull is easily distinguished by its size and well-developed incisor teeth, which are pigmented deep orange on the front surfaces.

Geographical Range: The beaver occurs throughout the entire Southeast, except for the southern two-thirds of Florida. In the United States, it occurs nationwide where habitats are suitable. The beaver was extirpated from much of its former range well before the 1900s by excessive trapping for the early fur trade. Starting in the 1950s, conservation and management practices were initiated to reintroduce and restore the

Geographical range of the beaver in the Southeast.

beaver to its former range using stocks from the Great Lakes area. These efforts were very successful, and beavers have increased in number and invaded nearly all habitats where they can possibly live successfully.

Habitat: Beavers are active nocturnally and live in almost every stream, pond, swamp, or lake having a suitable adjacent supply of trees available for food. They feed on the inner bark, twigs, and buds of a wide variety of trees, including sweet gum, cottonwood, elm, willow, tupelo gum, ironwood, wax myrtle, cottonwood, yaupon, chinaberry, box elder, and spruce pine. The degree of utilization of a tree species for food seems related to what is available at a given site and whether the trees are small enough to cut down. Beavers seldom cut down trees greater than twelve inches in diameter, and most are in the one-inch to six-inch class. They bark and girdle many larger trees.

Natural History: Beavers are famous for their diligent dam building and maintenance activities. The dams are made of limbs and branches from trees cut down by the beavers' large front teeth. Hundreds of pieces are sectioned to workable size, floated or dragged to the dam, and interwoven with considerable engineering skill into an effective water-retaining structure. Beavers tend the dam carefully each night, and whenever it is damaged, they quickly repair it.

In some areas of the Southeast, where the streams are fairly deep and maintain a good year-round flow, beavers do not build dams. Many southern beavers also do not build the massive stick lodges that are associated with more northern colonies. Southeastern beavers occasionally construct such stick lodges in quiet water, such as lakes and marshes, but most of them live in deep dens in the banks of streams. Entrances to dens are usually below water level, and the tunnel slopes upward to a dry chamber above water level, well back in the bank.

Beavers are social animals that live in family units, which consist of the adult male and female and their offspring from two breeding seasons (called yearlings and kits). They are primarily nocturnal, but occasionally venture forth during the day in protected or remote areas. They can remain under water for ten to fifteen minutes and have been known to swim as far as almost a half mile before coming up for air.

When felling a tree, the beaver stands on its hind feet propped by the tail and gnaws at a convenient height, removing large chips with the incisor teeth. They are not able to control the direction in which a tree falls. The tree merely snaps when the circling cut reaches a critical depth, and the beaver scurries away to avoid being hit. On rare occasions, beavers are killed or pinned by a falling tree. One beaver can cut down a willow tree five inches in diameter in as little as three minutes. Large trees often take more than one night to fell, and frequently they are only girdled and abandoned. Beaver colonies eventually "eat themselves out of house and home," so to speak. When most of the suitable trees within 300 to 600 feet of the water's edge have been depleted, beavers usually abandon the site and move to a new location, generally upstream or downstream along the same waterway. Beavers do consume some nonwoody vegetation, including aquatic plants, cattails, water weeds, streamside shrubs, acorns, and even corn where available.

The main sound associated with beavers is a large slap of the tail on the surface of the water just before they dive. It serves as a warning signal to other members of the colony that danger is near.

The reproductive season begins in December or January, and adults apparently form a pair bond for life. Usually one litter (rarely two) is produced per year, and the gestation period is about four months. The litter size ranges from one to eight, but usually numbers two, three, or four. The kits are born precocial, with a full coat of fur, the eyes open, and weighing about one pound each. They leave the den for the first time when about one month old and wean at about six weeks of age. They continue to live with their parents and work cooperatively on all colony projects until they are two years old. They are then driven away by the parents just prior to the birth of a new, third litter. They become transients for a while, and during this period is when the highest mortality occurs. Most of them eventually find a mate and start their own colonies, and they first breed when they are three years old. Maximum longevity in the wild is about 15 years, although some in captivity have lived to the age of 20.

Remarks: Beaver trapping was one of the main commercial inducements for the early exploration and settlement of the United States and Canada. Beaver pelts were made into all types of fashionable hats, coats, jackets, etc. They are still trapped and sold for pelts in northern states, but the market value of the fur is a fraction of its former worth.

Beavers have large "castor glands," or scent glands, located at the base of the tail. They use them to mark scent posts, which signify the territorial boundaries of the colony and warn off beavers who are transients or members of an adjacent colony. Dried castor glands are also sold by trappers to form an important ingredient of high-quality perfumes. Most castor glands from the United States are shipped to France or the Orient for processing today.

Beavers are legendary for their flood-control and pond-forming activities along streams. A series of beaver dams will often slow silt-laden floods and contribute to clearing of the water. The creation of ponds also causes the water temperatures to increase, and this affects fish culture.

The flooding of low areas by beavers often conflicts with forestry operations and farming activities. Pine plantations and cornfields are sometimes damaged extensively.

Selected References:

Aleksuik, M. 1968. Scent-mound communication, territoriality, and population regulation in beaver (Castor canadensis). J. Mamm. 49: 759–62.

Jenkins, S. H., and P. E. Busher. 1979. Beaver (Castor canadensis). Mammalian Species, No. 120: pp. 1–8.

Morgan, L. H. 1868. The American Beaver and His Works. Lippincott, Philadelphia. 330 pp.

Rue, L. L., III. 1964. The World of the Beaver. J. B. Lippincott Co., Philadelphia. 155 pp.

Svendsen, G. E. 1980. Seasonal changes in the feeding patterns of beaver in southeastern Ohio. J. Wildl. Mgmt. 44: 285–90.

Swank, W. G. 1949. Beaver ecology and management in West Virginia. Cons. comm. of W. Va. 65 pp.

Tevis, L., Jr. 1950. Summer behavior of a family of beavers in New York state. J. Mamm. 31: 40–65.

van Nostrand, F. C., and A. B. Stephenson. 1964. Age determination for beavers by tooth development. J. Wildl. Mgmt. 28: 430–34.

Eastern Woodrat
Neotoma floridana

Eastern woodrat, *Neotoma floridana*. Larry Brown

Identification: This species is also known as the pack rat because of its habit of building bulky stick nests. The eastern woodrat is a medium-sized rodent with large, rounded, leaflike ears, bulging black eyes, long whiskers, and a moderately well-haired tail which is slightly shorter than the head and body combined. The tail is also distinctly bicolored (blackish brown above and white below) and the feet are white. The woodrat's dorsal fur is brownish gray mixed with black and the ventral side is white.

The skull is identified by the presence of a slight depression on the top between the eye sockets, which is not present in other rats which live in the Southeast. The cheek teeth also have looping enamel folds surrounding dentine in the center of each fold.

Geographical Range: The eastern woodrat occurs over the entire southeastern area, except for a band through the Piedmont that extends from Georgia to Maryland. It is also absent from the upper and lower coastal plains of North Carolina, Virginia, and Maryland. Woodrats are common throughout the western portion of the southeastern region. In the United States, the eastern woodrat ranges from Connecticut westward to eastern Colorado and southward to Florida and Texas.

Habitat: In the coastal plain, the eastern woodrat occurs in lowland hardwood forests and swamps. In the northern mountains, the woodrat occurs in rich deciduous forest associated with rocky outcrops, cliffs with boulders, bluffs along rivers, talus slopes, caves, and boulder fields. Woodrats often nest in hollow logs, in stumps on the forest floor, under rocks and boulders, and they definitely have a fondness for old cabins.

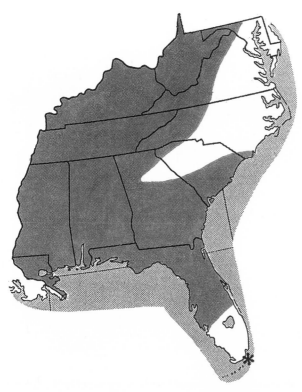

Geographical range of the eastern woodrat in the Southeast.

Natural History: Woodrats are nocturnal and almost never venture forth in the daytime. They are active the year round and do not hibernate. Evidence of woodrats often comes from accumulations of their oval droppings (about one-half inch long), which are deposited in piles not far from the nest. Such latrines, plus piles of sticks, are obvious indicators of their presence.

Woodrats are good climbers and are known to forage frequently in trees. Their diet is almost entirely vegetarian, and they eat all types of plant parts, including leaves, stems, seeds, buds, tubers, roots, fruit, and nuts. They also take a few insects, such as beetles and lepidoptera, as well as mushrooms and other fungi.

The woodrat is not nearly as prolific as most small to medium-sized rodents. They produce small litters and few litters per year. In the coastal plain, the breeding season may extend almost year round, but in the Appalachian Mountains and other northern areas it does not breed during the winter. Females breed two or three times a year and give birth to one to six offspring (usually two) per litter. Gestation averages 35 days, and the young are naked, helpless, and blind at birth. They attach themselves so firmly to their mother's teats that they are often dragged along the ground, without apparent harm, when she leaves the nest. When the young woodrats are about 15 days old, they are fully furred and the eyes open. Weaning takes place at about four weeks of age, but the young woodrats do not reach adult size or start breeding until about eight weeks.

Remarks: The eastern woodrat seldom if ever has an economic impact on man, but they sometimes receive blame for damage caused by two introduced species (the black rat and Norway rat). Woodrats do frequently move into cabins and summer cottages built in the deep woods. Rat-size snap traps or live traps are very effective for removing nuisance individuals.

The stick nests of eastern woodrats serve as homes for a variety of other creatures, including several rare insects, mice, shrews, spiders, snakes, frogs, toads, and lizards.

The Key Largo, Florida, race of the eastern woodrat was recently listed as endangered by the U.S. Fish and Wildlife Service. I first nominated it for endangered status in 1972 (due to habitat destruction from local developments), but it was almost 20 years before the federal government took the proper action; obviously, bureaucracies are often very slow.

Selected References:

Hamilton, W. J., Jr. 1953. Reproduction and young of the Florida wood rat, *Neotoma floridana floridana*. (Ord). J. Mamm. 34: 180–89.

Hersh, S. L. 1981. Ecology of the Key Largo woodrat *(Neotoma floridana smalli)*. J. Mamm. 62: 201–16.

Poole, E. L. 1940. A life history sketch of the Allegheny woodrat. J. Mamm. 21: 249–70.

Post, D. M., O. J. Reichman, and D. E. Wooster. 1993. Characteristics and significance of the caches of eastern woodrats *(Neotoma floridana)*. J. Mamm. 74: 688–92.

Rainey, D. G. 1956. Eastern wood rat, *Neotoma floridana*: Life history and ecology. Univ. Kansas, Mus. Nat. Hist. Publ. 8: 535–645.

Schwartz, A., and E. P. Odum. 1957. The woodrats of the eastern United States. J. Mamm. 38: 197–206.

Wiley, R. W. 1980. Eastern Woodrat *(Neotoma floridana)*. Mammalian Species, No. 139: pp. 1–7.

Cotton Rat
Sigmodon hispidus

Cotton rat, *Sigmodon hispidus*. Larry Brown

Geographical range of the cotton rat in the Southeast.

Identification: Often called the "field rat," this is a robust, medium-sized rodent with a tail which is a good deal shorter than the head and body combined. The ears are blackish, rounded, and buried in the neck fur. The upper pelage has a coarse, grizzled appearance and is a combination of brown, black, and light, tan-banded hairs. The belly is grayish or buff. The tail is sparsely haired and weakly bicolored, black above and buff below.

The skull is the size of a small rat and identified by cheek teeth which show an S-shaped pattern of enamel folds on the grinding surfaces.

Geographical Range: The cotton rat has a regionwide distribution in the Southeast and is one of our most common mammals. In the United States, the geographical range occupies the southern half of the country. It is also found in Mexico, Central America, and parts of South America.

Habitat: Cotton rats occur in a wide variety of open and semi-open habitats. They are most abundant in old fields composed of dense grasses (especially broom sedge) and weeds. They are also common in brush and vines where some grass is still present. During periods of high cotton rat populations, they tend to invade other adjacent plant communities.

Natural History: Cotton rats almost always make well-defined runways (two to three inches wide) through the grass, which is a good field indication of their presence. In areas where grassy vegetation is sparse, they do not always make runways. A small, spherical nest is constructed of dry grass or fibers stripped from the stems of larger plants. The nest is usually placed underground in a shallow tunnel, but sometimes it is built on the surface in dense vegetation. Cotton rats eat the leaves, stems, roots, and seeds of many grasses, sedges, legumes, and other herbaceous plants. They also take some insects, bird eggs, and carrion.

Cotton rats tend to show a three- to five-year population cycle, reaching peak numbers as high as 10–28 individuals per acre in some areas. This high point is followed by a die-off of most of the population to very low densities of less than one cotton rat per acre. They then slowly increase in numbers over several years to a peak once again. Cotton rats seldom live more than a year in the field, but in captivity they sometimes live three to four years.

Cotton rats are active both day and night. It is common to see them in the daytime, running rapidly along a runway into their habitat to escape an intruder. It is also not unusual to set a snap trap across one of their runways, take a few steps, and hear the trap go off because a cotton rat has run across it.

The reproductive rate of cotton rats is very high. In Florida and along the Gulf Coast, breeding occurs year round, but farther north it is curtailed during the winter months. Breeding peaks often occur in the early spring and in late summer or early fall for both regions. The mean litter size is five, but ranges from two to ten. Litters tend to be slightly larger in more northern populations. The gestation period is 27 days, and females come into estrus and breed again three to six hours after the birth of a litter. Thus, adult females produce several litters each year and are normally pregnant and nursing most of the time. The eyes open when the offspring are two days old. The young grow rapidly and are weaned within two weeks. Sexual maturity is attained at the age of 40–50 days, and adult size is reached at five months of age.

Cotton rats are a staple food item for many predators, including hawks, owls, cats, bobcats, coyotes, foxes, minks, skunks, weasels, among others. When cotton rats are numerous, many other prey species feel considerably less predation pressure.

Remarks: Cotton rats are destructive to many cultivated crops, including sugar cane, small grains, sweet potatoes, cotton, legumes, and truck garden vegetables. They also sometimes cause damage to bobwhite quail by eating the eggs or consuming plants the quail could use for food. The best control methods involve removing heavy plant cover used by the rats.

Selected References:

Cameron, G. N., and S. R. Spenser. 1981. Hispid Cotton Rat (*Sigmodon hispidus*). Mammalian Species, No. 158: pp. 1–9.

Gregory, M. J., and G. N. Cameron. 1988. Examination of socially induced dispersal in *Sigmodon hispidus*. J. Mamm. 64: 251–60.

Kilgore, D. L., Jr. 1970. The effects of northward dispersal on growth rate of young, size of young at birth, and litter size in *Sigmodon hispidus*. Amer. Midl. Nat. 84: 510–20.

Meyer, B. J., and R. K. Meyer. 1944. Growth and reproduction of the cotton rat, *Sigmodon hispidus hispidus*, under laboratory conditions. J. Mamm. 25: 107–29.

Odum, E. P. 1955. An eleven–year history of a *Sigmodon* population. J. Mamm. 36: 368–78.

Sealander, J. A., and B. Q. Walker. 1955. A study of the cotton rat in northwestern Arkansas. Proc. Ark. Acad. Sci. 8: 153–62.

Stickel, L. F., and W. H. Stickel. 1949. A *Sigmodon* and *Baiomys* population in ungrazed and burned Texas prairie. J. Mamm. 30: 141–50.

Rice Rat
Oryzomys palustris

Rice rat, *Oryzomys palustris*. Larry Brown

Identification: This is a small to moderate-sized rodent having a slender, scantily haired tail that is about equal to the length of the head and body combined. The underparts are buff brown, slightly sprinkled with black. The color is darkest down the middle of the back with more brown on the sides. The underparts are grayish white and the feet are white. The tail is bicolored, brownish above and grayish white below. The body fur is fairly coarse and moderately long. The ears are medium-sized, rounded, leaflike, and extend beyond the body fur.

The skull is identified by a prominent ridge (supraorbital ridge) running anteriorly just above the eye socket on each side. The grinding surfaces of the cheek teeth have small, rounded cusps covered with enamel.

Geographical Range: The rice rat has a regionwide distribution in the Southeast. In the United States, the rice rat occurs roughly in the southeastern quadrant of the country, from New Jersey southwestward to Kansas, Oklahoma, and Texas.

Habitat: This species is most abundant in freshwater marshes, saltwater marshes, swamps, wet hammocks, and wet, grassy meadows. It is sometimes also found along wet ditches and marshy edges of lakes and streams. It seldom occurs in dry fields or woodlands. The rice rat is a good swimmer and very much at home in the water.

Natural History: Rice rats are active both day and night. They eat the seeds of grasses and sedges, tender green plants, berries, fruits, fungi, insects, snails, crustaceans,

Geographical range of the rice rat in the Southeast.

and bird eggs and young. The nests are grapefruit-sized, globular masses made of dried grasses and are built in a shallow burrow on land or suspended in thick vegetation over water. Small feeding platforms of matted vegetation are normally constructed in marshy environments.

The breeding season extends from late winter to late autumn and may occur year round in Florida. Females are prolific and can produce as many as five to eight litters per year. The gestation period is 25 days, and females normally become pregnant again the day they give birth. When born, the babies are covered with a sparse coat of hair, but the eyes do not open until the sixth day. The litter size is two to seven and averages four. Young rice rats become sexually active when about six weeks old and reach adult body size at about eight weeks of age. They rarely live more than a year in the wild, but in captivity rice rats have survived up to five years.

Remarks: The rice rat can cause serious economic losses to agricultural crops such as rice and sugar cane. Population densities as high as 25 rice rats per acre have been reported in Louisiana.

The lower Florida Keys race of the rice rat (sometimes called the silver rice rat) is listed as endangered by the U.S. Fish and Wildlife Service due to destruction of its habitat.

Selected References:

Hamilton, W. L., Jr. 1946. Habits of the swamp rice rat (*Oryzomys palustris palustris*) (Harlan). Amer. Midl. Nat. 36: 730–36.

Negus, N. C., E. Gould, and R. K. Chipman. 1961. Ecology of the rice rat, *Oryzomys palustris* (Harlan), on Breton Island, Gulf of Mexico, with a critique of social stress theory. Tulane Studies, Zoology, 8: 93–123.

Svihla, A. 1931. Life history of the Texas rice rat (*Oryzomys palustris texensis*). J. Mamm. 12: 238–42.

Wolfe, J. L. 1982. Marsh Rice Rat (*Oryzomys palustris*). Mammalian Species, No. 176: pp. 1–5.

———. 1985. Population ecology of the rice rat (*Oryzomys palustris*) in a coastal marsh. J. Zool. 205: 235–44.

———. 1990. Environmental influences on the distribution of rice rats (*Oryzomys palustris*) in coastal marshes. Fla. Sci. 53: 81–84.

Eastern Harvest Mouse
Reithrodontomys humulis

Eastern harvest mouse, *Reithrodontomys humulis*. James Parnell

Identification: This is the smallest mouse that lives in the Southeast and one of the least-known mammals in the region. The upper side is grayish brown sprinkled with black hairs, and the underparts are white or gray. The tail measures one and three-quarters inches to two and one-quarter inches and is sparsely haired. The ears are fairly short, broad, rounded, and leaflike. The feet are white or light gray.

The skull is identified by its small size and by a longitudinal groove located on the front surface of each upper incisor. A similar species, the house mouse, lacks a groove on its upper incisors.

Geographical Range: This little mouse probably has a regionwide distribution, but records of it are rather sparse in many areas. In the United States, The geographical range occupies the southeastern quadrant of the country, from Maryland southwestward to eastern Texas.

Habitat: The eastern harvest mouse prefers old fields where tall grasses, such as broom sedge, predominate. It is also found in weedy fields, blackberry brier patches, grassy meadows, and roadside ditches.

Natural History: This species is not often collected and is apparently rather wary of entering mammal traps. Skeletal remains of harvest mice are often found in cast pellets of owls, but few are taken in traps set in those areas.

The nest is a small, spherical ball of dried grasses constructed above the ground in a thick clump of grass. Harvest mice are active nocturnally and feed on a variety of grass and weed seeds as well as some green vegetation.

Eastern harvest mice breed throughout the warmer months of the year. The gestation period is 21–22 days, and the litter size averages three (ranging from two to six). Their eyes open at seven to ten days of age, and the young are weaned in about three weeks. They become sexually mature and can breed when around twelve weeks old.

The home range size of these diminutive mice is not large, varying only from one-half acre up to one acre. Males have significantly larger home ranges than females.

Remarks: As a result of its seed-harvesting habits, the eastern harvest mouse aids in the dispersal of certain grasses and forbs. The species has little or no economic significance.

Although eastern harvest mice and cotton rats generally occupy the same type of habitat, they seldom coexist together. When cotton rats are abundant in a field, harvest mice tend to be absent, and vice versa. This strongly suggests that there is some degree of mutual exclusion (possibly behavioral) in the two species.

Selected References:

Dunaway, P. B. 1962. Litter-size record for eastern harvest mice. J. Mamm. 43: 428–29.

Kaye, S. V. 1959. A study of the eastern harvest mouse, *Reithrodontomys humulis humulis.* M.A. Thesis. North Carolina State College. 93 pp.

Layne, J. N. 1959. Growth and development of the eastern harvest mouse *(Reithrodontomys humulis).* Bull. Fla. State Mus. 4: 61–82.

Fulvous Harvest Mouse
Reithrodontomys fulvescens

Fulvous harvest mouse, *Reithrodontomys fulvescens.* Guy Cameron

Identification: The fulvous harvest mouse looks somewhat like a large house mouse with a longer tail and whitish feet. The upper pelage is golden brown with a blackish band down the center of the back. The tail is longer than the head and body combined and is not sharply bicolored. The sides, face, and ears are golden brown, and the belly is grayish white.

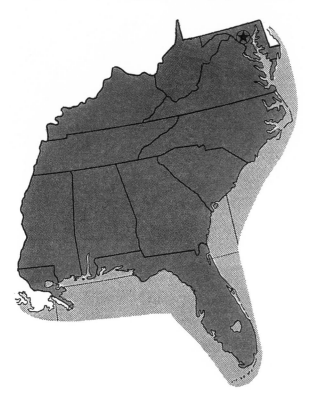

Geographical range of the eastern harvest mouse in the Southeast.

The skull is easily identified by the presence of deep grooves on the front of the upper incisors, and it is about one-third larger than the skull of the smaller eastern harvest mouse.

Geographical Range: In the Southeast, this mouse occurs only in southwestern Mississippi and eastern Louisiana. In the United States, this species ranges from the Lower Mississippi Valley southwestward into Texas, the southwestern United States, through Mexico, and into northern Central America.

Habitat: This harvest mouse lives in various stages of old-field succession. It is particularly abundant in the broom sedge (tall grasses) stage and in transitional areas of bushes and mixed grasses.

Natural History: The fulvous harvest mouse is primarily nocturnal and feeds mainly on succulent plant parts and on the seeds of weeds and grasses. They usually construct a ball nest above ground made of dried grasses and with a single entrance hole in one side.

The reproductive season begins in February and extends through November, unless there is a mild winter, in which case the fulvous harvest mouse will breed year round. The litter size ranges from two to seven with an average of four young per litter. The gestation period is 22–23 days long, and each female produces four to five litters per year. The young are weaned when they are three to four weeks old. Sexual maturity occurs when the young mice are two to three months of age.

A peak density of 19 fulvous harvest mice per acre was reported in one Louisiana study. The home ranges of females were found to be larger than those of males, which is the reverse of what is normally recorded for small mammal species. Both sexes exhibited larger home ranges in winter than summer (presumably in order to secure enough seeds and grasses to eat). Males were also reported to far outnumber females, but I suspect this data resulted from the greater susceptibility of males to being trapped.

Remarks: On wetter sites or in seasonally flooded fields, the fulvous harvest mouse often builds its softball-sized nest one to three feet above the ground in tall grasses and weeds.

Selected References:

McDaniel, V. R., J. C. Huggins, J. A. Huggins, and M. W. Hinson. 1978. A summary of the status of harvest mice, Cricetidae: Reithrodontomys, in Arkansas. Proc. Ark. Acad. Sci. 32: 63–64.

Packard, R. L. 1968. An ecological study of the fulvous harvest mouse in eastern Texas. Amer. Midl. Nat. 79: 68–88.

Spencer, S. R., and G. N. Cameron. 1982. Fulvous Harvest Mouse (Reithrodontomys fulvescens). Mammalian Species, No. 174: pp. 1–7.

Common Deer Mouse
Peromyscus maniculatus

Common deer mouse, *Peromyscus maniculatus*. Roger W. Barbour

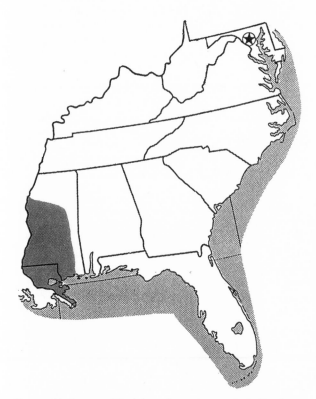

Geographical range of the fulvous harvest mouse in the Southeast.

Identification: The common deer mouse is brown or grayish brown above, with a slightly darker band that extends down the middle of the back. The venter and feet are white. The tail is moderately long, about equal to half the total body length, and sharply bicolored (dark brown, above and white below), with a small tuft of hairs at the tip. The ears are large, naked, and dusky gray in color. The deer mouse's summer pelage is slightly brighter than the winter coat. Juveniles are always dark gray above or white below.

The skull is difficult to distinguish accurately from the other deer mice and should be referred to an expert.

Geographical Range: The common deer mouse occurs in the Appalachian Mountains from Maryland south to Georgia as well as much of Tennessee and Kentucky. In North America, the geographical range extends from coast to coast, being absent only from parts of the Midwest, Deep South, and the Atlantic coast. It has the widest range of any species of *Peromyscus.*

Habitat: This species occurs in some of the higher mountains and foothills, as well as in the rolling hill country in Tennessee and Kentucky. It occurs in oak-hickory forest, mountain hemlock, and mixed hardwoods of various types. The nests are built in hollow logs, in tree stumps, and under rocks.

Natural History: The breeding season extends from March to November, but may decline somewhat in the hotter months. Each female produces three or four litters each year of three to eight young each (the average is five). The offspring are altricial, but they grow rapidly and wean at about three and one-half weeks. The gestation period is 23 days, and there is a postpartum estrus, with the females normally becoming pregnant while nursing the previous litter. Young deer mice become sexually mature at one and one-half months.

Like other members of the genus, deer mice are strictly nocturnal, and they sleep during the daylight hours. The diet consists of seeds, nuts, berries, fruits, mushrooms, snails, slugs, insects, and various other arthropods. They frequently make food caches in or near the nest to be eaten when food is scarce.

In nature, deer mice reach a maximum age of one and one-half to two years. The longevity record in captivity is eight years. They are taken by nearly every terrestrial and avian predator present in the area.

Deer mice are rather sedentary and have home ranges which only vary from one-half to one and one-half acres. Males have larger home ranges than females, and juveniles have the smallest.

Remarks: Deer mice are commonly used in medical and genetic research in the laboratory, but not as extensively as the house mouse or Norway rat. Genetic stocks of various *Peromyscus* species are maintained, bred, and sold to researchers at the Peromyscus Stock Center at the University of South Carolina, Columbia, South Carolina.

Selected References:

Brown, L. N. 1966. Reproduction of *Peromyscus maniculatus* in the Laramie Basin of Wyoming. Amer. Midl. Nat. 76: 183–89.

Howard, W. E. 1949. Dispersal, amount of inbreeding, and longevity in a local population of prairie deer mice in the George Reserve, southern Michigan. Univ. Mich. Contr. Vert. Biol. No. 43: 50 pp.

Millar, J. S., and E. M. Derrickson. 1992. Group nesting in *Peromyscus maniculatus.* J. Mamm. 73: 403–7.

Whitaker, J. O., Jr. 1966. Food of *Mus musculus, Peromyscus maniculatus bairdii,* and *Peromyscus leucopus* in Vigo County, Indiana. J. Mamm. 47: 473–86.

Geographical range of the common deer mouse in the Southeast.

Wolff, J. O. 1985. Comparative population ecology of *Peromyscus leucopus* and *Peromyscus maniculatus*. Canad. J. Zool. 63: 1548–55.

Wolff, J. O., and D. S. Durr. 1986. Winter nesting behavior of *Peromyscus leucopus* and *Peromyscus maniculatus*. J. Mamm. 67: 409–12.

Old-field Mouse
Peromyscus polionotus

Old-field mouse, *Peromyscus polionotus*. Larry Brown

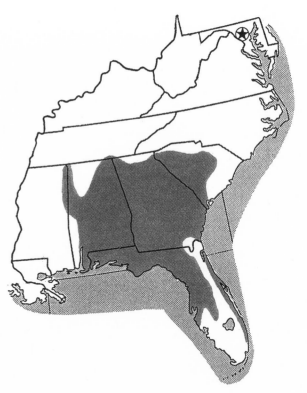

Geographical range of the old-field mouse in the Southeast.

Identification: The old-field mouse, sometimes called the beach mouse, is the smallest species of deer mouse. The upper pelage is dull buff-gray to cinnamon-brown, and the tail is sharply bicolored and rather short (one and one-half inches to two inches) for a deer mouse. The tail is white except for a thin brown stripe on the top (which is lacking on some beach forms). The anterior venter and feet are also white. The ears are medium-sized, rounded, leaflike, and dusky gray. In general, the pelage of old-field mice living on light-colored, sandy soils is light-colored, and mice from areas of dark soils are dark.

The skull is somewhat smaller than those of other deer mice, but positive identification requires an expert.

Geographical Range: This species occurs only in the southern third of the southeastern region, and it is most common in the coastal plains and coastal sand dunes. The geographical range in the United States is restricted to the southeastern states from South Carolina southwestward to Florida and eastern Mississippi.

Habitat: As suggested by the common name, these mice prefer the early weed-grass stages of old-field succession. They do not thrive in dense, vegetative ground cover, but are ideally suited for disturbed open areas having much bare soil.

Natural History: The old-field mouse always constructs a very stylized and predictable burrow. It consists of three parts: 1) a downward-sloping entrance tunnel that is loosely plugged with soil during the daytime to a depth of approximately four to eight inches back from the entrance; 2) a spherical nest chamber six to eight inches in diameter at a depth of two to three feet below the surface; and 3) an "escape tunnel" that rises steeply from the back side of the nest chamber to within an inch of the surface. I have excavated hundreds of burrows to collect old-field mice, and every single burrow system exhibited all three components. The mice always enter the escape tunnel when danger threatens, and often they will pop through to the surface if pressed, then run for the nearest cover. The nest is a cup-shaped pad of dried grasses, plant fibers, and sometimes even shredded paper or rags if these materials are available.

It is common to find a paired male and female in the burrow or a female and her young. Old-field mice are quite social, sometimes forming sizable groups in a single nest during the colder months. They feed nocturnally, mainly on insects and seeds of grasses and herbs (such as drop-seed, bluestem, lespedeza, buttonweed, sheep sorrel, wild oats, etc.).

Breeding can occur year round, but is at its maximum in the later fall and winter (October–January). The average litter size is three to four (but ranges from one to six), and the gestation period is 21–24 days (longer in lactating females). The babies are naked and blind at birth, but grow rapidly and wean when three weeks old. Under laboratory conditions, first breeding has occurred when young old-field mice are about 30 days old.

Remarks: The old-field mouse has little or no economic impact on agriculture, because it lives in fallow fields and abandoned farmland. In mature cornfields which are not yet harvested, they sometimes consume a little of the grain.

This species is preyed upon by owls, skunks, foxes, raccoons, snakes, cats, weasels, and most other small carnivores. In disturbed, sparsely vegetated areas, they are often the most abundant rodent present and a staple food item in the food chain.

Old-field mice are also known as "beach mice" in those regions of the Atlantic and Gulf coast where they live on beach dunes and barrier islands. These coastal populations of the old-field mouse tend to be much paler in coloration (some are almost all white) than more inland old-field mice. The pale coloration results from thousands of years of natural selection to match the pale beach sands. Most beach mouse populations have been decimated by habitat destruction for condominiums and other beach-front developments, as well as by periodic hurricanes. As result, the U.S. Fish and Wildlife Service has listed four races of the beach mouse as endangered and one as threatened in Florida and Alabama.

Selected References:

Bowen, W. W. 1968. Variation and evolution of Gulf Coast populations of beach mice, *Peromyscus polionotus*. Bull. Fla. State. Mus., (Biol. Sci.). 12: 1–91.

Extine, D. D., and I. J. Stout. 1987. Dispersion and habitat occupancy of the beach mouse *(Peromyscus polionotus nivliventris)*. J. Mamm. 68: 297–304.

Rave, E. H., and N. R. Holler. 1992. Population dynamics of beach mice *(Peromyscus polionotus ammobater)* in southern Alabama. J. Mamm. 73: 347–55.

Summer, F. B., and J. J. Karol. 1929. Notes on the burrowing habits of *Peromyscus polionotus*. J. Mamm. 10: 213–15.

White-footed Mouse
Peromyscus leucopus

White-footed mouse, *Peromyscus leucopus.* Roger W. Barbour

Identification: The white-footed mouse, or woodland deer mouse, is about the same size as the common deer mouse, but the tail is equal to or shorter than the total body length, and it is indistinctly bicolored (grayish brown above and white below, moderately haired). The upper pelage is chestnut brown or gray-brown, with a slightly darker mid-dorsal stripe, while the belly and feet are white. The ears are large, naked, and dusky gray in color. Summer pelages are more reddish than winter pelages. Its body size is smaller and less stocky than in cotton mice, but the two species are difficult to tell apart.

The skull is difficult to separate from the other deer mice and its identification should be left to an expert in mammalogy.

Geographical Range: The white-footed mouse occurs across the northern two-thirds of the Southeast from the Appalachian fall line northward. It is largely absent from the coastal plain except in the western portion of the range. In the United States, the geographical range covers the eastern two-thirds of the country, with the exclusion of the southeastern lowlands.

Habitat: This mouse prefers hardwood forests throughout its range. White-footed mice are prevalent in forests of the Appalachian Plateau, the mountains, and Mississippi River drainage. They nest in fallen logs, hollow stumps, tree cavities, and under rocks or boulders on the forest floor. They also often invade and live in cabins or houses located in the woods.

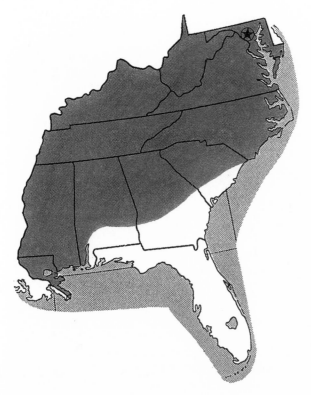

Geographical range of the white-footed mouse in the Southeast.

Natural History: As with other deer mice, this species is nocturnally active and sleeps during the daylight hours. The diet is very similar to that of the common deer mouse and cotton mouse.

The breeding season begins in early spring and continues until late autumn with some decline in activity during the hotter summer months. Three or four litters are produced each year, and there is a postpartum heat, so they are frequently lactating and pregnant at the same time. The litter size is two to seven, and the average is four. The length of gestation in nonlactating females is 21 days. The baby mice are altricial and their eyes do not open until they are two weeks old. Weaning occurs in a little over three weeks if a new litter arrives, or at four weeks if the mother is not pregnant. Young white-footed mice become sexually active when they are two months old. Those born in the spring usually mate later that summer or in early fall.

Remarks: White-footed mice are often the staple prey species of woodland-dwelling carnivores. These mice are also numerous enough to be a significant factor in the dispersal of seeds of many species of trees and shrubs.

White-footed mice sometimes do considerable damage to the interior parts of cabins and homes located in the woods. When they become a nuisance, these mice are readily controlled by the use of traps or rodent poisons.

Selected References:
Brown, L. N. 1964. Ecology of three species of *Peromyscus* from southern Missouri. J. Mamm. 45: 189–202.

Knuth, B. A., and G. W. Barrett. 1984. A comparative study of resource partitioning between *Ochrotomys nuttalli* and *Peromyscus leucopus*. J. Mamm. 65: 576–83.

McShea, W. J., and A. B. Gilles. 1992. A comparison of traps and fluorescent powder to describe foraging for most by *Peromyscus leucopus*. J. Mamm. 73: 218–22.

Rintamaa, D. L. , P. A. Mazur, and S. H. Vessy. 1976. Reproduction during two annual cycles in a population of *Peromyscus leucopus noveboracensis*. J. Mamm. 57: 593–95.

Terman, C. R. 1993. Studies of natural populations of white-footed mice: Reduction of reproduction at varying densities. J. Mamm. 74: 678–87.

Wolff, J. O. 1985. Comparative population ecology of *Peromyscus leucopus* and *Peromyscus maniculatus*. Canad. J. Zool. 63: 1548–55.

Cotton Mouse
Peromyscus gossypinus

Cotton mouse, *Peromyscus gossypinus*. Larry Brown

Identification: The cotton mouse is one of the largest, most robust deer mice living in the Southeast. The upper parts in adults can vary from chestnut brown to dark brown or grayish brown. The middle of the back is more deeply pigmented than the sides. The underparts and feet are white, and the ears are large, rounded, naked, and dusky gray. The tail is slightly shorter than the total length of the rest of the body. It is also sparsely haired and indistinctly bicolored (the top is dusky brown and the underside is white). Cotton mice and white-footed mice are often difficult to distinguish from one another.

The skull is very similar to that of other deer mice and must be examined by a mammalogist for positive identification.

Geographical Range: The cotton mouse occurs in the southern half and throughout the western portion of the southeastern region. The geographical range in the United States is confined to the southern states from southeastern Virginia southward to Florida and westward to eastern Texas.

Habitat: Cotton mice live in a wide variety of woodland habitats, ranging from the low swampland of the coastal plain all the way to open mountain hardwoods. They occur in almost any forest or forest-edge environment.

Natural History: Cotton mice are one of the most numerous rodents living in the Southeast. They are active nocturnally and usually nest in fallen logs, hollow

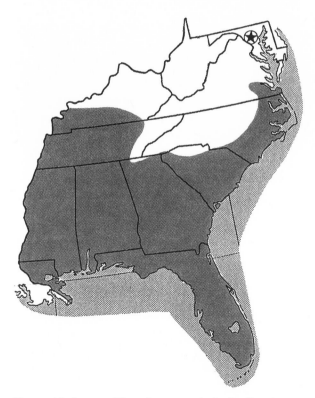

Geographical range of the cotton mouse in the Southeast.

stumps, holes dug in the ground, and old cabins. They also climb trees readily and build a spherical nest of leaves and plant fibers in a hollow cavity of their choice.

Cotton mice eat acorns, nuts, fungi, and seeds of many trees, as well as animal food such as snails, slugs, spiders, insects, and other arthropods.

The cotton mouse breeds throughout the year, but reproduction declines somewhat in both the hottest and coldest months. The peak breeding time is usually from September through December. The gestation period is 23 days, and the mean litter size is four young (but ranges from two to seven). Females usually produce four or five litters per year and frequently exhibit a postpartum estrus. The young are pink, naked, and blind at birth, but they grow rapidly and are weaned when 20–25 days old. The juvenile pelage is dusky gray dorsally, and they do not turn brown until the post-juvenile molt. Breeding can occur as early as 10 weeks old.

The longevity of cotton mice in the wild is fairly short, seldom exceeding one and one-half years. In captivity they will live up to five or six years of age. Cotton mice are eaten by every medium and small-sized woodland predator. In spite of predation, their high reproductive rate ensures that cotton mice maintain substantial population levels.

Remarks: Cotton mice are an important link in the food chain for many carnivores, and they also aid in the dispersal of many tree seeds. Further, they occasionally forage on the seeds of crops, such as corn, cotton, and soybeans, planted adjacent to wooded cover. They frequently invade corncribs and granaries to consume stored grain, and they will invade homes and cabins that are located in wooded areas. Snap traps or poison baits are normally quite effective for control of cotton mice in buildings and grain-storage areas.

There are several races of cotton mice that live on the coastal islands. One of these, the Key Largo cotton mouse, occurs in the Florida Keys and was recently added to the endangered species list by the U.S. Fish and Wildlife Service. The populations of this cotton mouse are threatened by habitat destruction due to development; they are also threatened by tropical storms which could wipe out their entire island habitat. I first nominated the Key Largo cotton mouse for endangered species status back in 1972, but due to bureaucratic shuffling and inaction, it was almost 20 years before the species received its listed status.

Selected References:

Bigler, W. J., and J. H Jenkins. 1975. Population characteristics of *Peromyscus gossypinus gossypinus* and *Sigmodon hispidus* in tropical hammocks of South Florida. J. Mamm. 56: 633–44.

Pearson, P. G. 1953. A field study of *Peromyscus* populations in Gulf Hammock, Florida. Ecology 34: 199–207.

Pournelle, G. H. 1952. Reproduction and early postnatal development of the cotton mouse, *Peromyscus gossypinus gossypinus*. J. Mamm. 33: 1–20.

St. Roamin, P. A. 1976. Variation in the cotton mouse *(Peromyscus gossypinus)* in Louisiana. Southwestern Nat. 21: 79–88.

Wolfe, J. L., and A. V. Linzey. 1977. Cotton Mouse *(Peromyscus gossypinus)*. Mammalian Species, No. 70: pp. 1–5.

Young, B. L., and J. Stout. 1986. Effects of extra food on small rodents in a south temperate zone habitat: Demographic responses. Canad. J. Zool. 64: 1211–17.

Florida Mouse
Peromyscus floridanus

Florida mouse, *Peromyscus floridanus*. Larry Brown

Identification: This species is one of the Southeast's largest deer mice. It is sometimes called the "gopher mouse" because of its association with gopher tortoise burrows. The upper parts are buff-cinnamon or buff-brown mixed with dusky hairs. There is a bright orange-cinnamon wash down each side at the junction with the all-white underparts. The feet are white and the ears are large, rounded, leaflike, and dusky gray. The tail is three inches to three and one-half inches long, dusky brown above, and grayish white below, but not sharply bicolored.

The skull is difficult to separate from the other deer mice, and an expert is required for identification.

Geographical Range: This species is confined mainly to the Florida peninsula. There is also an isolated population found in Franklin County, Florida, at the base of the Panhandle. Populations of this mouse are often spotty and isolated in distribution. The Dade and Pinellas County populations have been largely extirpated in recent decades by urban development. The Florida mouse occurs nowhere else in the United States except Florida.

Habitat: This species lives on high, well-drained sandy ridges covered by pine-turkey oak or sand pine scrub vegetation. Many of these sites represent old beach dunes formed along the edges of the Florida peninsula at a time when sea levels were higher and farther inland.

Natural History: The burrow of the Florida mouse is often located within the large tunnels dug by gopher tortoises. The mouse either nests in the main tortoise burrow or digs a short tunnel and nest chamber at right angles to the gopher turtle burrow. Since armadillos are also widely established in Florida, Florida mice also use their numerous burrows for nesting sites. The nest is usually a simple cup composed of leaves and grasses. Florida mice normally have several burrows in an area and tend to rotate their usage.

Florida mice are nocturnally active and semifossorial in their habits, doing some of their foraging in the underground tunnel system of the gopher turtle. They also forage on the surface, and favorite foods include acorns,

Geographical range of the Florida mouse in the Southeast.

pine seeds, palmetto berries, mushrooms, insects, and various other arthropods found in the burrow system.

Florida mice reproduce year round, but breeding is most concentrated in the fall and early winter. The gestation period is 23–24 days, and the average litter size is three and one-half young (but ranges from one to six). Females often produce two litters per year.

Remarks: As a seed eater, the Florida mouse aids in the dispersal of a sizable number of trees and other plants that grow in dry, sandy plant communities.

The habitats to which the Florida mouse is restricted are rapidly disappearing because of their prime value for citrus production, and for commercial and residential developments of all types. Thus, much sand pine scrub and pine-turkey oak habitats have been lost and the Florida mouse with them. Unless these plant communities are set aside and protected, this unique "endemic" species will become very rare except for a few protected parks and preserves. Due to habitat destruction, it is already gone from most of the east coast ridge located in Dade, Broward, and Palm Beach Counties, and from nearly all of the sand pine scrubs found in Pinellas, Manatee, and Sarasota Counties of Florida.

The life span of the Florida mouse in the field seldom exceeds two years, but in captivity they have lived as long as seven and one-half years.

Certain taxonomists have placed this species in the genus *Podomys* rather than *Peromyscus*, but the characteristics cited to classify it in that genus are both weak and superficial. Therefore, the long-used and preferred genus of *Peromyscus* will be retained here.

Selected References:
Eisenberg, J. F. 1984. Ecology of the Florida mouse, *Peromyscus floridanus*. Abstracts Amer. Soc. Mamm. 64th Ann. Meeting. Humbolt State Univ., Arcata, Calif.
Eisenberg, J. F., and C. A. Jones. 1985. Long-term residence patterns shown by *Peromyscus floridanus*. Abstracts Amer. Soc. Mamm. 65th Ann. Meeting. Humbolt State Univ., Arcata, Calif.
Jones, C. A., and J. N. Layne. 1993. Florida Mouse (*Peromyscus floridanus*). Mammalian Species, No. 427: pp. 1–5.
Layne, J. N. 1963. A study of the parasites of the Florida mouse, *Peromyscus floridanus*, in relation to host and environmental factors. Tulane Studies, Zoology, 11: 1–27.
———. 1969. Nest building behavior in three species of deer mice, *Peromyscus*. Behavior 35: 288–303.
———. 1970. Climbing behavior of *Peromyscus floridanus* and *Peromyscus gossypinus*. J. Mamm. 51: 580–91.

Golden Mouse
Ochrotomys nuttalli

Golden mouse, *Ochrotomys nuttalli*. Larry Brown

Identification: This medium-sized mouse has a strikingly beautiful coat that is golden cinnamon or burnt orange in coloration. The belly and feet are white, usually tinged with some cinnamon or gold. The tail is slightly shorter (between two and three-eighth inches and three and three-quarters inches long) than the body and head combined, scantily furred, and not bicolored. The ears are medium-large, rounded, leaflike, and the same color as the body.

The skull looks much like those of the closely related deer mice, and must be examined by a mammalogist for positive identification.

Geographical Range: The golden mouse is found throughout the entire southeastern region. In the United States, the range of the golden mouse occupies the southeastern quadrant, extending from Virginia west to eastern Oklahoma and southwest to eastern Texas.

Habitat: This mouse prefers dense woodland with heavy vines and underbrush in the understory, usually in moist environments. The golden mouse is an arboreal species, nesting and foraging above the ground in thick vegetation, vines, or brush.

Natural History: Golden mice build a spherical domed nest (five to eight inches in diameter) with a single small entry hole located on one side. Each mouse

Geographical range of the golden mouse in the Southeast.

usually builds several nests within its home range, each composed of a finely woven mass of shredded leaves and fibers, sometimes combined with animal hair, bird feathers, and inner tree bark. The nest is a neat, compact woven ball, and is placed in the fork of a branch, in a tangle of vines or in a hollow limb. The height of the nest varies, ranging from a few inches above the ground to over 15 feet in the air. These mice are known to forage even higher than that into the treetops. They also construct flat feeding platforms, well above the ground, scattered throughout the home range. The ratio of feeding platforms to nests is about six to one. Golden mice sleep during the day and forage nocturnally. The diet consists of seeds, berries, buds, fruits, leaves, and some insects. Preferred seeds include those of sumac, dogwood, magnolia, wild cherry, oak, and greenbrier.

The breeding season of the golden mouse in Florida extends throughout the year, but peaks in the spring and fall months. In northern areas, breeding extends only from March to October. The gestation period is 25–30 days, and the litter size averages two and one-half young (ranging from one to four). Litters born in the fall tend to be larger than spring ones, and several lit-

ters may be produced each year. Newborn babies are pink, blind, and helpless. The first hair appears on the fifth day, and the eyes open on the thirteenth day. Weaning occurs at three to four weeks of age. Females frequently come into estrus immediately after birth of a litter and are impregnated again. Adult females are known to produce as many as five or six litters per year in the southern part of the range, and only three or four litters in the northern part. Young golden mice become reproductively active when about two months of age.

Remarks: This beautiful mouse has little or no economic impact on humans. It is a valuable disperser of tree seeds and is a consumer of certain harmful forest insects.

Golden mice can be readily captured by hand from their globular nests. Interestingly, the nests are often made of reddish brown plant fibers that closely match the coat color of the golden mouse. They are excellent climbers, as would be expected, and are able to cling tenaciously to vertical objects. This species is a rather docile rodent which is not inclined to bite and can be readily handled. They make attractive and interesting pets.

Longevity in the wild rarely exceeds two and one-half years, but in captivity I have had several of them live five to six years. The longest life span ever recorded for a golden mouse in captivity was just under eight and one-half years, which is also the maximum longevity record for any small rodent in North America.

Selected References:

Dietz, B. A., and G. W Barrett. 1992. Nesting behavior of *Ochrotomys nuttalli* under experimental conditions. J. Mamm. 73: 577–81.

Goodpaster, W. W., and D. F. Hoffmeister. 1954. Life history of the golden mouse, *Peromyscus nuttalli*, in Kentucky. J. Mamm. 35: 16–27.

Linzey, D. W. 1968. An ecological study of the golden mouse, *Ochrotomys nuttalli*, in the Great Smoky Mountains National Park. Amer. Mid. Nat., 79: 320–45.

Linzey, D. W., and R. L. Packard. 1977. Golden Mouse (*Ochrotomys nuttalli*). Mammalian Species, No. 75: pp. 1–6.

McCarlsy, W. H. 1958. Ecology, behavior, and population dynamics of *Peromyscus nuttalli* in eastern Texas. Texas J. Sci. 10: 147–71.

Rock Vole
Microtus chrotorrhinus

Rock vole, *Microtus chrotorrhinus*. American Society of Mammalogists

Geographical range of the rock vole in the Southeast.

Identification: The rock vole is very similar to the meadow vole, but its nose is marked by a reddish orange blaze on either side and on the cheeks. The rest of the upper pelage is dark brown, flecked with black hairs. The belly fur and feet are dull gray to silvery gray.

The skull is identified by the presence of a longer tooth row than found in the meadow vole.

Geographical Range: This vole occurs at scattered locations along the Appalachian Mountain chain, as far south as the Great Smoky Mountain National Park. It also ranges northward into the more rugged parts of New England and eastern Canada, as far as the Gaspe Peninsula.

Habitat: The rock vole shows a distinct affinity for areas in the mountains having piles of moss-covered boulders. They usually build runways threading between the rocks, and they are active both at night and during the day. In the Smoky Mountains, I have found them common in rocky outcrops on the high, grassy balds of the mountain summits.

Natural History: The rock vole appears to live in isolated colonies and feeds on grasses, sedges, herbs, and berries of all types found growing in its rocky habitat.

The breeding season extends from early spring to mid-autumn. The females exhibit a postpartum estrus and become pregnant with a second litter immediately after the birth of the first litter. The gestation period is 19–21 days, and the litter size ranges from 2 to 5, averaging 2.8.

Remarks: The rock vole is considered rare by many mammalogists who have unsuccessfully set traps for them. In fact, these voles are relatively abundant in certain rock-strewn habitats. Snap traps or box traps set at right angles to their runways or paths are almost always successful. I trapped a series of rock voles along Highway 441, east of Gatlinburg, Tennessee, among moss-covered boulders of the Smoky Mountains.

Selected References:
Kilpatrick, C. W., and K. L. Crowell. 1985. Genetic variations in the rock vole, *Microtus chrotorrhinus*. J. Mamm. 66: 94–101.
Kirkland, G. L., Jr., and F. J. Jannett, Jr. 1982. Rock Vole *Microtus chrotorrhinus*. Mammalian Species, No. 180: pp. 1–5.

Meadow Vole
Microtus pennsylvanicus

Meadow vole, *Microtus pennsylvanicus.* American Society of Mammalogists

Identification: The meadow vole is a fairly large mouse having a dark brown upper coat and a short tail which extends well beyond the hind foot when extended. The underparts are silvery gray and the ears are small, rounded, leaflike, and partly hidden in the fur.

The skull is identified by the number of angular enamel loops surrounding dentine islands on the grinding surface of the cheek teeth. In the meadow vole there are five (or very rarely six) dentine islands on the second upper molar, instead of four as in the pine vole.

Geographical Range: The meadow vole occurs in the Appalachian Plateau and mountain regions of the northern third of the Southeast. It is largely absent from the coastal plains. In the United States, the meadow vole ranges over the northern two-thirds of the country. In the East, there are small, relict populations present on the west coast of the Florida peninsula and in the coastal region of South Carolina.

Habitat: This vole lives in wet meadows, grassy upland fields, in orchards having good ground cover, and in grassy openigs in forests and open woodlands. The Florida population lives in a coastal salt marsh.

Natural History: Meadow voles are active both day and night, and they are highly herbivorous, with over 90 percent of the diet being vegetable matter. They construct extensive runway systems similar in appearance to those of the cotton rat, but only about half as wide (about one and one-half inches in width). They feed on the stems and leaves of grasses and herbs. Piles of cuttings can be found scattered along the runways.

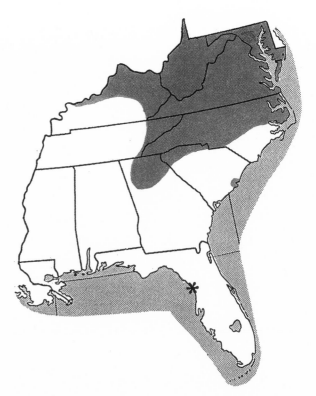

Geographical range of the meadow vole in the Southeast.

Nests are globular stuctures made of dried grasses, constructed on the surface of the ground or just below it.

Breeding usually occurs throughout the year in the meadow vole. The gestation period is 21 days, and the average litter size is five (ranging from three to ten). They are very prolific, becauser there is a postpartum estrus and breeding occurs again right after birth. Young meadow voles mature rapidly, sometimes weaning when just two weeks old, and breeding when they are one month of age. Very few meadow voles survive in the field beyond one year, but in the laboratory they have lived as long as five years.

Remarks: The meadow vole is one of the most important prey species for predators which forage in fields and meadows. These voles sometimes reach densities which damage field crops, pastures, gardens, and orchards.

The Florida race of the meadow vole is locally called the "saltmarsh vole" and was recently listed as an endangered species by the U.S. Fish and Wildlife Service. This designation occurred because mammalogists have been able to capture very few voles in the vast saltmarsh habitat near Cedar Key, Florida.

Selected References:

Bailey, V. 1924. Breeding, feeding, and other life habits of meadow mice (Microtus). J. Agr. Res. 27: 523–35.

Boonstra, R., and F. H. Rodd. 1983. Regulation of breeding density in *Microtus pennsylvanicus*. J. Animal Ecol. 52: 757–80.

Fisler, G. F. 1961. Behavior of salt marsh *Microtus* during winter high tides. J. Mamm. 42: 37–43.

Harper, S. J., E. K. Ballinger, and G. W. Barrett. 1993. Effects of habitat patch shape on population dynamics of meadow voles *(Microtus pennsylvanicus).* J. Mamm. 74: 1045.

Reich, L. M. 1981. Meadow Vole *(Microtus pennsylvanicus).* Mammalian Species, No. 159: pp. 1–8.

Woods, C. A., W. Post, and C. W. Kilpatrick. 1982. *Microtus pennsylvanicus* (Rodentia: Muridae) in Florida: A Pleistocene relict in a coastal salt marsh. Bull. Fla. State Mus., Biol. Sci. 28: 25–52.

Zimmerman, E. G. 1965. A comparison of the habitat and food of two species of *Microtus*. J. Mamm. 46: 605–12.

Prairie Vole
Microtus ochrogaster

Prairie vole, *Microtus ochrogaster.* American Society of Mammalogists

Identification: The prairie vole resembles the meadow vole but has a shorter tail, a more grizzled upper pelage, and buff belly fur (rather than silvery gray as in the meadow vole). The feet are pale buff, and the tail has a narrow dark dorsal stripe and buff underparts. The ears are nearly concealed in the relatively coarse fur, and the eyes are small.

The skull is very similar to those of other voles. The second upper molar has four triangles of dentine surrounded by enamel.

Geographical Range: The prairie vole is found in the northwestern portion of the southeastern states, primarily in western West Virginia, most of Kentucky, the western half of Tennessee, and in northern Alabama.

Geographical range of the prairie vole in the Southeast.

In the United States, the prairie vole ranges throughout the Midwest, the Great Plains, and eastward into the central prairie and south-central states.

Habitat: This mouse is characteristic of grassy fields, meadows, roadsides, railroad rights-of-way, and cattle pastures. Prairie voles also occur in grassy borders to forest ecotones, but do not invade continuous woodlands.

Natural History: Prairie voles are sociable and construct an extensive runway system beneath the grass canopy. These pathways can virtually honeycomb an entire field of grass. They also maintain an underground tunnel system. In good cover, prairie voles will build a globular nest above ground made of grass clippings. In short cover, they construct the nest just below the ground in a tunnel system. They feed primarily on grasses and forbs and cache the excess in underground chambers near the nest.

This vole often breeds year round, but peaks in reproduction occur in the spring and fall each year. Females average four to five litters per year of two to nine young each (the average is five). The gestation period is about 21 days, and the females can have a post-partum estrus and breed again while lactating. The first litter is weaned promptly upon arrival of the next litter at day 21. Young voles reach sexual maturity rapidly and first breed when four to six weeks of age. Laboratory research has revealed that female prairie voles exhibit induced ovulation, i.e., the presence of a fecund male induces receptivity to breeding in females and subsequent ovulation. This is a very efficient breeding strategy which insures successful reproduction.

Prairie voles, like other microtines, show marked fluctuations in population numbers related to changes in reproductive output and survival of individuals. The population density usually peaks every three to four years, when voles seem to be running everywhere one might look, followed by low densities for several years, when voles are very scarce.

Remarks: Prairie voles are active diurnally as well as nocturnally in their complex runway systems. It is not unusual for a previously set trap to capture a vole even as the collector proceeds along a runway system setting additional traps. Active runways are easily detected by the presence of green grass clippings and fresh droppings, distributed along the bare floor of each runway.

Voles sometimes do considerable damage to hay crops, alfalfa, and even row crops in early stages. Elimination of dense ground cover in or near the crop is normally the most efficient, nonpolluting way to control this vole. In small gardens, the use of snap traps or poisons is feasible, but no nonbiodegradable pesticides should be used, because it also poisons the environment and the biological food chain which are so vital to all of us.

Selected References:

Danielsen, B. J., and M. S. Gaines. 1987. Spatial patterns in two syntropic species of microtines (*Microtus ochrogaster* and *Synoptomys cooperi*). J. Mamm. 68: 313–22.

Davis, W. H., and P. J. Kalisz. 1992. Burrow systems of the prairie vole, *Microtus ochrogaster,* in central Kentucky. J. Mamm. 73: 582–86.

Jamison, E. W., Jr. 1947. Natural history of the prairie vole. Mus. Nat. Hist., Univ. Kansas Publ. 1 :125–51.

Mankin, P. C., and L. L. Getz. 1994. Burrow morphology as related to social organization of *Microtus ochrogaster.* J. Mamm. 75: 492–99.

Martin, E. P. 1956. A population study of the prairie vole (*Microtus ochrogaster*) in northeastern Kansas. Mus. Nat. Hist., Univ. Kansas Publ. 8: 301–416.

Stalling, D. T. 1990. Prairie Vole (*Microtus ochrogaster*). Mammalian Species, No. 356: pp. 1–9.

Wang, Z., and M. A. Novak. 1994. Parental care and litter development in primiparous and multiparous prairie voles (*Microtus ochrogaster*). J. Mamm. 75: 18–23.

Woodland Vole
Microtus pinetorum

Woodland vole, *Microtus pinetorum.* Roger W. Barbour

Identification: The woodland vole is also known as the pine vole. It is a small, blocky mouse having a short tail (barely longer than the hind foot), and a chestnut brown or cinnamon-brown upper pelage. The underparts are grayish, washed with buff or chestnut. The flanks are paler than the back, and the tail is not sharply bicolored. The ears are small, rounded, leaflike, and nearly concealed in the fur. The eyes are small and beady. The Florida and south Georgia form of the woodland vole is only about half the size of more northern races of this mouse and may be another species.

The grinding surfaces of the upper cheek teeth have a pattern of triangular folds surrounding dentine islands. The second upper molar has only four triangles of dentine surrounded by enamel, while the meadow vole has five or more.

Geographical Range: The woodland vole occurs over the entire southeastern region except for the southern half of Florida. In the United States, the geographical range occupies roughly the eastern half of the country.

Habitat: The woodland vole prefers to live underground in the humus and decomposing leaf litter of the hardwood forest floor. They also occur in fruit or-

Geographical range of the woodland vole in the Southeast.

chards and in fallow fields bordering forests. They sometimes occur in pine lands (where they were first trapped), thus the source of the common name, "pine vole." The species is quite fossorial, spending nearly all of its time in an extensive underground tunnel system, which the voles excavate. They often take over the old tunnels of moles as well. Their tunnel systems always have multiple entrances that are left open and not plugged (contrary to moles).

Natural History: Woodland voles forage both day and night in their underground burrow systems. They eat mainly roots, tubers, bulbs, sprouts, tender bark, and occasionally insects encountered underground. Food is cached in subterranean storage chambers as a hedge against periods of scarcity. The home range of a pine vole is small, covering only one-third to one-half acre. A globular nest of dead leaves and shredded bark is constructed just beneath the ground's surface, often at the base of a tree or stump or under a rotting log. Woodland voles are surprisingly social; small groups of adults or several females with litters have been recorded in a single nest.

The breeding season occurs year round, but is

somewhat reduced during the hot or cold months of the year. The gestation period averages 21 days (ranging from 20 to 24), and the mean litter size is three young (ranging from one to eight). Each adult female can produce five or six litters per year, and she normally comes into estrus and is impregnated again on the day the litter is born. The offspring are blind, naked, helpless, and pink at birth. When they are five or six days old, hair appears, and the eyes open around day 10. Young voles are weaned when about 20 days of age, just prior to the birth of another litter. They breed for the first time at two and one-half to three months of age.

In the wild few woodland voles survive more than two years and most die much sooner. Most medium- and small-sized predators take woodland voles, but the voles' semifossorial lifestyle helps protect them to some extent from heavy predation losses. Most voles are probably captured at the burrow entrances or during their short excursions above ground (only snakes and weasels tend to pursue the voles underground).

Remarks: This vole often causes damage to the root systems of trees and shrubs, including blueberries, apples, peaches, and various ornamentals. Tunneling severs small roots, and foraging even results in the girdling of larger roots or stems. They can damage row crops and gardens located near wooded areas. On the plus side, tunneling by voles aerates the soil and mixes organic matter to deeper levels where plant roots can benefit.

Woodland voles are best trapped by placing snap traps set at right angles across their underground burrows. By probing with the fingers, one can easily expose their tunnels, which are usually less than one inch below the surface.

Selected References:

Benton, A. H. 1955. Observations on the life history of the northern pine mouse. J. Mamm. 36: 52–62.

Goertz, J. W. 1971. An ecological study of *Microtus pinetorum* in Oklahoma. Amer. Midl. Nat. 86: 1–12.

Hamilton, W. J., Jr. 1938. Life history notes on the northern pine mouse. J. Mamm. 19: 163–70.

Paul, J. R. 1970. Observations on the ecology, populations, and reproductive biology of the pine vole, *Microtus pinetorum,* in North Carolina. Illinois State Mus. Repts. 20: 1–28.

Smolen, M. J. 1981. Woodland Vole *(Microtus pinetorum).* Mammalian Species, No. 147: pp. 1–8.

Southern Bog Lemming
Synaptomys cooperi

Southern bog lemming, *Synaptomys cooperi*. Roger W. Barbour

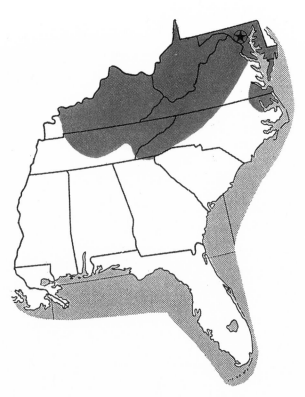

Geographical range of the southern bog lemming in the Southeast.

Identification: The southern bog lemming is a chunky, medium-sized vole with small eyes, a short tail that does not extend beyond the hind leg when extended, a blunt nose, and short ears that are the same length as the fur. The upper pelage is a grizzled brown with gray, black, and yellow-brown hairs sprinkled through it. The underside is grayish white, and the feet and tail are brownish black.

The skull has a short rostrum and there is a quadrate shape to the braincase. It is identified by the presence of a shallow, longitudinal groove on the front surface of each upper incisor (lateral edge).

Geographical Range: This is a boreal species that occurs throughout the Appalachian Mountain chain as far south as northeastern Georgia. In the northern portion of the southeastern region, it also occurs at lower elevation in the rolling foothills of Kentucky, West Virginia, Tennessee, Maryland, and Virginia. It occurs only rarely in the lowest elevation of the coastal plains in the northeastern parts of its range. In the United States, the geographical range occupies approximately the northeastern quadrant of the country as well as much of eastern Canada.

Habitat: This species lives in moist meadows, weedy fields, sphagnum bogs, moist woodlands, damp, grassy clearings in forests, and orchards.

Natural History: The bog lemming constructs extensive surface runway systems in dense ground cover and deposits little piles of green grass and sedge clippings, as well as green fecal pellets, along the runways. A subterranean globular nest, four to six inches in diameter, is constructed from leaves and grasses. Its diet consists of succulent sedges, various grasses, fungi, and an occasional berry. Bog lemmings forage both day and night, but show activity peaks in the early morning and late evening hours.

Breeding occurs from February to November. The gestation period averages 23 days, and litters range in size from one to eight (the average is three). There is usually a postpartum estrus, and three or four litters are produced annually. Babies are blind, naked, and pink. Hair appears on day six, and the eyes open around day 12. They wean at three and one-half weeks and become reproductively active when about two months old.

Remarks: In some areas, bog lemmings do damage to the roots and bark of fruit trees in orchards. Otherwise, they have very little economic impact. Bog lemmings rarely respond to baited traps, but they can be easily trapped by placing each snap trap at right angles across their surface runways. The lemmings are captured as they run across the trap treadle while traveling the runways.

Selected References:

Conner, P. F. 1959. The bog lemming, *Synaptomys cooperi*, in southern New Jersey. Mich. State Univ. Publ., Museum Series, 1: 161–248.

Danielson, B. J., and M. S. Gaines. 1987. Spatial patterns in two syntopic species of microtines (*Microtus ochrogaster* and *Synaptomys cooperi*). J. Mamm. 68: 313–22.

Linsdale, J. 1927. Notes on the life history of *Synaptomys*. J. Mamm. 8: 51–54.

Linzey, A. V. 1983. Southern Bog Lemming *(Synaptomys cooperi)*. Mammalian Species, No. 210: pp. 1–5.

Southern Red-backed Vole
Clethrionomys gapperi

Southern red-backed vole, *Clethrionomys gapperi*. American Society of Mammalogists

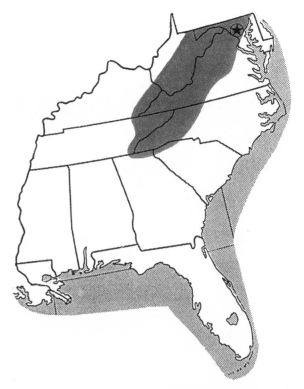

Geographical range of the southern red-backed vole in the Southeast.

Identification: This species is a medium-sized vole having small eyes, a fairly short tail (it is slightly longer than the hind foot), ears that extend just beyond the fur, and a prominent rusty red stripe down the back. The dorsal stripe grades to grayish brown on the flanks. The belly is gray or silver, and the feet are gray. The tail is distinctly bicolored, dark above and buff-white below. Juveniles are gray and lack the dorsal rusty red stripe found in adults.

The skull has a short rostrum, and there is a quadrate shape to the braincase. The upper incisors lack grooves, and the cheek tooth row is short compared to those of *Microtus* species.

Geographical Range: This is another boreal species found only in the higher mountains of the Appalachian chain in the Southeast, as far south as Georgia. In the United States, the geographical range extends across the northern third of the country, with southward extensions into the Appalachian Mountains and southward extensions into the Rocky Mountains to Arizona and New Mexico.

Habitat: The southern red-backed vole lives in montane coniferous forests (such as stands of hemlock) having moss-covered rocks, many logs, and cool, damp, shady slopes. These voles are also occasionally found in rock slides, on mountain balds, in montane deciduous forests, and in thickets of rhododendron. They tend to avoid dry and extremely open habitats.

Natural History: The southern red-backed vole is active year round and primarily nocturnal. They eat a wide variety of plant material and seldom take insects or other arthropods. The nest is globular (three to five inches in diameter) and made of leaves and mosses. It is constructed in a burrow chamber placed under a rock, root, log, or stump.

The breeding season extends from early spring to late autumn. The gestation period is short, averaging only 18 days (ranging from l7 to 19), and the litter size ranges from two to eight (averaging four). The babies are altricial with the eyes opening on day 12. Weaning occurs with the birth of the next litter, and there is normally a postpartum pregnancy in the nursing females. Two to four litters are produced by each female annually, and sexual maturity in the young voles occurs when they are about three months old.

The maximum longevity observed in the wild is about two years. In captivity, I have observed them living five years.

Remarks: Under favorable conditions in certain years, the woods seem to swarm with red-backed voles. This suggests they may have a regular population cycle which peaks every few years, a cycle similar to those of the meadow vole and certain lemmings. Red-backed voles are a staple food item for most woodland predators.

Sometimes these voles girdle small trees and shrubs during the winter months when food is in short supply. This girdling is mainly a problem in yard plantings in the mountains.

Selected References:

Manville, R. H. 1949. A study of small mammal populations in northern Michigan. Univ. Michigan, Misc. Publ. Mus. Zool. 73: 44–51.

Merritt, J. F. 1981. Southern Red-backed Vole *(Clethrionomys gapperi)*. Mammalian Species, No. 210: pp. 1–9.

Svihla, A. 1930. Breeding habits and young of the red-backed mouse, *Evotomys*. Papers Mich. Acad. Sci., Arts and Letters 11 :485–90.

Round-tailed Muskrat
Neofiber alleni

Round-tailed muskrat, *Neofiber alleni*. U.S. Fish & Wildlife Service

Identification: This aquatic vole is also called the Florida water rat. The body size is less than half that of the common muskrat, and its sparsely haired tail is round rather than laterally compressed. The dorsal fur is a shiny blackish brown or deep chocolate brown, and the underside is grayish white with a buff wash.

The ears are small, rounded, leaflike, and hidden in the fur. The tail is blackish brown and sparsely covered with bristlelike hairs.

The skull is much larger than those of other voles and the bog lemming. The first lower molar has five dentine triangles on the grinding surface, surrounded by enamel loops (rather than six in the common muskrat). The postorbital processes are prominent and project forward into the orbital area.

Geographical Range: The round-tailed muskrat occurs only in the southernmost portions of the southeastern region. In the United States, the entire geographical range includes only Florida and southern Georgia.

Habitat: This muskrat is an animal of the lower coastal plain. There it occurs in grassy freshwater marshes and some brackish coastal marshes. In freshwater it shows a strong affinity for strands of maiden cane, which is an emergent aquatic grass. It tends to be most abundant in those areas which are heavily choked with vegetation. In southern Florida, it is also prevalent in sugarcane fields.

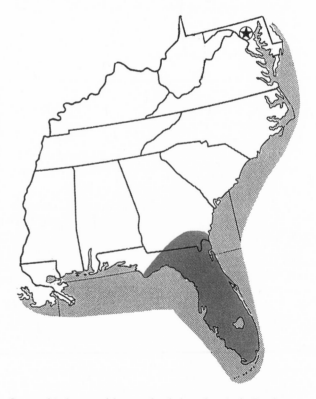

Geographical range of the round-tailed muskrat in the Southeast.

Natural History: Round-tailed muskrats construct a small, dome-shaped nest slightly above the water level composed of grasses and stems of water plants. It is anchored to emergent vegetation, such as maiden cane, willows, buttonbush, cattails, or small cypress trees, and is 10–24 inches across and 10–15 inches high. All nests have two escape openings, or "plunge holes," located in the bottom leading downward into the water. The muskrats leave or enter the nest quickly via these paired entrances, which are about three inches in diameter. Round-tailed muskrats normally build and maintain more than one house, usually two each (and ranging from one to four).

Breeding occurs throughout the year in round-tailed muskrats if food is available and weather conditions are favorable. Peaks in the number of pregnant females have been noted in April, August, and November. The gestation period is 26–29 days, and the average litter size is just over two young (the range is one to four). The babies are naked, blind, and helpless at birth. They are fully furred by one week of age, and the eyes open at about two weeks. Weaning takes place when they are about four weeks of age. Young muskrats become sexually mature when 90–100 days old. Adult females produce four or five litters per year.

Round-tailed muskrats also construct feeding platforms of matted vegetation throughout the marsh. Plant cuttings and fresh droppings are readily visible on active platforms.

If the marsh dries up, muskrats make runways through the marsh vegetation, much like other voles. They probably suffer much greater stress and mortality during periods of drought, but the colony can survive. The list of predators that are known to consume muskrats includes marsh hawks, owls, bobcats, raccoons, foxes, mink, snakes, and alligators.

Remarks: This muskrat periodically causes damage to sugarcane and rice crops in parts of its range. The best control practices involve habitat manipulation and elimination of cover for round-tailed muskrats in or near croplands.

The observed longevity in the wild seldom exceeds two years for the round-tailed muskrat. They have not been maintained for long periods of time in captivity, so the maximum potential life span is not known.

The spherical houses and feeding platforms built by these muskrats are also utilized by a variety of other marsh residents, including rice rats, cotton rats, snakes, frogs, wrens, rails, bitterns, herons, egrets, grebes, ducks, ants, spiders, insects, and many other arthropods. This species thus has an important ecological impact on its environment.

Selected References:

Birkenholz, D. E. 1963. A study of the life history and ecology of the round-tailed muskrat (*Neofiber alleni* True) in north-central Florida. Ecol. Monogr. 33: 255–80.

——. 1972. Round-tailed Muskrat (*Neofiber alleni*). Mammalian Species, No. 15: pp. 1–4.

Lifebore, L. W. 1982. Population dynamics of the round-tailed muskrat (*Neofiber alleni*) in Florida sugarcane. Ph.D. Diss., Univ. Fla., Gainesville. 204 pp.

Steffen, D. E., N. R. Holler, L. W. Lifebore, and P. F. Scanlon. 1981. Factors affecting the occurrence and distribution of Florida water rats in sugarcane fields. Proc. Amer. Soc. Sugar Cane Technology 9: 27–32.

Muskrat
Ondatra zibethicus

Muskrat, *Ondatra zibethicus.* Unknown

Identification: This large water vole is highly adapted for an aquatic mode of life. It is about three times the size of the round-tailed muskrat and possesses a long, flat, laterally compressed tail that is largely devoid of hair except for a fringe along the ventral edge. The dorsal fur is shiny chestnut brown or blackish brown, and the underside ranges from pale gray to cinnamon, often with a silvery cast. The ears are small, rounded, leaflike, and hidden in the fur. The tail is black or blackish brown.

The skull is approximately three times larger than that of the round-tailed muskrat and almost exactly the same shape. Also, the first lower molar has six dentine triangles surrounded by enamel loops on the grinding surface (there are five in the round-tailed muskrat). The postorbital process is prominent and extends forward into the orbital area.

Geographical range of the muskrat in the Southeast.

Geographical Range: This species occurs across the northwestern two-thirds of the Southeast. In the United States, it has been recorded in every state except Florida.

Habitat: The muskrat lives in a wide variety of aquatic habitats, including ponds, lakes, freshwater marshes, swamps, brackish coastal marshes, and rivers.

Natural History: Muskrats living in marsh situations usually build bulky houses (or lodges) composed of aquatic vegetation such as cattails, sedges, bulrushes, etc., which may reach eight feet in diameter and four feet high. The lodge is a heaping conical pile of stems, leaves, and roots of aquatic plants that sits on the bottom of a marsh or pond and contains a single nest chamber or occasionally two. The walls of the lodge are at least one foot thick and sometimes cemented with mud. This insulation keeps the nest chamber relatively cool in the summer and warm in the winter. From one to several tunnels exit the nest cavity and lead into the water. If the marsh is shallow, muskrats may deepen the bottom around the lodge to form a series of canals leading to deeper water. They also construct numerous feeding platforms in the general vicinity of the house.

Muskrats that live in streams, rivers, and some ponds and lakes seldom build homes in the open, but instead live in bank dens having submerged entrances. The burrows they dig vary in length from 10 to 50 feet and have a diameter of five to eight inches. A nest chamber is located well above the high water level at the terminal end of the burrow. A saucer-shaped nest of grasses lines this cavity.

Muskrats are more active nocturnally, but they can also be frequently seen foraging during the daytime. They eat mainly plant materials supplemented by an occasional snail, crustacean, clam, or minnow.

The breeding season extends over most of the year except in areas of cold winter weather. Muskrats are very prolific, producing two to five litters annually of two to ten young each (the average is six). The gestation period ranges from 25 to 30 days and averages 28. The shorter gestation periods occur when the female is not yet nursing a litter when she becomes pregnant. Like most other members of the vole family, females experience a postpartum heat or estrus period. Baby muskrats are altricial, but grow rapidly, having hair in about one week, the eyes are open at two weeks, and they are weaned at four weeks of age. They do not breed until they are about one year old.

Mortality is quite high in muskrats, and the maximum life span recorded in the wild is about five years. In captivity they have lived eight years. Many different predators take muskrats, but the major carnivore largely dependent upon them is the mink.

Muskrats can rapidly swim long distances underwater without breathing. The maximum distance they can swim without coming up for air is about 180 to 200 feet. They accomplish this feat by incurring considerable oxygen debt and buildup of lactic acid (a metabolic waste product) in the muscles and bloodstream. This ability is called the "diving-mammal reflex," which is common to nearly all diving species. After the muskrat surfaces, the oxygen debt which built up is cleared out and the lactic acid level drops back to normal.

Remarks: Muskrats are considered the number-one furbearing mammal in North America today. Many youths have made their first real money by running a trap line for them during the winter months. Millions of muskrats are harvested and sold each year in Canada and the United States for the fur trade.

On the negative side, muskrats will readily feed on field crops and gardens which are located adjacent to their aquatic habitats. They can often be discouraged by mowing or clearing a cover-free zone between the crop and the water. They can also be controlled by trapping if the need arises.

In Louisiana, the introduction and spread of the nutria has led to direct ecological competition between the native muskrat and the exotic rodent from South America. The much larger and more competitive nutria has largely replaced the muskrat in vast areas of coastal marshland in Louisiana. This trend could continue in other areas of the South.

The common name muskrat is based on the presence of two preputial, or "musk," glands located under the skin on either side of the penis in males. These glands enlarge considerably during the reproductive season and produce a musky secretion.

Selected References:

Erickson, H. R. 1966. Muskrat burrowing damage and control procedures in New York, Pennsylvania, and Maryland. N.Y. Fish and Game Jour. 13: 176–87.

Errington, P. L. 1963 *Muskrat Populations.* Iowa State Univ. Press, Ames, Iowa. 665 pp.

———. 1978. *Muskrats and Marsh Management.* Univ. of Nebr. Press, Lincoln, Nebr. 183 pp.

Svihla, A. and R. D. Svihla. 1931. The Louisiana muskrat. J. Mamm. 12: 12–28.

Shanks, C. E., and G. C. Arthur. 1952. Muskrat movements and population dynamics in Missouri farm ponds and streams. J. Wildl. Mgmt. 16: 138–48.

Willner, G. R., G. A. Feldhamer, E. E. Zucker, and J. A. Christain. 1980. Muskrat. Mammalian Species, No. 141: pp. 1–8.

Norway Rat
Rattus norvegicus

Norway rat, *Rattus norvegicus.* American Society of Mammalogists

Identification: The Norway rat, also known as the "wharf rat," is an introduced rodent having a large, robust body and a long, bare, scaly tail whose length is slightly shorter than or equal to the head and body combined. The upper side is a grizzled grayish brown, and the underparts vary from pale gray to grayish brown. The ears are large, rounded, leaflike, and naked; the nose is noticeably long and pointed.

The skull is difficult to separate from those of the black rat and eastern woodrat and should be examined by a mammalogist for positive identification.

Geographical Range: Norway rats have been recorded throughout the entire Southeast in both urban and rural habitats. It was first introduced into the United States from Europe around 1775. In the United States, it now has a nationwide geographical range.

Habitat: The Norway rat is about as widespread and abundant as its smaller cousin, the black rat. Populations are found on farms, at shipping wharves, in warehouses, in slums, in grain storage areas, in feed stores, factories, and many other buildings where there is cover and food.

Geographical range of the Norway rat in the Southeast.

Natural History: Norway rats are sedentary animals that remain near a food source and rarely have home ranges greater than 200 feet in diameter. However, they readily disperse to a new location if food and cover are no longer available.

Norway rats like to make tunnels in the ground where conditions are suitable. The burrow systems usually have several entrances and a labyrinth of interconnecting tunnels, which contain one or more nest chambers. They commonly live in colonies containing 10–20 individuals. A dominance hierarchy is maintained within the colony, with the largest, most aggressive male usually at the top of the pecking order.

Norway rats are probably the most omnivorous of all mammals, feeding on any vegetable or animal source available. They breed all year round, and the gestation period is 22 days. The litter size averages nine young and ranges from two to sixteen. Baby rats are pink, blind, naked, and helpless at birth. The eyes open at 14 days, and the young are weaned at about 21 days of age, just prior to the birth of the next litter. Norway rats can breed when they are as young as three months of age. Most females produce six to eight litters per year, but in captivity under laboratory conditions they have produced as many as 14 litters. Thus, this species has one of the highest fecundity rates of any mammal on earth.

Remarks: Because of their large body size and aggressive nature, Norway rats are even more destructive to human business and agricultural activities than the ubiquitous roof (or black) rat. They often cause problems in both urban and rural areas of the South. They are especially destructive to food storage warehouses, shipping docks, and wharf storage areas, and to animal feed-mixing operations. Control is best achieved by exterminating them from those areas which have food and cover. Poison baits can also be used successfully in most situations.

This species is the source of the famous lab rat or white rat, which is widely used in medical and biological research. Lab rats are highly inbred strains of the Norway rat (most of them are true pink-eyed albinos) that have been maintained and propagated in captivity for decades. White rats are extremely docile and easy to handle compared to normal field-type Norway rats, which are noticeably aggressive, wild, and high strung. In its laboratory form, the Norway rat is extremely beneficial to mankind as an all-purpose experimental animal.

Selected References:

Calhoun, J. B. 1966. The ecology and sociology of the Norway rat. U.S. Dept. Health, Education, and Welfare, Public Health Service. 288 pp.

Davis, D. E. 1953. the characteristics of rat populations. Quart. Review of Biology 28: 373–401.

Davis, D. E., J. T. Emlen, Jr., and A. W. Stokes. 1948. Studies on home range in the brown rat. J. Mamm. 29: 207–25.

Perry, J. S. 1944. The reproduction of the wild brown rat (*Rattus norvegicus*). Proc. Zool. Soc., London, 115: 19–46.

Pisano, R. G., and T. I. Storer. 1948. Burrows and feeding of the Norway rat. J. Mamm. 29: 374–83.

Silver, J. 1927. The introduction and spread of house rats in the United States. J. Mamm. 8: 58–59.

Roof Rat
Rattus rattus

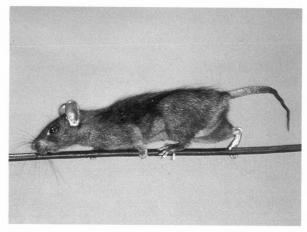

Roof rat, *Rattus rattus.* American Society of Mammalogists

Identification: Although the roof rat is also commonly called the black rat, this introduced rat is usually not black, but grayish brown on the upper side (the black form is one of its rarer color phases in the Southeast). This species is smaller then the Norway rat, but the long, bare, scaly tail is longer than the Norway rat's. The tail's length is much longer than the head and body combined. The underparts are variable in color, but usually slate gray, creamy, or white. The ears are large, rounded, naked, and leaflike; and the nose is extremely long and pointed.

The skull is difficult to distinguish from those of the Norway rat and the eastern woodrat, and it should be examined by a mammalogist for positive identification.

Geographical Range: The roof rat occurs throughout the entire southeastern region. It was first brought to

Geographical range of the roof rat in the Southeast.

the United States accidentally on the ships of early European explorers and colonists. It has been taken nationwide in association with humans, but seems to thrive best in coastal areas and especially throughout the southern states.

Habitat: This rat is widely associated with the buildings of humans or with our garbage dumps, granaries, warehouses, wharves, factories, etc. These rats are very agile climbers, quite at home in the roofs, attics, and rafters of any house or building. The name "roof rat" is based on their tendency to nest in the attics of buildings. Despite its common association with humans, a sizable portion of the roof rat population lives in feral situations completely separate from man. These rats build arboreal leaf nests in all types of dense forest habitats, including floodplain forests, oak hammocks, oak scrub, and coastal strand vegetation. They are agile climbers and forage throughout the canopy as well as on the ground.

Natural History: Roof rats, with their longer tails and smaller body size, are much better climbers than Norway rats. Sometimes both species will coexist in the same building, with the bigger, more aggressive Norway rats living on the ground floor and the slim, agile roof rats living in the rafters, attics, and upper floors. The two species are behaviorally incompatible; likewise, they never hybridize.

Roof rats prefer vegetative food but consume a wide range of animal material as well. In poultry houses they commonly eat eggs and kill young chicks.

This rat breeds year round and is almost as prolific as the Norway rat. The gestation period is 21 days, and the average litter size is six young (but ranges from two to twelve). The babies are pink, blind, naked, and helpless. The eyes open when they are about 14 days old, and they are weaned at three weeks. Adult females have a postpartum estrus and immediately become pregnant again. Young roof rats become sexually active when three to four months old. Females could potentially produce as many as 14 litters per year, but the average is six to eight litters, depending on the food supply.

Remarks: As already noted black rats are destructive to agricultural activities and cause a great deal of damage to homes and businesses. Their habit of gnawing off the insulation of electrical wires in the attics and walls of older buildings can be a serious fire hazard. Roof rats, like Norway rats, carry fleas which sometimes spread diseases such as typhus, bubonic plague, spotted fever, leptospirosis, and sylvatic plague.

The best way to control roof rats is to exclude them from the premises with good rat-proof barriers and to eliminate or protect all potential food sources. If these control measures are not successful, then trapping and the use of poison baits is the main recourse. Poisons, however, always carry a risk to children, pets, poultry, and livestock. Also, sick rats often crawl into some inaccessible location before they die, and the decomposition of their bodies can create strong odors for some time.

Selected References:
Davis, D. E. 1947. Notes on commensal rats in Lavaca County, Texas. J. Mamm. 28: 241–44.
———. 1953. The characteristics of rat populations. Quart. Rev. of Biol. 28: 373–401.
Spencer, H. J., and D. E. Davis. 1950. Movement and survival of rats in Hawaii. J. Mamm. 31: 154–57.
Storer, T. I. 1948. Control of rats and mice. Agr. Extension Service, Univ. Calif., Circular 142. 37 pp.
Worth, C. B. 1950. Field and laboratory observations on roof rats, *Rattus rattus* (Linnaeus) in Florida. J. Mamm. 31: 293–304.

House Mouse
Mus musculus

House mouse, *Mus musculus*. James Parnell

Identification: The house mouse is a small rodent with a long, scaly tail that is only slightly shorter than the length of the head and body combined. The upper pelage is grayish brown or olive-brown, and the underparts are ashy gray, buff-gray, or whitish. The ears are large, naked, and leaflike. The snout is elongated and pointed, and the eyes are small.

The skull is identified by small size and by the presence of a notch in the cutting surface of the upper incisors, readily visible from the side. There is no longitudinal groove on the front border of the upper incisors as present in the eastern harvest mouse.

Geographical Range: The house mouse is an introduced species found living throughout the entire Southeast. It occurs throughout the entire United States and southern Canada. In early historic times it was restricted to Europe and Asia, but it was brought to the New World by the ships of the early explorers.

Habitat: This is a cosmopolitan species which occurs in virtually all habitats in association with humans. In addition to dwellings, house mice live in granaries, factories, warehouses, restaurants, offices, supermarkets, farm buildings, garbage dumps, etc. House mice can also live in more natural habitats such as abandoned fields, fencerows, grain fields, beach dunes, weedy roadsides, pastures, etc.

Natural History: House mice tend to be social and form colonies both in buildings and in the wild. They will consume almost anything edible, but prefer grain and vegetable products. They also eat a wide variety of animal foods, when available.

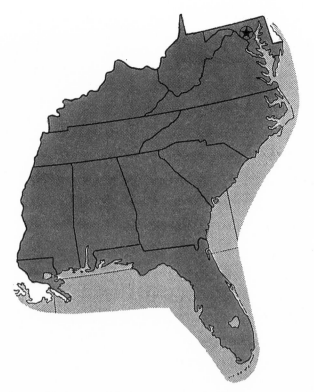

Geographical range of the house mouse in the Southeast.

House mice are extremely prolific and breed the year round. The gestation period is only 19–21 days, and the litter size varies from two to twelve, averaging about six. There is a postpartum estrus in adult females, and they could theoretically produce as many as 14 litters per year, but five to ten is the normal number. If all these young survived and bred, we would be hip-deep in house mice in just a few months. Fortunately most do not reach maturity. The babies are born naked, blind, and helpless. They are fully furred when 10 days old, and their eyes open at about 14 days of age. Young house mice wean at 20 days, and become sexually mature in four to six weeks.

Remarks: House mice are obnoxious and destructive pests in homes, where they gnaw holes in walls and woodwork, consume and contaminate food, and chew up clothing and books for nest material. On farms and in agricultural feed stores, they are particularly destructive to stored grain, seeds, fruits, and vegetables. Control is achieved either by trapping or poison baits or by establishing barriers which the house mice are not able to penetrate.

The highly inbred albino form of the house mouse is one of the world's basic laboratory animals (along with the Norway rat) for medical and scientific research. White mice and other colored phases of the house mouse are commonly sold as pets or as food for pet snakes, lizards, hawks, owls, and a variety of other small to medium-sized carnivores. All house mice have strong scent glands (called musk glands) located near the anus. If their cages and nest material are not kept quite clean, they develop a characteristic pungent odor because of the powerful scent glands and the accumulation of droppings and urine.

Longevity of house mice in feral populations is rarely greater than one year, but in the laboratory they often live four or five years. In the wild, house mice are preyed upon by every kind of bird, reptile, or mammal that consumes rodents.

Selected References:

Brown, L. N. 1965. Selection in population of house mice containing mutant individuals. J. Mamm. 46: 461–65.

Brown, R. Z. 1953. Social behavior, reproduction, and population changes in the house mouse (*Mus musculus*). Ecol. Monogr. 23: 17–40.

Catlett, R. H., and H. S. Shellhammer. 1962. A comparison of behavioral and biological characteristics of house mice and harvest mice. J. Mamm. 43: 133–44.

DeLong, K. T. 1967. Population ecology of feral house mice. Ecology 48: 611–34.

Smith, W. W. 1954. Reproduction in the house mouse, *Mus musculus* L. in Mississippi. J. Mamm. 35: 509–15.

Wooten, M. C., and M. H. Smith. 1986. Fluctuating asymmetry and genetic variability in a natural population of *Mus musculus*. J. Mamm. 67: 725–32.

Meadow Jumping Mouse
Zapus hudsonius

Meadow jumping mouse, *Zapus hudsonius*. Roger W. Barbour

Identification: The meadow jumping mouse has enlarged hind legs and feet and relatively short, weak front legs. The dorsal pelage is dark yellowish orange with a distinctly darker mid-dorsal stripe of blackish brown which runs down the back. The belly and feet are white. The tail is much longer than the rest of the body, is sparsely haired (brownish above and paler below), and tufted with dark hair at the end.

The skull is small with deep longitudinal grooves present on the front of each upper incisor and four upper cheek teeth on each side.

Geographical Range: This species has been taken sparingly over the northern half of the southeastern region in the Appalachian Plateau and mountain regions. The range in the United States covers the northern two-thirds of the country east of the Rocky Mountains.

Habitat: Meadow jumping mice are associated with wet meadows and fields with streams running through them. They also occasionally occur in woodlands having a lush carpet of grasses, sedges, and herbs.

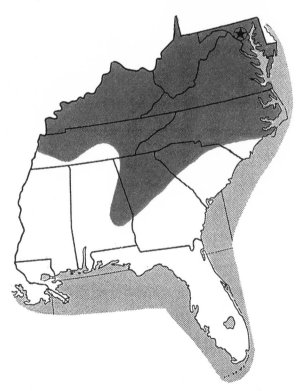

Geographical range of the meadow jumping mouse in the Southeast.

Natural History: This species is primarily nocturnal, but on cloudy days they occasionally venture forth to forage. They eat sedges, grasses, seeds, roots, nuts, insects, berries, fungi, and other invertebrates.

Meadow jumping mice are deep hibernators and are active only from spring to late autumn. They put on a heavy layer of subcutaneous fat (they look like furry butterballs), enter torpor in November, and sleep through the winter months in a well-insulated underground nest chamber. Their nests are usually two or three feet underground, composed of dried grass and leaves, and shaped like a sphere. A dormant jumping mouse is always rolled up in a tight ball with the long tail and hind legs curled up around the torso. Summer nests are usually built on the surface of the ground in thick ground cover or in hollow logs and stumps.

Hibernating meadow jumping mice have very low heart rates, breathing rates, and body temperatures (approximately that of the environment). They arouse from torpor once every 30–40 days during the long winter to defecate and urinate. In the spring, the males generally emerge from hibernation in April about one week before the females. Most of the stored fat has been utilized for energy by the time they emerge in the spring.

Breeding begins right after the females emerge from hibernation, and the gestation period is only 18–21 days. They usually produce two litters of three to eight young each year; the average litter size is five. Newborn meadow jumping mice are naked, blind, and helpless. The hair erupts in nine days, the eyes open in two weeks, and they wean when about three weeks old. There is no postpartum pregnancy in females. The second litter is born in late summer or early fall.

The predators of the meadow jumping mouse forage in grassy environments or along small streams and include mink, hawks, owls, skunks, weasels, raccoons, foxes, bobcats, and domestic cats.

Remarks: Meadow jumping mice make very interesting, unusual, and attractive pets. The long hibernation period makes them easy to care for, and they are clean and not odorous like many mice. However, when excited they have been observed to jump as high as seven or eight feet in a single hop.

There is no economic impact exerted by this species. They appear to be fairly rare in most areas. The longevity of meadow jumping mouse in the wild is apparently somewhat longer than for most rodents, probably due to its long hibernation. They have lived five to six years in captivity.

Selected References:

Blair, W. F. 1940. Home ranges and populations of the jumping mouse. Amer. Midl. Nat. 23: 244–50.

Brown, L. N., and R. B. McMillan. 1964. Meadow jumping mouse in southern Missouri. J. Mamm. 45: 150–51.

Hamilton, W. J., Jr. 1935. Habits of jumping mice. Amer. Midl. Nat. 16: 187–200.

Quimby, D. C. 1951. The life history and ecology of the jumping mouse, *Zapus hudsonius*. Ecol. Monogr. 21: 61–95.

Whitaker, J. O., Jr. 1963. A study of the meadow jumping mouse, *Zapus hudsonius* (Zimmerman) in central New York. Ecol. Monogr. 33: 215–54.

———. 1972. Meadow Jumping Mouse (*Zapus hudsonius*). Mammalian Species, No. 11, pp. 1–7.

Woodland Jumping Mouse
Napaeozapus insignis

Woodland jumping mouse, *Napaeozapus insignis*. Roger W. Barbour

Identification: The woodland jumping mouse has enlarged hind legs and feet and relatively short, weak front feet. Jumping mice have a tripedal, hopping type of locomotion, balancing on the two large hind feet and the long tail. The dorsal pelage is burnt orange with a distinctly darker median stripe of blackish brown running down the back. The belly and feet are white. The tail is much longer than the rest of the body, is sparsely haired (brownish above and pale below), and tufted with varying amounts of white hair at the tip.

The skull is small with deep longitudinal grooves present on the front of each upper incisor, and only three upper cheek teeth on each side.

Geographical Range: In the Southeast, this attractive species occurs along the Appalachian Mountain chain at moderate to high elevations. In the United States, the geographical range includes the northeastern states, Great Lakes region, southward in the Appalachian Mountains to northern Georgia.

Geographical range of the woodland jumping mouse in the Southeast.

Habitat: Woodland jumping mice occur in cool, damp forests located in the mountains. They are most common among the moss-covered rocks bordering cascading brooks or seeps in the hemlock-hardwood forest.

Natural History: These mice are most active at night, but they also forage during the daytime on cloudy days. Fully one-third of the diet consists of subterranean fungi, in addition to seeds, berries, green plant parts, and a few insects, worms, or other invertebrates. It is not clear how or where the woodland jumping mouse locates the subterranean fungi, but it probably finds the fungi by smell.

Woodland jumping mice are very long hibernators, being active only about half the year (from spring to autumn). By late summer, a heavy layer of subcutaneous fat accumulates on them, and these jumping mice are extremely plump by early fall. They enter torpor in October and hibernate until April or May, depending on the elevation and severity of the winter. Nests are well-insulated, globular structures (made of mosses, leaves, and grasses) placed in an underground chamber, under a fallen log, at the base of a hollow stump, or in a brush pile.

The characteristics of hibernation in the woodland jumping mouse are almost identical to those cited for the meadow jumping mouse. Males emerge from hibernation about a week before females in the spring. Breeding takes place very shortly after the females emerge from hibernation. The gestation period ranges from 20 to 23 days, and two to seven young (the average is five) are born in late May or early June. Normally only a single litter is produced annually, but occasionally a female will give birth to a second litter in August. It is difficult for the offspring of the second litter to store enough fat to carry them successfully through the six months of hibernation: death caused by depletion of fat reserves in juvenile jumping mice is known to be an important mortality factor. One study found that 75 percent of juveniles died over the winter from all causes.

Newborn woodland jumping mice are altricial. By the time they are two weeks old, the juvenile coat is fully developed, but the eyes do not open until they are over three weeks old. Weaning occurs when the juveniles are five weeks old. They do not become sexually active until the following year.

Remarks: Woodland jumping mice have no economic impact worthy of consideration. They make very interesting, unusual, and attractive pets compared to other kinds of mice. Due to their scent glands, jumping mice emit sort of a pleasant nutty smell in contrast to the pungent musk of house mice.

The hopping type of locomotion exhibited by the jumping mice is called "saltatorial locomotion." It is the same type of hopping gait shown by kangaroos, wallabies, gerbils, and kangaroo rats.

Selected References:

Brower, J. E., and T. J. Cade. 1966. Ecology and physiology of *Napaeozapus insignis* (Miller) and other woodland mice. Ecology 47: 46–63.

Sheldon, C. 1938. Vermont jumping mice of the genus *Napaeozapus.* J. Mamm. 19:444–53.

Whitaker, J. O., Jr., and R. E. Wrigley. 1972. Woodland Jumping Mouse *(Napaeozapus insignis).* Mammalian Species, No. 14: pp. 1–6.

Wrigley, R. E. 1972. Systematics and biology of the woodland jumping mouse, *(Napaeozapus insignis).* Illinois Biol. Monogr., U. Ill. Press, Urbana, Ill. 47: 59–113.

Nutria
Myocaster coypu

Nutria, *Myocaster coypu*. Larry Brown

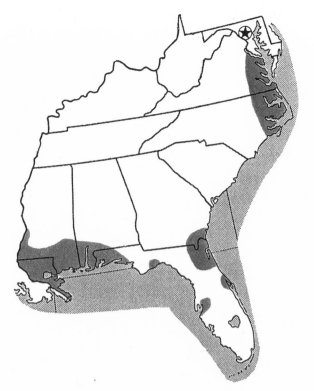

Geographical range of the nutria in the Southeast.

Identification: The nutria, or "coypu," is a giant introduced aquatic rat having a long, round, scaly tail and large, orange-edged front teeth. It is somewhat smaller than the beaver, and the upper parts are glossy dark amber or blackish brown. The belly is a slightly paler gray-brown, and the ears are short, rounded, and almost completely buried in the fur.

The skull is quite large and identified by an immense opening (the infraorbital foramen) located at the anterior junction of the cheekbone with the snout. The opening is large enough to admit the end of an observer's little finger (the beaver skull lacks this large opening).

Geographical Range: The nutria has been released and become established in a number of scattered locations throughout the southeastern states. In the United States, there are feral populations established in many southern, eastern, and western states. The nutria is native to the southern third of South America and was introduced to the United States for its fur.

Habitat: Nutria live in freshwater or slightly brackish marshes, ponds, canals, and lakes. They are adaptable to many aquatic environments which have emergent, floating, or submergent vegetation.

Natural History: Nutria feed on a wide variety of aquatic plants, including some that are likewise introduced and troublesome, like water hyacinth, hydrilla, and milfoil. Unfortunately, most of these aquatic plants grow faster than nutria can consume them. Nutria are active both day and night, but their primary foraging takes place during the nocturnal hours. They do not consume animal food and are strict vegetarians.

Nutria sometimes construct feeding and resting platforms composed of matted and interwoven vegetation. They live in sizable tunnels dug into banks or levees and construct crude nests made of plant cuttings. Often there are two or more entrances to each burrow system, one frequently below water level and one or more escape entrances above.

Breeding occurs in all months of the year in the Southeast. The gestation period is about 130 days (ranging from 127 to 132 days), and the litter size averages six offspring (ranging from two to twelve). Baby nutria are precocial, and they are born completely furred and with the eyes open. Following birth of a litter, the female usually comes into estrus and is bred again. Young nutria can swim shortly after birth, and they are sometimes nursed while in the water. This is possible because the mother's nipples are located along the sides rather than being placed ventrally. Nutria wean when they are six to eight weeks old. Sexual maturity can occur before nutria reach their adult size. This phenomenon is called "juvenile breeding" and may take place when nutria are as young as four months old. Most nutria, however, do not breed until they are eight months of age.

Alligators are the nutria's chief predator in the Deep South, and they take a heavy toll. Young nutria are also killed by owls, hawks, gars, snakes, coyotes, foxes, dogs, and bobcats, but the adults are too large to be vulnerable to most of these predators.

Remarks: Nutria have at times been extolled as a valuable fur animal, but actually the pelt is not of great quality, and only the belly fur is usable because the dorsal hair is so coarse. Breeding stock has often been sold to would-be nutria farmers by unscrupulous operators for high prices. When such breeding operations fail, the nutria have usually been released into the wild. Many introductions of nutria into new areas of the United States have resulted from failed attempts at nutria farming. This species is widely established in the Louisiana marshlands, where they have largely out-competed and replaced the native muskrat, which is the more valuable fur animal. Nutria also do considerable damage to dikes and levees by tunneling into them.

A few years ago I studied a population of nutria living on a large dairy farm in Hillsborough County, Florida, and discovered that they often fed on the commercial dairy feed intended for the cows. The nutria were also able to thrive and breed in the dairy ponds and canals which contained water that was highly polluted with fecal material and urine from the cattle feedlots and milking areas.

Selected References:

Bailey, J. W., and G. A. Heidt. 1978. Range and status of the nutria, *Myocaster coypu,* in Arkansas. Proc. Ark. Acad. Sci. 32: 25–27.

Brown, L. N. 1975. Ecological relationships and breeding biology of the nutria in the Tampa, Florida, area. J. Mamm. 56: 928–30.

Evans, J. 1970. About nutria and their control. Bur. Sports Fish and Wildl., Denver, Col., Resource Publ. 86. 65 pp.

Newsom, R. M. 1966. Reproduction of the feral coypu (*Myocaster coypu*). Zool. Soc. Lond. Symp. 15: 323–44.

Warkinton, M. J. 1968. Observations on the behavior and ecology of the nutria in Louisiana. Tulane Studies in Zool. and Bot. 15: 10–17.

Woods, C. A., L. Contreras, G. Willner-Chapman, and H. P. Whidden. 1992. Coypu (*Myocaster coypu*). Mammalian Species, No. 398: pp. 1–8.

Porcupine
Erethizon dorsatum

Porcupine, *Erethizon dorsatum.* Larry Brown

Identification: This large, sluggish, spiny rodent is about the size of a beaver. The body is chunky and covered with yellowish, black-tipped quills (modified hairs) on the dorsal and lateral sides. The pelage itself is brownish black with some long hairs tipped in white. The tail is long, flexible, and covered with the needle-like quills that dislodge readily into the victim when it is struck with force. The belly and muzzle are covered with stiff black hairs and quills are lacking.

The skull is large and rugged and contains a pair of large, beaverlike incisors, which are orange on the anterior surface. A large-diameter infraorbital foramen pierces the anterior base of each zygomatic arch (cheekbone).

Geographical Range: Porcupines have been collected in eastern West Virginia and southeastern Tennessee in the Appalachian Mountain chain. They are quite rare in the southeastern mountains. Porcupines also range northward through New England, across all of Canada and much of Alaska, and throughout the western mountains of the United States.

Habitat: Porcupines lives in both deciduous and coniferous forests, where they eat the cambium layer of the inner bark of many species of trees. Much of their time is spent foraging or resting in the treetops.

Natural History: On the ground, porcupines appear slow and clumsy, but they are well protected by a sheet of sharp quills. When approached, the porcupine shows little fear, but keeps its back turned toward the offender and shakes the massive, pin-cushion tail as a

Geographical range of the porcupine in the Southeast.

warning. Quills are never thrown, but they detach easily when touched. The needlelike tip of each quill is covered with small, backward-projecting scales, which prevent the free withdrawal of the quill from flesh. The quills actually work deeper into the flesh, not out, as a would-be attacker tries to dislodge them. A porcupine is covered by about 30,000 quills.

Except for the breeding season and during winter denning, porcupines are solitary and antisocial. Breeding occurs in the fall and early winter, and the gestation period is long, lasting from 205 to 216 days. Usually only one precocial baby (rarely two) is born from March to early June. Young porcupines weigh about one pound at birth (twice the weight of a newborn black bear) and are fully furred (the juvenile fur is black) with their eyes open. The quills are soft at birth but harden quickly in about one hour.

Porcupines are surprisingly sedentary for their large body size. A study of tagged individuals revealed that they ranged over only about 35 acres of habitat in a 30-day period. They are largely active at night but occasionally forage in the daytime. Population densities have been measured at 20–28 porcupines per square mile in Maine in good habitat. During the summer months, porcupines eat a wide variety of green leaves from trees, shrubs, and forbs. In the winter, they rely on the deeper layers of bark, twigs, and on buds of trees.

Remarks: Porcupines have lived up to nine or ten years in captivity, but the average life span in the wild is only about five years. Although the porcupine's defenses are formidable, several carnivores are able to prey upon them regularly. Examples include the fisher, wolverine, cougar, great horned owl, and bobcat.

Porcupines are greatly attracted to the minerals found in shed antlers and bones, which they often chew down to amorphous shapes. They are also attracted to roads where salt has been sprinkled to melt snow, which often leads to road kills. Porcupines also sometimes chew on cottages, sheds, and tool handles in search of salt and other minerals.

During very cold and stormy weather, porcupines will enter rock crevices, caves, and other underground cavities to den up until weather conditions improve.

Porcupines often cause serious forestry damage by debarking trees. In Maine, for example, porcupines have been reported to kill 10–15 percent of planted conifer and broadleafs annually. Girdling of the bark in young stands of trees with a DBH (diameter at breast height) of less than six inches appears to cause the greatest damage. Control techniques usually involve reducing the porcupine population by shooting, trapping, or poisoning.

Selected References:

Costello, D. F. 1966 *The World of the Porcupine.* J. B. Lippincott Co., Philadelphia, Pa. 157 pp.

Dodge, W. E. 1982. Porcupine. In *Wild Mammals of North America.* Johns Hopkins Univ. Press, Baltimore, Md., pp. 355–66.

Strathers, P. H. 1928. Breeding habits of the Canadian porcupine *(Erethizon dorsatum).* J. Mamm. 9: 300–308.

Woods, C. A. 1973. Porcupine *(Erethizon dorsatum).* Mammalian Species, No. 29: pp. 1–6.

Order Carnivora
Flesh-Eating Mammals

The flesh-eating mammals, known as carnivores, are mainly specialized for killing other animals and feeding on their bodies. Their adaptations include large conical canine teeth located near the front corners of the mouth, which are excellent at penetrating and holding the prey. Many carnivores also have specialized flesh-cutting and bone-shearing teeth (called carnassials) located toward the back of the jaw. The carnassials are bladelike, and they function much like scissors. When they slide by one another, they have tremendous shearing power. The carnassial teeth consist of the last upper premolar and the first lower molar. The jaw muscles of carnivores are powerful, and jaw movement is in the vertical plane. They also tend to have a keen sense of smell and/or sight, which enhance their ability to locate and catch prey.

Carnivores possess a highly developed brain, and the group exhibits a fairly high order of intelligence. The dogs and cats are specialized to walk up on their toes (called digitigrade locomotion), while most other carnivores walk on the soles of their feet (called plantigrade locomotion). Carnivores tend to travel with a running gait, which is called "cursorial locomotion." Some carnivores (bears and raccoons for example) are not exclusively flesh eaters but consume much vegetable matter as well. A few live on insects (the aardwolves of Africa), and others are scavengers (the hyenas of Africa). All carnivores have a well-developed "penis bone" in the males.

Carnivores have a worldwide distribution except for some of the oceanic islands. There are sixteen species of carnivores living in the wild in the Southeast. One extirpated species, the red wolf, is in a captive breeding program.

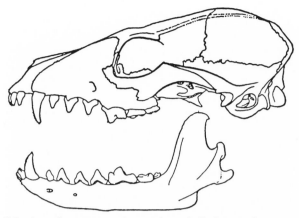

Side view of a representative carnivore skull, the gray fox (*Urocyon cinereoargenteus*). Note the long, sharp canine teeth.

Black Bear
Ursus americanus

Black bear, *Ursus americanus*. Florida Game & Fresh-Water Fish Commission

Identification: The black bear is the largest terrestrial carnivore which lives in the Southeast. It is a heavily built, bulky carnivore with long, dense, and glossy black hair over the entire body. The tail is very short and inconspicuous, but well haired. The face is rather blunt and broad, the eyes are small, and the nose pad is large. The muzzle is yellowish brown, and white spotting often occurs on the throat and chest. There are five toes, which have short, heavy, downward-curved claws, on each foot. In the western states and Canada there are brown, cinnamon, blue-gray, and creamy white color phases of the black bear, but none of these forms occur in southeastern populations.

The skull is identified by its large size, broad profile, large, pointed canines, and flat-topped molars (called bunodont molars).

Geographical Range: Historically, the black bear occurred throughout the entire southeastern region. Many areas are now too developed or ecologically modified to support a bear population. Black bears are still found in the more remote natural areas such as in the mountains and in large swamps. In the United States, the geographical range extends from coast to coast, but the black bear is now absent from some of the prairie states.

Habitat: Black bears live in all types of heavily wooded terrain. They are most often found in large tracts of remote swampland, undisturbed upland forest, and in rugged mountain ravines.

Natural History: Black bears make dens in a variety of environments, including large, hollow logs and stumps, tree cavities, caves, under overhanging banks, and even in culverts. They are good climbers and frequently make their dens in cavities well above ground level. One black bear in Louisiana was recorded denning in a hollow cypress tree with an entrance hole almost 100 feet above ground.

Most black bears hibernate for extended periods of time in the winter months. They enter a shallow tor-

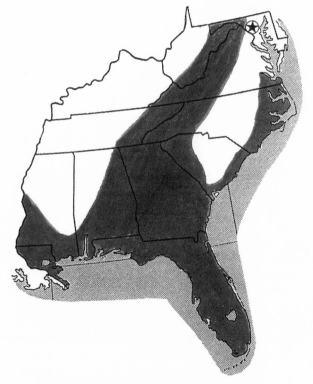

Geographical range of the black bear in the Southeast.

por, but can arouse within minutes when disturbed. Each bear usually dens alone, but a female may be accompanied in some cases by her yearling cubs.

Bears forage and move about mostly at dawn, dusk, and during the night. Occasionally they will also forage during the daytime, especially when a berry or fruit crop is ripe. Black bears walk with an ambling, flat-footed gait (called plantigrade locomotion), but can run as fast as 30 miles per hour in short charges or sprints. They often rear up on the back legs to get a better view of their surroundings.

Black bears eat a great deal of vegetable material and are truly omnivorous, much like humans. They eat berries, honey, fruits, grass, nuts, seeds, roots, tubers, buds, the inner bark of twigs, insects of all types, grubs, lizards, frogs, snakes, rodents, fish, bird eggs, armadillos, fawns, and carrion of all kinds. When searching for food, they often do a lot of digging; they also turn over logs and claw open rotten stumps. Bears sometimes leave long scratches in the bark of trees when sharpening their claws. In some parts of the country, bears become obnoxious feeders at garbage dumps and are sometimes dangerous at campgrounds as they steal food and tear up equipment.

Adult females breed only in alternate years during June or July, after which the sexes separate and return to solitary living. The female releases one to four eggs (usually two) from the ovaries, and these are fertilized by the sperm immediately after mating. The tiny embryos then undergo a period of arrested development (called delayed implantation) for the next five to six months. During midwinter, the embryos finally implant in the uterus and complete development rather rapidly. The total length of gestation ranges from 200 to 240 days, depending on the duration and depth of hibernation. Most young are born in January or February, and the cubs are tiny (weighing only six to eight ounces), naked, and blind at birth. They grow slowly, with the eyes opening and the first tooth erupting at about 40 days of age. By this time they are also well furred and weigh about two pounds. When they are about two months old, the cubs leave the den for the first time with their mother. They stay with her and continue to nurse throughout the summer and part of the fall. They usually do not leave their mother's side until the spring of their second year, at which time they weigh about 100 pounds. After leaving the mother, the cubs usually stay together through their second summer. Adult males take no part in rearing the young.

Females sometimes give birth when they are as young as three years of age, but most are five to seven years old before having young. Black bears do not reach their full body growth until they are about six years old, and they have a life expectancy of 15–20 years in the wild. In zoos they sometimes live 25–30 years.

The most famous black bear ever was "Smoky the Bear," the mascot of the United States Forest Service and its prevent forest fires campaign. He was found as a burned cub after a forest fire in New Mexico in 1950, and lived to the ripe old age of 27 years.

Determination of age in black bears is accomplished either by examining tooth wear or by counting the number of growth rings (called annuli) in the roots of the canine teeth or first premolars. The latter method requires the removal of a tooth, but is much more accurate than measuring age by tooth wear.

Bears have large home ranges, and adult males cover much larger areas than do females. One study in Louisiana found that the minimum home range of males averaged over 27,000 acres, and the home range of females was just under 5,000 acres. Studies in Florida found that individual bears range over 25 to 100 square miles. Radio tracking of black bears wearing transmitters reveals that they can move as much as 20 miles in a single 24-hour period. On occasion, transplanted black bears have wandered as far as 300 miles from their release point in just a few days.

Bears also gain weight rapidly when food is abundant. One adult gained 60 pounds in a single month in the fall as a result of feeding on a heavy mast crop (nuts and acorns). This represents a gain of roughly two pounds per day.

Remarks: Bears are hunted as game animals primarily to secure a "trophy," but the meat, especially of the younger bears, can also be eaten. The pelts are tanned and used for wall decorations or floor rugs.

Occasionally, black bears kill calves, pigs, sheep, goats, or poultry, and they sometimes damage corn crops and vegetable gardens in remote forested areas. Bears also have a taste for honey and honey bees, so they often do considerable damage to hives. The use of electric fences or elevated bearproof platforms for beehives is recommended where bears are numerous.

On fairly rare occasions, humans have been attacked, clawed, bitten, or even killed by black bears. I was once clawed by a large female bear in the Rocky Mountains when I approached too closely to take pictures of her twin cubs. She swatted me out of the way with one blow to the head and then quickly retreated, herding her babies before her. I then went for stitches at a nearby park aid station.

Black bears have been gradually declining in numbers in recent years, primarily because of continued habitat loss and overharvesting. If the downward trend in black bear populations continues and habitat destruction keeps its present pace, then this species will no longer be a viable big-game animal.

Selected References:

Garshelis, D. L., and M. R. Pelton. 1980. Activity of black bears in the Great Smoky Mountains National Park. J. Mamm. 61: 8–19.

Hellgren, E. C., M. L. Vaughan, and D. F. Stauffer. 1991. Macrohabitat use by black bears in a southeastern wetland. J. Wildl. Mgmt. 55: 442–48.

Horner, M. A., and R. A. Humphrey. 1990. Internal structure of the home ranges of black bears and analyses of home-range overlap. J. Mamm. 71: 402–10.

Kane, D. M., and J. A. Litvaites. 1992. Age and sex composition of live-trapped and hunter-killed samples of black bears. J. Mamm. 73: 215–17.

Marks, S. A., and A. W. Erickson. 1966. Age determination in the black bear. J. Wildl. Mgmt. 30: 389–410.

Schooley, R. L., C. R. McLaughlin, G. J. Matula, Jr., and W. B. Krohn. 1994. Denning chronology of female black bears: effects of food, weather, and reproduction. J. Mamm. 75: 466–77.

Willey, C. H. 1974. Aging black bears from first pre molar tooth sections. J. Wildl. Mgmt. 38: 97–100.

Wooding, J. B., and T. S. Hardisky. 1992. Denning by black bears in north central Florida. J. Mamm. 73: 895–98.

Van Wormer, J. 1966. *The World of the Black Bear.* J. B. Lippincott Co., Philadelphia, Pa. 163 pp.

Raccoon
Procyon lotor

Raccoon, *Procyon lotor.* Florida Game & Freshwater Fish Commission

Identification: The raccoon is about the size of an average dog and has a black mask across the eyes and a long, bushy tail with five to seven black rings around it. The upper coat is grizzled gray, brown, and black, washed with yellow, and the underparts are pale brown, mixed with grayish yellow. The face is whitish except for the prominent black mask, and the ears are grayish, with black on their posterior surfaces. There is a great deal of color variation in raccoons, ranging all the way from a pale, yellowish brown coat to one that is almost totally black.

The skull is broad and robust, and the hard palate extends well posterior to the bunodont (flat-topped) molars.

Geographical Range: The raccoon is abundant throughout the entire southeastern region. In the United States, the geographical range includes every state, as well as southern Canada, Mexico, and Central America.

Habitat: This species occurs in every ecological community having trees. Raccoons are probably most numerous in mature forests that have many hollow trees. The highest densities are usually recorded in the rich coastal hammocks and floodplain forests of the coastal plain.

Geographical range of the raccoon in the Southeast.

Natural History: The raccoon, like its relative, the black bear, is truly omnivorous, eating both plant and animal material readily. Raccoons are also very opportunistic, eating whatever is available. They often forage at garbage cans, dumps, and campgrounds.

Raccoons usually sleep during the daytime in a tree or on a platform of sticks in a tree, but they become active in the late afternoon and continue foraging through the night. If hungry, they will continue foraging into the daytime hours as well. It is commonly believed that raccoons always wash their food before eating, but this is incorrect. Most of the time they are not near water when food is found, and even when water is available, they do not wash food before eating.

Male raccoons usually occupy a home range about one mile in diameter, but they will sometimes travel much greater distances, especially during the mating season. Females have smaller home ranges that are about three-fourths of a mile in diameter. Within each home range there are several den sites, which are used on a rotating basis as the raccoon moves from place to place. One study found the average distance between den sites is about 1,400 feet. Raccoons do not hibernate, but I have seen them sleep so deeply that they were difficult to arouse when shaken vigorously. Since raccoons normally den in trees, they are agile climbers. When descending from trees, they can go either head-first or tail-first, and they frequently jump the last few feet. They are good fighters and usually give a dog plenty to handle in a scrape.

Raccoons generally produce one litter per year, and mating usually occurs in December or January, but sometimes later. The gestation period is 63 days and the average litter size is three and one-half offspring (ranging from one to seven). Males are promiscuous, and only the female provides care for the young, which are called pups, kits, or cubs. Newborn raccoons are fully furred, but their eyes are closed. Their eyes open when they are about two weeks of age, and pups leave the den for the first time when 8–10 weeks old to forage with mother. They are not completely weaned until 14–16 weeks. Some young females can breed near the end of their first year, but virtually all males and about 60 percent of females do not mature sexually until their second year.

Raccoons are most accurately aged by the use of concentric growth rings or annuli found in the roots of the incisor and canine teeth. The rate of tooth wear is also used for classification into age groups. Males can also be aged by measuring the increasing size and weight of the elaborately curved penis bone *(os baculum)*. Most raccoons in the wild live a maximum of six to eight years, but the record longevity reported in a free-ranging population is 16 years (based on tooth annuli). In captivity they have lived to 18 years of age.

Remarks: Raccoons are hunted extensively for sport, for food, and for their fur. Coon hunting is a time-honored sport in the rural South. Hounds are especially bred and trained for coon hunting, and they are adept at trailing and treeing the raccoon. The hunter then uses a gun to secure the raccoon from the treetops if he is so inclined. Some purists, however, let the coon go to be hunted another night. My grandfather, who lived in the Ozarks of southern Missouri, was content to listen to the coon hounds bay and yelp during the pursuit and eventual treeing of the raccoon. I never knew him to kill a "treed coon," although he enjoyed hunting untreed raccoons throughout his long lifetime.

Raccoons make reasonably good pets when captured young, and they possess an intelligence level about the same as domestic dogs and cats. They are very inquisitive by nature, inclined to explore every nook and cranny of a house, and often make messes as a result of climbing or tipping things over. They also may become aggressive and "nippy" when sexually mature.

Raccoons sometimes damage crops such as corn, watermelons, grapes, cantaloupes, tomatoes, and other vegetables. Often, they will kill chickens, ducks, baby turkeys, game birds, and other poultry. Problem raccoons are usually controlled by shooting, trapping, poisoning, or by coon dogs. In many areas, raccoon pelts or carcasses are sold to supplement rural incomes. The fur is of moderately good quality and often used to trim coats and jackets. The meat from raccoons is of debatable quality, but certain groups tout it as a delicacy. Raccoons have few predators except humans and their dogs. However, young ones are sometimes taken by bobcats, great horned owls, and coyotes. Prior to the decline or disappearance of the panther and red wolf in the eastern United States, these larger carnivores were no doubt significant predators of the raccoon.

Regarding disease transmission, most rabies outbreaks in the southern states have been associated with raccoons. The disease has a long incubation period, and, for this reason, adopting pet raccoons (even as babies) carries some risk that rabies might manifest itself later. Therefore, health agencies recommend that raccoons not be kept as household pets (unless they are bred and reared in captivity for several months). In addition to rabies, raccoons are sometimes subject to distemper, tuberculosis, and fungal skin diseases.

Raccoons are major predators of some of our most endangered and threatened species, including the eggs of several marine turtles, the American crocodile, several species of colonial nesting birds, and many others.

Selected References:

Berner, A., and L. W. Gysel. 1967. Raccoon use of large tree cavities and ground burrows. J. Wildl. Mgmt. 31: 706–14.

Grau, G. A., G. C. Sanderson, and J. P. Rogers. 1970. Age determination in raccoons. J. Wildl. Mgmt. 34: 364–72.

Johnson, A. S. 1970. Biology of the raccoon (*Procyon lotor varius* Nelson and Goldman) in Alabama. Auburn Univ. Agr. Exper. Stat. 148 pp.

Kennedy, M. L., G. D. Baumgardner, M. E. Cope, F. R. Tabatabui, and O. S. Fuller. 1986. Raccoon (*Procyon lotor*) density as estimated by the census-assessment line technique. J. Mamm. 67: 166–68.

Lotze, J. H., and S. Anderson. 1979. Raccoon (*Procyon lotor*). Mammalian Species, No. 119: pp. 1–8.

Rue, L. L., III. 1964. *The World of the Raccoon*. J. B. Lippincott, Co., Philadelphia, Pa. 145 pp.

Sanderson, G. C. 1961. The lens as an indicator of age in the raccoon. Amer. Midl. Nat. 65: 481–85.

Stuewer, F. W. 1942. Raccoons, their habits and management in Michigan. Ecol. Monogr. 13: 203–57.

Whitney, L. F., and A. B. Underwood. 1952. *The Raccoon*. Practical Science Publ. Co., Orange, Conn.

Mink
Mustela vison

Mink, *Mustela vison*. Karl Maslowski

Identification: The mink is a medium-sized, slender carnivore similar to but larger than the weasel. Both the dorsal and ventral pelages are a uniform glossy chocolate brown. The tail is long, bushy, and dark chocolate brown on the basal half and becoming progressively blacker toward the tip. The chin is white, and there are irregular white splashes on the throat and sometimes the belly and chest. The ears are short and round, and the head is flattened. Male mink average about one-third larger in body size than females.

The skull has 34 teeth, the last upper molar is dumbbell shaped, and the palate extends well beyond the last molar. The mink skull closely resembles the skull of the long-tailed weasel but is considerably larger, and the auditory bullae protecting the inner ear are proportionally smaller than in the weasel.

Geographical Range: The mink has a regionwide distribution in the Southeast. In the United States, the geographical range of the mink covers the entire country except for the southwestern desert areas.

Habitat: Mink live mainly in freshwater habitats such as streams, ponds, lakes, swamps, and marshes. There are also mink in some of the coastal salt marshes of Florida and Georgia.

Geographical range of the mink in the Southeast.

Natural History: Mink are always semiaquatic in their habits. They are mainly active at night, but on several occasions I have encountered them foraging along the shore of a stream or swimming in a lake in the daytime. Mink den in a variety of places, including hollow stumps, bank cavities, under logs, and even in rodent nests. Males have a large home range up to five miles in diameter. Females are much more sedentary and have a home range that averages only about one-fifth the size of males. Mink living along a river or stream have much more linear home ranges than mink living in a marsh.

The diet is strictly animal matter, including both aquatic and terrestrial species, such as frogs, crayfish, snails, fish, muskrats, rice rats, cotton rats, clams, insects, mice, rabbits, birds, and reptiles. In many areas the welfare of the mink is tied closely to the population cycle of the muskrat, but in other regions it is a more general feeder and catches whatever aquatic species is most abundant.

The breeding season begins in late winter and extends into spring. One litter is produced annually, and the gestation period ranges from 40 to 75 days (the average is 51 days) because of suspended development for various lengths of time by the tiny embryos in the mother's uterus. After implantation finally occurs, development of the embryos to term requires only 30 days. The average litter size is around three and one-half offspring but ranges from one to twelve in the wild. The kits weigh about one-half ounce at birth, are blind, and covered with a fine silvery white fur. By two weeks of age the fur color has changed to a pale cinnamon-gray. The eyes finally open when they are about three weeks old, and weaning occurs shortly thereafter. An adult male usually mates with several females each breeding season, but he sometimes remains with the last one and assists in the care of the young. Juvenile mink usually catch their own food by eight weeks of age, but they typically remain with their mother as a family group until late summer. They reach full adult size when five months old. Both sexes become reproductively active when about ten months of age. A few mink live as long as six to eight years in the wild, but in captivity, ranch mink have lived twelve years.

Mink in the Southeast are preyed upon by alligators, foxes, coyotes, bobcats, great horned owls, and occasionally by large cottonmouth water moccasins and eastern diamondback rattlesnakes.

Remarks: Mink have a fur coat that is of the highest quality of any southeastern mammal. The winter coat is much heavier, thicker, and much more valuable than the summer coat. Mink are raised or "ranched" in large numbers for their fur. There are many beautiful color mutations in these tame mink.

Selected References:

Enders, R. K. 1952. Reproduction in the mink *(Mustela vison)*. Proc. Amer. Phil. Soc. 96: 691–55.

Gerell, R. 1970. Home ranges and movements of the mink *(Mustela vison)* in southern Sweden. Oikos 21: 160–73.

Humphrey, S. R., and H. W. Setzer. 1989. Geographic variation and taxonomic revision of mink *(Mustela vison)* in Florida. J. Mamm. 70: 241–52.

Korschgen, L. J. 1957. December food habits of mink in Missouri. J. Mamm. 39: 521–27.

Marshall, W. H. 1936. A study of winter activities of the mink. J. Mamm. 17: 382–92.

Smith, A. T. 1980 An environmental study of the Everglades mink *(Mustela vison)*. South Fla. Research Center, Everglades Nat'l. Park. Report T-555, 1–17.

Yeager, L. E. 1943. Storing of muskrats and other food by minks. J. Mamm. 24: 100–101.

Fisher
Martes pennanti

Fisher, *Martes pennanti*. American Society of Mammalogists

Identification: The fisher resembles a large, dark cat with a gray head, but its body is more slender, its tail is longer and bushy, and its limbs are shorter. The ears are short and rounded and the face is broad, but the nose is pointed. The fur is dense, dark brown on the back to black on the underside, and much coarser than the fur of the marten or mink. The face and shoulders are streaked with gray and pale brown fur.

The skull is much larger and heavier than that of the marten. There are four premolars in the skull.

Geographical Range: The fisher has been recorded along the Appalachian mountain chain as far south as western North Carolina and eastern Tennessee. There are also records in western Virginia and western Maryland. In North America, the fisher ranges northward through New England, across Canada and the Great Lakes region, and down the Rocky Mountain chain to Wyoming, Utah, and California.

Habitat: This species is clearly associated with the old-growth coniferous forest where it prefers to live in the vicinity of streams. Unlike the marten, it can also be found in mature deciduous forest and even old second-growth stands of evergreens.

Natural History: Fishers are known to travel along regular hunting circuits much like wolves. The circuits may be as much as sixty miles long and encircle a home range which is about ten miles in diameter.

Mammals form about 80 percent of the fisher's diet. The favored food items are red squirrels, red-backed voles, snowshoe hares, shrews, flying squirrels, porcupines, and deer mice. They also consume a few birds, insects, berries, and nuts to spice the mammal diet.

The fisher has an unusually long gestation period due to greatly delayed implantation following fertilization. Breeding occurs in March or April, and the gestation period lasts a full year, to the next March or April when one to five offspring are born (the average is three). Thus, the full length of gestation ranges from 348 to 358 days (the average is 352 days). The undeveloped embryos actually implant in late January or early February, so the bulk of development takes place in 30–51 days. The female mates again during the first week after parturition, and she is pregnant and lactating at the same time. The newborn fishers are covered with a fine, white fur, but the eyes and ears are closed. The babies grow slowly and the eyes open at about seven weeks of age. Sexual maturity does not occur until the young fishers are two years old.

Remarks: The fisher is adept a preying on porcupines by attacking their soft, unprotected belly area. Occasionally, a fisher will catch a face full of quills, but this is rare, because they are normally agile enough to avoid this danger.

The hide of the fisher is considered a prize pelt by fur trappers. The skins are used for coat collars, stoles, and capes. The males produce a larger skin than females (about one-third bigger), but the fur is more coarse, so the smaller female pelts are more valuable.

The fisher has never been as common as the marten, and its numbers have declined in most areas, due to fur trapping and the cutting of old-growth forests for lumber. It is being reintroduced to some of its former range in the Appalachian and Rocky Mountains by various state game and fish commissions, so there is a good chance the fisher will be re-established in a number of areas.

Selected References:

Arthur, S. M., and W. B. Krohn. 1991. Activity patterns, movements and reproductive ecology of fishers in southcentral Maine. J. Mamm. 72: 379–85.

Cook, D. B., and W. J. Hamilton Jr. 1957. The forest, the fisher, and the porcupine. J. Forestry 55: 719–22.

Eadie, W. R., and W. J. Hamilton Jr. 1958. Reproduction in the fisher in New York. N.Y. Fish and Game Jour. 5: 77–83.

Powell, R. A. 1981. Fisher (Martes pennanti). Mammalian Species, No. 156: pp. 1–6.

———. 1982. The Fisher: Life History, Ecology, and Behavior. Univ. Minn. Press, Minneapolis, Minn. 219 pp.

———. 1994. Effects of scale on habitat selection and foraging behavior of fishers in winter. J. Mamm. 75: 349–56.

Geographical range of the fisher in the Southeast.

Pine Marten
Martes americana

Pine marten, *Martes americana*. Dan Hartman

Geographical range of the pine marten in the Southeast.

Identification: The pine marten is a mink-sized weasel that is arboreal (that is, it lives in the trees). The pelage is long, soft, and yellowish brown, and richer and darker above. The throat and chest are blazed with a pale buff-orange wash. The tail is bushy, about half the length of the body, and tipped in black.

The skull is relatively long and slender with rounded cranium and inflated tympanic bullae. There are four premolars in the skull, and it is much smaller than the fisher.

Geographical Range: In the Southeast, the marten has been recorded only in northern West Virginia and Virginia. In North America, it ranges through the northern Appalachians to Canada, across Canada to Alaska, and southward into the Rocky Mountains of the western United States.

Habitat: The marten is a native of mature northern coniferous forests. In the Appalachians it occurs in spruce-fir-hemlock and in spruce-cedar swamps at lower elevations. In the western states, it prefers fir-cedar-hemlock forests.

Natural History: Most of the marten's foraging activities are conducted in the treetops where it spends most of its time. It feeds almost exclusively on the red squirrel *(Tamiasciurus hudsonius)*. Martens also capture some birds, and they will eat fruit and berries when they are in season.

Mating occurs in late summer, but the implantation of the tiny embryos in the uterus is delayed for several months until late winter or spring. The young are usually born in April after a development period of 30–35 days. The total gestation period, including the delay over winter, is 7–8 months. Baby martens are blind, helpless, and covered with fine, yellowish fur. The eyes do not open until they are five to six weeks old, and they are weaned at about eight weeks of age. Juveniles reach adult size in about three and one-half months, but they do not mature sexually until the following year, and some do not breed until they are two years old.

Remarks: Marten are one of the most valuable furbearers found in North America. The pelts are used to make expensive capes, coats, stoles, and collars.

Its larger cousin, the fisher, is also one of the marten's major predators where the two species occur together. The marten is no match for the powerful jaws of the fisher.

Marten sometimes forage on the ground, especially when there is snow cover. I have trapped several of them in the western United States using steel foot traps, baited with meat, set on the ground at the base of trees in coniferous forest.

Selected References:

Clark, T. W., E. Anderson, C. Douglas, and M. Strickland. 1987. American Marten (*Martes americana*). Mammalian Species, No. 289: pp. 1–8.

Cowan, I. M., and R. H. Mackey. 1950. Food habits of the marten (*Martes americana*) in the Rocky Mountain region of Canada. Canad. Field Nat. 64: 100–104.

Hawley, V. D., and F. E. Newby. 1951. Marten home ranges and population fluctuations. J. Mamm. 38: 174–84.

Hodgman, T. P., D. J. Harrixon, D. D. Katnik, and K. D. Elowe. 1994. Survival in an intensively trapped marten population in Maine. J. Wildl. Mgmt. 58: 593–99.

Katnik, D. D., D. J. Harrison, and T. P. Hodgman. 1994. Spatial relations in a harvested population of marten in Maine. J. Wildl. Mgmt. 58: 600–607.

Marshall, W. H. 1946. Winter food habits of the pine marten in Montana. J. Mamm. 27: 83–84.

Long-tailed Weasel
Mustela frenata

Long-tailed weasel, *Mustela frenata*. Roger W. Barbour

Identification: The long-tailed weasel is a small, slender carnivore having short legs and a long tail, which is tipped in black. The dorsal pelage is chestnut brown, and the hair is short and uniform in color. The underparts are yellowish white or cream-white. The ears are short, rounded, furry, and not conspicuous. The tail length is about 40 percent of the head and body combined, and the tail is brown dorsally, except for the black tip. The eyes are small and somewhat beady, and the snout tapers to a rather well-defined point.

The skull is identified by its small size for a carnivore and by its inflated, elongated auditory bullae, surrounding the inner ear.

Geographical Range: This species occurs throughout the entire southeastern region. In the United States, the geographic range includes all the contiguous states in the country, as well as Mexico and Central America. This is the broadest distribution of any small carnivore in North America.

Habitat: The long-tailed weasel appears to have no real habitat preference among the terrestrial communities. It has been taken in virtually every plant community, including both forested and open habitats.

Natural History: This weasel is an aggressive little carnivore and does not hesitate to attack and kill prey larger than itself. It is extremely fast, agile, and usually leaps on the back of the prey and sinks its sharp teeth into the brain or severs the jugular veins in the neck. They are strictly meat eaters and prey largely on rodents, birds, reptiles, and rabbits. They sometimes invade the farmyard to take rats and mice as well as poultry.

The weasel's home is a shallow burrow in the ground, in a log, or in a stump—a residence often taken over from one of its prey species. With their long, slender build, weasels can easily forage in the burrows of various medium- and small-sized rodents. The presence of a weasel is sometimes indicated by a pile of discarded

Geographical range of the long-tailed weasel in the Southeast.

bones, bits of skin and fur, or a fresh kill cached within a burrow entrance. They hunt both day and night, but tend to be more active nocturnally. They are very inquisitive and will explore every nook and cranny of a habitat or structure looking for prey.

Males have larger home ranges than females, averaging about 400 acres in size. It usually takes several days for a weasel to cover its entire home range. Females are more sedentary and have an average home range size of about 150 acres.

Almost nothing is known about the breeding of weasels in the South, because they are usually rare and difficult to study. Farther north, the long-tailed weasel breeds in July or August and produces a single annual litter, usually born in April or May. The gestation period is extremely variable in length because weasels can delay implantation of the fertilized eggs for up to six to seven months. Once the embryos implant in the uterus, the development to full term requires only about 25 days. Thus, the total gestation period may be as long as eight to nine months. The one annual litter contains one to twelve young but averages six. At birth the babies are pink, blind, nearly hairless, and quite helpless. They are well furred by three weeks of age, but the eyes do not open until the young weasels are about five weeks old. Adult males sometimes assist in caring for the young. Weaning takes place shortly after the eyes open, after which the young begin foraging with their mother until they are nearly full grown. Young females reach sexual maturity when three to four months old, but males do not become sexually active until they are a year old.

The size and weight of the penis bone (os baculum) is sometimes used to age male weasels. In the wild, weasels seldom live beyond three to four years, but in captivity they have survived as long as seven years.

Remarks: Weasels are beneficial in consuming a number of destructive kinds of rats and mice. Occasionally, they are reported to attack poultry and apparently will kill more than they can eat. The excess food is often cached and eaten at a later time when a fresh kill is not available. Control of problem weasels is usually achieved by the use of traps, by shooting, or by dogs.

In the northern part of its range, the long-tailed weasel molts to an all-white winter pelt with the tail still remaining tipped in black. This protective coloration makes them almost invisible on a snowy background. In the southern half of the United States, wea-

sels remain brown the year round. Long-tailed weasels are an economically important furbearer only in the northern portion of their range, where fur dealers usually refer to them as "ermine."

I can personally attest to the fearless nature of the long-tailed weasel. I once kept a large male in a cage to observe its habits. One day it somehow unlatched the cage door and got out. I chased it several times around the room, while wearing heavy leather gloves to protect my hands during the recapture effort. As I cornered it under a bench, the weasel jumped almost three feet into the air, on the attack, and aimed for the general direction of my head and throat. I deflected him to the side and subdued him, but gained a healthy permanent respect for the aggressive, fearless nature of this little predator.

Selected References:

Hamilton, W. J., Jr. 1933. The weasels of New York, their natural history and economic status. Amer. Midl. Nat. 14: 289–344.

Polderboer, E. B., L. W. Kuhn, and G. O. Hendrickson. 1941. Winter and spring habits of weasels in central Iowa. J. Wildl. Mgmt. 5: 115–19.

Sanderson, G. C. 1949. Growth and behavior of a litter of captive long-tailed weasels. J. Mamm. 30: 412–15.

Svendsen, G. E. 1976. Vocalizations of the long-tailed weasel (Mustela frenata). J. Mamm. 57: 398–99.

Wright, P. L. 1942. Delayed implantation in the long-tailed weasel (Mustela frenata), the short-tailed weasel (Mustela erminea), and the marten (Martes americana). Anat. Record 83: 341–53.

———. 1947. The sexual cycle of the male long-tailed weasel (Mustela frenata). J. Mamm. 28: 343–52.

———. 1948. Breeding habits of captive long-tailed weasels (Mustela frenata). Amer. Midl. Nat. 39: 338–44.

Short-tailed Weasel
Mustela erminea

Short-tailed weasel, *Mustela erminea*. American Society of Mammalogists

Identification: The short-tailed weasel, or ermine, is smaller than the long-tailed weasel and is very similar in markings. The upper pelage is a uniform chocolate brown and the underparts are white. The tail is fairly long (four to six inches), and the last third of it is tipped in long black hairs. the ermine's pelage is short and fine throughout and exhibits a pronounced color change when it molts in the late fall to pure white all over, except for the black markings on the tip of the tail. The white winter coat is thicker than the brown summer coat. Adult males are about one-third larger than females.

The skull is medium-sized, long, narrow, and flattened. There are only three premolars, and the tympanic bullae are elongated.

Geographical Range: This little carnivore is at home in the conifers and mixed conifer-hardwood forests of the Appalachian Mountains. Farther north, it also occurs in the tundra and subalpine boreal forests, so it is adaptable to a number of different cold temperate and Arctic habitats.

Natural History: Ermines are opportunistic carnivores. They are active both day and night and capture all types of prey in their size range, including mice, small birds, ground squirrels, chipmunks, small rabbits, pocket gophers, reptiles, shrews, and other small mammals. They seldom make their own dens, but take over the vacant nest of a prey species. Populations of weasels often undergo drastic fluctuations, depending on the density of the rodent populations.

Prey is subdued by attacking the shoulder or throat region and biting through the base of the skull. As winter approaches, they store extra carcasses in their den to feed upon when food is scarce.

The breeding season begins in late summer, at which time mating occurs. The eggs are fertilized, but implantation and further embryonic development is delayed until the following March or April. Birth of the young occurs about 30 days after implantation of the embryos in the uterus. Thus, a single litter is born each year in April or May, roughly 10 months after insemination by the males. The litter size ranges from four to nine and averages six. Newborn weasels are tiny and covered with fine white fur, and the eyes and ears are closed. Young ermine grow rapidly, but the eyes do not open until they are five weeks old. Juvenile females mature and breed their first summer, but males do not become sexually active until the following spring, after which they mate in the summer.

Remarks: It appears that the short-tailed weasel may remain paired throughout the year. Males assist the females by bringing food to the young while they are nestlings.

The name ermine refers to the white winter coloration. It is a very valuable fur species in this color phase. The small skins are used extensively for trimming coats, stoles, and other items. Unfortunately, the fur industry makes no distinction between the pelts of the three species of weasels found in North America (long-tailed weasel, short-tailed weasel, and least weasel). They are all lumped together as ermine. However, the short-tailed weasel makes up the bulk of the trapper's catch. This is because they appear to be more abundant than the other two species in most areas.

Weasels which are changing from brown to white or white to brown when trapped are called "graybacks" in the trade, and they are worth only a fraction of regular white pelts.

Geographical range of the short-tailed weasel in the Southeast.

Selected References:

Hall, E. R. 1951. *Mustela erminea*. In American Weasels. Mus. Nat. Hist., Univ. Kan. Publ. 4: 87–167.

Hamilton, W. J. Jr. 1933. The weasels of New York: their natural history and economic status. Amer. Midl. Nat. 14: 289–344.

King, C. M. 1983. Short-tailed Weasel or Ermine (*Mustela erminea*). Mammalian Species, No. 195: pp. 1–8.

Wright, P. L. 1942. Delayed implantation in the long-tailed weasel (*Mustela frenata*), the short-tailed weasel (*Mustela erminea*), and the marten (*Martes americana*). Anat. Record 83: 341–53.

Least Weasel
Mustela nivalis

Least weasel, *Mustela nivalis*. American Society of Mammalogists

Identification: The least weasel is the smallest member of the mustelid family, as it is no bigger than a medium-sized mouse. It is also the world's smallest carnivore, with a walnut brown upper coat and white underparts. The tail is quite stubby, brown above, white below, and there are just a few black hairs at its very extreme tip. In the winter, they are totally white except for the few black hairs on the tip of tail. The skull is much smaller and more delicate in appearance than those of the larger weasels.

Geographical Range: The least weasel occur in the Appalachian chain as far south as the Smoky Mountains. In North America, it also ranges westward through the Great Lakes region to the Pacific Northwest, across Canada, Alaska, Asia, and Europe (it has a truly "holarctic" distribution).

Habitat: The least weasel lives in a wide variety of habitats, including conifers, mixed conifers and hardwoods, meadows, stream banks, and mixed forest–open park lands.

Geographical range of the least weasel in the Southeast.

Natural History: The least weasel is active year round and secretive in its habits. It is seldom observed or captured except by accident. Least weasels are primarily nocturnal and are very agile hunters. The least weasel seldom builds its own nest, but takes over the burrows of its prey species, which consist of most small animals. They cache food extensively in underground burrows. Least weasels are relatively sedentary, having a home range size of only about two acres. Males are only slightly larger than females.

Reproduction differs from that of the larger weasels. Implantation is not delayed and occurs only 10–12 days after fertilization. Breeding tends to occur two to three times per year, whenever food is abundant. The gestation period is only 35–37 days, and litters have been discovered in all four seasons of the year. The litter size ranges from one to six and averages four young. Eyes open in about one month, but adult males play no part in rearing the young. Weaning of the young weasels occurs at about six to seven weeks.

Remarks: While least weasels molt to a white coat over most of their range, in the middle and southern Appalachians they only change to a slightly paler brown coat in the winter. The timing of molt in the least weasel is not tied to the amount of snow cover, but is determined by the length of the photo period (day length) and genetics of each weasel.

The least weasel is seldom taken by trappers, probably because of its small size. Most of the traps are too large to be effective on a mouse-sized carnivore. Therefore, it is of little significance in the ermine fur trade.

The least weasel, the world's smallest carnivore, has only about .001 the body weight of the world's largest group of carnivores, the bears.

Selected References:

Heidt, G. A. 1970. The least weasel, *Mustela nivalis* Linnaeus: Developmental biology in comparison with other North American *Mustela*. Mich. State Univ., Publ. of the Mus., Biol. Series, 4: 227–82.

Heidt, G. A., M. K. Peterson, and G. L. Kirkland Jr. 1968. Mating behavior and development of least weasels (*Mustela nivalis*) in captivity. J. Mamm. 49: 413–19.

Ponderboer, E. B. 1942. Habits of the least weasel (*Mustela rixosa*) in northeastern Iowa. J. Mamm. 23: 145–47.

Richmond, N. D., and R. D. McDowell. 1952. The least weasel (*Mustela rixosa*) in Pennsylvania. J. Mamm. 33: 251–53.

Sheffield, S. R., and C. M. King. 1994. Least Weasel (*Mustela nivalis*). Mammalian Species, No. 454: pp. 1–10.

Swanson, G., and P. O. Fryklund. 1935. The least weasel in Minnesota and its fluctuation in numbers. Amer. Midl. Nat. 16: 120–26.

Striped Skunk
Mephitis mephitis

Striped skunk, *Mephitis mephitis*. Larry Brown

Identification: The striped skunk is about the size of a house cat, stout bodied, and entirely black except for two white stripes that run down the back. Occasionally the white stripes on the back are very narrow or fused into a single stripe. This skunk has a small head, short stocky legs, and a large, plumelike black tail, sometimes marked with white. Each foot has long, slightly-curved claws, and males tend to be slightly larger than females.

The skull is about the same size as that of the mink, but the auditory bullae protecting the inner ear are relatively small. The region above the eye sockets is well rounded and arched upward.

Geographical Range: Striped skunks live throughout the entire Southeast. The geographical range in the United States extends from coast to coast and includes portions of Mexico and all of Canada.

Habitat: This skunk occurs in virtually every terrestrial community in the region. Striped skunks are probably most abundant in forest-edge plant communities, brushy fields, and farming areas with heavily overgrown fencerows. They sometimes live in suburban and residential areas.

Natural History: Striped skunks can be active at any time day or night, but they usually venture forth in the

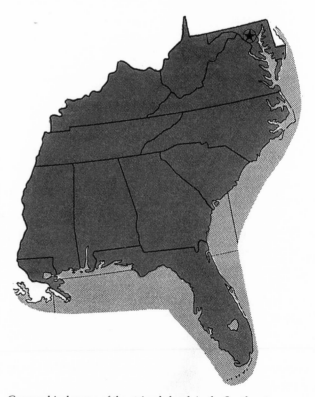

Geographical range of the striped skunk in the Southeast.

late afternoon and continue to be active during the night. They have a keen sense of hearing and smell but fairly poor vision. Skunks usually dig their own dens, but they also may remodel those of foxes, armadillos, gopher turtles, etc., to suit their needs.

The striped skunk is infamous for its potent scent glands located on either side of the anus. The scent glands can spray droplets of an acrid, pungent musk on intruders up to 15 feet away. The smell itself can be detected for much greater distances, up to one and one-half miles downwind. Skunks cannot squirt the musk if the tail is depressed toward the ground, but they spray it with considerable accuracy when the tail is up.

Striped skunks are omnivorous, eating both plant and animal foods in about equal amounts. They are very opportunistic and feed on about anything they can catch or reach.

The breeding season begins in February or March and continues into early summer. The gestation is variable, ranging from 59 to 77 days, but averages 65 days. The tiny embryos often undergo a period of arrested development before implantation in the mother's uterus, which extends the length of gestation. One litter is normally produced annually, containing two to ten young, but averaging five. Young females tend to have smaller litters than older females. At birth, the kits weigh about one ounce, the eyes are closed, and they are almost naked, but they do show delicate black-and-white skin markings where the hair will erupt. At the end of two weeks they will be well furred. Their eyes open by about 22 days of age, and the young skunks will assume a characteristic defensive pose if they are approached. They leave the nest and accompany their mother on foraging trips for the first time when six to seven weeks old. Weaning occurs at eight to ten weeks of age. Young striped skunks are not able to throw scent until they are about one month old. After weaning, the mother and young usually stay together as a family until late summer.

In the wild, striped skunks generally live a maximum of five or six years. In captivity, however, when they are often kept as pets, some have lived for ten years. Skunks do not hibernate, but they become very obese in the fall and sleep for extended periods during cold weather, living off their stored fat.

Remarks: Striped skunks are trapped and sold for their pelts in many northern areas; the fur is used to trim garments. Striped skunks occasionally become pests by killing young chickens and other poultry, but this is not common.

Skunks are sometimes kept as pets if they are captured young and then descented. To deodorize a skunk, the large musk glands on either side of the anus must be surgically removed while the skunk is anesthetized. It is a tricky operation for the beginner, and many accidents have occurred during attempted descentings.

The odor from being sprayed by a skunk is very difficult to completely eradicate. Clothes are usually burned, but various solvents and deodorants may be tried in order to salvage them. Cleaning preparations often recommended include laundry bleaches, ammonia, turpentine, tomato juice, and vinegar. I have found none to be totally effective, however.

Since skunks sometimes carry and transmit rabies and leptospirosis, there is some danger in handling skunks from wild populations. There is also a risk in buying skunks as pets because the incubation period for rabies is long, and the past history of a skunk is often unknown. Almost 50 percent of all animal rabies cases reported in the United States each year occur in skunks of various kinds, so the danger is real.

Striped skunks have very few predators because of their potent defense system. The bold black-and-white color pattern of skunks is considered a strong warning coloration, which potential predators quickly learn to recognize and avoid. Great horned owls, however, are not deterred by the scent (they apparently have a very poor sense of smell), so they frequently catch and eat skunks. A few young skunks are also taken by hungry bobcats, foxes, and coyotes. It is not unusual for dogs to attack and kill adult skunks, but they seldom repeat the performance.

Selected References:
Dean, F. C. 1965. Winter and spring habits and density of Maine skunks. J. Mamm. 46: 673–75.
Hamilton, W. J., Jr. 1963. Reproduction of the striped skunk in New York. J. Mamm. 44: 123–24.
Shirer, H. W., and H. S. Fitch. 1970. Comparison from radio tracking of movements and denning habits of the raccoon, striped skunk, and opossum in northeastern Kansas. J. Mamm. 18: 194–202.
Storm, G. L. 1972. Daytime retreats and movements of skunks on farmlands in Illinois. J. Wildl. Mgmt. 36: 31–45.
Verts, B. J. 1967. The biology of the striped skunk. Univ. of Illinois Press, Urbana. 218 pp.
Wade-Smith, J., and B. J. Verts. 1982. Striped Skunk(*Mephitis mephitis*). Mammalian Species, No. 173: pp. 1–7.

Eastern Spotted Skunk
Spilogale putorious

Eastern spotted skunk, *Spilogale putorious*. Larry Brown

Geographical range of the eastern spotted skunk in the Southeast.

Identification: The eastern spotted skunk, or "civet cat," is a small carnivore the size of a squirrel which has a black coat with numerous conspicuous white stripes and spots scattered over its upper parts. There is always a large white spot on the forehead and another located in front of the ear. The tail is long, bushy, and usually all black, but it may have a prominent white tip. The legs are short and stocky, the ears and eyes are small, and the toes have long claws.

The skull is much smaller than that of the striped skunk, and the region above the eye socket is flat, lacking an arch. The auditory bullae over the internal ears are slightly inflated.

Geographical Range: Eastern spotted skunks occur throughout the entire southeastern region. In the United States, the geographical range covers the eastern two-thirds of the country with the exception of the Great Lakes area and northeastern states. Spotted skunks also occur in Mexico and most of Central America.

Habitat: Those habitats preferred by the eastern spotted skunk are old fallow fields, weedy pastures, brush and vines, dry prairies, field fencerows, and open disturbed areas. In the mountains, they often occur in open forests with rocky outcrops. They do not live in wet, swampy, or marshy habitats.

Natural History: Spotted skunks sleep during the day in underground dens and are active primarily at night. They usually dig their own burrows, but sometimes they modify the tunnels of other burrowing animals

to suit their needs. They have a particular fondness for denning under barns, sheds, old foundations, woodpiles, rockpiles, logs, brush heaps, and even occupied houses (where they are seldom appreciated).

The spotted skunk has potent anal musk glands like those of the striped skunk. The evil-smelling scent is often described as having a more sickening, sweeter smell than that of the striped skunk. The droplets are sprayed for a distance of 12–15 feet, but the odor travels for long distances downwind. The defensive posture of the spotted skunk is very unusual and stereotyped. Before spraying scent, they do a series of rapid handstands while holding the rear end of the body and the tail high in the air. When approached too closely, they drop to all fours, assume a U-shaped stance with the tail lifted and the anus and head directed toward the intruder, and let fly with the spray.

Spotted skunks are omnivorous and consume a wide variety of plants and animals. Insects make up a large part of the diet, but they also eat mice, rats, amphibians, reptiles, small birds, eggs, fruits, nuts, mushrooms, and plant tubers. They are very good climbers and can scurry up and down trees, much like a squirrel.

The breeding season begins in the late winter and young are born in the spring. The gestation period varies from 50 to 65 days, but averages about 58 days. ~~9-12 months check other reference~~ There can be a delay of a week or more before the tiny embryos implant in the mother's uterus. The litter size varies from two to nine and averages four and one-half offspring. The kits are blind and naked at birth, and weigh about one-half ounce, but their black-and-white color patterns are clearly visible. By three weeks of age, dense fur covers the entire body, but the eyes do not open until they are about 32 days old. Young spotted skunks can first throw musk when 46 days of age, and they are weaned at about 8 weeks old. Adult size is reached at three to four months, and breeding occurs when they are 10–12 months of age. Some adult females mate a second time in the late summer and produce a fall litter.

Spotted skunks in the wild usually live a maximum of five to six years, but in captivity they have survived up to ten years of age.

Remarks: The pelts of spotted skunks are sold in most northern areas for use as trim on clothing. This species rarely kills poultry, but individuals sometimes develop a fondness for chicken eggs. Sometimes the skunk will straddle an egg and give it a quick kick backward with the hind feet, forcefully propelling the egg against the wall to crack it open. They may repeat this action to achieve the desired result. Spotted skunks sometimes carry rabies and leptospirosis.

Selected References:

Crabb, W. D. 1941. Food habits of the prairie spotted skunk in southeastern Iowa. J. Mamm. 22: 349–64.

———. 1944. Growth, development, and seasonal weights of spotted skunks. J. Mamm. 25: 213–21.

———. 1948. The ecology and management of the prairie spotted skunk in Iowa. Ecol. Monogr. 18: 201–32.

Mead, R. A. 1967. Age determination in the spotted skunk. J. Mamm. 48: 606–16.

Mead, R. A. 1968. Reproduction in eastern forms of the spotted skunk (Genus *Spilogale*). J. Zool. 156: 119.

Van Gelder, R. G. 1959. A taxonomic revision of the spotted skunks (Genus *Spilogale*). Bull. Amer. Mus. Nat. Hist. 117: 229–392.

River Otter
Lutra canadensis

River otter, *Lutra canadensis.* Larry Brown

Identification: The river otter is a large, elongated, torpedo-shaped carnivore with a small, flattened head and a broad muzzle. The tail is long, muscular, and tapers gradually from the broad base to a point at the end. The legs are short and stout, and the feet have webbed toes. The upper fur is glossy brown, and the underparts are paler brown or grayish tan. The ears are small, rounded, and rather inconspicuous.

The skull is large, broad, and possesses a very short rostrum in front of the eye sockets. There is also a narrow constriction of the upper surface of the skull between the eye sockets.

Geographical Range: The river otter is found throughout the entire southeastern region. In the United States, the geographical range is nationwide, excluding only the southwestern desert region. However, it has been exterminated or decimated by humans and their pollution in a number of states where it once occurred widely. River otters also range through Canada and Alaska.

Habitat: This carnivore lives in almost every aquatic habitat available. Otters do very well in rivers, lakes, ponds, swamps, marshes, bayous, and small streams. They are less often found in brackish water and saltwater, except on the tidal zones of some large rivers. They never occur far from water, unless they are dispersing in search of a new home.

Natural History: Otters live in bank burrows, usually located under the roots of a tree, stump, or thick vegetation. They may excavate their own tunnels, but frequently

Geographical range of the river otter in the Southeast.

take over and remodel the den of another animal such as a beaver or nutria. Otters feed almost exclusively on animals, and crayfish and fish are their favorite items. They will also eat frogs, salamanders, snakes, turtles, snails, clams, rodents, birds, and even large aquatic insect larvae. River otters are among the most playful of all mammals and take particular delight in repeatedly sliding head first (torpedo style) into the water. They are very sociable carnivores that appear to enjoy many types of intraspecific group interactions.

River otters have large home ranges that may cover three to ten linear miles along a stream, lakeshore, or marsh. They are mainly nocturnal, but I have occasionally observed them foraging during the daytime, especially in protected reserves with ample cover. Otters, like all members of the weasel family, have very strong musk glands located in the anal area. They make scent posts throughout their home range by marking clumps of leaves or sticks with their pungent musk. Such scent markings are important in the various social and reproductive interactions of river otters. I once caught a half-grown river otter with my bare hands. I had no cage in my truck, so I merely tossed him loose into the back of the carry-all. I was able to drive only a

few hundred yards before stopping to liberate the otter back into the wild. The pungent musk released by this aroused animal was enough to gag a person in a confined space.

The mating season occurs in the late summer or fall. This is the only time when males are not sociable, for they engage in fighting and combat in an attempt to breed the females. There is a period of dormancy in the tiny embryos that lasts several months, but after implantation development to term requires only nine weeks. The total length of the gestation period averages eleven months but varies from ten to twelve months. The litter size ranges from one to six kits and averages three. The mother remates for the next year's litter immediately after giving birth. The babies are born blind, helpless, and are dark brown in color. The eyes open around 35 days of age, but young otters do not leave the den until they are 10–12 weeks old. The mother will not tolerate adult males near her young until they are about six months old, although weaning occurs around four months of age. The young otters accompany their mother until they are about one year old and fully grown. A few breed at one year of age, but most do not become sexually active until they are two years old.

River otters live fairly long, and some reach 12–15 years of age in the wild. In zoos they have lived as long as 20 years. Males can be aged by measuring the increasing size and configuration of the penis bone. The amount of tooth wear can also be used to age both sexes, but the most accurate method is to count the annuli in tooth enamel.

Otters are preyed upon by alligators in some portions of the Southeast, but they have almost no other enemies except humans. The nets of commercial fisherman occasionally drown river otters in certain areas. Also, I have noted a sizable number of otters hit by cars in those areas where the roads pass near or through wet habitats.

Remarks: The fur of the river otter is among the most valuable and durable of all carnivores. It is harvested by trappers during the winter months when the fur is thickest, and the pelts are sold for substantial prices.

River otters make entertaining and playful pets if raised from a young age. Unfortunately, they often cache a portion of the food given them, which can become a rather smelly habit. They also require a large aquarium or pool in which to frolic.

Some fishermen believe that otters damage fishing catches, but studies have shown that otters consume mainly nongame species. They may in fact benefit game fish by reducing competition.

Selected References:

Fitch, C. E., Jr. 1949. Age determination, by use of the baculum, in the river otter, *Lutra canadensis canadensis* Schreber. J. Mamm. 30: 102–10.

Hamilton, W. J., Jr., and W. R. Eadie. 1964. Reproduction in the otter in Michigan. J. Wildl. Mgmt. 6: 244–54.

McDaniel, J. C. 1963. Otter population study. Proc. Annual Conf. S.E. Assoc. Game and Fish Comm. 17: 163–68.

Park, E. 1971. *The World of the Otter.* J. B. Lippincott Co., Philadelphia, Pa. 159 pp.

Severinghaus, C. W., and J. E. Tanck. 1948. Speed and gait of an otter. J. Mamm. 29: 71.

Yeager, L. E. 1938. Otters of the delta hardwood region of Mississippi. J. Mamm. 19: 195–201.

Coyote
Canis latrans

Coyote, *Canis latrans*. U.S. Fish & Wildlife Service

Geographical range of the coyote in the Southeast.

Identification: This is a large, doglike carnivore that somewhat resembles a German shepherd dog. The upper pelage is light gray to yellowish buff, with the outer hairs (guard hairs) tipped with black. The underparts are whitish, cream, or pale gray. The backs of the ears are rust colored, and the muzzle is yellowish or rusty. The tail is somewhat bushy and colored like the back, but the tip is black. The front legs are whitish, and the outer sides of the hind legs are rust colored. Considerable variation in the pelage occurs, and there are nearly all-black and nearly all-white color phases.

The skull is doglike and much larger than those of foxes. Compared with dogs, coyotes have longer canine teeth and a lower "brow ridge" (the bump on top of the skull between the eyes).

Geographical Range: The coyote is not native to the Southeast, but has been introduced from time to time by fox-hunting groups. There are now well-established populations throughout much of the region. In the United States, the geographical range of the coyote is nationwide. It also occurs in Canada, Mexico, Alaska, and Central America.

Habitat: Coyotes are very adaptable, but they prefer open rangeland, fallow fields, and brushy pastures. They are most numerous in the coastal plains and Appalachian plateau habitats of the Southeast. They are least common in deep forest areas.

Natural History: Coyotes are noted for their vocalizations, which include howls, barks, whimpers, yips, and growls. Howling is more prevalent at the mating season and usually occurs at night. Other coyotes in the area usually respond to a howl with answering calls.

Coyotes dig large dens, often located in a bank or under some protective obstacle. Sometimes they merely enlarge the burrow of a fox, armadillo, gopher turtle, or other large tunneling species. There are usually at least two openings into the den, which measure approximately 10–12 inches wide by 20–24 inches high. The burrow may be 10–30 feet long with an enlarged nest chamber at the end.

Coyotes often travel over an area of 20–30 miles in diameter, and males have much larger home ranges than females. They deposit urine, feces, and scent at locations which mark their territorial boundaries for the benefit of other coyotes. They kill a variety of animals and are very opportunistic feeders, but rabbits and rodents make up about two-thirds of their diet. Coyotes also eat some fruits, seeds, and berries. They likewise take birds, reptiles, amphibians, carrion, and even garbage.

The breeding season occurs in the late winter and early spring. Gestation ranges from 58 to 65 days (the average is 63 days), and females produce only one litter per year averaging five young (ranging from two to twelve). Larger litters are born in years of good food supply (e.g., when there is high rodent or rabbit populations). Some coyotes mate for life, and others pair only for one reproductive season. Both parents tend the young, which are blind and helpless at birth and covered by a grayish brown, woolly fur. The eyes open when coyote pups are ten to fourteen days old. The pupils of the eye are round in the coyote pup, unlike the vertical slits of both red fox and gray fox pups. Young coyotes first leave the den when about three weeks old. The adult male often brings food to the female, which she tears into bits for the offspring. Juvenile coyotes are weaned at about eight weeks of age, then both parents bring food to the den in their stomachs and disgorge it at the entrance for the offspring to eat. The pups are taught to hunt by both parents when they are between 8 and 12 weeks old. The coyote family then abandons the den but stays together as a family group until late summer or early fall, when dispersal of the juveniles takes place. Young coyotes have been known to travel as far as 150 miles before setting up their own home ranges. A few young coyotes breed when one year old, but most do not become sexually active until two years old.

Coyotes have been known to survive for a maximum of twelve years in the wild and up to twenty years in captivity. The degree of tooth wear on the canines and incisors is often used as an aging criterion in coyotes, but counting the annuli in the enamel or cementum layers of the teeth is a more accurate method of measuring age among most carnivores.

Remarks: Coyotes consume large quantities of harmful rodents and rabbits. They also occasionally kill young sheep, goats, calves, and poultry. Sometimes, however, coyotes get blamed for the depredations of free-running packs of dogs. Problem coyotes can generally be trapped, hunted, or poisoned with some effort. Coyotes have no serious predators in the Southeast except humans and their dogs. Coyotes can carry and transmit rabies, scabies, mange, canine distemper, and leptospirosis.

Coyotes readily hybridize with domestic dogs and produce fertile offspring, which are called "coy-dogs." A coy-dog cross can look like either parent or, more commonly, like an intermediate between the parents. Coy-dogs with a German shepherd parent usually look so much like coyotes that it is difficult to determine that they are hybrids. Coy-dogs are normally fully fertile and can breed with either parental line or among themselves.

Selected References:

Andelt, W. F. 1985. Behavioral ecology of coyotes in south Texas. Wildl. Monogr. 94: 1–45.

Bekoff, M. 1977. Coyote (*Canis latrans*). Mammalian Species, No. 79: pp. 1–9.

———. 1978. Coyote: Biology, behavior, and management. Academic Press, N.Y., 384 pp.

Holzman, S., M. J. Conroy, and J. Pickering. 1992. Home range, movements, and habitat use of coyotes in southcentral Georgia. J. Wildl. Mgmt. 56: 139–46.

Mengel, R. M. 1971. A study of dog-coyote hybrids and implications concerning hybridization in *Canis*. J. Mamm. 52: 316–36.

Young, S. P., and H. H. Jackson. 1951. *The Clever Coyote*. Stackpole Co., Harrisburg, Pa. 411 pp.

Van Wormer, J. 1964. *The World of the Coyote*. J. B. Lippincott Co., Philadelphia, Pa. 150 pp.

Red Fox
Vulpes vulpes

Red fox, *Vulpes vulpes*. American Society of Mammalogists

Identification: The red fox is a medium-sized carnivore having a reddish yellow or tawny red upper coat and a long tawny, bushy tail in which the terminal portion is black and tipped with white. The cheeks, throat, and belly are white, but the legs and feet are black. The muzzle and ears are pointed, and the ears are black on the posterior side.

The skull is distinguished from that of the gray fox by having a shallow depression above and between the postorbital processes rather than a deep one. Also, the parietal and frontal ridges on top of the skull are not pronounced or elevated. The upper incisors are distinctly lobed on each side, but they are evenly rounded in the gray fox.

Geographical Range: The red fox has a regionwide distribution in the Southeast. In the United States, the geographical range extends from coast to coast. It also occurs throughout Canada and Alaska.

Habitat: The red fox prefers deciduous woodlands which are generously interspersed with fallow fields and weedy pastures. Unlike the gray fox, it tends to avoid heavy forest.

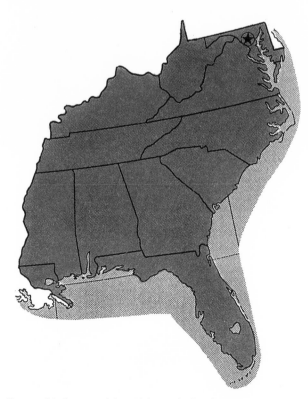

Geographical range of the red fox in the Southeast.

Natural History: Although primarily nocturnal, red foxes occasionally forage in the daytime and still more often at dawn and dusk. They normally excavate their own underground dens, but sometimes take over and enlarge the burrow of another animal. The den invariably has more than one entrance and is usually 20–40 feet long and three to four feet deep.

Breeding takes place in the late fall or early winter. The gestation period is around 53 days (and ranges from 50 to 56 days), and one litter is produced per year, averaging five young (in a range from one to ten). Red foxes are monogamous and apparently remain mated for life. The number of young per litter produced by a female increases until she is five to seven years old and then declines. At birth the pups are blind, helpless, and dark grayish brown in color and weigh about four ounces. The eyes open when they are seven to nine days old, and the pups first leave the den to play when they are about three weeks of age. They lose their woolly juvenile fur when about one and one-half months old, and the subsequent pelage is much like that of the parents. Weaning takes place at about two months of age, and they leave the parents when six months old. Young foxes sometimes disperse long distances before establishing their own home sites.

Red foxes eat mainly small mammals, including rabbits, rats, and mice. They also consume wild birds, amphibians, and reptiles when available. If food is plentiful, they may kill more than they can eat and cache the excess in the ground or cover it with grass and leaves.

In the wild, red foxes live eight to ten years, but in captivity some have survived fifteen years. They have very few enemies except humans, their dogs, bobcats, and coyotes. Great horned owls may also take a few pups at the mouth of the den.

Remarks: Red foxes are trapped and sold for fur in many parts of the country. The pelts are used extensively for trimming coats and jackets. Foxes feed heavily on rats, mice, and other small mammals and therefore are very beneficial in rodent control. However, they occasionally also make serious inroads in poultry populations.

In the northern United States and Canada, red foxes—especially the valuable "silver fox" variation, which is just a mutation of the normal coat color in this species—are raised on "farms" in captivity for their fur.

The red fox has historically always been much admired by hunters who love the sport of the chase. It has greater speed, endurance, and stamina than the gray fox and is generally considered to give a pack of trailing foxhounds a much better test of their abilities. Fox hunt clubs in the United States are usually patterned after the elaborate and formal sporting groups which originated in England. There are fox hunt clubs active in several parts of the Southeast.

Red foxes can carry and transmit such diseases as rabies, mange, scabies, canine distemper, and leptospirosis.

Selected References:

Nelson, A. L. 1933. A preliminary report on the winter food of Virginia foxes. J. Mamm. 14: 40–43.

Rue, L. L., III. 1969. *The World of the Red Fox.* J. B. Lippincott Co., Philadelphia, Pa. 204 pp.

Sargeant, A. B., S. H. Allen, and J. O. Hastings. 1987. Spatial relationships between sympatric coyote and red foxes in North Dakota. J. Wildl. Mgmt. 51: 285–93.

Scott, T. G., and W. D. Klimstra. 1955. Red foxes and a declining prey population. Southern Ill. Univ., Monogr. Series No. 1. 123 pp.

Sheldon, W. G. 1949. Reproductive behavior of foxes in New York State. J. Mamm. 30: 236–46.

Stanley, W. C. 1963. Habits of the red fox in northeastern Kansas. Univ. Kans., Mus. Nat. Hist. Misc. Publ. 34: 1–31.

Storm, G. L., R. D. Andrews, R. L. Phillips, R. A. Bishop, D. B. Siniff, and J. R. Tester. 1976. Morphology, reproduction, dispersal, and mortality of midwestern red fox populations. Wildl. Monogr. 49: 11–82.

Gray Fox
Urocyon cinereoargenteus

Gray fox, *Urocyon cinereoargenteus.* American Society of Mammalogists

Identification: The gray fox is a medium-sized carnivore having grizzled salt-and-pepper gray upper parts and a long, bushy tail with a distinct black stripe on its upper side. The underparts are white along the cen-

ter of the belly and tawny-orange along the sides. The muzzle is pointed with a blackish patch located on the top and on the chin. There are areas of tawny-orange on the sides of the neck, back of the ears, and sides of the legs. The orange flank and leg markings often lead to the erroneous identification of this species as the red fox, which is orangish red over all its sides and back. Young gray foxes have a juvenile fur that is quite distinct from the colorful adult pelage. It is a woolly gray-brown color that is replaced at about one and one-half months of age by fur similar to the adult markings.

The skull is easily identified by the presence of a prominent pair of elevated, lyre-shaped ridges running lengthwise on the top of the cranium (located on the frontal and parietal bones). Also, the upper incisors are evenly rounded on each side, but in the red fox they are lobed.

Geographical Range: This species has a regionwide distribution in the Southeast. In the United States, the gray fox is found everywhere except the northern Rocky Mountains and portions of the High Plains. They also range throughout Mexico, Central America, and into northern South America.

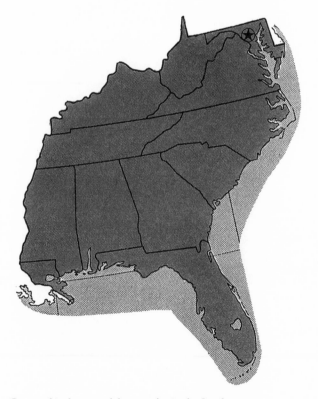

Geographical range of the gray fox in the Southeast.

Habitat: The gray fox occurs at least occasionally in almost every terrestrial habitat, but is most abundant in hardwood forests, wooded floodplains, and pine-oak woodlands bordering fallow fields and weedy pastures. This fox is very adaptable and tolerant of human activities. I have even found them to be common in semideveloped suburban areas.

Natural History: Gray foxes are often overlooked by the casual observer because they are active primarily at dawn and dusk and during the nocturnal hours. They spend their days sleeping in underground dens and in hollow logs or stumps. The gray fox is the only member of the dog family that routinely climbs trees in pursuit of prey or to escape hounds.

They prey heavily on rabbits, which usually make up nearly half of the total food consumed. Also important are mice, rats, birds, large insects, acorns, and fruits.

Mating in gray foxes occurs during the late winter or early spring. The gestation period averages 53 days (ranging from 51 to 63), and one litter per year is produced in March or April. The litter size averages four young and ranges from one to seven. The offspring (called pups) are blackish in color, blind, scantily furred, and weigh about three and one-half ounces. Their eyes open between the ninth and twelfth day after birth, and the young foxes first leave the den for short periods when about three weeks old. For the first five or six weeks, only the female cares for the young, but after that the male also brings food to the family. When they are about three months old, young foxes begin to forage for food with their parents, but the family breaks up by late summer. Gray foxes begin breeding in the year following their birth.

This species has few enemies other than people and their dogs, but bobcats and great horned owls take a few pups. Gray foxes are rarely hit by automobiles, presumably because of their speed, agility, and cunning nature. They normally live a maximum of eight to ten years in the wild, but there are records of them living up to fifteen years in captivity.

Remarks: The pelt of the gray fox is of fairly high quality, particularly in colder states, where it is widely trapped and sold for use in making coats. Gray foxes sometimes prey on chickens, ducks, turkeys, and other poultry from the farmyard.

I have noticed on several occasions that gray foxes often show little fear of humans when bright lights are shown on them at night. They are normally much more wary when they encounter humans. This tameness in response to spotlights has probably led to individuals' demise from time to time.

Gray foxes sometimes carry rabies, canine distemper, mange, scabies, or leptospirosis. These diseases are rare in most populations, however.

Selected References:

Fritzell, E. K., and K. J. Haroldson. 1982. Gray Fox (*Urocyon cinereoargenteus*). Mammalian Species, No. 189: pp. 1–8.

Heidt, G. A., J. H. Peck, and L. Johnson. 1984. An analysis of gray fox (*Urocyon cinereoargenteus*) fur harvests in Arkansas. Proc. Ark. Acad. Sci. 38: 49–52.

Layne, J. N. 1958. Reproductive characteristics of the gray fox in southern Illinois. J. Wildl. Mgmt. 22: 157–63.

Layne, J. N., and W. H. McKeon. 1956. Some aspects of red fox and gray fox reproduction in New York. N.Y. Fish and Game Jour. 3: 44–74.

Sampson, G. W. 1980. Missouri fur harvests. Mo. Dept. of Conserv., Terrestrial Series No. 7.

Sheldon, W. G. 1949. Reproductive behavior of foxes in New York State. J. Mamm. 30: 236–46.

Sullivan, E. G. 1956. Gray fox reproduction, denning, range, and weights in Alabama. J. Mamm. 37: 346–51.

Cougar
Felis concolor

Cougar, *Felis concolor.*

Identification: The cougar is also sometimes called the panther, puma, or mountain lion in various parts of its range. It is a large, powerfully built cat with a long, heavy, cylindrical tail. The upper parts are dark buff to tawny, and the underparts are dull white overlaid with buff in some areas. The head is relatively broad, and the ears are small, rounded, blackish on the posterior side, and never tufted. The sides of the muzzle are black, as is the dorsal portion of the furry tail.

The cougar skull is at least twice the size of a bobcat skull, and it contains three premolars on each side in the upper jaw, while the bobcat has two.

Geographical Range: The cougar once had a region-wide distribution in the Southeast, but it is now extirpated over most of the region. A small remnant population of 30–40 animals still occurs in southern Florida. Occasional sightings are also recorded in the swamplands of extreme southeastern Georgia and northern Florida, but most or all of these animals are escaped or released cougars from the West. In the United States, this big cat once had a geographical range from coast to coast, but it is now mainly confined to the Rocky Mountain and Pacific Coast states, plus the south Florida population, which is restricted to the Florida Everglades and Big Cypress Swamp. Cougars also occur in western Canada, Mexico, Central America, and all the way across South America to its southern tip. The cougar has the largest range of any mammal found in North America or the Western Hemisphere.

Habitat: The cougar lives in a wide variety of wilderness habitats, but tends to avoid those areas occupied by humans and their dogs. Because the southeastern states have little or no true wilderness left, the cougar has declined to the point of being extirpated or nearly extinct.

Natural History: Studies of marked and collared cougars using radio telemetry reveal that they range over vast areas. Males have much bigger home ranges—sometimes as large as 400 square miles—than females. Females have a home range that is only about one-fifth that of males.

Cougars are very secretive, solitary predators that are active mainly during the night and at dawn and dusk. These cats are mainly terrestrial foragers, but they swim very well and climb trees with agility. When pursued by dogs, they normally climb a tree to avoid harassment.

Present geographical range of the cougar in the Southeast.

Various species of deer, as well as wild pigs where they occur, are the principal prey of the cougar. Cougars also eat rabbits, hares, rodents, armadillos, and raccoons, but they cannot thrive without an abundant supply of large-bodied prey. A cougar catches its food by stealthily stalking the prey, then pouncing and biting the throat or back of the neck. After eating its fill, the carcass is dragged into a thicket or under dense cover and concealed with leaves, sticks, and debris. A cougar will return to this cache and feed for several days, either until the meat is all consumed or until it putrefies.

Females are two and one-half to three years old before they first breed, and thereafter they have a litter only once every two to three years. Breeding can occur at any time of the year. Adults only tolerate each other during the brief breeding encounter, so males play no part in caring for their offspring. The gestation period is between 82 and 96 days (the average is 90 days), and the litter size ranges from one to six, averaging two and one-half young. Kittens weigh about one pound at birth and are approximately 12 inches long, including the tail. They are covered with a soft, buff fur spotted with black, they have brownish black rings on the tail, and they are blind. Their eyes open at seven to ten days of age. Young cougars are weaned and start accompanying their mother on nightly hunting trips when three to four months old.

The life span of cougars in the wild is unknown, but seldom exceeds 12–15 years. In zoos they have lived a maximum of 25 years. The age of a cougar can be estimated by examining tooth wear, or it can be determined accurately by counting the annual growth rings in the cementum of teeth.

Remarks: The cougar is fully protected throughout the Southeast and is listed as officially endangered by the U.S. Fish and Wildlife Service.

In earlier times the cougar was beneficial in culling and controlling our deer populations, which tend to overpopulate their habitat. Humans now fulfill this function with an annual hunting season, so the natural role of the big cat is mainly obsolete. It remains today as an elegant reminder of our rich wildlife heritage that is largely gone.

Cougars are the "top carnivore" in the ecological food chain in North America. There are only a few scattered records of them attacking humans. They occasionally kill livestock and have to be controlled.

Numerous sightings of so-called "black panthers" are reported throughout the Southeast each year; these usually represent misidentified large dogs, hogs, cattle, etc., because there has *never ever* been a melanistic (black-colored) cougar collected or identified anywhere in North America. Perhaps some of these sightings may be of real panthers, glimpsed in very dim lighting, which makes them appear to be black.

Cougars have no serious natural enemies except humans and dogs. The latter frequently trail, harass, and tree them. Cougars can easily outrun trailing dogs, but they apparently feel secure in trees, because they almost always climb one when persistently trailed by dogs. This tendency becomes their undoing if hunters accompany the dogs.

Selected References:

Belden, R. C., W. B. Frankenberger, R. T. McBride, and G. T. Schwikert. 1988. Panther habitat use in southern Florida. J. Wildl. Mgmt. 52: 660–63.

Currier, M. J. P. 1983. Cougar or Panther (*Felis concolor*). Mammalian Species, No. 200: pp. 1–7.

Maehr, D. S. 1987. Florida panther movements, social organization, and habitat utilization. E-1-11 annual performance report. Fla. Game and Fresh Water Fish Comm., Tallahassee.

———. 1990. The Florida panther and private lands. Conservation Biology 4: 167–70.

Maehr, D. S., E. D. Land, J. C. Roof, and J. W. McCown. 1989. Early maternal behavior in the Florida panther. Amer. Midl. Nat. 122: 34–43.

Maehr, D. S., R. C. Belden, E. D. Land, and L. Wilkins. 1990. Food habits of panthers in southwest Florida, 1990. J. Wildl. Mgmt. 420–23.

Seidensticker, J. C., IV, M. G. Hornocker, W. V. Wiles, and J. P. Messick. 1973. Mountain lion social organization in the Idaho Primitive Area. Wildl. Monogr. 35: 1–60.

Young, S. P., and E. A. Goldman. 1946. *The Puma, Mysterious American Cat*. Amer. Wildl. Inst., Washington, D.C. 358 pp.

Bobcat
Lynx rufus

Bobcat, *Lynx rufus*. Florida Game & Freshwater Fish Commission

Identification: The bobcat, or "wildcat," is a carnivore about halfway in size between a cougar and a domestic cat. It has a short tail, which is four to six inches long, long legs, and pointed ears that usually have small tufts of hair (about one inch long) at the tips. Bobcats have a short, broad face and ruffs of fur extending out from each cheek like sideburns. The upper parts are tawny-brown to olive-brown, with scattered black spots or streaks giving the coat a splattered-paint appearance. The underparts are whitish with black spots, and there a few black bars on the inner sides of the front legs. The tail is tawny-brown with several transverse black bars, the last of which is rather broad, followed by a tiny white tip. The toes are all equipped with large curved, retractable claws. The backs of the ears and ear-tufts are black.

The skull is broad, rounded, and short-faced. It is identified by having two upper premolars on each side rather than the three present in the cougar and domestic cat.

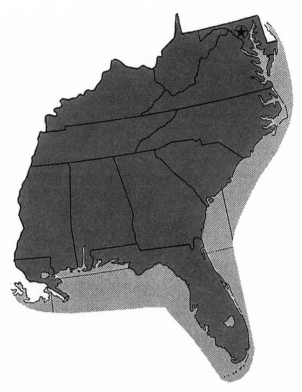

Geographical range of the bobcat in the Southeast.

Geographical Range: Bobcats are abundant throughout the entire southeastern region. In the United States, the geographical range is nationwide, and it is also present in most of Mexico.

Habitat: Bobcats occur in a wide variety of terrestrial habitats, ranging from dense forest to open grassy areas extending from the coastal plain to the northern mountains. They are missing only from extensive aquatic environments. It is not unusual for bobcats to live even on the fringes of semideveloped residential areas and open suburban habitats.

Natural History: Bobcats sometimes forage during the daylight hours, but they are most active at night and at sunrise and sunset. They are excellent climbers and often forage or rest in trees. On one occasion, I was searching for fox squirrels and discovered a large bobcat sleeping in the fork of a large cypress tree about 40 feet above the ground. When I rapped on the tree with a stick, he awoke, but showed no alarm, apparently feeling secure in his lofty perch.

Bobcats are solitary carnivores that have sizable home ranges varying from 15 to 25 square miles in diameter. Male home ranges are much larger than those of females, and they defend territories against other males. The boundaries of the territories are marked with scent posts, which consist of feces, urine, and/or scratchings in the dirt. When marking a territory, bobcats typically back up to an object and spray copious amounts of urine on it. In contrast to the male bobcats, females are not territorial, having home ranges that overlap broadly.

Bobcats are strict carnivores but very opportunistic in their foraging, taking whatever animal is most available at a given time. Rabbits usually make up the largest percentage of the diet, but rats, mice, squirrels, opossums, quail, turkeys, perching birds, snakes, lizards, and an occasional fawn are also included.

Breeding can occur year round, but it usually peaks during the late winter or early spring. Most births occur from April through September, with the peak parturitions in April through May and in July. Adult females normally produce one litter each year, though occasionally they produce two. The gestation period is about 62 days, followed by the birth of one to six kittens (the average is two and one-half). At birth, the kittens are covered with a soft, spotted fur, have sharp claws, and are blind. In about ten days the eyes open, and the kittens leave the den to play for the first time. The mother starts bringing food to the den for the young when they are seven to eight weeks old. Weaning takes place when the young bobcats are about three to four months old, but they stay with their mother until the following spring. Some females mate when as young as one year of age, but most females and all the males wait to breed until they are two years old.

In the wild, bobcats normally live a maximum of 10 to 12 years, but in captivity they reach 25 years of age. The most accurate method of measuring their age is to count growth rings in the cementum layer of the canine teeth.

Humans and their dogs appear to be the major enemies of the bobcat. Kittens may also be taken by great horned owls, foxes, coyotes, or cougars, but these are probably not major sources of mortality. Road kills by automobiles are fairly common, however.

Remarks: Bobcats are often hunted or trapped to be mounted as trophy specimens by hunters. The fur is also valuable as a trim for coats and other garments. The ban on importing the fur of most spotted cats into the United States has greatly increased the demand for pelts of the native bobcat.

This carnivore is an important consumer of many problem rodents such as the cotton rat, black rat, rice rat, Norway rat, etc., and they do a great deal to help control cottontail rabbit populations. On the negative side, bobcats, like most carnivores, occasionally carry rabies or feline distemper.

Selected References:

Fritts, S. H., and J. A Sealander. 1978a. Diets of bobcats in Arkansas with special reference to age and sex. J. Wildl. Mgmt. 42: 533–37.

———. 1978b. Reproductive biology and population characteristics of bobcats in Arkansas. J. Wildl. Mgmt. 59: 347–53.

Maehr, D. S., and J. R. Brady. 1986. Food habits of bobcats in Florida. J. Mamm. 67: 133–38.

Rolley, R. E. 1985. Dynamics of a harvested bobcat population in Oklahoma. J. Wildl. Mgmt. 49: 283–92.

Rucker, R. A., M. L. Kennedy, and G. A. Heidt. 1989. Population density, movements, and habitat use of bobcats in Arkansas. Southwestern Nat. 34: 101–8.

Wassmer, D. A., D. D. Guenther, and J. N. Layne. 1988. Ecology of the bobcat in south-central Florida. Bull Fla. State Mus., Biol. Sci., 33: 159–228.

Young, S. P. 1978. *The Bobcat of North America*. Univ. of Nebr. Press, Lincoln, Nebr. 193 pp.

Harbor Seal
Phoca vitulina

Harbor seal, *Phoca vitulina*. Tom French

Identification: The harbor seal is fairly small (five to six feet long) and the color is variable, but it is usually dark grayish brown, yellowish gray, or whitish gray, often mottled with dark spots, blotches, or rings. The front flippers are small and the hind flippers always point backwards. The eyes are large, nose whiskers are prominent, and there are no external ears.

The skull has four bladelike cheek teeth on each side of the upper and lower jaw, all of which are double-rooted. The third upper cheek tooth is the largest.

Geographical Range: The harbor seal has been recorded only rarely along the southeastern Atlantic Coast. The species is a northern one, but it has been recorded all the way down the East Coast to a peripheral limit near Cape Kennedy in peninsular Florida. Harbor seals occur over a wide range along the shores of all oceans in the Northern Hemisphere.

Habitat: These seals, as their name suggests, inhabit harbors, bays, inlets, and other estuarine areas along the coast. They spend a good deal of time resting on shore and forage in shallow coastal waters, but occasionally they are found well out at sea.

Natural History: Harbor seals feed on a wide variety of shallow-water fishes and shellfish. They tend to migrate seasonally up and down the marine coasts. Individuals tend to be widely scattered during most of the summer months. In New England, by August they congregate in small herds of mixed ages and sexes. In September, mature adults swim to secluded, inshore areas and mate. Males do not maintain harems of females as is common among some other species of seals. The winter is often spent at sea away from the mainland.

The gestation period is about 280 days, and one or two pups are born in the spring. The newborn seals are covered by a soft coat of white or yellowish-white fur. It is shed and replaced by a darker coat within a week or two. Young seals are precocial and can swim shortly after birth. They nurse for a few weeks, grow rapidly, and are soon foraging on their own for various fishes. Young harbor seals become sexually active at about two years of age. The maximum life expectancy is around 20 years. Killer whales, sharks, and polar bears are considered the seal's main predators.

Remarks: In some areas harbor seals are believed to compete seriously with commercial fishing interests. In the Arctic, they are utilized by native populations for meat and hides.

Selected References:

Lawson, J. W., and D. Renouf. 1985. Parturition in the Atlantic harbor seal, *Phoca vitulina concolor*. J. Mamm. 66: 345–98.

Sullivan, R. M. 1982. Agonistic behavior and dominance relationships in the harbor seal, *Phoca vitulina*. J. Mamm. 63: 554–69.

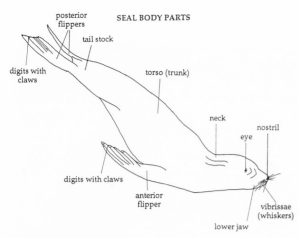

SEAL BODY PARTS

posterior flippers
tail stock
digits with claws
torso (trunk)
neck
nostril
eye
digits with claws
anterior flipper
vibrissae (whiskers)
lower jaw

Seal body parts.

Hooded Seal
Cystophora cristata

Hooded seal, *Cystophora cristata.* Sea World

Identification: This seal is large (sometimes reaching ten feet long), mottled gray and black, and exhibits an elastic nose pouch. When inflated with air this "hood," as it is called, looks like a rubber football extending from the nostrils to the forehead. The snout is wrinkled when the hood is deflated. Inflatable nose pouches are absent in females and immature males.

The skull has only two pairs of upper incisors, one pair of lower incisors, and the cheek teeth are simple pegs.

Geographical Range: The hooded seal rarely wanders south along the Atlantic Coast into southeastern waters. It is a northern species, but wandering individuals have been recorded as far south as southern Florida. This species is most abundant in the North Atlantic off the coasts of Canada and Greenland.

Habitat: Hooded seals are animals of the open ocean and northern ice packs. They are highly migratory and usually occur in small groups. They are also deep divers and feed mostly on clams, squids, octupi, shrimp, fish, and starfish.

Natural History: Hooded seals are most gregarious during the breeding, migrating, and molting seasons. Each year they undertake long, pelagic migrations extending from the birthing areas (in March) on the winter pack-ice off Labrador, northward to Greenland (by June). In late summer they return southward to feed off the coasts of Newfoundland and Labrador.

Each female gives birth to a single pup in the early spring, weighing about 50 pounds. They are nursed for only about two weeks and then abandoned by the mothers to fend for themselves. Adult females mate right after the end of lactation, and breeding is monogamous. The gestation period is thus about 11 $1/2$ months long. Young seals grow very rapidly on the rich milk produced by their mothers. Sexual maturity in young seals does not occur until they are four to six years old. The maximum life expectancy is approximately 32 to 35 years. Sharks, killer whales, and polar bears are the primary predators of the hooded seal, in addition to humans.

Remarks: This species is extensively hunted for its pelt and meat in Arctic waters. The young seals, or "bluebacks," possess the most sought-after fur. They are harvested in large numbers and are a significant economic factor in some countries.

Southern records of the hooded seals apparently represent lost or widely wandering individuals. No colonies of this species have occurred in southeastern waters in historic times.

Selected References:

Rasmussen, B. 1960. On the stock of hooded seals in the North Atlantic. Fisheries Res. Board, Artic Unit. Ste. Anne de Bellevue, Quebec. No. 387.

Sergeant, D. E. 1965. Exploitation and conservation of harp and hooded seals. The Polar Record 12: 541–51.

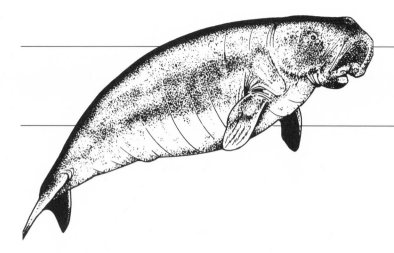

Order Sirenia
Manatees

The manatees, or "sea cows," are a bizarre-looking group of aquatic mammals found in coastal waters of tropical and subtropical areas. They are massive, blimp-like vegetarians that sometimes occur in herds. They are considered to be quite social and gentle creatures. The forelimbs are modified into paddlelike appendages, and the tail is stubby, muscular, and horizontally flattened into a broad, spatulate flipper used for propulsion through the water. There are no hind limbs or dorsal fin present.

Manatees consume copious amounts of submerged and floating vegetation. They spend the winters inland in large, spring-fed rivers, and the warmer months in coastal marine waters. Sirenians may be solitary, live in pairs, or associate in larger social groups of various sizes.

Sirenians are considered to be the source of the legendary mermaid stories. Sailors returning from months or years at sea apparently let their imaginations run wild when they glimpsed the amorphous, cigar-shaped bodies of manatees in the water. The fact that manatees have two mammary glands located in the chest area at the base of each flipper for suckling the young no doubt contributed to the mermaid myth.

Sirenians occur along the coasts of warm seas and in the associated large rivers of southern Asia, eastern Africa, northern Australia, southern North America, and northern South America. In many areas of the world their populations have been decimated as result of the actions of humans.

Manatees have no close relatives, but it is believed that elephants and sirenians evolved from a common ancestor. The cheek teeth of the two groups are very similar in their structure and replacement. They also share a number of other anatomical characteristics. Only one species of manatee lives in the southeastern United States, and there are only four living species of sirenians in the whole world.

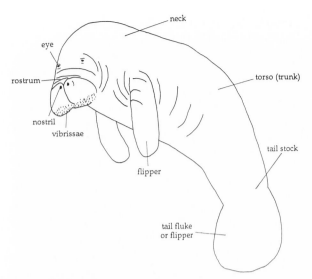

Manatee body parts.

Manatee
Trichechus manatus

Manatee, *Trichechus manatus*. Florida Game & Freshwater Fish Commission

Identification: This species is also referred to as the West Indian or Florida manatee because of its regional distribution pattern. Manatees are shaped like overstuffed cigars, with a small, blunt head and no visible neck. The tail is broad and rounded, the forelimbs are short, stocky flippers, and hind limbs are absent. The body is almost hairless and the thick, blubbery skin is dull gray to dusky gray in color. The snout is broad and square, and the lips are generously covered with tactile bristles.

The skull has a narrow, forward-projecting rostrum, and the molar teeth wear off anteriorly and are replaced by the next ones in line posteriorly. The lower jaw is rather massive and slightly curved downward.

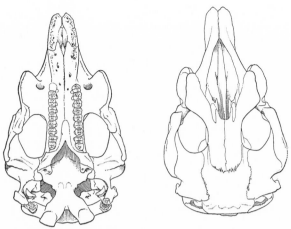

Lower view (left) and upper view (right) of the manatee (*Trichechus manatus*) skull.

Geographical Range: Manatees migrate northward from Florida to the marine coastal waters of Georgia in the summertime. In the winter months, they move back south to reside in the large spring-fed rivers of central and southern Florida. In the United States, the range of this species extends from South Carolina along the South Atlantic Coast through Florida to the Gulf of Mexico, and all the way around to the southern tip of Texas. It also occurs throughout most of the islands of the West Indies, the east coast of Mexico and Central America, and the north and east coasts of South America.

Habitat: The manatee prefers shallow marine bays and estuaries during the warmer months of the year. When the ocean temperatures drop in the fall, manatees move into freshwater to spend the winter. They select the large spring-fed rivers because of the constant warm water temperatures during the winter months. They usually congregate in large numbers near spring heads and in the channels downstream from the springs.

Natural History: Manatees are very intolerant of cold temperatures. Their metabolic rate is so slow that they cannot maintain body heat when surrounding temperatures are below 65 degrees Fahrenheit. In the winter, a long cold snap can result in the deaths of significant numbers because of colder than average water temperatures, pneumonia, and other respiratory ailments. Manatees tend to congregate during the winter at warm water sources such as artesian springs and power plants. They have a very gentle disposition, are completely harmless to humans, and almost defenseless as well. Skin divers often swim among them and are often ignored or at least tolerated. It is also not uncommon for manatees to solicit a back scratch from divers.

In the winter, manatees usually gather in small herds of five to twenty-five individuals to forage and socialize. Occasionally, larger congregations of fifty or more take place in especially favorable locations. Manatees can remain submerged for as long as fifteen minutes, but normally they surface for a breath every two to three minutes or less.

When an adult female comes into heat, which can occur at any time during the year, several bulls usually follow her around and attempt to mate. Courtship activities include nuzzling and embracing a prospective mate, and actual copulation usually takes place in shallow water. The females are promiscuous, i.e., they mate with a large number of pursuing males. Gestation is approximately 12–13 months long, and a single calf (rarely two) is produced once every three to five years. More calves are born in the spring and summer than at other times of the year. The babies weigh 30–60 pounds at birth, are about four feet long, and their coloration is pinkish. The mother nudges her offspring to the surface to breathe immediately after birth, and holds it there for about an hour. In a short time it is able to surface and breathe on its own without assistance. Calves nurse underwater at each of two mammary glands located in the mother's axillary region. Young manatees start taking vegetation within a few months, but they remain with their mother for up to two years. Young females reach sexual maturity and start breeding when about seven years of age. Young males are seldom successful breeders even though they are sexually mature because they must attain bulk and size to compete with the older bulls.

Adult manatees measure eight to fourteen feet long (but seldom do they exceed twelve feet), and they weigh from 600 to 2,500 pounds. The adult females are usually somewhat larger and heavier than adult males. The maximum longevity of manatees in the wild is unknown, but it may approach 40–50 years (they have lived over 30 years in zoos). There is presently no reliable method for aging adult manatees. Humans appear to be the only serious predator of adults, but alligators, sharks, or crocodiles may account for occasional mortality in the young.

Remarks: Manatee meat was considered a delicacy by early Indian cultures and pioneer settlers. The hides were made into leather, and oil derived from the blubber was once used for cooking and burned in lamps. Today, of course, the manatee is fully protected as an endangered species by both the state and federal governments. The total population of manatees in the Southeast is estimated not to exceed 2,500 individuals, and the stability of this population is not clear. As with most of our endangered species, humans are the major decimating factor that brought manatee populations down. Boat propellers clearly do the most damage in killing and maiming manatees. Many adults show the tell-tale scars of old or recent propeller cuts. Over the last few years, there has been a major campaign to post and enforce lower boat speed limits in most manatee wintering areas. Even more important, some areas near springs are now closed to motorboats entirely when the manatees are there for the winter. Other human-caused mortality factors include poaching, vandalism, and harassment by curious divers and swimmers. The periodic outbreaks of "red tide" (caused by the release of toxic poisons by certain microorganisms) along the marine coasts are responsible for some manatee deaths.

Manatees are becoming more appreciated by the public for their unique aesthetic value and unusually gentle nature. They are major tourist attractions almost everywhere they congregate. Perhaps their popularity means they can be increased in number and saved from any possibility of extinction.

Selected References:

Beeler, I. E., and T. J. O'Shea. 1988. Distribution and mortality of the West Indian manatee (*Trichechus manatus*) in the southeastern United States. National Tech. Inf. Ser., Springfield, Va. 2 vols. 613 pp.

Domning, D. P., and L. C. Hayck. 1986. Interspecific and intraspecific morphological variation in manatees (*Sirenia: Trichechus*). Marine Mammal Science 2: 87–144.

Garrott, R. A., B. B. Ackerman, J. R. Cary, D. M. Heisey, J. E. Reynolds III, P. M. Rose, and J. R. Wilcox. 1994. Trends in counts of Florida manatees at winter aggregation sites. J. Wildl. Mgmt. 58: 642–53.

Hartman, D. S. 1979. Ecology and behavior of the manatee (*Trichechus manatus*) in Florida. Amer. Soc. Mammal., Spec. Publ. 5: 1–153.

Irvine, A. B. 1983. Manatee metabolism and its influence on distribution in Florida. Biol. Conserv. 25: 315–34.

Kochman, H. I., G. B. Rothbun, and J. A. Powell. 1985. Temporal and spatial distribution of manatees in Kings Bay, Crystal River, Florida. J. Wildl. Mgmt. 49: 921–24.

O'Shea, T. J., C. A. Beck, R. K. Boude, H. I. Kochman, and D. K. Odell. 1985. An analysis of manatee mortality patterns in Florida, 1976–81. J. Wildl. Mgmt. 49: 1–11.

Reynolds, J. E., III, and J. R. Wilcox. 1986. Distribution and abundance of the West Indian manatee, *Trichechus manatus*, around selected Florida power plants following winter cold fronts: 1984–85. Biol. Conserv. 38: 103–11.

U.S. Fish and Wildlife Service. 1989. Florida manatee *(Trichechus manatus latirostris)* recovery plan. Atlanta, and Georgia. 98 pp.

Order Artiodactyla
Even-Toed Hoofed Mammals

This group of mammals includes deer, elk, moose, pigs, cattle, antelope, caribou, goats, llamas, camels, and sheep. Among all of them, the tips of the second and third toes on each foot support the weight of the body and are sheathed in large hooves. The other toes (called dew-claws) are reduced in size or absent. The limbs are elongated, and some of the ankle and foot bones are fused to form a single lower leg, or "cannon bone."

A closely related group, the odd-toed hoofed mammals (Order Perissodactyla) has no wild representatives in the Southeast, but includes our domestic horses, asses, donkeys, and mules, as well as tapirs, zebras, and rhinoceroses. Among the odd-toed hoofed mammals the body weight is borne either on one toe (the third) or on three toes (the second, third, and fourth).

Artiodactyls often have horns or antlers developed as outgrowths of the frontal bones. In the deer family they grow each year and are shed, but in the cattle family they are permanently growing structures that are not shed. All artiodactyls are herbivores, but they are variously adapted to feed on a wide diversity of plant materials. Many of them have complex, multichambered stomachs (the first chamber is called a rumen) and will regurgitate food, chew it a second time, and reswallow (the whole process is called rumination).

Native species of artiodactyls occur throughout the world except Australia and New Zealand. There were three species of native artiodactyls in the Southeast when the European explorers arrived. Two of these (the bison and elk) were quickly extirpated, and the other, the white-tailed deer, is common. In addition, man has introduced the wild boar (or feral pig), the fallow deer, sika deer, and sambar deer to various locations throughout the southeastern United States, and they have become well-established residents.

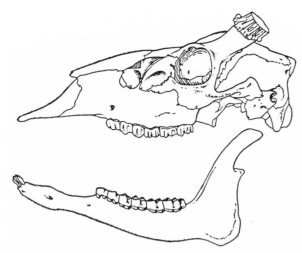

Side view of a representative artiodactylid skull, the white-tailed deer *(Odocoileus virginianus).*

Wild Boar
Sus scrofa

Wild Boar, *Sus scrofa.* Larry Brown

Identification: The wild boar, or feral pig, looks much like the domestic pig except that it is more lean and rangy and has a narrower, longer skull containing large, sharp tusks. The predominant pelage color of feral pigs is black or dark brown. However, spotted and mottled color patterns of black, brown, orange, russet, yellow, or white are also relatively common. A typical population studied in central Florida consisted of 60 percent black individuals, and 40 percent were spotted. The pelage of feral pigs is generally coarser and denser than that of domestic pigs, which presumably provides better protection against cold weather.

The skull is long and narrow with a downward-sloping forehead and snout. Males possess enlarged, sharp-edged recurved canines in both upper and lower

jaws, which are formidable weapons. The tusks of females are rather small and inconspicuous by comparison. Cheek teeth are of the bunodont type, with low rounded cusps.

Geographical Range: Wild boars are not native to the Southeast; they are said to have been first brought here from Europe by Hernando DeSoto in 1539 and subsequently by many other groups. Feral populations now occur in many locations throughout the region. In the United States, the geographical range extends throughout the south from Maryland and Kentucky to Texas and Arkansas. Isolated populations also occur in California, Hawaii, Puerto Rico, the Virgin Islands, and many other places.

Habitat: Wild pigs occupy many types of plant communities, including oak-hickory woodlands, mixed hardwood forests, swamp borders, live oak hammocks, pine-oak woodlots, beech-maple forests, etc.

Natural History: Wild pigs are omnivorous and forage extensively on food they pick up on the surface of the ground or just below the surface as a result of root-

Geographical range of the wild boar in the Southeast.

ing with their broad, shovel-like noses. An area recently foraged by feral swine usually looks like an unevenly plowed field of dirt or mud. They damage or eliminate many plants growing in the understory, eating large quantities of bulbs, roots, and tubers in the process. Pigs also love acorns, hickory nuts, pecans, seeds, mushrooms, fleshy fruits, and berries. They will also consume all types of small animals, including snakes, lizards, frogs, toads, worms, eggs, grubs, mice, rats, baby birds, arthropods, and even carrion. Wild pigs forage mainly from dusk till dawn, but they are also active during the daytime, especially in areas of heavy cover or on cloudy, overcast days.

Wild pigs breed throughout the year. When a female comes into estrus, she normally breeds repeatedly with the dominant boars in the area. Subordinate boars then usually breed with the still receptive sow. Such copulatory activity and fighting among the boars may extend over a two-day period. Gestation is 112–14 days long, and the litter size varies from one to twelve piglets, averaging about five. Baby pigs are precocial, and they are born with their eyes open, fully haired, and able to walk and move about shortly after birth. The piglets grow rapidly and wean within a few weeks, but often remain with the female to form a foraging family group for several months. Young sows can reach sexual maturity as young as three months of age. I once collected a small female that weighed only 50 pounds but whose uterus contained three small embryos. Young boars reach puberty at about five months of age, but rarely have the opportunity to participate in breeding until they reach 12–18 months old, due to dominance by older males.

Feral pigs characteristically travel in herds composed of several adult females and their offspring of various ages. Adult boars are normally solitary except at breeding time. A herd of feral pigs tends to gradually drift through a fairly large home range area as they forage. Movement within the home range is usually linked to seasonal changes in the type of food available. The home range size varies from 500 to 750 acres, depending on habitat quality and cover density.

The age of wild pigs can be measured, when young, by the sequence of tooth eruptions and, later on, by examining tooth wear in the molars. The weight of the eye lens is also an accurate method of aging if an autopsy is being performed. In the wild, feral pigs live a maximum of 10–15 years. In captivity some have lived 20 years.

Other than humans and their dogs, wild pigs do not have a long list of enemies. In the few areas where bears or cougars remain, pigs can be a prey for these carnivores. Young pigs are also consumed by bobcats, coyotes, and alligators.

Remarks: Wild boars are an important big-game animal. They provide, along with deer, a significant share of big-game sport hunting throughout the South. The heads of large boars with long tusks are usually mounted and proudly displayed as trophy specimens.

Feral pigs seriously damage all types of ground cover in their foraging activities. Some rare and delicate plants and some animals can be completely decimated by foraging hogs. Particularly vulnerable are orchids, lilies, ferns, bog plants, amphibians, small reptiles, and eggs or young of ground-nesting birds. Also, at the edges of some urbanizing areas, they cause damage to lawns, golf courses, road shoulders, parks, and recreational areas.

Problem wild pigs can usually be trapped and removed by using corral-type pens that have trigger-release, swinging-trap doors. The trap can be baited with rancid corn. Multiple catches of sows and young pigs are frequent in these traps, but wily old boars are often difficult to lure into the corral trap. Boars and other pigs can also be captured using trained "hog dogs," such as pit bulldogs and trailing hounds. Most trained dogs will lock their jaws upon the ears (or wherever they can secure a hold) of a cornered wild boar and hang on for dear life until the hunter arrives to tie-up or dispatch the quarry. There is a high injury and mortality rate in hunting dogs due to the powerful, slashing tusks of larger boars.

The European or Russian wild boars established in the North Carolina, Tennessee, and Georgia mountains tend to be larger, heavier, and better trophy specimens than the average wild pig found in the South. They were introduced in 1912.

Selected References:

Brown, L. N. 1985. Elimination of a small feral swine population in an urbanizing section of central Florida. Fla. Scientist 48: 121–23.

Baron, J. 1982. Effects of feral hogs (Sus scrofa) on the vegetation of Horn Island, Mississippi. Amer. Midl. Nat. 107: 202–5.

Belden, R. C. 1989. History and biology of feral swine. In Proc. Feral Pig Symposium, Orlando, Fla. Livestock Conserv. Inst., Madison, Wisc.

Bratton, S. P. 1975. The effects of the European wild boar, *Sus scrofa*, on gray beech forest in the Great Smoky Mountains. Ecology 56: 1356–66.

Frankenberger, W. B., and R. C. Belden. 1976. Distribution, relative abundance and management needs of feral pigs in Florida. Proc. SE Game and Fish Comm., 30: 641–44.

Mayer, J. L., and I. B. Brisbin, Jr. 1991. *Wild Pigs in the United States: Their History, Morphology, and Current Status.* Univ. Ga. Press, Athens, Ga. 313 pp.

Wood, G. W., and R. H. Barrett. 1974. Status of wild pigs in the United States. Wildl. Soc. Bull. 7: 237–46.

White-tailed Deer
Odocoileus virginianus

White-tailed deer, *Odocoileus virginianus*. Florida Game & Freshwater Fish Commission

Geographical range of the white-tailed deer in the Southeast.

Identification: White-tailed deer are fairly large and have long, slender legs and a broad, well-haired tail which flashes white on the underside. Antlers are normally present only in the bucks, and these are grown and shed each year. Deer walk on the tips of the toes (called digitigrade locomotion) which are sheathed in hooves. The upper parts of the white-tailed deer are grayish brown to russet-brown, and the underparts and inside of the legs are white. They have a white eye ring, a white spot around the nose, and the ears are large and cowlike.

The skull can be identified in males by the presence of bifurcating antlers or antler pedicles on the frontal bones. The pointed forks of the antlers are called "tines," and in the white-tailed deer there is usually one main antler beam off which the tines branch. Both bucks and does lack upper incisor and canine teeth, and there is a gap in the bones (the lacrimal opening) in front of the eye socket that is at least one-half inch wide.

Geographical Range: White-tailed deer occur throughout the entire southeastern region. In the United States, the geographical range is nationwide, except for portions of the arid Southwest and western mountain areas. The species also ranges through Canada, Mexico, Central America, and northern South America. In the eastern two-thirds of the United States, it is normally the most common deer present.

Habitat: White-tailed deer live in almost every terrestrial habitat found in the Southeast. They tend to be most abundant in various forest-edge habitats, where they can find both good cover and ample forage to feed upon.

Natural History: Deer are mainly browsing and grazing mammals, which means they feed upon the twigs, leaves, and tender shoots of many trees and shrubs as well as on grasses. They forage mainly from dusk to dawn and bed down in a thicket or clump of dense grass during the daytime. On cloudy, overcast days when they are hungry, foraging may also occur during the daylight hours. In the fall, acorns and hickory nuts are important foods, and they also eat fruits (especially apples and pears), berries, and mushrooms when available.

Individual home ranges of white-tailed deer are not as large as one might expect. Bucks have larger home ranges (averaging from one to one and one-half square miles) than do females (which average only one-half to three-fourths of a square mile). During the mating season, bucks often cover an even larger area in search of females to breed with. Deer have several scent glands, which are located on the legs near the hoofs. These glands are important in marking scent posts and trails, which aid deer in locating one another. They have a very keen sense of smell, as well as good hearing and excellent eyesight.

The breeding season for white-tailed deer is fairly long in the Southeast, extending from September to early March. Most of the does are impregnated in the fall or early winter, but stragglers usually represent young does of the previous year that are late in reaching sexual maturity or have foraged on poor range. Each doe is in heat for only 24 hours, and should she not encounter a buck during this short period, she will recycle each lunar month (every 28 days) for several times during the breeding season. The gestation period is six and one-half to seven months long and averages 202 days. The litter size ranges from one to three fawns, but the average is two. Young females that are breeding for the first time usually produce a single offspring. On poor deer range, even older females will tend to produce one fawn each year instead of the normal two. At birth, the fawns weigh three to seven pounds. They are precocial, the eyes being open, and they are able to run shortly after delivery. Fawns are very well camouflaged by numerous pale-white spots on a cinnamon-brown background. They hide motionless in thick vegetation while the mother is gone foraging. They also have little or no scent, which makes them difficult for many predators to find.

When the fawns are three to four weeks old they begin to follow the doe around and start eating some solid food. Fawns are usually weaned when three to four months old, and the spots fade at about that time, giving them a uniform brown coloration on the upper parts. Young deer usually continue to accompany their mothers until they are old enough to breed. Some young females breed at six to eight months of age, but most does and all bucks are about one and one-half years old before they enter the breeding population.

In the wild, the majority of white-tails do not survive to a ripe old age, especially if they are hunted. Most deer harvested in the Southeast are between one

and one-half and three and one-half years old. A few deer (especially does, where they are not hunted) will survive in the wild to about 15 years. The maximum longevity in a zoo is about 25 years.

It is interesting to note that the oldest bucks do not possess the largest antlers. A peak is normally reached in antler size during the prime of breeding life (usually from six to ten years old), after which the antlers of aging males decline in size. Deer can be placed into age classes by examining the sequence of tooth replacement and by measuring the rate of tooth wear.

Remarks: The white-tailed deer is the number-one big-game mammal over most of the eastern United States. State wildlife departments have historically put more emphasis on its study and management than on any other game species. Deer hunting is a major recreational business with strong economic impact in most rural, undeveloped areas of the region.

White-tailed deer sometimes cause agricultural damage by foraging heavily on field crops or gardens. They can usually be frightened away with noise-making devices or by erecting electric fences.

Young deer are sometimes kept as pets, but this practice is against state wildlife regulations and can even be dangerous, particularly if the fawn grows up to become a buck with antlers. Bucks in rut become extremely aggressive and joust with other males to determine dominance for breeding. There are cases on record of owners of previously docile deer being attacked, injured, or even killed by their pets. The increase in aggressiveness is due to high levels of male sex hormone (testosterone) secreted by the testes into their systems. Antler growth and maturation is caused by the same hormone. As antlers grow and branch from buds on the frontal bones, they are covered with a very vascular, soft, fuzzy skin called "velvet." By early fall, antler growth is complete and the blood supply to the velvet shuts off because of hormonal changes. The velvet then dies and sloughs off, leaving the hard, bonelike antlers. At this time, the bucks vigorously rub and polish the antlers on shrubs and saplings, usually leaving evidence in the form of broken branches and stripped bark. The antlers remain functional throughout the fall and winter months. In the late winter or early spring, a portion of the bony core of the antler is resorbed near the antler base, causing a weak zone, called the "abscission" layer. The antlers then break off because of their weakened condition, usually one at a time, and this completes the annual cycle. Bucks are then antlerless for six to eight weeks before the buds on the frontal bones begin to grow again.

The race of white-tailed deer found in southern Florida are small compared to individuals located farther north. The smallest deer of all are the endangered Key deer of Florida. The largest white-tails live in the northern half of the Southeast region.

Deer do not regulate their own population numbers, and they tend to gradually increase in density to the point of damaging and reducing the carrying capacity of their habitat. Large carnivores such as the cougar or red wolf probably used to help offset this innate tendency of deer to overpopulate, but these carnivores are now rare or extirpated, so there is essentially no regulator of deer populations available except humans. The carefully controlled harvest of surplus animals, particularly does, in the deer population is desirable and necessary for the future health of the species. Bucks tend to breed with a sizable number of does, but the ideal ratio is roughly eight females for each adult male.

Packs of stray dogs often run, harass, or even kill white-tailed deer. Free-running dogs should be eliminated from deer habitat to ensure the deer's well-being and survival. Bobcats, coyotes, and bears kill a few fawns in some parts of the southeastern region.

Selected References:

Beier, P., and D. R. McCullough. 1990. Factors influencing white-tailed deer activity patterns and habitat use. Wildl. Monogr. 109: 1–51.

Hirth, D. H. 1977. Social behavior of white-tailed deer in relation to habitat. Wildl. Monogr. 53: 55 pp.

Johns, P. E., R. Baccus, M. N. Manlove, J. E. Pinder III, and M. H. Smith. 1977. Reproductive patterns, productivity, and genetic variability in adjacent white-tailed deer population. Proc. Annual Conf. SE Game and Fish Comm. 31: 167–72.

Karlin, A., G. A. Heidt, and D. W. Sugg. 1989. Genetic variation and heterozygosity in white-tailed deer in southern Arkansas. Amer. Midl. Nat. 121: 273–84.

Leberg, P. L., and M. H. Smith. 1993. Influence of density on growth of white-tailed deer. J. Mamm. 74: 723–31.

Smith, M. H., R. K. Chesser, F. G. Cothrum, and P. E. Johns. 1982. Genetic variability and antler growth in a natural population of white-tailed deer. In *Antler Development in Cervidae*. Kleburg Wildl. Res. Inst., Kingsville, Texas.

Smith, W. P. 1992. White-tailed Deer (*Odocoileus virginianus*). Mammalian Species, No. 388: pp. 1–13.

Taylor, W. P., ed. 1956. The Deer of North America. Stackpole Books, Harrisburg, Pa. 668 pp.

Wilson, S. N., and J. A. Sealander. 1971. Some characteristics of white-tailed deer reproduction in Arkansas. Proc. Annual Conf. S.E. Assoc. Game and Fish Comm., pp. 53–65.

Schultz, S. R., and M. K. Johnson. 1992. Chronology of antler velvet shedding in captive Louisiana white-tailed deer. J. Wildl. Mgmt. 56: 651–55.

Shea, S. M., T. A. Breault, and M. L. Richardson. 1992. Herd density and physical condition of white-tailed deer in Florida flatwoods. J. Wildl. Mgmt. 56: 262–67.

Sambar Deer
Cervus unicolor

Sambar deer, *Cervus unicolor*. U.S. Fish & Wildlife Service

Identification: This introduced species is an elk-sized deer, several times larger than the native white-tailed deer. The hair of the sambar deer is coarse and ranges from dark chocolate brown in winter to rusty chestnut brown in summer. The calves are uniformly brown and unspotted. This deer has a large muzzle, brown ears, and a black-tipped, bushy tail which is about one foot long. Antlers are well developed and present only in males.

The skull is identified by the presence of small canines in the upper jaw of both sexes.

Geographical Range: The sambar deer was introduced from India to St. Vincent Island, Franklin County, Florida, in 1908 by the owner of the island. The initial release consisted of only four animals, but they thrived and multiplied to several hundred individuals within several decades. Deer occasionally swim the short distance from St. Vincent Island to the mainland, but these individuals have been shot by hunters, preventing their establishment on the mainland of the Florida panhandle thus far.

The native range of sambar deer in southeast Asia includes India, Sri Lanka, Burma, South China, Taiwan, Java, Borneo, Thailand, Malaysia, Sumatra, Celebes, and the Philippines.

Habitat: Studies in Florida reveal that sambar deer favor wetland habitats, particularly freshwater marshes and adjacent dense brush and trees.

Geographical range of the sambar deer in the Southeast.

Natural History: In Florida, sambar deer breed over a ten-month period from September through June. The peak of the rut occurs in midwinter (December–February). Females (also called "hinds") normally produce one calf per year, but twinning occurs on rare occasions. Stags are sexually mature at the age of one and one-half years, but the older dominant males do most of the breeding. Hinds become sexually active when they are two and one-half years old. The gestation period is approximately eight months. Calves are born in the summer, fall, and winter.

Adults were known to live up to 12–15 years on St. Vincent Island, when it had an unhunted population. The present population on the island is estimated to be 150–200 individuals. Most of the diet of the sambar consists of aquatic plants.

Remarks: The sambar deer have been under federal protection since 1968 when the U.S. Fish and Wildlife Service took control of St. Vincent Island and made it a wildlife refuge. Initially, federal planners sought to remove these exotic deer from the refuge. The deer proved difficult to trap, however, and local opposition to removal was quite strong. It was eventually decided that the sambar deer would be retained and managed as a game animal. A controlled harvest of sambar deer through public hunts was begun in 1987 to help keep the population at proper density.

Selected References:

Lewis, J. C., L. B. Flynn, R. L. Marchinton, S. M. Shea, and E. M. Marchinton. 1990. Ecology of Sambar deer on St. Vincent National Wildlife Refuge, Florida. Tall Timbers Research Station Bull. 25: 107 pp.

Mary, E., and M. Balakrishnan. 1984. A study of olfactory communication signals in sambar deer (*Cervus unicolor*). Proc. Indian Acad. Sci. Animal Series 93: 71–76.

Shea, S. M. 1986. The ecology of sambar deer: Social behavior, movement ecology, and food habits. M.S. Thesis, Univ. of Georgia, Athens, Ga.

Sika Deer
Cervus nippon

Sika deer, *Cervus nippon*. American Society of Mammalogists

Geographical range of the sika deer (two upper symbols) and the fallow deer (all four symbols) in the Southeast.

Identification: This small deer is identified by the presence of white spots on a reddish brown upper coat, by a black line down the middle of the back, and by a broad white patch across the rump and tail. Also, the underside of the tail has less white than the native white-tailed deer. The male sika deer have erect antlers with the individual tines branching from the front of the main beam, much like a miniature American elk. Males are a great deal larger than females. Winter coats are paler and grayer than summer ones.

Geographical Range: This species was introduced in the early 1900s and established on the eastern shore of Maryland and Virginia. It also thrives on Assateague Island and Chincoteague Island of Virginia and Maryland. Sika deer are native to Japan and China.

Habitat: Sika deer occur in pine forests, dense woody thickets, and along the borders of brackish marshes where they feed. The species is adaptable to a variety of coastal plains habitats.

Natural History: Bucks establish territories during the summer and spar with other males to attract a harem of females. They breed during the fall rutting season. After mating, the gestation period is seven months, with a single fawn born in mid- to late spring. Young deer grow rapidly, and they are weaned by late summer. Does normally breed for the first time in the fall of their birth year.

Remarks: The Chincoteague National Wildlife Refuge contains a sizable population of sika deer. Regulated hunts are being used by the U.S. Fish and Wildlife Service to help control the size of the herd and prevent it from overpopulating. There is little evidence that these deer are significantly expanding their range on the mainland in Maryland and Virginia. Sika deer are hunted legally each fall and winter, along with the native white-tailed deer, where land is under state control.

Selected References:

Feldhamer, G. A. 1980. Sika deer *(Cervus nippon)*. Mammalian Species, No. 128: pp. 1–7.

Feldhamer, G. A., and M. A. Marcus. 1994. Reproductive performance of female sika deer in Maryland. J. Wildl. Mgmt. 58: 670–73.

Flyger, V., and N. W. Davis. 1964. Distribution of sika deer *(Cervus nippon)* in Maryland and Virginia in 1962. Chesapeake Sci. 5: 212–13.

Koga, T., and Y. Ono. 1994. Sexual differences in foraging behavior of sika deer, *Cervus nippon*. J. Mamm. 75: 129–35.

Fallow Deer
Dama dama

Fallow deer, *Cervus dama.* American Society of Mammalogists

Identification: Fallow deer are somewhat smaller than white-tailed deer. The summer coat is reddish brown, dappled with white spots on the sides and back. They are blackish on the rump and upper tail, and creamy white on the throat, belly, and underside of the tail. In males, the antlers are erect, directly above the skull, and palmate in shape like those of a moose. Winter coats are grayish brown and have no spots.

Geographical Range: This species was introduced and established at scattered locations in coastal Virginia, Maryland, and North Carolina, and in southeastern Alabama. Fallow deer are native to England, Europe, and Asia Minor.

Habitat: These deer prefer open deciduous and coniferous woodlands and park lands. They also thrive in bushy, hilly areas which provide good cover, with grassy meadows nearby to forage upon.

Natural History: The bucks spar almost continuously for breeding rights in the fall. Most matings take place in October, and the gestation period is eight months. A single fawn (occasionally two) is born in June. Young fallow deer are weaned at about three months of age, but retain their spots, unlike white-tailed deer fawns.

Remarks: Fallow deer tend to run in small herds, except when the does have fawns to care for. This species is not as abundant or as successful in the Southeast as the sika deer.

Selected References:

Feldhamer, G. A., K. C. Farris-Renner, and C. M. Barker. 1988. Fallow Deer *(Dama dama)*. Mammalian Species, No. 317: pp. 1–8.

Gilbert, B. K. 1964. Social behavior and communication in fallow deer *(Dama dama)*. M.S. Thesis, Duke Univ., Durham, N.C. 79 pp.

Order Cetacea
Whales

The whales, dolphins, and porpoises are wholly aquatic forms, found almost exclusively in saltwater. There are two major subgroups of cetaceans with markedly different feeding mechanisms and physical characteristics. One group is the toothed whales, which possess varying numbers of well-developed, cone-shaped teeth in the mouth. The other group is the baleen whales, which are completely toothless and obtain their food by filtering large quantities of water through their strainerlike mouth parts called "baleen plates" (which trap the small marine organisms they eat). The baleen whales are the largest creatures that have ever lived on earth. The blue whale, or sulphur-bottomed whale, is the largest species of the group, sometimes attaining a length of 100 feet and a weight of 200 tons.

All cetaceans have a streamlined body shape like a torpedo or cigar, adapted for moving through water with minimal resistance. Their skins are smooth and thick, with hair virtually absent except for a few bristles around the mouth. Their tails are broad and flat, designed for propulsion with an up-and-down motion of the body torso. Whales have relatively large brains proportional to body size, and they appear to have a fairly high level of intelligence. They also exhibit a well-developed biological "sonar," or echolocation system. Whales emit sounds that bounce off objects in the water, and they navigate in response to the echoes returning to their ears.

There are 32 species of whales present in the marine waters off the southeastern coasts. All species were included for which there are records along the Atlantic or Gulf Coasts. Many species of whales spend most of their lives in the pelagic zone, far from land, and only on rare occasions do they come near shore or actually beach themselves on the shore. We know the least about these open water species. The names "dolphin" and "porpoise" are generally applied to the smaller species of toothed whales.

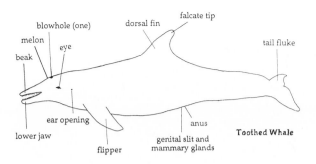

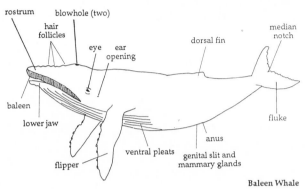

Whale body parts.

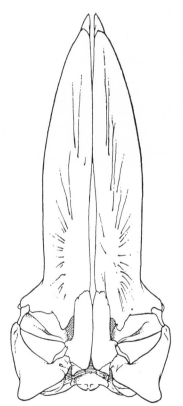

Ventral view of the skull of a representative baleen whale, the blue whale (*Balaenoptera musculus*).

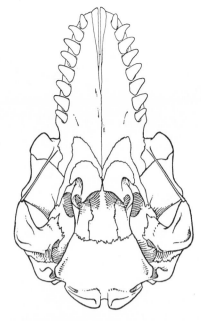

Ventral view of the skull of a representative toothed whale, the false killer whale (*Pseudorca crassidens*).

Rough-toothed Dolphin
Steno bredanensis

Identification: The rough-toothed dolphin is small (six to eight feet long), purplish black on the back, with yellowish white to pinkish white spots on the sides. The beak and underparts are white, tinged with rose or purple. The snout is long and slender and not set off from the rest of the head by a groove or indentation. The flippers and tail flukes are dark.

The skull is very similar to that of the bottle-nosed dolphin, but the rostrum is much longer and slimmer. The teeth all have rough vertical ridges and wrinkles on their outer surfaces, giving the species its common name. There are 20–27 teeth present on each side of the upper and lower jaws.

Geographical Range: The rough-toothed dolphin occurs sparingly off the Atlantic coast as far north as North Carolina and Virginia, but is seldom stranded or washed ashore. It is a warm-water species which also lives in the Pacific Ocean, Indian Ocean, Mediterranean Sea, and Red Sea.

Habitat: This species prefers warm temperate and tropical seas, generally far from shore, off the edge of the continental shelf.

Natural History: The habits if this dolphin are virtually unknown, but they are clearly social and travel in groups. Examination of the stomach contents of stranded individuals has revealed octopus beaks and marine algae.

Remarks: This small pelagic dolphin has no economic importance and is only rarely encountered by humans.

Selected References:
Norris, K. S., and W. E. Evans. 1967. Directionality of echolocation clicks in the rough-tooth porpoise, *Steno bredanensis* (Lesson). In *Marine Biacoustics*, Vol. 2. Pergamon Press, Oxford, pp. 305–16.

Layne, J. N. 1965. Observations on marine mammals in Florida waters. Bull. Fla. State Mus. Biol. Sci. 9: 131–81.

Rice, D. W., and V. B. Scheffer. 1968. A list of the marine mammals of the world. U.S. Fish and Wildl. Serv., Spec. Rep. No. 579, pp. 1–16.

Long-snouted Spinner Dolphin
Stenella longirostris

Identification: The long-snouted spinner dolphin is small (six to seven feet long), grayish black on the back grading to gray on the sides, and white on the belly. The pectoral fins are black, as are the lips of the beak.

The rostrum of the skull is extremely long and slender, being greater than twice the length of the cranial portion of the skull. There are 47–64 teeth present on each side of the upper and lower jaws.

Geographical Range: The long-snouted spinner dolphin occurs sparingly in the Gulf of Mexico and along the Atlantic Coast as far north as New Jersey, but is seldom stranded or washed ashore. Besides the Atlantic Ocean, it also occurs in the Indian Ocean and eastern Pacific Ocean.

Habitat: This dolphin lives in warm temperate and tropical seas and prefers the deeper open areas well away from shore.

Natural History: The habits of the long-snouted spinner dolphins are poorly known, but from the species of fish and squid found in stomach contents it is suggested that they feed at considerable depths (800 feet deep or more). They occur in herds of up to several hundred individuals. They are called spinner dolphins because of their habit of spinning or rotating around the long axis when jumping clear of the water. The reasons for this behavior are unknown.

Remarks: This species is frequently seen in the company of tuna schools in the Pacific Ocean. Fishermen keep a lookout for these dolphins as an indication of where and when to set purse seines or other nets. As a result, a large number of the dolphins are accidentally drowned because of entanglement in tuna nets. Regulations and modifications of the nets have recently been adopted to encourage escape of the helpful dolphins before drowning occurs.

Long-snouted spinner dolphins appear to take particular delight in riding the bow wake of ships, and they often continue this behavior for considerable distances.

Selected References:
Norris, K. S., and T. P. Dohl. 1980. The behavior of the Hawaiian spinner dolphin, *Stenella longirostris*. Fishery Bull. 77: 821–49.

Perrin, W. F. 1972. Color patterns of spinner porpoises of the eastern Pacific and Hawaii, with comments on delphinid pigmentation. U.S. Fish and Wildlife Service Fishery Bull. 70: 983–1003.

Perrin, W. F., D. B. Smith, and R. B. Miller. 1977. Growth and reproduction in the eastern spinner dolphin, a geographical form of *Stenella longirostris* in the eastern tropical Pacific. U.S. Fish and Wildlife Service Fishery Bull. 75: 725–50.

Perrin, W. F., and J. R. Henderson. 1979. Growth and reproduction rates in two populations of spinner dolphins, *Stenella longirostris* with different histories of exploitation. SW Fisheries Center, Nat'l Marine Fisheries Service, Adm. Rep. LJ-79-29.

Short-snouted Spinner Dolphin
Stenella clymene

Identification: The short-snouted spinner dolphin is small (five to six and one-half feet long), the back is black to dark gray with lighter gray on the sides, and the belly is white. The pectoral fins are black, and the beak has white on the top adjacent to the black tip and lips.

The skull is rather similar to that of the long-snouted spinner dolphin, but the rostrum is slightly shorter and more stout. There are 38–49 teeth present on each side of the upper and lower jaws.

Geographical Range: This species occurs in the Gulf of Mexico and the Atlantic Ocean from New Jersey to the northern edge of South America. It does not often strand or wash ashore.

Habitat: This species lives in warm temperate and tropical seas and prefers the open ocean and deep coastal waters near islands.

Natural History: Until recently, this species was confused with the long-snouted spinner dolphin, and it has similar habits. However, its spins and jumps are not quite as complex nor high as those of long-snouted species. The purpose of the spinning motion is unknown for both species. The diet consists of small fishes and squids.

Remarks: This dolphin was only recently described as a separate species. It apparently has little or no economic importance.

Selected References:

Minasian, S., K. C. Balcomb III, and L. Foster. 1984. Short-snouted spinner dolphin *Stenella clymene*. In *The World's Whales*. Smithsonian Books, W. W. Norton and Co., New York, N.Y., pp. 132–33.

Perrin, W. F., E. D. Mitchell, J. G. Mead, D. K. Caldwell, and P. J. H. Van Bree. 1981. *Stenella clymene*, a rediscovered tropical dolphin of the Atlantic. J. Mamm. 62: 538–48.

Striped Dolphin
Stenella coeruleoalba

Identification: The striped dolphin, or Gray's dolphin, is small (six to nine feet long), bluish black on the upper side and white below. A narrow black stripe runs from the eye along the side to the anus, with two shorter stripes branching off and extending toward the base of the pectoral fin. The lips are black and the eyes have a dark ring around them.

The skull has a rostrum that is almost one and one-half times the length of the cranium, and there are 39–55 teeth present on each side of the upper and lower jaws.

Geographical Range: The striped dolphin is fairly common in the Gulf of Mexico and along the Atlantic Coast, but is rarely stranded or washed ashore. It occurs widely throughout the oceans of the world.

Habitat: This dolphin lives in warmer temperate and tropical seas, generally far from shore in the pelagic zone.

Natural History: Little is known about the life habits of these beautiful dolphins. They often occur in large pods of several hundred individuals, and they feed at mid-depths on squids, fishes, and crustaceans. Striped dolphins are sometimes observed riding the bow wakes of ships.

Remarks: Like long-snouted spinner dolphins, these dolphins often travel with schools of tuna, and this association tells fishermen where to set purse seines. Many striped dolphins are accidentally drowned when trapped in the nets. Procedures are available which may greatly reduce this senseless loss.

Selected References:

Hubbs, C. L., W. F. Perrin, and K. C. Balcomb. 1973. *Stenella coeruleoalba* in the eastern and central tropical Pacific. J. Mamm. 54: 549–52.

Miyazaki, N. 1977. Growth and reproduction of *Stenella coeruleoalba* off the Pacific Coast of Japan. Whales Res. Inst., Sci. Rep. 29: 21–48.

Miyazaki, N., T. Kusaka, and M. Nishiwaki. 1973. Food of *Stenella coeruleoalba*. Whales Res. Inst., Sci. Rep. 25: 265–75.

Miyazaki, N., and M. Nishiwaki. 1978. School structure of the striped dolphin off the Pacific coast of Japan. Whales Res. Inst., Sci. Rep. 30: 65–115.

Spotted Dolphin
Stenella frontalis

Identification: The spotted dolphin is small (six to eight feet long), dark purplish gray, heavily flecked with small spots of white on the upper side, and the underside is whitish and densely spotted with dark gray. The lips are white, blotched with gray, and there is a distinct transverse groove at the base of each flipper.

The skull is similar to that of the striped dolphin, but it has fewer teeth. There are 34–37 teeth present on each side of the upper and lower jaws.

Geographical Range: The spotted dolphin is fairly common in the Gulf of Mexico and the Atlantic Ocean from North Carolina southward to the Caribbean Sea. It occasionally washes ashore. This species also ranges in the tropical Atlantic southward to northern South America.

Habitat: The spotted dolphin lives in both warm temperate and tropical seas, preferring deep water (over 100 fathoms) at least five miles from shore.

Spotted dolphins travel in social groups or pods of various sizes, and they forage well offshore in pelagic waters. Deep-sea fisherman often report seeing them in groups of a dozen or more, breaking the water in unison in graceful arcs. They sometimes frolic about ships or boats and can swim at 12–15 knots. Their diet consists primarily of squids and fishes. Spotted dolphins occur in herds of up to several hundred individuals.

Copulation has been observed in July, and, as with most dolphins, the female gives birth to a single calf about nine months after mating. The baby dolphin usually swims alongside the mother, staying between the front flipper and the tail fluke, the two mammals rising and sinking in unison.

Sucker fish, which are up to two feet long, sometimes attach to spotted dolphins and are carried along like trailing streamers in the water. This probably gave rise to the erroneous tale, often repeated, that baby spotted dolphins are towed along by grasping a front flipper or tail fluke of the mother.

Remarks: This small deep-water dolphin has no economic importance. It is common enough in offshore waters that its biology could be studied more extensively.

Selected References:
Caldwell, D. K., and M. C. Caldwell. 1966. Observations on the distribution, coloration, behavior, and audible sound production of the spotted dolphin. Los Ang. City Mus. Contrib. Sci. 104: 1027.
———. 1974. Marine mammals from the Southeastern United States Coast: Cape Hatteras to Cape Canaveral. Virginia Inst. of Marine Sci. Journ. 3: 704–72.
Sutherland, D. L., and L. L. May. 1977. Spotted dolphins, underwater observations using an unmanned submersible. Cetology 27: 1–9.

Bridled Dolphin
Stenella attenuata

Identification: The bridled dolphin is small (five to seven feet long), its back is dark gray, fading to light gray on the sides and belly, and there are small light gray spots scattered dorsally and small dark gray spots scattered ventrally. There is a distinct beak, and the lips are white or pinkish. The sides of the head are light gray, and there is a black circle around the eyes. A broad black stripe extends from the corner of the mouth to the front flipper.

The rostrum of the skull is less than twice the length of the cranium, and there are 35–47 teeth present on each side of the upper and lower jaws

Geographical Range: The bridled dolphin has been recorded sparingly in the Gulf of Mexico and along the Atlantic Coast as far north as North Carolina. It ranges southward in the Caribbean as far as the Lesser Antilles.

Habitat: This species lives in warm temperate and tropical waters, usually well offshore, but occasionally near coastal areas and islands.

Natural History: Bridled dolphins travel in small herds of five to thirty animals and often ride the bow waves of ships. They feed on fishes, shrimp, and squids, but their life habits are poorly known.

Remarks: Specimens of this rare species have been recorded mainly on shore during or after a severe oceanic storm. The bridled dolphin has little or no economic importance.

Selected References:
Kasuya, T. 1976. Reconsideration of life history parameters of the spotted and striped dolphins based on cementum layers. Whales. Res. Inst., Sci. Rep. 28: 73–106.
Perrin, W. F. 1969. Color pattern of the eastern Pacific spotted porpoise, (*Stenella attenuata*) (Cetacea, Delphinidae). Zoologica 54: 135–42.
———. 1975. Distribution and differentiation of populations of dolphins of the genus *Stenella* in the eastern tropical Pacific. J. Fish. Res. Board, Canada 32: 1059–67.
Perrin, W. F., F. D. Smith, and G. T. Sakagawa. 1975. Status of population of spotted dolphin (*Stenella attenuata*), and spinner dolphin (*Stenella longirostris*), in the eastern tropical Pacific. Scientific Consultation on Marine Mammals, Bergen, Norway. 27 pp.

Saddle-backed Dolphin
Delphinus delphis

Identification: The saddle-backed dolphin, or common dolphin, is small (six to eight and one-half feet long), black on the upper side, and the sides are marked with saddle-shaped (or hour-glass-shaped) patterns of yellow or tan mixed with bands of white. The underparts are white, and there are two narrow black lines which bifurcate on the sides of the tail region and extend forward along the flank, one passing through the base of the front flipper, the latter being black. The eyes are surrounded by black circles, from which a black line runs forward to the base of the beak.

The rostrum of the skull is about one and one-half times the length of the cranium, and two long grooves run just inside the tooth rows on the roof of the mouth. There are 48–50 teeth present on each side of the upper and lower jaws.

Geographical Range: The saddle-backed dolphin is common in the Gulf of Mexico and Atlantic Ocean from Newfoundland to Florida and southward in the tropics, but it is seldom stranded or washed ashore on beaches. This dolphin occurs widely throughout most of the oceans of the world.

Habitat: The saddle-backed dolphin lives in both temperate and tropical seas, generally well offshore and over the outer continental shelf.

Natural History: Groups of saddle-backed dolphins are often sighted during the summer months 70–100 miles off the Atlantic and Gulf coasts. They are fast swimmers and have been clocked at speeds up to thirty miles per hour by boats. Although the saddle-backed dolphin is an offshore pelagic species, it occasionally enters the mouths of large, deep rivers. It also migrates northward during the summer months, no doubt following schools of fish. Saddle-backed dolphins are quite social, occurring in groups of ten to a thousand or more. They feed almost exclusively on fishes and squids living near the surface. In captivity, saddle-backed dolphins are timid and much less aggressive than the bottle-nosed dolphin. Females produce a single offspring, which is born from spring to fall after a gestation period of about nine months.

Remarks: In those areas where saddle-backed dolphins are abundant, they probably have some impact on schools of small fishes and squids. Their impact is generally of minor economic importance.

These dolphins are bow wake riders and often come to a boat from considerable distances. Once on the bow wake, they often ride for extended periods of time.

Selected References:

Gurevich, V., and B. Stewart. 1978. The use of tetracycline marking in age determinations of *Delphinus delphis*. Proc. Internat. Conf., Determ. Age Odontocete Cetaceans. Scripps Instit. Oceanography, La Jolla, Calif., p. 9.

Jefferson, J. A., S. Leatherwood, L. K. M. Soda, and R. L. Peterson. 1992. *Marine Mammals of the Gulf of Mexico.* Texas A&M Univ., Galveston, Tex. 92 pp.

Mitchell, E. 1970. Pigmentation pattern evolution in delphinid cetaceans: an essay in adaptive coloration. Can. J. Zool. 48: 717–40.

Sleptsov, M. M. 1957. Determination of the age of *Delphinus delphis*. Bull. MOIP., Otdel. Biologic. 49: 43–51.

Bottle-nosed Dolphin
Tursiops truncatus

Identification: The bottle-nosed dolphin is small (eight to twelve feet long), purplish gray to light gray on the upper side, and whitish on the under side back to the anus. The front flippers are dark gray.

The rostrum of the skull is short, about the same length as the cranium. There are only 20–26 teeth present on each side of the upper and lower jaws.

Geographical Range: The bottle-nosed dolphin is abundant in the coastal and inshore marine waters of the Southeast. In the Atlantic, it occurs from Massachusetts southward through the Caribbean and Gulf of Mexico to South America. Bottle-nosed dolphins are found in coastal areas throughout most of the oceans and seas of the world.

Habitat: This species prefers the shallow-water coastal and estuarine areas along southeastern shores. It is found in greatest numbers in the vicinity of passes that connect larger bays with the ocean and is also present in back bays that have lower salinity. It is the only whale commonly seen in inshore marine waters. Bottle-nosed dolphins are also frequently found just beyond the surf in the open ocean but seldom venture beyond the 100 fathom line.

Natural History: More is known about the life habits of this small whale than about any other cetacean. This is because it is abundant inshore and adaptable to life in a sea aquarium. The bottle-nosed dolphin is the species most commonly trained to perform the entertaining acrobatic feats that often form the main feature at marine mammal shows. A bottle-nosed dolphin was also used to portray "Flipper" of television fame. Some of the oceanaria, in addition to presenting public entertainment, have also conducted research on the biology of these dolphins.

Breeding activity peaks in March and April. The adult males fight viciously for breeding dominance and acquire numerous battle scars. Posturing on the part of the male is the initial feature of courting behavior, which includes rubbing, stroking, nuzzling, mouthing, snapping the jaws closed, and barking. The male frequently positions himself in front of the female vertically with his body held in an S-shaped curve. The pair also swim about in close proximity, with their bodies in contact. Copulation occurs when the female rolls over on her side, presenting her lower surface to the male. The process lasts for only ten seconds or less but is usually repeated several times.

The gestation period is about twelve months, and one calf is produced every other year, beginning when a female is about six years old. Births occur from February to May, and a single baby dolphin emerges tail-first. A newborn bottle-nosed dolphin weighs about thirty pounds, is approximately three and one-half feet long, and is precocial, being able to move about and fend for itself. Each infant swims well from the moment of birth and immediately surfaces to breathe. If the newborn hesitates in any way, the mother will push it up to the surface to take its first breath. Babies begin suckling milk almost immediately from one of the mammary glands. During the first month of life, the calf stays very close to its mother, but gradually it gains confidence and moves about some on its own. Weaning, however, does not occur until the young are about one and one-half years old.

Males in the groups (or "pods" as they are called by whale biologists) of bottle-nosed dolphins have a definite social hierarchy, and dominance is closely associated with larger body size. Jaw snapping is one of the main forms of antagonistic behavior employed to enforce the social structure. The females do not appear to compete in or form part of the hierarchy.

The bottle-nosed dophin's diet consists of various common fish species, including mullet, sheepshead, pinfish, pufferfish, speckled trout, black drum, eels, catfish, flounder, croaker, and sand trout. The dolphins also eat shrimp, crabs, and squids.

Bottle-nosed dolphins have a wide range of vocalizations. Some of these function in a system of echolocation. Dolphins not only locate objects by sound, but also they can discriminate between objects of different shapes and sizes.

Dolphins will sometimes cooperate to support a sick or injured individual at the surface to permit it to breathe. Usually two dolphins place their heads beneath the front fins of the injured or sick companion and buoy it to the surface. The swimming speed of the bottle-nosed dolphin has often been exaggerated. Actual measurements in captivity of a frightened, rapidly swimming dolphin record maximum speeds of 22 miles per hour.

In captivity bottle-nosed dolphins are very playful and apparently rather intelligent. In recent years, the U.S. Navy has successfully trained them to retrieve various objects, including divers in trouble, lost rockets, and even nuclear bombs, from considerable depths.

Remarks: Bottle-nosed dolphins are an important asset to various oceanaria because they can be trained to provide an interesting show. Some facilities have come under criticism recently for keeping dolphins confined in small and inadequate holding cages, which is considered very cruel treatment for animals with free-ranging habits in the ocean. This species is very highly regarded by the public for its intelligence and aesthetic value.

Bottle-nosed dolphins sometimes become entangled in shrimp and fishing nets set in coastal and near-offshore areas, and they can do considerable damage to the nets. They also eat some shrimp and crabs for which humans are competing, but their overall economic impact is considered to be minor compared to the impact of other types of marine predators.

Other than humans and sharks, bottle-nosed dolphins have no natural enemies. Some of the larger, more aggressive species of sharks occasionally attack, kill, and eat bottle-nosed dolphins. Dolphins sometimes defend themselves quite successfully by ramming the attacking shark in the sensitive gill or nose regions.

During the whaling era in the United States, the bottle-nosed dolphin was captured and processed at a fishery based in Cape Hatteras, North Carolina. The meat was marketed in eastern cities, and the oil was used for lamps. All dolphins are now protected by state and federal law from such harvesting or from any type of wanton killing.

Selected References:

Bragen, S., B. Wursig, A. Acevedo, and T. Henningsen. 1994. Association patterns of bottlenose dolphins (*Tursiops truncatus*) in Galveston Bay, Texas. J. Mamm. 75: 431–37.

Caldwell, D. K., and M. C. Caldwell. 1972. *The World of the Bottlenosed Dolphin*. J. B. Lippincott Co., Philadelphia, Pa. 157 pp.

Hogan, T. 1975. Movements and behavior of the bottle-nosed dolphin in the Savannah River mouth area. M.S. thesis, Univ. of Rhode Island, Kingston, R.I.

Leatherwood, J. S. 1975. Observations on the feeding behavior of bottlenosed dolphins, *Tursiops truncatus* in the northern Gulf of Mexico, etc. Marine Fish. Rev. 37: 10–16.

Odell, D. K. 1975. Status and aspects of the life history of the bottlenose dolphin, *Tursiops truncatus*, in Florida. J. Fish. Res. Board, Canada. 32: 1055–58.

Shane, S., and D. J. Schmidly. 1979. The population biology of the bottlenose dolphin, *Tursiops truncatus*, in the Aransas Pass area of Texas. Nat. Tech. Inf. Serv., Springfield, Va.

Fraser's Dolphin
Lagenodelphis hosei

Identification: Fraser's dolphin is small (six to eight feet long), robust in build, and has a very short beak. The body is dark gray on the back and tail, but white on the belly, with a pronounced dark, narrow lateral stripe running from the rostrum to the tail. Above the stripe, there is a creamy white band beginning on the head and running almost to the tail. A second creamy white band lies below the lateral black stripe and parallel to it, separating the gray color on the sides from the white belly. There is also a dark gray ring around each eye, and the rostrum and pectoral flippers are dark gray. There is a thin dark line running from the base of each pectoral flipper forward to the corner of the mouth.

The rostrum of the skull is short and broad, and there are 40–44 teeth present on each side of the upper and lower jaws.

Geographical Range: In the Southeast, Fraser's dolphin has been recorded only in Florida (at the Marquesas Keys in Monroe County) at the extreme southern tip of the state. In the world, the species is known only from a few scattered specimens taken in the tropical Pacific and Atlantic Oceans.

Habitat: This dolphin normally occurs well out at sea in warm subtropical and tropical waters.

Natural History: So few specimens of Fraser's dolphin have been collected or observed that its biology is poorly known. They are fast, aggressive swimmers and appear to be deep divers. The stomach of one specimen taken near the island of St. Vincent in the Lower Antilles contained large red shrimp, fish otoliths (ear stones), and squid beaks.

The record of Fraser's dolphin presence in the Florida Keys occurred in the fall of 1981 and consisted of a mass stranding of at least 17 individuals and probably more. Only the skulls and skeletons remained by the time the discovery was made. This evidence verifies that Fraser's dolphin is gregarious and travels in sizable herds.

Remarks: Fraser's dolphin has no economic importance. There have been several records of this species in the Atlantic Ocean in recent years where none existed before, which is a possible indication it has become slightly more common.

Selected References:
Fraser, F. C. 1956. A new Sarawak dolphin. Sarawak Mus. J. 8: 478–502.

Jefferson, T. A. and S. Leatherwood. 1994. Fraser's dolphin (*Lagenodelphis hosei*). Mammalian Species, No. 470, pp. 1–5.

False Killer Whale
Pseudorca crassidens

Identification: The false killer whale is medium-sized (12–20 feet long), uniformly black over the entire body, and sometimes is marked with white on the lips. There is no beak and the head is narrow and bulbous. The flippers have a broad hump on the front margin near the middle. The false killer whale has a much shorter and more curved dorsal fin than the killer whale.

The rostrum of the skull is short, stout, and broad. There are only eight to eleven teeth on each side of the upper and lower jaws.

Geographical Range: The false killer whale has been recorded occasionally in the Gulf of Mexico and along the Atlantic Coast from Canada all the way to the tropics. It is known mainly for occasional mass strandings on beaches. It occurs throughout most of the oceans of the world.

Habitat: This species lives in warm temperate, subtropical, and tropical seas, generally in deep water far from land.

Natural History: False killer whales are social animals usually living in large pods. They sometimes beach in large numbers. Large pelagic fishes and squids have been found in the stomachs of beached false killer whales.

Breeding apparently can occur year round, because autopsies of females stranded around the world in various months of the year have revealed fetuses of all different sizes and stages of development. The young are five and one-half to six and one-half feet long at birth.

Remarks: False killer whales sometimes steal fish from both commercial fishing and sport fishing lines. In some open ocean areas where they are abundant, they may have an impact on populations of large pelagic fishes.

The killer whale has a reputation for being a much more fierce and aggressive predator toward other whales, seals, and sharks than does the false killer whale. Also, the two species are not particularly similar in appearance. Their lone shared feature is a well-developed dorsal fin, which often breaks the surface of the water as they cruise along.

Selected References:

Brown, D. H., D. K. Caldwell, and M. C. Caldwell. 1966. Observations on the behavior of wild and captive false killer whales, with notes on associated behavior of other genera of captive delphinids. Los Ang. City Mus. Contrib. Sci. 95: 1–32.

Caldwell, D. K., M. C. Caldwell, and C. M. Walker, Jr. 1970. Mass and individual strandings of false killer whales, *Pseudorca crassidens*, in Florida. J. Mamm. 51: 634–36.

Stacey, P. J., S. Leatherwood, and R. W. Baird. 1994. False killer whale *(Pseudorca crassidens)*. Mammalian Species, No. 456, pp. 1–6.

Killer Whale
Orcinus orca

Identification: The killer whale is the largest member of the porpoise and dolphin family (length 20–30 feet). The upper parts are black, except for a prominent white patch behind the eye and a light gray or white saddle behind the tall dorsal fin. In adult females and juveniles, the dorsal fin is somewhat curved backward (called "falcate"), but in adult males it is very tall and straight. The underparts are white, light tan, or pale yellow. The undersides of the tail flukes are white, but the front fins and large dorsal fin are entirely black. Males are a good deal larger than females.

The rostrum of the skull is broad, being wider than one-half its length at its base. There are ten to fourteen large teeth present in each side of the upper and lower jaw. The teeth are quite robust, long, and large in diameter at the base (up to one inch across).

Geographical Range: The killer whale occurs sparingly in the Gulf of Mexico and along the entire Atlantic Coast from the Arctic to the tropics, but is seldom stranded or washed ashore. It has a widespread distribution and lives in most of the oceans of the world.

Habitat: This species prefers to forage near the surface in cool to cold coastal marine waters. It occasionally enters large rivers, and also ventures into subtropical waters, but it is most abundant in the Arctic and Antarctic regions. These whales engage in considerable wandering and exploring.

Natural History: The killer whale has an amazing range of temperature tolerance, since it occurs from polar seas all the way to the equator. These whales forage in small packs or pods of five to fifty animals and have the reputation of being ferocious in their feeding habits. Each pack travels in close association, and the individual members often simultaneously attack prey much larger than themselves, such as a baleen whale. Killer whales have been known to slash, tear, and wound baleen whales mortally during an attack. They are impressive predators that can swim extremely fast, reaching top speeds of over thirty miles per hour. Killer whales feed on a wide range of species including seals, other whales, sharks and other large fishes, squids, sea turtles, seals, sea lions, walruses, and large marine birds. The approach of a pack of killer whales usually panics most marine vertebrates in the vicinity. When a killer whale observes a seal or penguin near the edge of pack ice, it sometimes dives deeply and rushes to the surface, breaking ice up to two feet thick and dislodging the prey into the water.

Killer whales are very social animals, as they travel, hunt, rest, feed, and play together in a "pod" apparently their entire lives. Different pods occupying the same general region sometimes join together for a few days (generally in the summer or fall) to form "superpods" of 100–200 individuals.

Sexual maturity is reached when killer whales are about 12 years old. Mating occurs in the spring and summer in the Pacific Northwest, but in warmer waters breeding has been reported near the end of the year. The gestation period is long, averaging about sixteen months, and a single offspring, about six to eight feet long, is produced no more than once every third year. Some females breed less frequently and produce a calf only once every six or seven years. A few whale researchers believe that adults may live as long as 100 years, but this is speculation that has not yet been verified.

The first baby killer whale to be born and survive in captivity was produced at Sea World near Orlando, Florida, in l985. It was a female, six feet long, weighing around 350 pounds at birth. The baby was born head first and was released rather explosively from the mother as she swam rapidly about the tank in spiraling circles. In just two and one-half weeks, the young killer whale had grown to seven and one-half feet long and weighed around 700 pounds, as result of drinking at least ten gallons of her mother's milk each day.

The social groups of killer whales appear to be centered around the adult females. Most pods are composed of older females and their offspring of various ages. Some females first observed as calves were still associated with their mother's pod ten years later, and this female family group type of association may go on for life. The males also form small pods, apparently only on a seasonal basis.

Killer whales emit a series of "clicks" which are used in echolocation of food and objects in the water. They also make pulsed calls (that sound somewhat like the screeching of a rusty hinge) and whistles, both involved in social behavior.

Remarks: This is the major "showcase" species used in marine mammal shows in the United States. Almost everyone has seen or heard of the impressive jumps and trainer-whale interactions of killer whales like "Shamu" or a "Namu." Considering the ferocious feeding actions of groups of killer whales in nature, it is remarkable how gentle and submissive captive individuals become. However, vicious attacks by one killer whale on another sometimes do occur in captivity. In August l989 at Sea World, one large adult female attacked and killed a second, smaller female almost instantly in a single slashing charge during a whale show. There are several documented attacks by killer whales on small boats, but no reliable records of them attacking human swimmers in the water.

The long, bladelike dorsal fin of the killer whale is sometimes misidentified by people as that of a shark, which certainly contributes to fear of killer whales.

Selected References:

Heyning, J. E., and M. E. Dehlheim. 1988. Killer whale (*Orcinus orca*). Mammalian Species, No. 304: p. 109.

Jonsgard, A., and P. B. Lyshoel. 1970. A contribution to the knowledge of the biology of the killer whale. Nytt. Mag. for Zool. 18: 41–48.

Nishiwaki, M., and C. Handa. 1958. Killer whales caught in the coastal waters off Japan for the recent ten years. Whales Res. Inst., Sci. Rep. 13: 85–96.

Rice, D. W. 1968. Stomach contents and feeding behavior of killer whales in the eastern North Pacific. Norsk Hvalfangstrid. 57:35–38.

Pigmy Killer Whale
Feresa attenuata

Identification: The pigmy killer whale is small (seven to nine feet long), and the entire body is dark gray or black, except for a small area of white in the anal region and along the lips (called a "goatee"). There is no beak and the head is blunt and rounded. This species closely resembles the false killer whale but is much smaller. The skull has a short, broad rostrum with nine to eleven teeth on each side of the jaw.

Geographical Range: In the Southeast, the pigmy killer whale has been recorded only in Florida waters. It lives in both the Atlantic Ocean and the Gulf of Mexico, but is seldom stranded or washed ashore. It also occurs throughout the tropical Pacific and Indian Oceans.

Habitat: This whale lives in warm tropical and subtropical seas and prefers deep pelagic areas well offshore.

Natural History: The pigmy killer whale has a reputation of being aggressive toward handlers and other species of marine mammals when in captivity. This vicious nature probably carries over into its feeding behavior as well. The diet consists of larger fishes, seals, squids, and porpoises.

Remarks: A group of five pigmy killer whales were stranded on Singer Island in Palm Beach County, Florida, in May l971. This and other more recent strandings suggest that the whale has a social nature and travels in small pods. Very little is known about the biology of this interesting species.

Selected References:

Caldwell, D. K., and M. C. Caldwell. 1971. The pigmy killer whale, *Feresa attenuata,* in the western Atlantic, with a summary of world records. J. Mamm. 52: 206–9.

Pryor, T., K. Pryor, and K. S. Norris. 1965. Observations on a pigmy killer whale (*Feresa attenuata*) from Hawaii. J. Mamm. 46: 450–61.

Risso's Dolphin
Grampus griseus

Identification: Risso's dolphin, or grampus, is small (9–13 feet long), the body is slate gray with underparts, and the head slightly paler. There are normally light-colored scars or scratches crisscrossing the torso. There is no beak, and the forehead is rounded and bulges "melon-like." The dorsal fin, pectoral fins, and tail flukes are dark to blackish. The dorsal fin is high and curved backward.

The rostrum of the skull is very broad, short, and stout. There are only two to seven teeth on each side of the lower jaw and one or two vestigial teeth or no teeth at all in the upper jaw.

Geographical Range: Risso's dolphin ranges throughout the Gulf of Mexico and along the entire Atlantic Coast from Maine to Florida. It is fairly common well offshore and only occasionally becomes beached or stranded. It occurs throughout most of the oceans of the world.

Habitat: This species lives in temperate and tropical seas, usually beyond the edge of the continental shelf, but occasionally near shore where the waters are deep.

Natural History: Risso's dolphin typically occurs in small groups of fewer than a dozen, but occasionally several small pods in an area may associate seasonally. The diet consists of squids and some fishes. The numerous scars and scratches found on adults are apparently produced both by intraspecific fighting and by squids defending themselves. A pregnant female (that had become stranded) was carrying a full-term fetus when it was recorded one December.

One famous Risso's dolphin lived in an area at the mouth of a bay in New Zealand. It delighted residents of the area by jumping and playing around incoming ships and by "guiding" them into the mouth of the sound. This specimen may give some hint to the longevity of the species, because this individual, which was fully protected by the New Zealand government, apparently died of natural causes after 20 years as an adult.

Remarks: Risso's dolphin is occasionally trained and used in oceanarium shows in some areas of the world. These dolphins are intelligent and jump readily in conditioned routines. Beyond this minor usage, the spe-

cies has little economic impact. They sometimes ride the bow waves of boats and often breach (that is, jump clear of the water) while doing so.

Selected References:

Jefferson, T. A., S. Leatherwood, L. K. M. Shoda, and R. L. Pitman. 1992. Marine mammals of the Gulf of Mexico. Texas A&M Printing Center, College Station, Texas. 92 pp.

Leatherwood, S., D. K. Caldwell, and H. E. Winn. 1976. Whales, dolphin, and porpoises of the western North Atlantic. Nat'l Oceanic Atmos. Adm., Marine Fish. Service Circ. 396: 176 pp.

Mitchell, E. D., ed. 1975. Report of the meetings on smaller cetaceans, Montreal. J. Fish. Res. Board, Canada 32: 889–983.

Short-finned Pilot Whale
Globicephala macrorhynchus

Identification: The short-finned pilot whale, or "black-fish," is medium-sized (13–23 feet long), entirely black above and below, and has a bulbous, globelike head. There is frequently a patch of gray on the chin and on the belly. The pectoral fins are rather short.

The rostrum of the skull is extremely broad and short, and there are seven to eleven conical teeth located on each side of the upper and lower jaw.

Geographical Range: This species has been recorded throughout the Gulf of Mexico and along the Atlantic Coast as far north as Virginia. From there it ranges southward into the tropics. It occurs widely in most of the world's oceans.

Habitat: Short-finned pilot whales live in both temperate and tropical seas, usually seaward of the outer edges of the continental shelf, but they sometimes forage closer to shore.

Natural History: This species is quite gregarious and usually seen in herds varying in size from a few dozen to several hundred individuals. They show a decided tendency to follow a single leader, which probably explains many of the strandings of pilot whales around the world. Pilot whales are migratory, moving north with the seasons in spring and summer months and back to warmer waters in the fall and winter. Their diet consists of squids, fishes, and cuttlefishes.

Pilot whales breed in tropical waters during the winter months. The gestation period is about twelve months, and a single calf is born approximately every third year. The babies are eight to nine feet long at birth, and they nurse for several months. Young females take about six to seven years to reach sexual maturity, but males are said to require twelve to thirteen years. The species is polygamous, with a few old, large males breeding most of the females. Older females stop bearing young at 38–40 years of age. The maximum life span of the pilot whale may reach 50 years.

Remarks: The short-finned pilot whale was once the mainstay of the Newfoundland whaling industry, with a harvest of several thousand each summer. The average yield of blubber oil per animal was about forty gallons and for head oil was about two gallons. The meat of pilot whales has been used on fox and mink farms for animal food.

In the islands of the Lesser Antilles, where pilot whales spend the winter, they are also sometimes killed for both meat and oil. Natives there have typically hunted the whales with harpoons in small, open boats rather than large ships.

Pilot whales sometimes rest by hanging vertically in the water with their heads out, but they seldom breach. When swimming, members of the herd often line up side-by-side in long lines facing forward and advance as a front. This behavior could be related to stalking prey or could be a way of being socially agreeable.

Selected References:

Sergeant, D. E. 1962. On the external characters of the blackfish or pilot whales *(Genus Globicephala)*. J. Mamm. 43: 395–413.

Walen, K. H., and S. H. Madin. 1965. Comparative chromosome analysis of the bottle-nosed dolphin *(Tursiops truncatus)* and the pilot whale *(Globicephala macrorhynchus)*. Amer. Natur. 99: 349–54.

Long-finned Pilot Whale
Globicephala melaena

Identification: The long-finned pilot whale is slightly smaller (18–20 feet long) than the closely related short-finned pilot whale. The pectoral fins are quite long (up to one-fifth the body length), and the overall body color is black with an anchor-shaped gray patch on the chin, a gray area on the belly, and a gray saddle be-hind the dorsal fin. The dorsal fin is more falcate (that is, hook-shaped) than in the short-finned pilot whale.

Geographical Range: In the Southeast, this whale occurs as far south as North Carolina and possibly Georgia. From there, it ranges northward in the Atlantic Ocean to Greenland, Iceland, and Russia. It also occurs in the Mediterranean Sea.

Habitat: This whale inhabits cold temperate and Arctic waters, where it lives a pelagic lifestyle, far out at sea.

Natural History: Mating occurs in the spring during April and May, before they leave the wintering grounds in the North Atlantic. The gestation period is about 15 $1/2$ months, and a single calf is born during the late summer (most appear in August) off Greenland and Iceland.

Baby pilot whales are $5 1/2$ to 6 feet long at birth. They wean at about 21–22 months of age. Young females breed when about 6 years old and 12 feet long. Males do not mature sexually until they are around 12 years old and 16 feet long.

Remarks: These whales have a bipolar distribution, but they are absent from the tropics and subtropics. They feed primarily at night on squids, cod, flounder, and amphipods.

Selected References:

Caldwell, M. C., D. H. Brown, and D. K. Caldwell. 1963. Intergeneric behavior by a captive pilot whale. Contrib. Sci. Los Angeles Co. Mus. 70: 1–12.

Sergeant, D. E. 1962. The biology of the pilot or pot-headed whale, *Globicephala melaena*, in Newfoundland waters. Bull. Fish. Res. Board, Canada 132: 1–84.

Melon-headed Whale
Peponcephala electra

Identification: The melon-headed whale is small (six and one-half feet to nine feet long) and somewhat similar to the false killer whale, but with a more rounded, bulbous head. The upper parts, including the sides, are dark gray with a dappling of fine white spots. It gives this whale a salt-and-pepper appearance. The underside is gray, but the upper and lower lips, anal area, genital aperture, and an anchor-shaped area between the flippers are all white.

The rostrum is equal to the length of the rest of the skull and the total number of teeth ranges from 76 to 96.

Geographical Range: In the Southeast, this species has only been recorded from the Maryland shore. It ranges throughout the tropical and subtropical waters of the Atlantic, Pacific, and Indian Oceans.

Habitat: This is a warm-water species that occasionally ventures into temperate waters. It lives a pelagic lifestyle, far from shore.

Natural History: Tropical storms, especially hurricanes, can occasionally move these whales onshore. Little is known about their biology or life history.

Remarks: A greater effort needs to be made by scientists to study the feeding habits and biology of the melon-headed whale. It probably feeds on squids and small fish.

Selected References:
Nishiwaki, M., and K. S. Norris. 1966. A new genus, *Peponcephala,* for the odontocete cetacean species, *Electra electra.* Whales Res. Inst., Sci Rep. 20: 95–100.

Hall, E. R. 1981. *The Mammals of North America.* John Wiley and Sons, New York, N.Y., p. 895.

Harbor Porpoise
Phocoena phocoena

Identification: The harbor porpoise is the smallest cetacean in Atlantic waters (four to five feet long). The body is chunky with a small, rounded head and no beak present. The back is dark brown to gray, fading to light brown or light gray on the sides. The belly is white, and the dorsal fin is small, dark, and triangular in shape.

The rostrum of the skull is short, broad, and rounded at the tip. There are 26–28 teeth on each side of the upper and lower jaws.

Geographical Range: This species is found sparingly along the Atlantic Coast from the Arctic south to Florida. It also lives along the Atlantic Coast of Europe and in the Pacific Ocean from Alaska to California. It is absent from the Gulf.

Habitat: The harbor porpoise is usually found inshore in fairly shallow waters and occasionally offshore out to the 100-fathom line. These porpoises also frequent bays, harbors, inlets, and the mouths of large rivers. They are found primarily in Arctic and temperate waters.

Natural History: These porpoises normally travel in pairs or small groups, but have occasionally been seen in schools of around 100 individuals. They seem to be less playful than many species of small dolphins, and they seldom jump out of the water and never ride the bow wakes of boats. They usually swim just beneath the surface of the water, rising to breathe three or four times per minute. Harbor porpoises have been trapped in fish nets up to 250 feet deep. Their principal foods are squids, herring, cod, mackerel, whiting, and other fishes.

Mating takes place in the spring and early summer. The gestation period is about eleven months long, and a single calf that measures approximately half as long as its mother is born tail-first.

Remarks: In earlier times, harbor porpoise fisheries existed in European waters. The meat was sold at markets, and the oil was used in lamps. Eskimo and coastal Indian populations still occasionally eat harbor porpoises in Arctic waters, but the species has no economic impact in more temperate areas.

Selected References:
Gaskin, D. E., P. W. Arnold, and B. A. Blair. 1974. Harbor Porpoise (*Phocoena phocoena*). Mammalian Species, No. 42: 1–8.

Neave, D. J., and B. S. Wright. 1968. Seasonal migrations of the harbor porpoise (*Phocoena phocoena*) and other cetacea in the Bay of Fundy. J. Mamm. 49: 259–69.

Watts, P., and D. E. Gaskin. 1985. Habitat index analysis of the harbor porpoise (*Phocoena phocoena*) in the Southern Coastal Bay of Fundy, Canada. J. Mamm. 66: 733–44.

Pigmy Sperm Whale
Kogia breviceps

Identification: The pigmy sperm whale is small (eight to twelve feet long), the back is dark steel gray grading to lighter gray on the sides, and the lower jaw is small and terminates well behind the tip of the snout. The dorsal fin is small and only slightly curved backward.

The skull is short, broad, and appears basically triangular in shape when seen from above. There are 12 to 16 large, conical teeth on each side of the lower jaw but none on the upper jaw.

Geographical Range: The pigmy sperm whale is fairly common off the entire Atlantic and Gulf Coasts. Individual strandings have been increasing in number in recent years. It ranges through most of the world's oceans, but is apparently rare in the South Atlantic Ocean.

Habitat: This species lives in warmer seas in deep offshore waters, but it comes closer to shore during the calving season.

Natural History: Pigmy sperm whales are migratory, moving northward in the summer and returning to warmer tropical waters in the fall. The diet consists of pelagic squids, cuttlefishes, shrimp, and some fishes that live near the surface.

Calves are born in the wintering areas, but breeding occurs the preceding spring or early summer. The gestation period is about nine months long, and adult females produce one calf about every two years. A ten-foot-long female is recorded to have given birth to a calf that is five and three-quarter feet long and weighed 176 pounds. The duration of nursing is unknown, but the calf stays with its mother for about one year.

Remarks: This small whale has little or no economic importance. There is a small spermaceti reservoir located in the head which contains sperm whale oil, a highly valued substance.

The pigmy sperm whale has an interesting defense mechanism. When startled, it releases a dark cloud of liquid, reddish brown feces from the anus into the water. This cloud is apparently intended to confuse potential predators while the whale escapes (the octopus and squid, of course, are famous for releasing "ink clouds" for a similar purpose).

Selected References:
Handley, C. O., Jr. 1966. A synopsis of the genus *Kogia* (pygmy sperm whales), in *Whales, Dolphins, and Porpoises.* Univ. of Calif. Press, Berkeley, Calif., pp. 62–69.

Raun, G. G., H. D. Holse, and F. Moseley. 1970. Pygmy sperm whales, genus *Kogia*, on the Texas coast. Tex. J. Sci. 21: 269–74.

Dwarf Sperm Whale
Kogia simus

Identification: The dwarf sperm whale, or "rat porpoise," is small (six to nine feet long), dark steel gray above with the sides lighter gray, and the belly is dull white with some gray splotched along the margins. This species is a slightly smaller version of the pigmy sperm whale, and both were once thought to be one species. However, the dorsal fin of the dwarf sperm whale is about twice the size of the dorsal fin of the pigmy sperm whale and is more curved. The name rat porpoise is based on its rather ratlike nose and face.

The skull is short, broad, and triangular in shape when viewed from above, and it is smaller in overall size than the pigmy sperm whale. There are only eight to eleven conical teeth on each side of the lower jaw, and occasionally there are one to three teeth present in the upper jaw.

Geographical Range: The dwarf sperm whale occurs in low numbers in the Gulf of Mexico and along the Atlantic Coast as far north as Virginia. It ranges throughout most of the world's oceans.

Habitat: This species lives in deep offshore waters of temperate and tropical seas, but it comes closer to shore during the calving season.

Natural History: The dwarf sperm whale was only recently recognized as a clearly separate species from the pigmy sperm whale, and its life habits are poorly known. It is migratory, moving north to cooler waters in the spring and summer, and returning to warm tropical oceans in the winter months. These whales travel in small groups of two to ten individuals. The gestation period is believed to be about nine months, and the calving season extends over a four- to five-month period during the winter. At birth, the calves are three to four feet long.

The diet consists of fishes, squids, cuttlefishes, crabs, and shrimp. According to the stomach contents of beached individuals, this whale appears to feed at considerable depths at the edge of the continental shelf. Its prey species live only on or near the ocean bottom at a depth of 800 feet or more below the surface.

Remarks: This small whale has no economic impact. Like the pigmy sperm whale, the dwarf sperm whale ejects a dark reddish brown fluid from the anus when alarmed. Such a cloud of pigment released into the water appears to aid its escape from predators.

Selected References:

Caldwell, D. K., and M. C. Caldwell. 1974. Marine mammals of the Southeastern United States Coast: Cape Hatteras to Cape Canaveral. Virginia. Inst. of Marine Sciences 3: 704–72.

Nagorsen, D. 985. Dwarf Sperm Whale (*Kogia simus*). Mammalian Species, No. 239: pp. 1–6.

Giant Sperm Whale
Physeter macrocephalus

Identification: The giant sperm whale is the largest of the toothed whales, and the males are nearly twice as big as the females. The length of adult males ranges from 40 to 69 feet, while the adult females range from 30 to 39 feet in length. Males can weigh from 40 to 60 tons. The most striking feature of the giant sperm whale is the enormous square head, one-quarter to one-third of the total length, combined with a long, slender lower jaw full of large, conical teeth. The body color is dark brownish gray or dark bluish gray, and much of the skin looks corrugated or shriveled. There are scattered areas of white in the anal area and on the upper and lower jaws. The single blowhole is located well to the left of the midline and far forward on the head. Sperm whales have a distinct dorsal hump on the body about two-thirds of the way back.

The skull is massive and out of proportion to the rest of the body size. There are 16–30 large cone-shaped teeth (each six to eight inches long) on each side of the lower jaw, and occasionally a few small nonfunctional teeth are present in the upper jaw (usually there are none).

Geographical Range: This huge whale occurs sparingly in the Gulf of Mexico and along the entire Atlantic Coast from Canada to the Caribbean Sea. Individual sperm whales do beach occasionally, but mass strandings of several whales are rather rare. The giant sperm whale is widely distributed throughout the oceans of the world.

Habitat: Giant sperm whales prefer to live in deep ocean waters off the edge of the continental shelf. They can tolerate both icy Arctic waters and warm tropical seas.

Natural History: The gigantic head of this species is clearly a specialization for diving to great depths in the ocean. When diving they descend almost vertically, head first. Giant sperm whales feed at great depths, exceeding 1,200 feet, and the diet is mainly squids (including the famous giant squid), cuttlefishes, octopuses, and fishes such as barracuda, sharks, skates, albacore, and angelfish. Giant sperm whales often bear the scars of battle with giant squids (sucker marks and beak bites). The maximum depth to which they are known to dive is well over one mile, and they have remained submerged well over an hour. After long dives, they may remain on the surface and blow for ten to fifteen minutes to recover from oxygen debt. Their usual swimming speed is five miles per hour, but when pressed they can reach fifteen miles per hour.

Females reach sexual maturity when they are about 28 feet long and 8 years old. Most matings occur in the spring, and the gestation period is about 16 months. A single calf or rarely two is produced, measuring 14–15 feet long and weighing about one ton. Immediately after birth the mother and nearby adults lift the newborn calf gently to the surface to breathe. Baby whales nurse at either of two teats located in deep, longitudinal grooves on each side of the vaginal opening. Each calf nurses for about two years, then is weaned when about twenty feet long. Adult females breed only once every three to five years. Sometimes females breed while they are still nursing, which is unusual in whales.

Giant sperm whales are gregarious and polygamous, usually traveling in pods of 15–20 individuals. They may also be found singly or in groups of up to 40 whales. Males tend to migrate to cold temperate waters during summer months, but the cows and calves stay behind in warm tropical waters. Adult males sometimes wander far northward or southward into polar seas, then return to warmer waters to winter and to breed. The harem is the basic social unit among sperm whales. It consists of adult cows (usually nursing and/or pregnant), young cows, young bulls, and an old bull, the "harem master." This large bull patrols the perimeter of his herd, guarding against raids from other harem masters or bachelor bulls.

Giant sperm whales have well-developed echolocation systems that permit them to locate and catch prey in the totally dark ocean depths several thousand feet below the surface. They emit a series of regular clicks at varying speeds and wavelengths that bounce off objects and return to their sensitive ears. Sperm whales forage mainly at night in hunting groups which sweep through a favorable area far below the surface. The younger whales do not participate in the long foraging dives, instead remaining at the surface with an adult female from the harems. She is apparently designated as the "baby-sitter." When sperm whales breathe, they make a characteristic spray, or "blow," which is at a low slanted angle (other whales blow straight up at a 90-degree angle).

Remarks: A gummy substance called ambergris is expelled from the large intestine of the giant sperm whale. It is apparently produced only by this species. After exposure to air and sunlight, it hardens into a semisolid, orange-yellow substance with a sweet, earthy smell. It was once thought to have medicinal properties, but is now used primarily in the manufacture of perfumes.

A large cavity in the forehead of the giant sperm whale contains "spermaceti," a waxy, oily material that is used as a high-grade lubricant, as a base for face creams and salves, and for several other purposes. Early whalers mistook the oil for real "sperm" and named the species and the substance accordingly. The teeth of the sperm whale are a favored material for ivory picture carvings called "scrimshaw." Such artifacts are very expensive at the marketplace, and many times more so if they are antiques.

The giant sperm whale once supported a great whaling industry in the United States and various countries around the world. Prior to overharvesting by the whaling ships, these huge whales were abundant throughout the Atlantic Ocean, Pacific Ocean, and Gulf of Mexico. They are now officially protected and classified as endangered by the U.S. Fish and Wildlife Service.

One of the most interesting novels to evolve around the whaling era, based partly on facts, is the epic Moby Dick, by Herman Melville. It is centered around a ship captain's quest for an "albino" giant sperm whale living in the Pacific Ocean during the mid-1800s. Such an albino animal is said to have really existed during whaling days, and it formed the basis for one of the most famous sea-adventure novels ever written.

Selected References:
Best, P. B. 1974. The biology of the sperm whale as it relates to stock management. In *The Whale Problem: A Status Report*. Harvard Univ. Press, Cambridge, Mass.

——. 1979. Social organization in sperm whales. *In Behavior of Marine Animals—Current Perspectives in Research, Vol. 3: Cetaceans*. Plenum Press, N.Y., pp. 227–89.
Caldwell, D. K., M. C. Caldwell, and D. W. Rice. 1966. Behavior of the sperm whale, *Physeter catadon*, in *Whales, Dolphins, and Porpoises*. Univ. of Calif. Press, Berkeley, Calif., pp. 677–717.
Donovan, G. P., ed. 1980. Sperm whales: Special Issue. Rep. Int. Whal. Comm. (Special Issue 2). 275 pp.
Ohsumi, S. 1966. Sexual aggression of the sperm whale. Whales Res. Inst., Sci. Rep. 20: 1–16.
Rice, D. W. 1989. Sperm whale, *Physeter macrocephalus* Linnaeus. In *Handbook of Marine Mammals*. Academic Press, London, Eng., pp. 177–233.

Goose-beaked Whale
Ziphius cavirostris

Identification: The goose-beaked whale, or Cuvier's beaked whale, is medium-sized (16–25 feet long), the body color is dark grayish brown or rust-brown with scattered light spots sometimes occurring throughout, and the entire head and jaws are creamy white. The dorsal fin is small and located well toward the tail fluke. The head is small and drawn out into a beak anteriorly, with the lower jaw protruding forward beyond the tip of the lower jaw.

The rostrum of the skull is long, narrow, and lacking any functional teeth. The lower jaw of males contains only two visible teeth located at the front tip of the mandible, but in females these usually do not erupt.

Geographical Range: The goose-beaked whale occurs sparingly in the Gulf of Mexico and along the entire Atlantic Coast of the United States. It is more often encountered when it becomes stranded than any of the other beaked whales. It is widely distributed throughout most of the oceans of the world.

Habitat: This species occurs in both temperate and warm tropical seas, generally in the deep water zones well away from land but occasionally near shore.

Natural History: The life habits of the goose-beaked whale are poorly known because the species is sparingly distributed and wary of humans and boats. Groups of 10 to 30 individuals have been seen traveling, diving, and feeding together. They are fast, vigorous swimmers and can remain underwater for periods of over 30 minutes. When beginning a deep dive, they raise the tail flukes above the surface and go down almost vertically. One adult female was found to have the remains of over 1,300 deep water squids (the whale's preferred food) in her stomach. Goose-beaked whales also take deep water fishes. The two teeth at the anterior tip of the lower jaw are used to grasp the squids they eat.

Males reach sexual maturity at a body length of about eighteen feet, and females first become pregnant at a body length of about nineteen feet. The gestation period is approximately twelve months long, and a single offspring is produced about once every third year by adult females. The age of goose-beaked whales can be measured by counting growth rings in the cementum layer of teeth. The maximum number of growth rings thus far reported is approximately 40, which presumably reflects the number of years the species lives.

Remarks: There is little or no economic impact associated with the goose-beaked whale.

Selected References:
Caldwell, D. K., and M. C. Caldwell. 1974. Marine mammals of the Southeastern United States Coast. Virginia. Inst. of Marine Sciences, 3: 704–72.
Jefferson, T. A., S. Leatherwood, L. K. M. Shoda, and R. L. Pitman. 1992. *Marine Mammals of the Gulf of Mexico.* Texas A&M Univ., Galveston, Texas, 92 pp.
Schmidly, D. J. 1981. *Marine Mammals of the Southeastern United States Coast and Gulf of Mexico.* Texas A&M Univ., College Station, Tex. 165 pp.

Dense-beaked Whale
Mesoplodon densirostris

Identification: The dense-beaked whale, or Blainville's beaked whale, is medium-sized (14–17 feet long), and the upper parts are black to dark gray, usually blotched with grayish white. On the belly, the color is white from the anal area forward to the tip of the lower jaws. The body is distinctly spindle-shaped and streamlined. The head is narrow, and the lower jaws have a prominent rise at the skull junction. The only teeth in the skull are a single large pair located on a prominence at the back of the jaws. In females the teeth usually do not erupt through the gums. The bones of the rostrum are extremely dense, compact, and heavy (about one-third more dense than elephant ivory).

Geographical Range: This species occurs occasionally in the Gulf of Mexico and along the entire Atlantic Coast, but strandings are uncommon. It is a rare species which occurs in most of the oceans of the world.

Habitat: Dense-beaked whales live well offshore in tropical and warm temperate seas.

Natural History: Very little is known about the life habits of this species because it is rarely seen. The stomach contents of stranded animals reveal they feed on squids. One subadult male stranded on a beach emitted a series of chirps and short whistles while still in the surf.

Remarks: The dense-beaked whale has no economic impact.

Selected References:
Gaskin, D. E. 1982. *The Ecology of Whales and Dolphins.* Heinemann Educational Books, Inc. Portsmouth, N.H. 459 pp.
Moore, J. C. 1968. Relationships between the living genera of beaked whales with classifications, diagnosis, and keys. Fieldiana Zool. 53: 209–98.

Antillean Beaked Whale
Mesoplodon europaeus

Identification: The Antillean beaked whale, or Gervais' beaked whale, is medium-sized (12–22 feet long), and the body color is dark grayish black, with white on the lips and anterior tip of the beak. The dorsal fin is small, curved backwards, and located well toward the tail.

The rostrum of the skull is long, pointed, and very narrow. The only teeth in the skull are one pair located about one-third of the way back from the tip of the lower jaw. These teeth are laterally flattened and pointed at the tip.

Geographical Range: This whale occurs rarely in the Gulf of Mexico and along the entire Atlantic Coast south of New England. The species lives only in the western Atlantic Ocean from the latitude of New York south to northern South America.

Habitat: The Antillean beaked whale appears to prefer the open sea in tropical and warm temperate waters.

Natural History: The diet of this species is almost exclusively squids. During the calving season, females come closer to shore than at other times. Little is known about this whale's life habits.

Remarks: This species is rarely encountered by humans and has no economic significance.

Selected References:

Arnason, U., K. Benirschki, J. G. Mead, and W. W. Nichols. 1977. Banded karyotypes of three whales: *Mesoplodon europaeus, M. carlhubbsi,* and *Balaenoptera acutorostrata.* Hereditas 87: 189–200.

Moore, J. C. 1968. Relationships between the living genera of beaked whales with classifications, diagnosis, and keys. Fieldiana Zool. 53: 209–98.

True's Beaked Whale
Mesoplodon mirus

Identification: True's beaked whale is medium-sized (14–18 feet long), the upper parts are dark gray to dull black, and the belly and lower sides are white to slate gray, often flecked with dark spots. The entire head and lips are dark gray to black.

The rostrum of the skull is long, very narrow, and pointed. The only teeth in the skull are a single pair located at the tip of the lower jaw, clearly visible in males but not always erupted in females.

Geographical Range: True's beaked whale occurs rarely off the entire Atlantic Coast from northern Florida northward. It lives only in the western Atlantic Ocean from Nova Scotia to northeastern Florida.

Habitat: This whale prefers deep offshore areas in temperate seas.

Natural History: True's beaked whale probably eats squids like other species in the genus. It is seldom encountered by humans, but individuals occasionally beach or wash ashore dead along the Atlantic beaches.

Remarks: Because of its rarity, True's beaked whale has no economic significance.

Selected References:

Mitchell, E. D., ed. 1975. Report of the meetings on smaller cetaceans. J. Fish. Res. Board, Canada 32: 889–983.

Moore, J. C. 1968. Relationships between the living genera of beaked whales with classifications, diagnosis, and keys. Fieldiana Zool. 53: 209–98.

North Sea Beaked Whale
Mesoplodon bidens

Identification: The North Sea beaked whale is medium-sized (13–16 feet long), shiny blue-black dorsally, and the underparts are blue-gray with irregular light spotting. The head tapers to a long, slender beak.

The skull contains a single pair of mandibular teeth which only erupt in males.

Geographical Range: In the Southeast, there is only one record of this species, which was reported in St. Joseph's Bay, Gulf County, Florida, in October 1984. The species ranges throughout the North Atlantic from the United States and Canada to Great Britain, France, and Norway.

Habitat: The North Sea beaked whale prefers deep, cold temperate waters. It is clearly a pelagic species.

Natural History: The biology of this and all the other beaked whales is poorly known because they have never been hunted commercially and they are rarely stranded inshore. The North Sea beaked whale is apparently not migratory and not gregarious (it is seldom observed in groups of more than two or three). The species is believed to feed primarily on squids. Nothing is known about its reproductive habits, except that one calf is produced when the females give birth.

Remarks: The Florida specimen probably represents a lost, widely wandering individual, but occasional strandings can be expected along the Mid-Atlantic Coast. This species is also called "Sowerby's beaked whale."

Selected References:

Moore, J. C. 1968. Relationships between the living genera of beaked whales with classifications, diagnosis, and keys. Fieldiana Zool. 53: 209–98.

Sergeant, D. E., and H. D. Fisher. 1957. Sowerby's beaked whale *(Mesoplodon bidens).* In The smaller cetaceans of eastern Canadian waters. J. Fish Res. Board, Canada 14: 83–115.

Fin Whale
Balaenoptera physalus

Identification: The fin whale, or fin-backed whale, is gigantic in size (60–80 feet long), and the second-largest mammal found in southeastern waters. The color is blue-black or brownish black above and white on the belly (with long parallel folds, or "pleats," in that area). The posterior portion of the back is distinctly ridged, topped by a small backward-pointed dorsal fin. There is also an asymmetrical color pattern on the head and jaws. The right lower jaw area is white, while the left lower jaw is blue-black. Large fin whales can reach a weight of 100 tons.

The rostrum of the huge skull is an elongated triangle, tapering to a distinct point when viewed from above. No teeth are present, but there are 350–400 baleen plates located in the mouth to strain and trap food. The plates vary in color from white to blue-gray or purplish gray, streaked with white.

Geographical Range: The fin whale occurs sparingly in the Gulf of Mexico and along the entire Atlantic Coast from Canada southward to the tropics. The species is widely distributed throughout all the oceans of the world and is one of the most common baleen whales.

Habitat: This species prefers the waters of the open ocean but may come inshore when migrating. Fin whales tolerate both the warm water of the tropics and the frigid polar seas.

Natural History: These huge whales sometimes travel in packs of fifty or more individuals, but small groups of only a few animals also occur. They can swim quite rapidly when pursued and have been clocked at speeds of up to about 30 miles per hour.

Fin whales tend to migrate to colder waters in the summertime and return to warm waters for the winter months. Some east–west movements of the pods for considerable distances have also been noted. Both mating and calving take place during the winter months. The gestation period is about one year, and one offspring is normally produced. Twins occur at a rate of roughly one pregnant female out of a hundred. The calves are 19–22 feet long at birth but grow at a tremendous rate. A baby fin whale drinks about 140 gallons of milk per day and puts on about 125 pounds of weight each 24-hour period. Whale's milk contains 30–40 percent fat, which compares to only 3–5 percent fat in cow's milk. Young fin whales are weaned at around 6 months of age, when about 35–40 feet long. Sexual maturity occurs when the young whales reach about six years old. The maximum life span is thought to be around 50 years, but no one is certain.

Fin whales feed on small sea creatures such as crustaceans, small swarming fishes, plankton, shrimp, copepods, and mollusks. They pass huge quantities of seawater through the baleen plates in the mouth and trap millions of organisms contained therein. They are thought to forage more deeply than other baleen whales (to a depth of more than 750 feet). Fin whales do not show their tail flukes when beginning a dive.

Remarks: Because of its gigantic size and relative abundance in some areas, the fin whale has historically been the second most important baleen whale harvested by the whaling industry, behind only the blue whale. Today, only the countries of the former Soviet Union and Japan still continue to support large whaling operations. These countries kill fin whales as one of their preferred species. There is a worldwide moratorium on capturing any blue whales because of their low numbers, which puts more pressure on the fin whale. The whale-oil yield from a large fin whale is around fifty barrels. The meat is sometimes used to feed furbearers such as foxes and mink which are raised on farms. The large bones are usually ground up to use as bone meal.

Because of the fin whale's relatively low population numbers, the U.S. Fish and Wildlife Service lists it as officially endangered.

Selected References:

Gambell, R. 1985. Fin whale—*Balaenoptera physalus*. In *Handbook of Marine Mammals*. Vol. 3. Academic Press, London, pp. 171–92.

Gaskin, D. E. 1976. The evolution, zoogeography, and ecology of cetacea. Oceangr. Mar. Biol. Annu. Rev. 14: 246–346.

Laws, R. M. 1959. The foetal growth rates of whales with special reference to the fin whale, *Balaenoptera physalus*. Disc. Rep. 29: 281–308.

Ratnaswamy, M. J., and H. E. Winn. 1993. Photogrammetric estimates of allometry and calf production in fin whales, *Balaenoptera physalus*. J. Mamm. 74: 323–30.

Ray, G. C., E. D. Mitchell, D. Wartzok, M. Kozicki, and R. Maiefski. 1978. Radio tracking of a fin whale (*Balaenoptera physalus*). Science 202: 521–24.

Tersky, B. R. 1992. Body size, diet, habitat use, and social behavior of *Balaenoptera* whales in the Gulf of California. J. Mamm. 73: 477–86.

Minke Whale
Balaenoptera acutorostrata

Identification: The Minke whale, or little piked whale, is large (23–33 feet long), yet it is the smallest baleen whale found off the Southeast coast. The body color is dark blue-gray or black above, and the belly and undersides of the pectoral flippers are white. The front half of the belly is furrowed, or "pleated." This is the only baleen whale with a patch of white on the upper side of the pectoral flippers, and the baleen plates (numbering 230–350) are yellowish white. The dorsal fin is tall and directed backward.

The long, pointed rostrum of the skull has straight, parallel lateral sides (rather than being outwardly bowed as its close relatives have) when viewed from above.

Geographical Range: The Minke whale is found sparingly in the Gulf of Mexico and along the entire Atlantic Coast from Canada southward into the tropics. It ranges throughout all of the oceans of the world.

Habitat: This whale prefers open seas above the continental shelf and both cold temperate and warm tropical waters. It sometimes enters bays, inlets, and estuaries to hunt food.

Natural History: The Minke whale migrates northward for the summer and returns to warmer waters to spend the winter and breed. Its seasonal distribution from year to year is also highly dependent on krill (small fishes, shrimp, and other invertebrates). Individuals often show little fear of boats or ships and can frequently be observed breaching free of the water's surface as they swim along.

Adult females give birth to a single calf once every 12–18 months on average after they reach maturity. The gestation period is about 10 months, and newborn calves are around nine feet long. Young Minke whales wean at six months, and reach sexual maturity at a length of about 21–23 feet (at approximately two years of age).

Remarks: Minke whales are ranked sixth from the top in terms of commercial value among baleen whales taken by the two remaining whaling fleets of Russia and Japan. Because they are much smaller than the other great whales of the baleen group, their oil and blubber yield is much smaller per individual. Most experts believe that the last remnants of the whaling industry should die a natural and timely death because the economic benefits of whaling are very marginal and because the great whale stocks of the world are being decimated to the brink of extinction by these two "outlaw" countries.

Minke whales often display an innate curiosity about ships and will approach them closely. This makes them easy targets for slaughter by whalers.

Selected References:

Bearnish, P., and E. Mitchell. 1973. Short pulse length audio frequency sounds recorded in the presence of a minke whale (*Balaenoptera acutorostrata*). Deep Sea Res. 20: 375–86.

Mitchell, E. D., ed. 1975. Report of the meetings on smaller cetaceans. J. Fish. Res. Board, Canada 32: 889–983.

Sergeant, D. E. 1963. Minke whales, *Balaenoptera acutorostrata*, of the western North Atlantic. J. Fish Res. Board, Canada 20: 1489–1504.

———. 1973. An additional food supply for humpback (*Megaptera novaeangliae*) and minke whales (*Balaenoptera acutorostrata*). Int. Counc. Expl. Sea Mammals Comm. 13 pp.

Tersky, B. R. 1992. Body size, diet, habitat use, and social behavior of *Balaenoptera* whales in the Gulf of California. J. Mamm. 73: 477–86.

Sei Whale
Balaenoptera borealis

Identification: The sei (pronounced "say") whale, or pollock whale, is gigantic (45–62 feet long), but somewhat smaller than the fin whale. The color is bluish black on the back, grading to dark steel gray on the sides and under the tail, and the pleated portion of the belly is grayish white. The undersides of the flukes and flippers are gray, not white. The ventral pleats extend only a short distance posterior to the pectoral flippers. The dorsal fin is tall, pointed, and falcate (directed backward). The baleen plates number 320–400 and are black, fringed with grayish white.

The skull is much more massive than those of Bryde's whale and the Minke whale, but smaller than that of the fin whale. An expert on whales must be consulted to make an accurate identification.

Geographical Range: The sei whale occurs rarely in the Gulf of Mexico and along the entire Atlantic Coast from Canada southward to the subtropics. It ranges widely throughout most of the oceans of the world.

Habitat: This species prefers the open deep waters of temperate and subtropical seas. These whales occasionally come inshore to feed, but normally stay far out at sea.

Natural History: Sei whales feed on surface plankton, shrimp and other crustaceans, small schooling fishes, and small squids. They are surface-skimmer feeders and do not normally dive deeply. Sei whales move long distances to follow seasonal changes that affect their food. They are usually found in groups of two to five individuals, but may congregate in larger numbers on rich feeding grounds. The breeding cycle is apparently similar to that of the fin whale. The gestation period is between 11 and 12 months long. Females normally produce one offspring, but there is an occasional record of twins occurring. The calves are about 15–16 feet long at birth, and, like all baleen whales, they grow at a tremendous rate. Weaning takes place at about nine months of age.

Remarks: The commercial value of the sei whale is ranked approximately fourth from the top among baleen whales harvested by the remaining whaling countries in the world (Japan and Russia).

Because of declining population numbers, the U.S. Fish and Wildlife Service lists the sei whale as officially endangered.

Selected References:

Gambell, R. 1985. Sei whale—*Balaenoptera borealis.* In *Handbook of Marine Mammals.* Academic Press. London. 362 pp.

Horwood, J. 1987. The sei whale: Population biology, ecology, and management. Crown Helm, London. 375 pp.

Lockyear, C. 1974. Investigations of the ear plug of the southern sei whale, *Balaenoptera borealis,* as a valid means of determining age. J. Cons. Int. Explor. Mer. 36: 71–81.

Johnsgaard, A., and K. Darling. 1975. On the biology of the eastern North Atlantic sei whale, *Balaenoptera borealis.* Univ. of Rhode Island, Kingston, R.I., M.S. thesis.

Mead, J. G. 1977. Records of sei and Bryde's whales from the Atlantic coast of the United States, the Gulf of Mexico, and the Caribbean. Intern. Whal. Commission, Special Issue 1, pp. 113–16.

Bryde's Whale
Balaenoptera edeni

Identification: Bryde's whale is very large (36–46 feet in length), the upper parts are blue-black, and the underside and front edges of the flippers are grayish white. The body is remarkably elongated and not as powerfully built as the sei whale or fin whale. This is the only whale having three longitudinal ridges located on top of the snout anterior to the blowhole. The dorsal fin is fairly large and directed backward, and the baleen plates are slate gray colored with a white or light gray front fringe. The pleats or belly folds extend all the way back to near the anal area.

The skull is less robust and smaller in size than those of both the fin and sei whales, and considerably larger than the skull of the Minke whale. There are 250–370 baleen plates in the mouth. A whale expert should be consulted to make an accurate identification.

Geographical Range: Bryde's whale occurs rarely in the Gulf of Mexico and along the Atlantic Coast from Virginia southward to the tropics. They range through all the oceans of the world.

Habitat: This whale prefers the open waters of warm temperate and tropical to subtropical seas. It sometimes comes inshore to feed but more often is found far at sea.

Natural History: Bryde's whale has long been confused with the sei whale and was not recognized as a valid species until fairly recently. For this reason, there is relatively little information on its biology. These whales are not surface skimmers but are deeper divers. Like the other baleen whales, they feed on small schooling fishes, crustaceans, and plankton. Surprisingly, they have also been reported to eat small sharks and penguins, obviously swallowing them whole since they have no teeth.

Remarks: The commercial value of Bryde's whales is ranked approximately fifth from the top among baleen whales harvested by the two remaining whaling countries in the world (Japan and Russia). Bryde's whales often appear to be curious about ships and will approach them for a closer inspection. This makes them easy targets for whalers.

In 1988, a young Bryde's whale was beached in Florida and nursed back to health at Sea World on a diet of squid and small fish. It was a two-year-old female which weighed 4,200 pounds and measured almost 23 feet long. It was eventually released by the U.S. Coast Guard back into the Gulf of Mexico. So far as can be determined, this is the first baleen whale to be rescued near death and later recover in captivity.

Selected References:

Gaskin, D. E. 1976. The evolution, zoogeography, and ecology of cetacea. Oceangr. Mar. Biol. Annu. Rev. 14: 246–346.

Jefferson, T. A., S. Leatherwood, L. K. M. Shoda, and R. L. Pitman. 1992. *Marine Mammals of the Gulf of Mexico*. Texas A&M Univ., Galveston, Texas. 92 pp.

Mead, J. G. 1977. Records of sei and Bryde's whales from the Atlantic coast of the United States, the Gulf of Mexico, and the Caribbean. Intern. Whal. Commission, Special Issue 1, pp. 113–16.

Schmidly, D. J. 1981. *Marine Mammals of the Southeastern United States Coast and Gulf of Mexico*. Texas A&M Univ., College Station, Tex. 165 pp.

Tersky, B. R. 1992. Body size, diet, habitat use, and social behavior of *Balaenoptera* whales in the Gulf of California. J. Mamm. 73: 477–86.

Blue Whale
Balaenoptera musculus

Identification: The gigantic blue whale, also called the sulphur-bottomed whale, is the largest animal ever to live (including the dinosaurs), measuring up to 100 feet long and weighing 200 tons. As the name implies, the basic color is dark blue-gray, mottled with light blue-gray oval spots on the back, flanks, and belly. Vertical throat grooves, or "pleats," are yellowish and extend back from the lower mandible to the naval. There are scattered short hairs on the rostrum, lips, and around the blowholes. The baleen plates are short, coarse, and uniformly blue-black. The plates number 250–400 on each side. Adult females are larger than adult males, and the Antarctic stocks are larger than those in the Northern Hemisphere.

Geographical Range: The blue whale is very rare in southeastern waters, but there are records of occurrences as far south as North Carolina on the Atlantic coast. The only Gulf coast record thus far is from the Texas Coast, so probably the whale turns up along the southeastern Gulf Coast as well. The blue whale ranges through all the oceans of the world in polar and cold temperate waters.

Habitat: Blue whales are pelagic dwellers in Arctic, Antarctic, and cold temperate oceans in both the northern and southern hemispheres. They seldom venture close to shore either to feed or migrate.

Natural History: The blue whale is usually encountered singly or in small groups of 2–3 individuals. This giant usually cruises at around 15 miles per hour when not alarmed, but can reach 20 to 25 miles per hour when alarmed and swimming at full speed. The maximum depth these whales reach in a dive is recorded at 194 fathoms, and they can remain submerged for up to a maximum of 50 minutes (10–15 minutes submerged is the more common length of time, however).

Blue whales are migratory, going north to the edge of the polar ice cap in the spring and summer, then traveling back to spend the winter in temperate waters each fall. Mating occurs from May to September, with a peak in activity in June and July. The gestation period is 10 $1/2$ months, and single calves (rarely twins) are born in April or May, while the females are migrating northward, still in temperate waters. Baby blue whales are around 23 feet long at birth and weigh about two metric tons. The calves grow very rapidly and wean in December when they are about seven months of age and 50 feet long. Both young males and females reach sexual maturity at about five years, but males are generally not successful breeders until they are much older and larger.

Remarks: Blue whales feed exclusively on planktonic crustacea, or "krill." Cold polar seas teem with krill during the summer months, and the whales gorge themselves by swimming repeatedly through the planktonic bloom.

The blue whales once dominated whaling in the 1930s after the decline of humpbacked whale populations from overharvesting. A single mature blue whale yields from 80 to 300 barrels of whale oil. Over 30,000 blue whales were killed in 1931 alone, so the population declined rapidly within a few short years.

The blue whale has been protected in the North Atlantic since 1955 and in the North Pacific since 1965. The world stocks of this animal are still at a low population level, but they are slowly increasing under the full protection of the International Whaling Commission. Blue whales are also listed as endangered by the U.S. Fish and Wildlife Service.

Selected References:
Gaskin, D. E. 1976. The evolution, zoogeography, and ecology of cetacea. Oceangr. Mar. Biol. Annu. Rev. 14: 246–346.

Gulland, F. B. 1972. Future of the blue whale. New. Sci. 54: 198–99.

Johnsgaard, A. 1966. The distribution of Balaenopteridae in the North Atlantic Ocean. In *Whales, Dolphins, and Porpoises*. Univ. of Calif. Press, Berkeley, Calif., pp. 114–24.

Tersky, B. R. 1992. Body size, diet, habitat use, and social behavior of *Balaenoptera* whales in the Gulf of California. J. Mamm. 73: 477–86.

Humpbacked Whale
Megaptera novaeangliae

Identification: The humpbacked whale is gigantic in size (40–53 feet long), the color is mostly black, and the belly is white or splotched with white. The pectoral flippers are extremely long (about 15 feet), nearly all white, and the front edges are scalloped. The tail flukes are marked with white in various patterns on the underside, and the rear edges also are scalloped. The top of the snout and border of the lower jaw has a series of raised fleshy "knobs" or protuberances scattered over the skin. The dorsal fin is quite small, directed backward, and positioned on a small hump two-thirds of the way back from the tip of the snout. The baleen plates (270–400 in number) are black in color with olive-black fringes anteriorly. Ventral pleats or folds extend from the throat to the mid-belly region. A large humpbacked whale weighs from 40 to 50 tons.

The rostrum of the skull is long, arched only slightly, and somewhat convex on the lateral edges.

Geographical Range: The humpbacked whale is found in the Gulf of Mexico and along the entire Atlantic Coast from northern Canada to Florida. It is found widely throughout both the Atlantic and Pacific Oceans, but rarely becomes stranded on the beaches.

Habitat: These large whales prefer to forage and live over the continental shelf or along island banks. They are also sometimes found far at sea in the pelagic region.

Natural History: The humpbacked whale is gregarious and highly migratory, inhabiting cold northern and southern polar waters in the summer, and then returning to warm tropical waters for the winter. During approximately six months each year (the migration period and while on the wintering grounds), humpbacked whales do not feed but rely on vast stores of fat in their blubber and other body tissues to meet their energy demands. During the summer months they feed on enormous schools of prey in polar inlets. Groups of humpbacked whales tend to concentrate in several distinct populations that are isolated from one another and between which there is little exchange of individuals. There may be some mingling of northern hemisphere herds with southern hemisphere herds near the equator during the winter months, but this is not certain.

The humpbacked whale's diet consists mainly of crustaceans and small schooling fishes. They are often observed to forage in groups and concentrate the food animals by forming "bubble curtains," created by releasing air bubbles while swimming in a wide circle well beneath the surface. The whales then rush upward in the center of the bubble column with their mouths agape, gorging on millions of small marine organisms. As many as three to eight of these huge whales may breach simultaneously, lunge for the sky, and then crash thunderously back into the water with their pleated throats greatly distended with water and food. This bizarre and interesting feeding mechanism in baleen whales has been named "bubble netting."

Humpbacked whales mate in the wintering areas and the gestation period is eleven to twelve months. Adult males compete aggressively with one another to mate with receptive females. While mating, both male and female whales have been observed to repeatedly administer alternate blows or "slaps" to the other. After the seasonal migration northward to forage, each pregnant female again returns to warm tropical waters where a single calf is born. On rare occasions, twins are born. As with most whales, the calves are born tail first and then lifted to the surface to begin breathing. A newborn baby humpback whale weighs about 3,000 pounds and is 13–15 feet long. In the early stages, each baby grows at the rate of 100 pounds a day because of mother's rich milk. The age of weaning is around eleven months. Female humpbacked whales become sexually mature when seven to eight years old, at a length of 37–40 feet. Adult females produce a calf only once every three years. The maximum life span is probably 50–70 years.

Remarks: The humpbacked whale is a species highly prized by the whaling industry. The yield from a 40 footer is about 40–45 barrels (about eight tons) of whale oil, one-half ton of bone meal, and two tons of frozen meat.

The stocks of the humpbacked whale have decreased to the point that they are listed as endangered by the U.S. Fish and Wildlife Service. The only countries still killing them are Russia and Japan.

The variation in the white splotches on the tail flukes of this species are used by whale researchers to identify individuals. Photographs are routinely taken of the tail flukes as they clear the water to begin a dive. Each whale has its own unique white markings which serve as a "signature" wherever and whenever it is seen again. In this way, humpbacks observed in Iceland in the summer have been tracked in their migration to specific areas of the Caribbean Sea in the winter.

Humpbacked whales are often heavily parasitized externally by amphipods called "whale lice." Mature whales are also encrusted with barnacles, much like a ship's hull. Researchers studying their seasonal migrations have found the placement patterns of the whale lice and barnacles to be useful in identifying individual whales.

Selected References:

Jurasz, C. M., and V. P. Jurasz. 1979. Feeding modes of the humpback whale, *Megaptera novaeangliae,* in southeast Alaska. Whale Res. Inst., Sci. Rep. 31: 69–83.

Katona, S. K. 1986. Biogeography of the humpback whale, *Megaptera novaeangliae,* in the North Atlantic. UNESCO Tech. Pap. Mar. Sci. 46: 66–171.

Payne, R., and S. McVay. 1971. Songs of humpback whales. Science 173: 585–87.

Stone, G. S., S. K. Katona, and E. B. Tucker. 1987. History, migration, and present status of humpback whales, *Megaptera novaeangliae,* at Bermuda. Biol. Conserv. 42: 133–45.

Swartz, S. L. 1989. The humpback whale; In Audubon Wildlife Report 1989/1990. Academic Press, San Diego, Calif., pp. 386–403.

Weinrich, M. T., C. R. Belt, M. R. Schilling, and M. E. Cappellino. 1986. Habitat use patterns as a function of age and reproductive status in humpback whales *(Megaptera novaeangliae).* In *Humpback Whales of the Southern Gulf of Maine.* Cetacean Research Inst., Glouchester, Maine. 41 pp.

Right Whale
Balaena glacialis

Identification: The right whale is gigantic in size (40–53 feet long), the body is dark brown to black in color (somewhat mottled), and there are usually white areas in the mid-belly region and on the chin. The head is enormous (one-fourth the body length), and the mouth is highly arched, curving upward in front of the eyes on the sides of the head. This species has neither a dorsal fin nor throat pleats. The top of the snout has a large rough, horny projection that is light colored, called the "bonnet," located in front of the blowholes. Bonnets are hard protuberances representing the accumulation of cornified layers of skin, commonly infested with parasitic crustaceans (whale lice) and worms. Smaller callosities of this type also occur along the margins of the lower jaw (called "beards" and "lip patches") and sometimes near the eye (called "eyebrows"). There are about 250 pairs of baleen plates which are very narrow, long (up to six feet) and black to dark brown in color. They hang like closely packed curtains from the roof of the huge yawning mouth. The pectoral flippers are short, broad, and rounded. Some specimens weigh 40–50 tons.

The rostrum of the skull has a pronounced downward curving arch and is quite narrow and tapered to a point anteriorly.

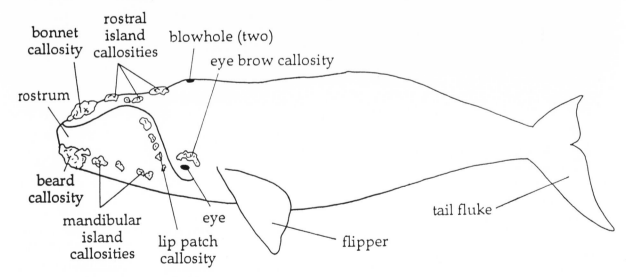

Decorative callosities found around the head of a right whale (*Balaena glacialis*).

Geographical Range: This large whale is found sparingly in the Gulf of Mexico and along the Atlantic Coast from Canada southward to Florida. It ranges throughout most of the oceans of the world.

Habitat: Right whales are migratory and found in both cold and temperate waters, but they tend to avoid tropical seas near the equator. They often forage near shore in shallow water and sometimes enter large bays. These whales move along the South Atlantic Coast between early January and late March and do not return until the following late summer or early autumn.

Natural History: This giant whale feeds on planktonic animal life, mainly copepods, shrimp, and mollusks. They use the skimming method of feeding, in which they swim through swarms of krill (mostly copepods) with yawning open mouths and their heads above water to just behind the nostril openings. When a sufficient mouthful of krill has been filtered from the water by the baleen plates, they dive, close their mouths, and swallow the food.

The name "right whale" was given to them by early whalers because this was the "right" or "correct" whale to harpoon. They were "right" for several reasons: 1) they swam slowly (only about five miles per hour); 2) they were abundant and easy to approach (being not at all wary of ships); 3) they were buoyant and did not sink when killed; and 4) they yielded copious amounts of whale oil.

Despite their great size, right whales are surprisingly agile, and seem to particularly enjoy breaching almost completely out of the water.

Breeding takes place in the late summer or fall and the gestation period is about 12 months. The young are born at the southern end of their north–south migration, in the Atlantic Ocean just off the area of the Georgia–Florida state line. One calf is normally produced, measuring 15–16 feet long at birth. They nurse for about one year before being weaned. Young right whales reach sexual maturity in about six years, and adult females give birth to an offspring only once every three years. The maximum life span is around 40 years. Collisions with ships are the main cause of mortality.

Remarks: Unrestricted whale hunting from the twelfth to the nineteenth centuries nearly exterminated the right whale because the females and calves that frequented inshore waters formed most of the kills. All right whales are now protected by international agreements of all the major nations of the world from any type of exploitation. They are also listed as endangered by the U.S. Fish and Wildlife Service, and they appear to be slowly increasing in numbers, but there are only about 300 living in the whole North Atlantic.

Scientists who study the right whale identify individual animals by the unique patterns and shapes of their "bonnets" and other callosities located around the head and mouth. They are photographed at close range when their heads are visible and reidentified at a later time and place using the pictures.

Selected References:

Brownell, R. L., Jr., P. B. Best, and J. H. Prescott, eds. 1986. Right whales: Past and present status. Rep. Int. Whal. Comm. (Special Issue 10). 289 pp.

Cummings, W. C. 1985. Right whales—*Eubalaena glacialis* and *Eubalaena australis*. In *Handbook of Marine Mammals.* Academic Press, London, pp. 275–304.

Kraus, S. D., M. J. Crone, and A. R. Knowlton. 1989. The North Atlantic right whale. In Audubon Wildlife Report 1989/1990. Academic Press, San Diego, Calif., pp. 684–98.

Kraus, S. D., J. H. Prescott, A. R. Knowlton, and G. S. Stone. 1986. Migration and calving of right whales (*Eubalaena glacialis*) in the western North Atlantic. In *Right Whales: Past and Present Status.* Rep. Int. Whal. Comm., Cambridge, Eng., pp. 139–44.

Reeves, R. R., J. G. Mead, and S. Katona. 1978. The right whale, *Eubalaena glacialis*, in the western North Atlantic. Rep. Int. Whal. Comm. 28: 303–12.

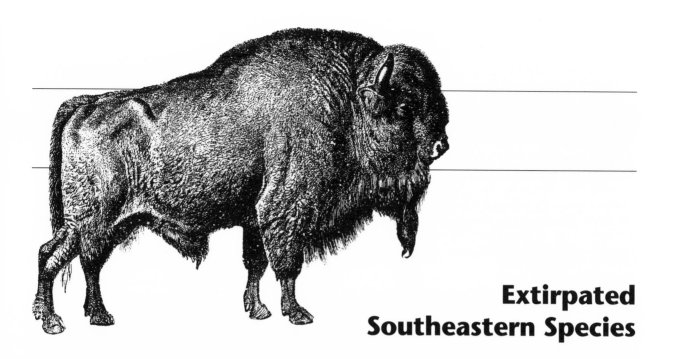

Extirpated
Southeastern Species

1. Red Wolf
Canis rufus

Red wolf, *Canis rufus*. U.S. Fish & Wildlife Service

The red wolf is very similar in coloration and general contours to the introduced coyote but slightly larger in overall body size. Some individuals are melanistic rather than tannish gray. They once ranged widely over the eastern half of the United States in the dense, mature hardwood forests present when the first European settlers arrived. They occurred throughout the Southeast, but disappeared by the 1800s. Recent DNA studies show that the red wolf is actually a hybrid between the gray or timber wolf (Canis lupus) and coyote (Canis latrans) and should not be recognized as a separate species. Specimens of the gray or timber wolf (Canis lupus) are recorded from the northern United States, but that species apparently did not occur in the Southeast. The demise of the red wolf was caused by three factors: 1) the cutting of virgin timber stands and opening up of the forests, i.e., habitat change; 2) poisoning, trapping, and shooting of wolves by farmers and settlers; and 3) the red wolf hybridized with the invading coyotes and/or they were out-competed by coyotes for space.

Elsewhere in the United States, the last remaining red wolves were captured in eastern Texas in the 1970s and placed in a captive breeding program by the U.S. Fish and Wildlife Service. Offspring from this effort have been released in the late 1980s and early 1990s in the Smoky Mountains and along both the Atlantic and Gulf coasts. If these restocking efforts are successful, the red wolf may eventually be reintroduced in other suitable southeastern habitats.

2. Elk
Cervus canadensis

Elk, *Cervus canadensis*. Larry Brown

The elk, or wapiti, is one of the largest species of deer found in North America. Only the moose (Alces alces) is larger. The coat is chestnut brown to brownish tan, and the tail is small and creamy yellow, surrounded by a large rump patch of the same color. Each year males grow and later shed large antlers that have several branches (the antlers reach a length of four to five feet). The skull of elk have upper canine teeth, unlike deer, which lack canines. The average weight of a bull elk is about 600 pounds, but 1,200-pound bulls have occasionally been recorded. A cow elk is only about two-thirds the size of a bull the same age, and cows do not have antlers.

The early European settlers in the Southeast made heavy use of elk and other big game they encountered with no thought as to the survival of the species. All the native elk found in the Southeast were gone by 1850 or earlier. Little is known regarding the preferred habitat of the eastern elk, but it probably consisted of a mixture of open meadows and hardwoods. They browsed on the leaves and twigs of many species of trees and shrubs as well as eating grasses and forbs. Elk are still fairly common in many western states and Canada, where they are carefully managed for sport hunting. It is a great loss that elk no longer roam the hills and valleys of the southeastern United States.

3. American Bison
Bison bison

American bison, *Bison bison.* Barry Mansell

When the first European explorers arrived, the American bison, or buffalo, occurred widely throughout the eastern United States and were especially abundant on the western plains. They were extensively slaughtered for meat and hides and disappeared in the East before 1800. Bison once occurred throughout the Appalachian Mountains and Plateau areas of the Southeast. They were probably the first native mammal eliminated from the region by the overharvesting by early settlers.

Bison are large, shaggy, dark brown members of the cattle family (Bovidae), with a prominent hump at the shoulders and pointed black horns that curve sharply upward and inward on a very broad, massive skull. The bulls are considerably larger and more robust than the cows. Calves are cinnamon brown, later changing to dark brown like the adults. Mature bulls sometimes reach a weight of 1,800 pounds and stand six feet at the hump. Cows are only about two-thirds as large as males. The eastern bison appear to have been primarily woodland and forest-opening dwellers, contrary to the bison of the vast western plains. Early records suggest that they sometimes occurred in small herds in open valleys and forest edges, but they were never as numerous as the western herds. The heavy hunting pressure eliminated them quickly.

4. West Indian Monk Seal
Monachus tropicalis

The West Indian monk seal was a tropical species that once occurred on the islands and keys at the southern tip of Florida and other parts of the Caribbean and Gulf of Mexico. They were docile, easily approached, and heavily exploited by early sailors for meat, hides, and oil. The last one reported in southeastern waters was taken near Key West, Florida, in March 1922. There were infrequent reports of isolated seals sighted on islands in the West Indies and along the east coast of Mexico up until about 1950, but West Indian monk seals are now apparently extinct, because none have been positively identified for over 40 years.

Their color was uniformly brown above, tinged with gray at the tips of the hair. The color was slightly lighter on the sides, and yellowish white on the belly. West Indian monk seals were about six to seven feet long with females slightly smaller than the males.

Appendix I
Dental Formulas of Southeastern Terrestrial Mammals

The dental formula of a mammal enumerates the number of incisors, canines, premolars and molars present in the mouth of that genus or species. The number of teeth and type of teeth present are vary useful in identifying the skull. The dental formulas of the southeastern terrestrial mammals are presented as follows:

	Incisors	Canines	Premolars	Molars	U/L Total	Mammal
U	5-5	1-1	3-3	4-4	50	*Didelphis*
L	4-4	1-1	3-3	4-4		
U	3-3	1-1	4-4	3-3	44	*Condylura,*
L	3-3	1-1	4-4	3-3		*Parascalops, Sus*
U	3-3	1-1	4-4	2-2	42	*Canis, Urocyon,*
L	3-3	1-1	4-4	3-3		*Ursus, Vulpes*
U	3-3	1-1	4-4	2-2	40	*Procyon*
L	3-3	1-1	4-4	2-2		
U	2-2	1-1	3-3	3-3	38	*Myotis*
L	3-3	1-1	3-3	3-3		
U	3-3	1-1	4-4	1-1	38	*Martes*
L	3-3	1-1	4-4	2-2		
U	3-3	1-1	3-3	3-3	36	*Scalopus*
L	2-2	0-0	3-3	3-3		

Continued on next page

	Incisors	Canines	Premolars	Molars	U/L Total	Mammal
U	2-2	1-1	2-2	3-3	36	*Lasionycteris,*
L	3-3	1-1	3-3	3-3		*Plecotus*
U	3-3	1-1	4-4	1-1	36	*Lutra*
L	3-3	1-1	3-3	2-2		
U	2-2	1-1	2-2	3-3	34	*Pipistrellus*
L	3-3	1-1	2-2	3-3		
U	3-3	1-1	3-3	1-1	34	*Mephitis, Mustela,*
L	3-3	1-1	3-3	2-2		*Spilogale*
U	3-3	1-1	3-3	3-3	32	*Blarina, Microsorex,*
L	1-1	1-1	1-1	3-3		*Sorex*
U	2-2	1-1	1-1	3-3	32	*Eptesicus*
L	3-3	1-1	2-2	3-3		
U	1-1	1-1	2-2	3-3	32	*Lasiurus, Tadarida*
L	3-3	1-1	2-2	3-3		
U	0-0	0-0	3-3	3-3	32	*Odocoileus*
L	3-3	1-1	3-3	3-3		
U	0-0	0-0		{8-8}	32	*Dasypus*
L	0-0	0-0		{8-8}		
U	3-3	1-1	2-2	3-3	30	*Cryptotis*
L	1-1	1-1	1-1	3-3		
U	1-1	1-1	1-1	3-3	30	*Nycticeius,*
L	3-3	1-1	2-2	3-3		*Lasiurus intermedius*
U	1-1	1-1	2-2	3-3	30	*Eumops*
L	2-2	1-1	2-2	3-3		
U	3-3	1-1	3-3	1-1	30	*Felis*
L	3-3	1-1	2-2	1-1		
U	3-3	1-1	2-2	1-1	28	*Lynx*
L	3-3	1-1	2-2	1-1		
U	2-2	0-0	3-3	3-3	28	*Lepus, Sylvilagus*
L	1-1	0-0	2-2	3-3		
U	1-1	0-0	2-2	3-3	22	*Glaucomys, Marmota,*
L	1-1	0-0	1-1	3-3		*Tamiasciurus,Sciurus carolinensis*

Continued on next page

	Incisors	Canines	Premolars	Molars	U/L Total	Mammal
U	1-1	0-0	1-1	3-3	20	*Castor, Erethizon,*
L	1-1	0-0	1-1	3-3		*Geomys, Myocastor, Sciurus niger, Tamias*
U	1-1	0-0	1-1	3-3	18	*Zapus*
L	1-1	0-0	0-0	3-3		
U	1-1	0-0	0-0	3-3	16	*Clethrionomys, Microtus,*
L	1-1	0-0	0-0	3-3		*Mus, Napaeozapus, Neofiber, Ondatra,*
						Oryzomys, Peromyscus, Rattus,
						Reithrodontomys, Sigmodon, Synaptomys

Appendix II
Standard Measurements and
Weights of Southeastern Terrestrial Mammals

Mammal	Total Length (mm)	Tail (mm)	Hind Ft. (mm)	Wt.
Virginia Opossum *Didelphis virginiana*	765 (680–830)	320 (285–345)	68 (59–75)	7 lb (5–9 lb)
Pigmy Shrew *Microsorex hoyi*	82 (78–86)	30 (28–32)	9.5 (8.5–10.5)	3 g (2.1–4.5 g)
Water Shrew *Sorex palustris*	140 (135–45)	65 (59–72)	20 (18–22)	15 g (11–18 g)
Smoky Shrew *Sorex fumeus*	117 (109–26)	43 (36–49)	13 (11–15)	7 g (6–12 g)
Long-tailed Shrew *Sorex dispar*	122 (118–27)	55 (50–59)	14.5 (12.5–17)	5.5 g (4.5–6 g)
Southeastern Shrew *Sorex longirostris*	79 (77–92)	29 (25–34)	10.5 (9.5–11.5)	3.5 g (3–4 g)
Masked Shrew *Sorex cinereus*	90 (86–94)	36 (31–40)	12 (10–13.5)	4 g (3–5 g)
Northern Short-tailed Shrew *Blarina brevicauda*	115 (100–120)	25 (22–29)	15 (13–16)	14 g (11–18 g)
Southern Short-tailed Shrew *Blarina carolinensis*	79 (75–84)	17 (16–18)	11 (9.5–12.5)	5 g (4–5.5 g)

Continued on next page

Mammal	Total Length (mm)	Tail (mm)	Hind Ft. (mm)	Wt.
Least Shrew *Cryptotis parva*	75 (70–79)	16 (14.5–17.5)	10.5 (9.5–11.0)	4.5 g (4–5 g)
Eastern Mole *Scalopus aquaticus*	148 (140–80)	21 (15–28)	19 (17–21)	40 g (30–50 g)
Star-nosed Mole *Condylura cristata*	186 (178–92)	65 (59–70)	26 (22–30)	50 g (45–56 g)
Hairy-tailed Mole *Parascalops breweri*	160 (150–71)	28 (23–32)	19 (17–21)	44 g (40–48 g)
Little Brown Bat *Myotis lucifugus*	90 (80–94)	35 (30–40)	9.5 (8.5–10.5)	4.5 g (4–5 g)
Southeastern Bat *Myotis austroriparius*	91 (84–96)	41 (35–45)	10.8 (10–12)	6 g (5–7)
Gray Bat *Myotis grisescens*	89 (80–97)	37.5 (32–43)	10 (8.5–11.5)	7.4 g (6.5–8.0 g)
Keen's Bat *Myotis keenii*	84 (80–88)	42 (36–45)	8.5 (7.0–9.5)	5.5 g (4.5–7 g)
Indiana Bat *Myotis sodalis*	82 (70–90)	36 (26–43)	8 (7.2–8.8)	6.5 g (5–8 g)
Small-footed Bat *Myotis leibii*	77 (72–82)	32 (29–35)	6.8 (6.6–7.1)	3.5 g (3–4 g)
Silver-haired Bat *Lasionycteris noctivagans*	105 (99–110)	42 (38–45)	8 (7.2–9)	6.5 g (7–9 g)
Eastern Pipistrelle *Pipistrellus subflavus*	85 (80–89)	40 (35–45)	8.8 (8–10)	4.5 g (3.5–6 g)
Big Brown Bat *Eptesicus fuscus*	115 (105–28)	46 (42–52)	11 (10–11.8)	15 g (12–18)
Red Bat *Lasiurus borealis*	113 (95–125)	50 (45–60)	9.5 (8.5–10.1)	12 g (9–15 g)
Seminole Bat *Lasiurus seminolus*	115 (109–19)	51 (44–58)	9.6 (8.5–10.2)	13 g (9.5–16 g)
Hoary Bat *Lasiurus cinereus*	135 (128–40)	60 (54–68)	13 (11.5–14.5)	30 g (21–36 g)
Yellow Bat *Lasiurus intermedius*	134 (126–38)	52 (46–58)	13 (11–14.5)	29.7 g (20–35 g)
Evening Bat *Nycticeius humeralis*	93 (88–97)	37 (32–41)	7 (6–8)	5.8 g (5–6.5 g)
Rafinesque's Big-eared Bat *Plecotus rafinesqii*	99 (92–103)	47 (42–51)	11 (9–13)	8 g (7–10 g)

Continued on next page

Mammal	Total Length (mm)	Tail (mm)	Hind Ft. (mm)	Wt.
Townsend's Big-eared Bat *Plecotus townsendii*	100 (95–106)	49 (42–52)	11.5 (10.5–12)	9.5 g (8–11 g)
Brazilian Free-tailed Bat *Tadarida brasiliensis*	92 (87–99)	30 (27–38)	8.5 (7.3–9.1)	6.5 g (5–8 g)
Wagner's Mastiff Bat *Eumops glaucinus*	130 (121–39)	48 (42–53)	11 (10–12)	41 g (35–48 g)
Little Mastiff Bat *Molossus molossus*	102 (90–107)	37 (34–40)	10 (9–11)	15 g (12–17 g)
Jamaican Fruit Bat *Artibeus jamaicensis*	80 (75–85)	—	17 (15–19)	42 g (38–45 g)
Nine-banded Armadillo *Dasypus novemcinctus*	825 (785–850)	365 (310–400)	104 (89–115)	12 lb (8–16 lb)
Eastern Cottontail *Sylvilagus floridanus*	440 (388–461)	55 (40–62)	92 (88–96)	3.5 lb (3–4 lb)
Appalachian Cottontail *Sylvilagus obscurus*	425 (380–450)	56 (48–62)	96 (90–101)	3.5 lb (3–4 lb)
Swamp Rabbit *Sylvilagus aquaticus*	525 (497–552)	68 (59–76)	106 (98–115)	4.8 lb (3.8–6 lb)
Marsh Rabbit *Sylvilagus palustris*	430 (400–50)	40 (34–46)	90 (80–97)	3.2 lb (2.3–3.6 lb)
Snowshoe Hare *Lepus americanus*	470 (420–500)	42 (37–46)	135 (122–40)	4 lb (3.2–4.5 lb)
Black-tailed Jackrabbit *Lepus californicus*	560 (470–640)	70 (55–110)	125 (110–40)	6.3 lb (4–8 lb)
Woodchuck *Marmota monax*	550 (501–610)	128 (100–140)	75 (64–80)	4,000 (2,780–5,950 g)
Eastern Chipmunk *Tamias striatus*	230 (190–245)	83 (68–89)	35 (30–40)	85 g (70–102)
Gray Squirrel *Sciurus carolinensis*	440 (395–488)	200 (178–225)	60 (51–69)	420 g (390–460 g)
Fox Squirrel *Sciurus niger*	625 (590–656)	305 (285–327)	85 (76–91)	850 g (725–960 g)
Red-bellied Squirrel *Sciurus aureogaster*	450 (410–506)	225 (185–240)	65 (55–72)	468 g (400–510 g)
Red Squirrel *Tamiasciurus hudsonicus*	292 (230–326)	132 (106–48)	46 (38–59)	180 g (130–210 g)
Southern Flying Squirrel *Glaucomys volans*	235 (198–255)	105 (98–112)	32 (29–35)	80 g (60–100 g)

Continued on next page

Mammal	Total Length (mm)	Tail (mm)	Hind Ft. (mm)	Wt.
Northern Flying Squirrel *Glaucomys sabrinus*	270 (245–95)	125 (110–38)	37 (30–44)	165 g (120–200 g)
Southeastern Pocket Gopher *Geomys pinetis*	260 (210–98)	85 (65–99)	35 (29–44)	225 g (125–355 g)
Beaver *Castor canadensis*	1,200 (1,090–1,305)	420 (390–480)	180 (150–205)	40 lb (30–85 lb)
Eastern Woodrat *Neotoma floridana*	400 (360–440)	184 (170–202)	38 (36–42)	310 g (220–380 g)
Cotton Rat *Sigmodon hispidus*	265 (210–84)	106 (74–110)	30 (25–34)	100 g (80–125 g)
Rice Rat *Oryzomys palustris*	265 (240–90)	135 (120–55)	32.5 (28–36)	63 g (43–80 g)
Eastern Harvest Mouse *Reithrodontomys humulis*	120 (112–30)	36 (50–62)	16 (14–18)	12.5 g (10–15 g)
Fulvous Harvest Mouse *Reithrodontomys fulvescens*	158 (140–200)	88 (80–100)	19 (15–22)	12 g (8.5–17 g)
Common Deer Mouse *Peromyscus maniculatus*	180 (165–210)	90 (77–105)	20.5 (18–23)	24 g (16–30 g)
Old-field Mouse *Peromyscus polionotus*	125 (120–35)	46 (40–50)	16.5 (15–18)	15 g (10–20 g)
White-footed Mouse *Peromyscus leucopus*	164 (150–80)	71 (59–82)	20 (19–22)	20 g (15–25 g)
Cotton Mouse *Peromyscus gossypinus*	182 (152–205)	72 (63–90)	22 (20–24)	32 g (24–40 g)
Florida Mouse *Peromyscus floridanus*	195 (185–208)	88 (84–94)	26 (23–29)	26 g (20–32 g)
Golden Mouse *Ochrotomys nuttalli*	175 (155–286)	85 (80–90)	20 (18–22)	23.5 g (20–27 g)
Rock Vole *Microtus chrotorrhinus*	166 (240–85)	48 (38–57)	20 (16–24)	35 g (30–40 g)
Meadow Vole *Microtus pennsylvanicus*	167 (147–91)	44 (34–56)	22 (19–25)	25.8 g (19–38 g)
Prairie Vole *Microtus ochrogaster*	145 (132–60)	30 (24–38)	19 (16.5–22.5)	37 g (25–50 g)
Woodland Vole *Microtus pinetorum*	115 (108–18)	18 (16–20)	15 (14–16)	28 g (20–35 g)
Southern Bog Lemming *Synaptomys cooperi*	126 (120–37)	24 (20–28)	20 (18.5–21.5)	30 g (25–35 g)

Continued on next page

Mammal	Total Length (mm)	Tail (mm)	Hind Ft. (mm)	Wt.
Southern Red-backed Vole *Clethrionomys gapperi*	135 (121–50)	37 (32–42)	19 (17–21)	24 g (20–28 g)
Round-tailed Muskrat *Neofiber alleni*	320 (285–365)	124 (98–136)	45 (38–48)	300 g (270–340 g)
Muskrat *Ondatra zibethicus*	545 (495–586)	235 (210–255)	76 (69–82)	2.2 lb (1.5–3 lb)
Norway Rat *Rattus norvegicus*	400 (320–480)	188 (152–219)	41 (36–45)	420 g (300–540 g)
Roof Rat *Rattus rattus*	395 (350–440)	212 (190–240)	36 (31–39)	200 g (175–230 g)
House Mouse *Mus musculus*	160 (145–200)	78 (68–90)	18 (16–20)	19 g (15–24 g)
Meadow Jumping Mouse *Zapus hudsonius*	195 (180–219)	118 (105–29)	30 (28–32)	16 g (14–18 g)
Woodland Jumping Mouse *Napaeozapus insignis*	224 (186–235)	140 (120–48)	30 (28–33)	24 g (20–28 g)
Nutria *Myocaster coypu*	940 (830–1,010)	344 (300–340)	131 (100–150)	12 lb (8–20 lb)
Porcupine *Erethizon dorsatum*	875 (785–945)	149 (130–62)	81 (69–91)	13 lb (10–24 lb)
Black Bear *Ursus americanus*	1,600 (1,480–1,900)	90 (81–99)	228 (190–255)	255 lb (200–600 lb)
Raccoon *Procyon lotor*	815 (700–892)	265 (230–86)	120 (105–30)	15 lb (10–24 lb)
Mink *Mustela vison*	550 (500–615)	185 (170–230)	68 (55–80)	2.1 lb (1.5–3 lb)
Fisher *Martes pennanti*	975 (890–1,080)	362 (314–402)	125 (110–39)	9.5 lb (7.5–12.5 lb)
Pine Marten *Martes americana*	575 (520–610)	192 (180–205)	84 (79–88)	2 lb (1.5–2.5 lb)
Long-tailed Weasel *Mustela frenata*	365 (305–448)	121 (96–158)	41 (34–51)	175 g (75–270 g)
Short-tailed Weasel *Mustela erminea*	254 (192–298)	63 (42–81)	31 (27–38)	67 g (40–83 g)
Least Weasel *Mustela nivalis*	170 (145–203)	28 (19–36)	20 (18.5–21.5)	43 g (22–68 g)
Striped Skunk *Mephitis mephitis*	680 (600–720)	295 (217–353)	70 (65–78)	7 lb (4–10 lb)

Continued on next page

Total Length Mammal	Tail (mm)	Hind Ft. (mm)	(mm)	Wt.
Eastern Spotted Skunk *Spilogale putorious*	440 (332–545)	165 (115–210)	42 (36–52)	3 lb (2–4 lb)
River Otter *Lutra canadensis*	1,000 (880–1,150)	360 (300–400)	100 (90–110)	16 lb (12–20 lb)
Coyote *Canis latrans*	1,180 (1,000–1,280)	342 (300–380)	184 (175–205)	30 lb (20–55 lb)
Red Fox *Vulpes vulpes*	975 (890–1,056)	370 (310–415)	165 (145–96)	9.5 lb (8.5–13 lb)
Gray Fox *Urocyon cinereoargenteus*	970 (885–1,045)	348 (300–390)	145 (105–78)	9 lb (7–12 lb)
Cougar *Felis concolor*	1995 (1,800–2,350)	715 (650–770)	276 (259–289)	140 lb (110–90 lb)
Bobcat *Lynx rufus*	990 (830–1,200)	128 (98–152)	160 (150–70)	22 lb (12–45 lb)
Wild Boar *Sus scrofa*	1,200 (1,000–1,500)	170 (150–200)	400 (350–450)	125 lb (75–400 lb)
White-tailed Deer *Odocoileus virginianus*	1,800 (1,600–2,150)	295 (230–360)	450 (400–500)	115 lb (80–400 lb)
Sambar Deer *Cervus unicolor*	2,000 (1,650–2,500)	135 (120–50)	600 (500–700)	330 lb (220–440 lb)
Sika Deer *Cervus nippon*	1,350 (1,200–1,500)	180 (165–200)	430 (380–480)	100 lb (80–120 lb)
Fallow Deer *Dama dama*	1,450 (1,300–1,600)	175 (160–190)	425 (375–475)	125 lb (65–185 lb)

Glossary

Aardwolf: a type of canid or dog found in Africa that eats termites, insects, and carrion.

Abscission layer: a weak layer which forms near the base of an antler to facilitate antler shedding in deer.

Alar membrane: the large gliding membrane that extends from front leg to back leg along the sides of flying squirrels.

Altricial: describes young that are born naked, blind, and helpless; requiring prolonged parental care.

Ambergris: a commercially valuable secretion from the large intestine of sperm whales, used in making perfumes.

Annuli: the yearly growth rings found in the teeth of carnivores and certain other mammals.

Antler: a branched, horny ornament that grows annually on the head of a male deer and is shed at the end of the breeding season. Antlers are covered with soft, vascular skin called "velvet" while they are growing. It later sloughs off.

Anus: the posterior opening of the digestive system.

Arboreal: adapted for living in trees.

Arthropods: those invertebrates having jointed legs and an external skeleton.

Auditory bullae: bulbous coverings on the skull that surround delicate middle- and inner-ear bones.

Baleen: platelike food strainers in the mouths of large whales that filter large amounts of water and trap small fish, shrimp, and other invertebrates.

Bifurcate: forked or split into two parts.

Blowhole: nostril opening of a whale.

Blubber: thick layer of fat beneath the skin of whales and seals.

Brackish marsh: a marsh having diluted saltwater.

Breaching: a spectacular swimming maneuver of whales whereby they leap totally or partially above the surface and crash back into the water.

Brow ridge: a prominent elevation or bump on the frontal bones of some mammal skulls.

Bunodont: type of molar tooth with low cusps and a flat grinding surface.

Cache: a food hoard made by an animal for later use.

Calcar: an elongated ankle bone which supports the trailing edge of the tail membrane of bats.

Canine tooth: one of the four basic types of teeth (located behind the incisors, usually long and cone shaped) and adapted for grasping and piercing.

Cannon bone: elongated leg bone in ungulates which is formed by fusion of foot and ankle bones to support the animal's weight .

Carnassial tooth: a type of cheek tooth in carnivores adapted for cutting or shearing flesh and bone.

Carnivorous: feeding primarily on flesh or meat.

Castor gland: the large scent gland located at the base of the tail in a beaver.

Cementum: a bonelike layer surrounding the root of tooth, which is often laminated and used for measuring the age of a mammal.

Class: in taxonomy, a group of related orders such as Chiroptera, Rodentia, Lagomorpha, etc., are placed together because of similarities.

Climax vegetation: the final, self-perpetuating stage of plant succession.

Community: a group of interacting organisms of various species living in a common environment.

Coniferous: cone-bearing trees such as pines and cypress.

Coy-dog: the hybrid offspring of a coyote and a dog.

Cranium: cavity of the skull which holds the brain.

Crepuscular: being active at dusk and dawn.

Cursorial: a running type of locomotion.

Cuttlefish: a squidlike marine mollusk eaten by whales.

Deciduous: 1) in plants, refers to those plants that undergo the yearly dropping of leaves at the end of each growing season; 2) in animals, refers to the milk teeth of young mammals which are replaced by permanent teeth as the mammals grow and mature.

Delayed fertilization: a process whereby fertilization of eggs is delayed over the winter after copulation. The sperm remain viable until spring in the female reproductive tract, as in many bats.

Dentary: the lower jawbone containing teeth in mammals.

Diastema: a gap between teeth in the jaw, usually between the incisors and cheek teeth, because canines are absent.

Digitigrade: adapted for walking on the tips of the toes.

Digits: the toes or fingers of an appendage, such as the foot and hand.

Diurnal: active during the daytime.

Dolphin: 1) any small species of toothed whale; 2) a species of marine fish.

Dorsal: pertaining to the back or upper side of an animal.

Echolocation: a means of locating objects by bouncing supersonic vocalizations off them, which are then picked up by the ear. This process is common in some mammals, including bats and whales.

Ecology: the study of interrelationships between living organisms and their environments.

Ecotone: a transition area between two adjacent ecological communities, generally exhibiting competition between organisms in both.

Endangered species: a species which is facing extinction if its downward population trend continues.

Epiphyte: a plant that obtains moisture and nutrients from the air as it grows upon another plant.

Estuary: a marine aquatic area where saltwater and freshwater water mix.

Evergreen: a plant having foliage that remains green the year round.

Extinction: the dying out or disappearance of a species on earth.

Extirpation: the disappearance of a species within a given geographical region or political subdivision (such as a state).

Falcate: hook-shaped or sickle-shaped, as in the dorsal fin of some sharks.

Fallow field: agricultural land that has not been farmed lately, but allowed to grow up in weeds, grass, vines, and brush.

Family: in taxonomy, a group of related genera and species that are placed together because of similarity.

Fecundity: the rate of reproduction.

Feral: living under natural conditions or in the wild.

Flipper: an appendage or limb which is adapted for aquatic locomotion with fully-webbed digits.

Floodplain: the area bordering a river which is subject is periodic flooding.

Forage: to search for food.

Fossorial: adapted for living under the ground, like the mole or pocket gopher.

Frontal bone: the bone forming the top of the skull above the eyes.

Frugivorous: feeding primarily on fruit.

Fusiform: shaped like a cigar, and tapering at both ends.

Gestation: the duration of pregnancy for a species of mammal.

Genus: a group of related species.

Guano: bat or bird droppings deposited at their roosting sites.

Guard hairs: the outer coat of course, longer hairs covering the underfur of mammals.

Habitat: the place where an organism is normally found living.

Hammock: a stand of hardwood trees, usually of the broadleaf evergreen type.

Hedgehog: a type of insectivore from Europe and Asia which is covered with spines and can roll up into a ball.

Herbivorous: feeding primarily on plants or vegetation.

Hibernation: a state of reduced metabolic and physical activity, usually occurring over winter.

Hierarchy: the behavioral pecking order of dominant animals in a population.

Hind: a female deer or doe.

Hispid: grizzled color pattern of the fur, resulting from a combination of brown, black, and light tan banding of the hairs.

Histoplasmosis: a fungal disease carried in the droppings of several species of bats.

Home range: the area that a mammal is familiar with and where it carries on its normal daily activities.

Horn: the hard, sheathlike projection growing from the head of some members of the cattle family. Each has a bony core and is not shed annually.

Hybrid: offspring resulting from the interbreeding of two species.

Implantation: the attachment of the tiny developing embryo to the wall of the mother's uterus.

Incisor tooth: one of the four basic types of teeth (located at the front of the mouth), usually adapted for biting off pieces.

Induced estrus: when the presence of an adult male triggers receptivity to copulation, or "heat," in an adult female.

Induced ovulation: when the presence of an adult male triggers the production of eggs in an adult female.

Insectivorous: feeding primarily on insects and other invertebrates.

Interfemoral membrane: the tail membrane of bats that stretches from one hind leg to the other and includes the tail.

Juvenile breeding: the occurrence of reproduction before the body has reached adult size.

Keeled calcar: in some species of bats, the bladelike lateral flange on the ankle bone supporting the tail membrane.

Kit: term for the young of certain mammals, such as beavers, mink, raccoons, etc.

Krill: tiny oceanic crustaceans eaten by whales in huge quantities.

Labyrinthine: having many complex chambers or tunnels.

Lacrimal: refers to the tear gland of the eye.

Lactation: secretion of milk by the mammary glands of a mammal with young.

Leptospirosis: any of several diseases of man and domestic animals that are caused by infection of leptospires, a genus of slender aerobic spirochetes.

Litter: the group of offspring produced by a female at birth.

Longevity: the length of life of a species.

Marsupium: the external pouch on the lower abdomen of marsupials which encloses the mammary glands and serves as an incubation chamber.

Mast: seeds or nuts of trees, such as oak, hickory, pecan, beech, etc., that are used as food by mammals and birds.

Maternity colony: in certain bats, adult females form unisexual colonies to give birth and care for the young.

Melanistic: a black color phase of an animal.

Migration: regular periodic, seasonal movements of a species from one part of its range to another.

Molar tooth: one of the two types of cheek teeth (located at the back of the mouth), often large and adapted for grinding.

Molt: the shedding and replacement of fur and hair.

Monogamous: when each sex of a species takes only one mate.

Montane: a biogeographical zone of relatively moist, cool upland slopes below timberline dominated by large evergreen trees.

Musk glands: the strong-smelling scent glands present in certain mammals such as shrews, skunks, and weasels.

Nocturnal: active at night or in the dark.

Omnivorous: feeding on both plant and animal material.

Order: in taxonomy, a group consisting of related families of animals that are placed together because of similarities.

Os baculum: the Latin name for the bone found in the penis of certain mammals such as carnivores and rodents.

Otolith: an ear bone found in the inner ear of some animals which is involved in balance and orientation.

Ovary: the egg-producing organ located in the abdomen of female mammals.

Ovulation: the release of an egg (ovum) or eggs (ova) from the ovary of a female.

Parietal bones: skull bones located on top of the cranium.

Parturition: the process of giving birth.

Pectoral: located in the chest or mid-trunk area, as the fins of whales or fish.

Pelagic: relating to the open ocean, far from shore.

Pelage: the hair or fur coat of a mammal.

Pelt: the skin and fur or hair of a mammal, which often has commercial value.

Pelvic: located in the hip or lower trunk area as the appendages of certain animals.

Penis: the male copulatory organ of an animal.

Pheromone: a chemical substance produced by one individual of a species to serve as a sexual stimulus to other individuals of the species.

Pinna: the largely cartilaginous projecting portion of the external ear.

Placenta: the vascular connection between the developing embryo and its mother within the uterus.

Plantigrade: adapted for walking with the sole and head of the foot touching the ground.

Pod: a social group or herd of whales.

Polyestrous: being reproductively active several times a year (in a female mammal).

Precocial: describes young that are born fully furred, with their eyes open, and able to move about; requiring parental care.

Prehensile: the ability of an appendage, such as the tail, to grasp or coil around objects.

Prey: an animal that is killed and eaten for food by a predator.

Polygamous: when one sex of the species mates with multiple individuals of the other sex, rather than forming a strong pair bond with one mate.

Porpoise: the smaller species of toothed whales.

Premolar tooth: one of the two types of cheek teeth (located just behind the canines and in front of the molars), usually adapted for grinding or for shearing.

Pseudo-rumination: reingestion of soft fecal pellets by certain lagomorphs to pass the partially digested food through the digestive track a second time.

Race: a geographically and morphologically distinct subspecies or subgroup of a species.

Relict population: a remnant population that has shrunk to a small size with time.

Riparian: relating to or living on the bank of a natural watercourse (such as a river).

Rostrum: a forward, noselike projection of the skull.

Rumen: the first compartment of the complex stomach of some ungulates.

Rumination: regurgitation, rechewing, and reswallowing of food by cattle as an aid to digestion.

Runway: the worn visible pathway resulting from repeated use by some animals, such as rodents.

Rut: the annual recurring state of sexual arousal; the time when breeding takes place.

Salamander: 1) a colloquial name used by some southerners for the pocket gopher (a rodent); 2) a rather slimy-skinned amphibian having a long tail and four limbs extending out at right angles to the body.

Saltatorial locomotion: a hopping type of gait characteristic of jumping mice, kangaroos, and some other mammals.

Scat: the fecal droppings of a mammal.

Scavenger: an animal that feeds on the dead bodies of other animals.

Secondary succession: the type of plant succession that occurs following a disruption, such as fire or plowing.

Sedentary: settled in one place or inactive.

Seral stage: one of the community stages of plant succession, such as grassland or forest.

Sexual dimorphism: Difference in sexual or other features (such as size) between males and females of a species.

Slug: a close relative of the snail which lacks a shell.

Sibling species: a closely related species.

Sign: indirect evidence of the presence of an animal, such as tracks, hair, scent post, etc.

Species: a freely interbreeding group of animals that are reproductively isolated from other kinds.

Species of special concern: a species that is not yet threatened or endangered but whose population numbers are declining and overall status is in question for the future.

Spermaceti: the oil from the large cavity in the skull of sperm whales.

Solenodon: a primitive shrewlike insectivore found in Cuba and Hispaniola.

Subspecies: a geographically and morphologically distinct race or subdivision of a species.

Succession: the orderly replacement of communities with time on a given site, terminating in a climax community that is self-perpetuating.

Supraorbital process: bony projection above the eye socket (orbit) on a mammal skull.

Supraorbital ridge: the prominent ridge of bone running anteriorly above the eye socket or orbit.

Tail fluke: the laterally flattened lobes of a whale or manatee.

Tenrec: a type of shrewlike insectivore found in Madagascar.

Terrestrial: adapted for living on dry land.

Territory: an area defended by an animal or group of animals from other individuals or groups.

Testis: the sperm-producing organ of male mammals.

Threatened species: a species whose numbers have declined to the point where it may eventually become endangered.

Tine: a spike or prong of a deer antler.

Torpor: a dormant or hibernating status.

Tragus: a thin, leaflike spike at the base of the ear opening of bats.

Underfur: coat of dense, fine hair, usually overlaid by guard hairs, that serves for insulation.

Understory: those plants growing on the forest floor beneath the canopy trees.

Unicusp: simple, cone-shaped teeth near the front of the mouth in shrews.

Uterus: the organ of the female reproductive system, within which embryos develop.

Vagina: the female reproductive tube that receives the penis during copulation.

Ventral: pertaining to the belly or underside of an animal.

Vertebrate: an animal which has a vertebral column down the back protecting the delicate nervous system.

Vestigial: the remnant of a structure which was once more developed and functional in a species.

Vibrissae: long, stiff hairs or whiskers on the snout, which serve as touch receptors.

Wean: to transfer the young mammal from mother's milk to other types of food.

Whale lice: parasitic amphipods (crustaceans) found attached to the skin of whales.

Zygomatic arch: the cheekbone of mammals.

Selected References

General References

Allen, T. B., ed. 1979. *Wild Animals of North America*. National Geographic Society, Washington, D.C.

Anderson, S., and J. K. Jones. 1984. *Orders and Families of Recent Mammals of the World*. John Wiley and Sons, New York, N.Y.

Barbour, R. W., and W. H. Davis. 1969. Bats of America. Univ. Press of Kentucky, Lexington, Ky.

Brown, L. N. 1991. *Sea Mammals, Atlantic, Gulf, and Caribbean*. Windward Publ., Miami, Fla.

Chapman, J. A. and G. A Feldhamer, eds. 1982. *Wild Mammals of North America: Biology, Management, and Economics*. Johns Hopkins Univ. Press, Baltimore, Md.

Current Mammalogy. 1987 to present. An annual published by Plenum Press, New York, N.Y.

Davis, D. E., and F. B. Golley. 1963. *Principles in Mammalogy*. Reinhold Publishing Corp., New York, N.Y.

Hall, E. R. 1981. *The Mammals of North America*. Vols. 1–2. John Wiley and Sons, New York, N.Y.

Harrison, R., and M. Bryden, eds. 1988. *Whales, Dolphins, and Porpoises*. Facts on File, Inc., New York, N.Y.

Jones, J. K., R. S. Hoffman, D. W. Rice, C. Jones, R. J. Baker, and M. D. Engstrom. 1992. *Revised Checklist of North American Mammals North of Mexico*. The Museum, Texas Tech University, Occasional Papers No. 146.

Journal of Mammalogy. 1919 to present. A quarterly published by the American Society of Mammalogists. Allen Press. Lawrence, Kans.

Journal of Wildlife Management. 1937 to present. A quarterly published by the Wildlife Society.

MacDonald, D., ed. 1984. *The Encyclopedia of Mammals*. Facts on File, Inc., New York, N.Y.

Mammalian Species. 1972 to present. Detailed accounts of the life history and biology of given mammal species. Published at intervals by the American Society of Mammalogists. Allen Press, Lawrence, Kans.

Minisian, S. M., K. C. Balcomb, and L. Foster. 1984. *The World's Whales*. Smithsonian Books, Washington, D.C.

Nowak, R. M., and J. L. Paradiso. 1983. *Walker's Mammals of the World*. Vols. 1–2. Johns Hopkins Univ. Press, Baltimore, Md.

Vaughan, T. A. 1986. *Mammalogy*. W. B. Saunders Co., Philadelphia, Pa.

Field Guides

Burt, W. H., and R. P. Grossenheider. 1976. *A Field Guide to the Mammals*. Houghton Mifflin Co., Boston, Mass.

Glass, B. P. 1973. *A Key to the Skulls of North American Mammals*. Okla. State Univ., Stillwater, Okla.

Murie, O. J. 1974. *A Field Guide to Animal Tracks*. Houghton Mifflin Co., Boston, Mass.

Smith, R. P. 1982. *Animal Tracks and Signs of North America*. Stackpole Books, Harrisburg, Pa.

Whitaker, J. O. 1980. *The Audubon Society Field Guide to North American Mammals*. Alfred A. Knopf, Inc., New York, N.Y.

State and Regional Publications

Banfield, A. W. F. 1974. *The Mammals of Canada.* Univ. of Toronto Press, Toronto, Canada.

Brown, L. N. 1997. *Mammals of Florida.* Windward Publ., Miami, Fla. (in Press).

Choate, J. R., J. K. Jones, Jr., and C. Jones. 1994. *Handbook of Mammals of the South-Central States.* Louisiana State Univ. Press, Baton Rouge, La., 304 pp.

Cothran, G., M. H. Smith, and J. E. Gentry. 1991. *Mammals of the Savannah River Site.* Savannah River Ecology Lab. Publ. No. 21, Aiken, S.C.

Golley, F. B. 1962. *Mammals of Georgia.* Univ. of Georgia Press, Athens, Ga.

———. 1966. *Mammals of South Carolina.* Contrib. of the Charleston Museum, No. 15, Charleston, S.C.

Lowrey, G. H. 1974. *The Mammals of Louisiana and its Adjacent Waters.* Louisiana State Univ. Press, Baton Rouge, La.

Schwartz, C. W., and E. R. Schwartz. 1959. *The Wild Mammals of Missouri.* Univ. of Missouri Press, Columbia, Mo.

Webster, W. D., J. F. Parnell, and W. E. Biggs. 1985. *Mammals of the Carolinas, Virginia, and Maryland.* Univ. of North Carolina Press, Chapel Hill, N.C.

Techniques Manuals

Anderson, R. M. 1965. *Methods of Collecting and Preserving Vertebrate Animals.* Bulletin of the National Museum of Canada, No. 69, Biol. Series 18, Ottawa, Canada.

Bookhowt, T. A., ed. 1994. *Research and Management Techniques for Wildlife Habitats.* 5th Edition. The Wildlife Society, Bethesda, Md.

Schemitz, S. D., ed. 1980. *Wildlife Management Techniques Manual, Revised.* The Wildlife Society, Washington, D.C.

Index

DATE			